D0931110

Building the Kaiser's Navy

Building the Kaiser's Navy

The Imperial Navy Office and
German Industry in the von Tirpitz Era

1890 – 1919

GARY E. WEIR

Naval Institute Press
Annapolis, Maryland

© 1992 by the United States Naval Institute
Annapolis, Maryland

All rights reserved.
No part of this book may be reproduced without written permission from the publisher.

Library of Congress Cataloging-in-Publication Data

Weir, Gary E.
    Building the Kaiser's navy : the Imperial Navy Office and German industry in the von Tirpitz era, 1890–1919 / Gary E. Weir.
        p.   cm.
    Includes bibliographical references (p.   ) and index.
    ISBN 1-55750-929-8
    1. Germany. Kriegsmarine—History. 2. Shipbuilding industry—Germany—History. 3. Tirpitz, Alfred von. 1849–1930. I. Title.
VA513.W255 1991
338.4′76238225′0943—dc20   90-19529
                                                  CIP

Printed in the United States of America on acid-free paper ∞

9 8 7 6 5 4 3 2

First printing

Frontispiece. Grand Admiral von Tirpitz, State Secretary of the Imperial Naval Office. (Bundesarchiv-Militärarchiv)

To Catherine,
who has filled my life with more joy than she knows

Contents

Acknowledgments

Over the past few years, while keeping company with von Tirpitz and the shipbuilding community of Imperial Germany, I have enjoyed the generosity of institutions and the patience, understanding, and expertise of a great many people. This book began as a dissertation under the direction of Professor John H. Morrow, Jr., of the University of Tennessee. No student could hope for a better or more attentive mentor. Professor Morrow has repeatedly allowed me to tap his knowledge, professional skill, and wisdom. I am thankful that over the years he has remained a generous teacher and valued friend.

My first research trip to Germany was sponsored by the McClure Foundation of the University of Tennessee in 1979, and thanks to the German Academic Exchange Service, I was able to return to the Federal Republic for the 1980–81 academic year. I am very grateful for the generosity of these organizations.

While in Germany I benefited from the expertise and hospitality of a number of excellent archivists. At the Bundesarchiv-Militärarchiv in Freiburg, where the bulk of the research for this book was done, Drs. Fleischer and Giessler as well as the late Dr. Sandhofer were extremely helpful. I am also indebted to the staff of the archive's research room, including Herr Wenzel, Frau Müller, and Herr Mahler for their guidance. At the Historisches Archiv Friedrich Krupp in Essen, Frau Köhne-Lindenlaub and Herr Müther graciously offered their hospitality and advice while helping me find sources vital to this study.

The Bundesarchiv-Militärarchiv and Historisches Archiv Friedrich Krupp also provided many of the illustrations in this book, and I wish to thank them for permission to use their photographs. Mr. Charles Haberlein of the Naval Historical Center in Washington, D.C., helped me find many of the other illustrations in the U.S. Navy's impressive collection, which he manages so well.

I also want to acknowledge the cooperation of the University of Freiburg Library and the expert assistance of Mr. John Vajda and Mr. Dale Sherrick of the Navy Department Library in Washington, D.C. These librarians and facilities were instrumental in the successful completion of this project.

I first developed in article form many ideas that found their way into this work. I am thankful to *Military Affairs*, now the *Journal of Military History*, and the *International History Review* for permission to use material that first appeared in their publications.

I am also indebted to Drs. Richard Abels, William Roberts, William Cogar, and the other participants in the works-in-progress seminar at the U.S. Naval Academy. As my colleagues during the 1986–87 academic year, these and other talented historians in the history department of the academy helped me refine my ideas and contributed many insights that became part of the final work.

Finally, I wish to thank my family for their support. In my late parents, Mary and Edward Weir, I had my first and best teachers. At home, my wife, Catherine, and my daughter, Lili, always help me keep history in proper perspective. They give me love, time, advice, and constantly remind me of the other marvelous things in life far more important than German history.

Abbreviations

ABA	Abnahameamt or RMA Purchasing Office
ABB	Allgemeine Baubestimmungen or general construction regulations
AEG	Allgemeine Elektricitäts Gesellschaft or the German General Electric Company
BA/MA	Bundesarchiv-Militärarchiv or German Federal Military Archive
BBS	Baubeaufsichtigung or supervisor of construction
KCA	Kriegschemikalien AG or the War Chemicals Company
KMA	Kriegsmetall AG or War Metals Company
KRA	Kriegs Rohstoff Abteilung or War Materials Office
Krupp/FAH	Historical Archive of the Krupp Firm/Family Archive
Krupp/WK	Historical Archive of the Krupp Firm/Works Archive
KW	Kaiserliche Werft or imperial shipyard
KWD	Imperial shipyard at Danzig
KWK	Imperial shipyard at Kiel
KWW	Imperial shipyard at Wilhelmshaven
LV	Lieferantenverzeichnis or suppliers' list

MAN	Maschinenfabrik Augsburg-Nürnberg (diesel engine company)
OHL	Oberste Heeresleitung or the Army High Command
PW	Privat Werft or private shipyard
RMA	Reichsmarineamt or Imperial Naval Office

RMA Construction Department divisions:
KI = Shipbuilding Division
KII = Machine Building Division
KIII = Department for Shakedown Cruises and Military Construction Matters
KIV = Department for the Administration of Construction Materials

RSA	Reichschatzamt or Imperial Treasury
SKL	Seekriegsleitung or Naval High Command (1918)
SMS	Seine Majestäts Schiff or His Majesty's Ship
SS/RMA	State Secretary of the Reichsmarineamt or Imperial Naval office
SS/RSA	State Secretary of the Reichschatzamt or the Imperial Treasury
SSW	Siemens-Schuckert Werke
UI	U-Boat Inspectorate
WUMBA	Waffen und Munitions Beschaffungsamt or Weapons and Munitions Procurement Agency

Equivalents

1 knot per hour = 1.15 miles per hour or 1.85 kilometers per hour
1 sea mile = 1 nautical mile = 1.85 kilometers or 1.15 miles
1 inch = 2.54 centimeters

Building the Kaiser's Navy

Introduction

At the turn of the twentieth century, possessing a navy was a sign of national greatness and power, and a strong naval force was virtually required for a nation to compete for economic and political influence around the world. In the 1890s, Imperial Germany, under the direction of Kaiser Wilhelm II, sought to enter this international contest by developing a navy on a par with that of Great Britain. This study focuses on the creation of the new German fleet from the perspective of the naval-industrial relationship between the Imperial Naval Office (RMA) and the various shipyards and industrial concerns responsible for ship construction from 1897 to 1919.

At the turn of the century, the often tempestuous relationship between naval policy makers and the armaments industry evolved into what historian William McNeill has dubbed a "command technology." Larger, faster, and more powerful ships were being built in response to the demands of naval leaders such as Admiral Alfred von Tirpitz, chief of the German Imperial Naval Office. In developing command technologies, the armaments industry and the navies of the major Western powers inaugurated an alliance that represented the first stage in the evolution of the naval-industrial complex.[1]

In refining this relationship, the RMA and industry had to identify and reconcile often conflicting viewpoints and practices. In many cases, the private sector developed and controlled the advanced naval technologies essential to the fabrication of ships and weapons systems. Thus companies that pioneered important innovations such as nickel-steel armor plate could determine the alternatives open to the navy, new directions in research and development, and the price of the final product.

Because of the important role of these companies and the limited market for many of the products the navy needed, von Tirpitz and his associates at the RMA encouraged competition. They thus precipitated a struggle between the navy and some of its most important contractors for control of technology, market, and price. The naval officers in the RMA frequently expressed frustration with what they perceived as the self-serving motives of industry. Industrial leaders, in turn, found themselves obliged to defend their business practices with a regularity they found disturbing and to contest naval procurement policies that required extraordinary research commitments and product guarantees.

In the final analysis, both parties had to overcome the ancient ambivalence between buyer and seller. Although such differences would never entirely disappear, the navy and industry identified and reconciled their contending motives, goals, and expectations in the process of composing solutions to their occasionally paralyzing confrontations. Their initial incompatibility gradually gave way to a greater degree of cooperation.

Traditional business practices and attitudes often posed the greatest obstacle to this process of evolution. Although they had become increasingly responsive to naval needs, companies like Krupp initially recoiled at the implications of a command technology. Many industrialists wanted to cooperate with the navy for reasons of patriotism and profit, but not to the extent of endangering their hold on the market or depriving them of the initiative in setting policy, prices, and research and development priorities.

Leading naval officers held a sharply contrasting point of view. Building warships was not business as usual, and the RMA refused to be treated as an ordinary customer. Instead, von Tirpitz demanded long-range commitments from industry and a degree of control over quality and price that went far beyond the traditional relationship between buyer and seller.

The admiral also felt that the navy had to assume the dominant role in its relationship with the arms merchants. If industry were dominant, he feared that market variations and the profit motive would become determining factors in the development of Imperial Germany's High Seas Fleet and providing the navy's domestic needs might become a function of supply and demand or monopoly. Therefore, determining relative roles and responsibilities for the RMA and industry in their relationship became a vital part of the debate that characterized this growing command technology.

This evolutionary aspect of the naval-industrial relationship has escaped some students of the period, such as Michael Epkenhans, who simply defend the patriotism and purpose of the industrialists.[2] This one-dimensional analysis fails to perceive the necessity and educational purpose of the conflicts precipitated by the very different views of the RMA and industry as they struggled to perfect a workable relationship. In searching for solutions to their frequent conflicts, the navy and its contractors achieved a familiarity with their respective policies and viewpoints that contributed to the evolution of an effective command technology. Over the long term, as they worked together to overcome the many problems involved in ship construction, especially during World War I, this alliance evolved into the naval-industrial complex.

The historical literature that provided the foundation for this study is split between two perspectives. Walther Hubatsch's well-known contributions to German naval historiography, particularly his analysis of command structure, reflect the traditional view that von Tirpitz built the fleet for military and economic defense. Hubatsch saw the fleet as Germany's response to foreign pressures.[3]

Eckart Kehr pioneered a new outlook by integrating interest-group politics, domestic economic issues, and the international implications of fleet construction. He challenged the German historical preoccupation with foreign affairs and focused on the primacy of domestic issues in German history. In his evaluation of the German naval construction program, Kehr concluded that internal financial and political interests, not the necessity of responding to foreign pressures, spawned the fleet.[4]

In the last twenty years historians have rediscovered the social, political, and economic themes stressed by Kehr during the interwar years. Paul Kennedy is but one illustration. His *Rise of Anglo-German*

Antagonism, 1860–1914 demonstrated how Germany's unification and subsequent emergence as a world-rank military and economic power created the conflict with Great Britain that contributed to the outbreak of World War I. In this study, the naval issue is placed in the wider national context of political, social, and economic elements.

Other historians have followed Kehr's lead. Jonathan Steinberg restated Kehr's thesis in *Yesterday's Deterrent,* which focused on the passage of the 1898 and 1900 naval laws through the Reichstag. Holger Herwig broadened German naval historiography by studying the social background of the officer corps. Michael Geyer examined the role of armaments and arms production as an ever-present process affecting national attitudes as well as domestic and foreign economic and political policies. Ivo Lambi has contributed an excellent study of the many factors affecting German naval operational planning covering the period 1862 to 1914. Wilhelm Deist has carefully explored the role of propaganda and the RMA News Bureau in von Tirpitz's plans to expand the fleet.[5]

More important for the issues essential to this work is Volker Berghahn's *Der Tirpitz Plan.* Berghahn's emphasis was on Admiral von Tirpitz, his aggressive motives, and the importance of the risk theory. He argues that the admiral was building the fleet for the explicit purpose of challenging Britain for mastery of the seas.

The works of Walther Hubatsch offered adept exposition and analysis of the naval command. Kehr, Kennedy, Steinberg, Geyer, Deist, and Herwig evaluated the navy's position in the politics, society, and economy of Germany at the turn of the century. Yet all of this literature overlooks one vital element—the difficulties involved in actually building ships, that is, the RMA's attempt to cope with the puzzle presented by daily business with civilian contractors. This study will fill that void.

When Holger Herwig published his history of the German Imperial Navy, *Luxury Fleet,* he performed a vital service. Rather than providing a comprehensive history, addressing every issue and personality, he recognized the high caliber and great diversity of current research and opinion on the German Imperial Navy and the pressing need for a synthesis to guide those interested in the subject. This study is an effort to add one more important piece to the historical mosaic which Herwig has so carefully crafted from the excellent contemporary historiography on the German Imperial Navy.

This book will not try to reiterate the historical insights and information so well presented by Herwig, Berghahn, Steinberg, Kehr, Deist, and others. Neither will it attempt to restate the excellent analysis of the German wartime economy and administration offered by Gerald Feldman in his classic *Army, Industry, and Labor in Germany, 1914–1918*. Rather, it will fill a conspicuous void in the literature on the Imperial Navy and complement both Feldman's work on the army and that of John H. Morrow, Jr., *Building German Airpower, 1909–1914*, and *German Airpower in World War One*, by analyzing the naval-industrial component for the period before and during World War I.

Most of the primary sources used in this work came from the naval holdings of the Bundesarchiv-Militärarchiv in Freiburg, West Germany. The majority of the documents used can be found in the files classified RM3, the signature for the RMA or Imperial Naval Office. These documents include material from all departments of the RMA, including correspondence from all the private firms employed by the navy in ship construction. Other sources made available in Freiburg covered the old Imperial Admiralty (RM1), the Naval High Command (RM4), the Admiralty Staff (RM5), and the Naval Cabinet (RM2). Also valuable were the personal papers of Admirals von Tirpitz, Eduard von Capelle, Gustav Freiherr von Senden-Bibran, and Paul Behncke.

Fortunately, the bulk of the military documentation was preserved at various locations throughout World War II. Most of the archives of the pertinent private firms and shipyards were destroyed between 1940 and 1945: the university libraries and private records centers in cities including Hamburg, Bremen, Kiel, and Wilhelmshaven. For example, all that remains of the pre-1945 company records at the Howaldtswerke shipyard in Kiel, a single contract for the battleship SMS *Bayern*, was sent to me in response to a written inquiry for available source material.[6]

There are very few major firms in Germany that still possess records covering their activities in the early twentieth century. Among the few naval-related firms that do are Krupp, Mannesmann, and Maschinenfabrik Augsburg-Nürnberg (MAN). Unfortunately, neither Mannesmann's nor MAN's archive was open to me during my working visit to Germany in 1981. But the most important of the three, Krupp, allowed more than enough time to do the research required for this work, especially in the area of armor production and U-boat development. Therefore, in spite of the problems of war damage and archive scheduling, the Militärarchiv and the Archives of the Krupp firm at the Villa Hügel in Essen supplied abundant source material. This evidence was more than adequate for a thorough investigation of both the naval and industrial perspectives on the problems of naval expansion.

Other valuable sources used in this work include the memoirs of various naval figures and politicians. The most important of these works describe the careers of von Tirpitz, Chlodwig von Hohenlohe-Schillingsfürst, Bernhard von Bülow, and Kurt Riezler. The nature of memoirs, however, is such that a historian must use them with care. Von Tirpitz's obvious purpose in his memoirs was to defend his political policies and naval construction program. The success of the U-boat and the unfulfilled expectations regarding the fleet during World War I forced him out of the RMA in 1916 under a barrage of criticism. Thus his statements, published ten years later, must be evaluated carefully. In too many instances he admits few errors and always defends his position uncritically as the logical and correct one. His decision to encourage only limited U-boat research and development within the navy is a case in point. Von Tirpitz's evaluation of his own actions was widely criticized by his contemporaries and later by historians. Similar works present the same difficulties, but the role of von Tirpitz in this study makes his memoirs at once very important and equally suspect.

The naval-industrial context of this inquiry also offers a new perspective on both prominent and relatively obscure historical characters. Alfred von Tirpitz's actions in his capacity as director of an expanding naval construction program were determined by the risk theory, a strategic concept defensive in appearance but offensive in reality. Von Tirpitz built the High Seas Fleet to give Germany enough seapower to discourage an attack by any potential adversary; the risk inherent in any such attack would not be worth the cost in men and machinery. Yet von Tirpitz's plans for the future of the fleet seemed to go far beyond the creation of this risk. Thus the suspicion that von Tirpitz actually intended to surpass the primary naval power of his time arose in the minds of British leaders over eighty years ago as it does for modern historians.

His dogged attachment to this theory takes on an interesting dimension when one correctly perceives the admiral's position. Von Tirpitz never had tactical command of the fleet he built between 1897 and World War I. Indeed, he came close to this opportunity only once, and his candidacy displeased too many to be taken seriously. Thus he became an administrator and shipbuilder relentlessly following a concept which those in command of the fleet did not unequivocally accept.[7] The influence of this conflict on both naval construction and the effective use of the fleet are issues central to this study.

Other naval figures appear here either for the first time or in a new light. Captain Lothar Persius and Admiral Karl Galster were two of von Tirpitz's strongest public critics. Von Tirpitz's successor in 1916, Admiral Eduard von Capelle, was an administrator of the highest caliber, and far more adaptable in his strategic ideas than his superior. His first experience with the RMA came as head of the Administrative Department during the early years of von Tirpitz's naval expansion.

There are key characters among other RMA departments as well. Both Admiral Rudolf von Eickstedt and his successor, Admiral Rollmann, were vital to the progress of the building program, directing the Construction Department of the RMA from 1899 to 1914. In addition, Admiral Harald Dähnhardt's role in determining the feasibility of many projects and in naval relations with the Reichstag were crucial to fleet development. As director of the RMA Budget Department, his views on the constantly rising price of armor plate on the domestic and international market were particularly valuable to the navy.

Although the creation of the High Seas Fleet has often been portrayed as the product of von Tirpitz's energy and imagination alone, these other characters hold the key to understanding relations between the navy and industry. Von Tirpitz set the policy, but these men turned the fleet into reality and tried, on a daily basis, to exert RMA control over the naval-industrial relationship that governed the progress of the construction program.

1

An Ambitious Beginning

1 8 9 0 – 1 8 9 8

The Navy and the Shipbuilding Industry

Shortly after young Kaiser Wilhelm II ascended the thrones of Prussia and the German Empire in 1888, he requested that a commission review suggestions for reorganizing the naval hierarchy. This commission proposed a new structure that was approved first by the Reichstag and then by the kaiser himself in 1889.

The old Admiralty was split into three parts (see Appendix A, Figure 1), the Supreme Command (Oberkommando der Marine), the Naval Cabinet (Marinekabinette), and the Imperial Naval Office (Reichsmarineamt or RMA).[1] The navy formulated strategy and the kaiser performed his function as commander in chief through the Supreme Command, whose first director was Vice-Admiral Max von der Goltz. The Naval Cabinet under Gustav Freiherr von Senden-Bibran followed the pattern established by the army's Military Cabinet and took responsibility for matters of personnel and all of the secretarial aspects of the kaiser's command role. The RMA, first directed by Rear Admiral Karl Eduard Heusner, functioned as the official ministry, charged with presenting all naval matters before the Reichstag (see Appendix A, Table

1).[2] While the Supreme Command initially determined ship types and advanced design, the RMA projected naval needs into the future through budget allocations and actually supervised construction. At this point, however, the RMA did not have a full-time chief of naval construction, and it was easily the least important of the three naval branches with direct access to the kaiser.

Under Karl Eduard Heusner (1889–91) and then Friedrich Hollmann (1891–97) the policy of the RMA lacked direction. Both of these officers came of age in a coastal defense navy that suddenly found itself caught in a period of chaotic redefinition.[3] Clearly, Wilhelm desired a program of naval expansion to support his image of Germany as a world power. But the absence of a widely accepted strategy for the future obscured the precise character and purpose of the kaiser's navy.

To complicate matters further, the Reichstag's approval of the funds essential to the kaiser's plan remained doubtful. To formulate a comprehensive strategy, a logical expansion plan, and a proper budget that might be defended successfully before the Reichstag would take considerable political talent. As career officers with little or no political background, Heusner and Hollmann lacked the necessary skills.

Relations between the RMA and industry reflected similar confusion and aimlessness. The flow of orders to the primitive naval armaments industry lacked uniformity and regularity because the fleet was a hodgepodge of different types of ships without a strategic plan to provide coherence. The industrialists rarely knew what the navy wanted and suspected that the Reichstag would not vote appropriations sufficient to justify sustained capital investment.

The appropriations problem approached a climax when State Secretary Hollmann failed to pilot a 1.56 billion mark naval budget through the Reichstag in the spring of 1897. He never presented well-defined spending proposals to the Reichstag and seldom made a concerted effort to support his budget requests with studies or plans showing present and future needs for increased appropriations. The parliamentary deputies found his tendency to base his budget requests on unclear general principles rather than calculated plans and considerations too vague.[4]

The Center and Progressive parties in the Reichstag thought the kaiser's proposed 1897 naval budget "limitless." The Progressive liberal leader, Eugen Richter, tried to challenge Hollmann's position as a minister of the crown, stressing his responsibility to the Reichstag as a cabinet minister. The kaiser denied that Hollmann was ultimately responsible to the Reichstag, which was technically true. But when Hollmann unwisely resurrected an 1873 memorandum on fleet composition and strategy as the basis of his Reichstag budget defense, the deputies cut 12 million marks off the naval appropriations for that year.[5]

The kaiser's impatience with the Reichstag's hesitation to accept increased naval spending then spilled over to include Admiral Hollmann's inability to alter that situation. As a contemporary political analyst put it: "One of his [Hollmann's] main difficulties with the Reichstag was his inability to justify his estimates by numerical demonstrations. . . . On the other hand, Admiral von Tirpitz's always lay chiefly in this, that he knew what he wanted and why he wanted it."[6]

Volker Berghahn suggests that the kaiser, in search of a solution to the budgetary dilemma, began to envision the RMA as a supraministry that could prepare and successfully guide a naval construction program through the Reichstag. Convinced that determined leadership would help him realize his ambitions for the navy, the kaiser recalled Rear Admiral von Tirpitz from the Far East Cruiser Squadron to take command of the RMA.[7]

From the outset, the Supreme Command's new director, Admiral Eduard von Knorr, recognized that von Tirpitz wanted to make the RMA the preeminent branch of the Imperial Navy. But in the wake of von Tirpitz's appointment, the navy's operational leadership failed to preserve its influence in matters of construction and fleet composition because Wilhelm gave his full support to the new RMA leader. Indeed, with his All-Highest Cabinet Order of 1898 the kaiser gave the RMA chief a free hand in construction and the selection of the types of ships that would join the fleet.[8]

German industry joined the kaiser in hailing von Tirpitz's energy and determined leadership. He provided a welcome respite from the uncertainty of the Heusner-Hollmann years, during which the RMA failed to provide a steady flow of contracts to ensure the future of naval shipbuilding. Because of poor planning on the part of RMA officials, insufficient naval appropriations, and the work traditionally absorbed by the navy's imperial shipyards, many German shipbuilding firms were forced to diversify before von Tirpitz's arrival in order to attract business outside the maritime world. Before 1898 they diversified as a matter of survival.

Historically, diversification was a fact of life for much of Germany's shipbuilding industry. In 1852 the first seagoing steamer of German construction came off the slipway at the Fürchtenicht and Brock Company, later the Vulcan Firm of Hamburg and Stettin. It was, of course, not an ironclad, nor was there a Germany to speak of at the time. The only domestic source of ironclad ship construction technology was a small school at Grabow (Stettin) opened in 1831. For the most part, German shipbuilders learned their trade abroad, in England or at the naval construction school at Copenhagen.[9] After the unification of Germany in 1871, Great Britain still built most of Germany's ships.

The first concerted effort to force the expansion and development of the German shipbuilding industry came from General Albrecht von Stosch, head of the Imperial Admiralty from 1871 to 1882, who performed the functions Wilhelm II would later distribute among the Reichsmarineamt, the Admiralty staff, and the Naval Cabinet. His post as chairman of the Committee on Naval Affairs enabled him to exert considerable political power and industrial influence.[10]

Von Stosch was the first to insist that a greater percentage of German naval construction be done within Germany. He ordered that the purchase of warships be limited exclusively to domestic shipyards (see Appendix A, Table 1).[11] By 1899 Germany had twenty-six shipyards of various capacities (Appendix A, Tables 2 and 3): eleven private firms on the Baltic, twelve more on the North Sea, and three imperial shipyards at Wilhelmshaven, Kiel, and Danzig. The six most important private yards were Krupp-Germaniawerft, owned and operated by Friedrich Krupp of Essen, Howaldtswerke in Kiel, Schichau in Elbing and Danzig, AG Weser in Bremen, Blohm und Voss in Hamburg, and Vulcan in Stettin and Hamburg.

Germaniawerft eventually became the largest shipbuilding company in Germany. Located at the south end of the Kiel docks, this concern, established in 1822, was initially a foundry for boilers and the manufacture of naval engines until it acquired the Norddeutsch Werft, also in Kiel. By 1881 the company was called the Schiff-und Maschinenbau AG Germania and began to acquire impressive shipbuilding credentials. Germaniawerft built the SMS *Kaiserin Augusta*, the first German warship with triple screws, capable of twenty-two knots, and the first armored German cruiser, SMS *Fürst Bismarck*. Under Krupp's direction it became an early center for research and development for surface ships and U-boats. Under the supervision of Krupp director Hanns

Jencke, a long-standing member of Germania's board of governors, the Essen firm acquired Germaniawerft gradually between 1896 and 1902. The process was completed only seven months before Fritz Krupp's suicide in November 1902.[12]

As a member of the Association of Shipyards, Germania became one of fourteen yards to respond collectively to von Stosch's plan to rely more on both German materials and production in domestic yards. Yet von Stosch's initial efforts to bring shipbuilding home could not suddenly bring stability to a firm. Germania experienced financial difficulties in the decade before von Tirpitz's appointment to the RMA that no doubt reflected the unpredictability of naval contracts and British domination of the commercial and warship market.[13]

In their relationship with the RMA after 1897, Germania and the Krupp firm often found Admiral von Tirpitz less than cordial. Very early in his term the new state secretary of the RMA correctly surmised that Krupp would just as soon profit from selling to Germany's enemies as supply the German navy. But as historian Willi Boelcke has pointed out, von Tirpitz and the navy were hopelessly dependent on the firm: "Although Admiral Tirpitz was truly a strong person of responsible position in Wilhelmian Germany, a man of unusual talents, hard and ruthless ambitions, and an initiator of modern warship construction, he was definitely not a friend of the House of Krupp. But the Reichsmarineamt could and would never be without the services of Krupp."[14]

The other major private shipyard in Kiel was the Howaldtswerke, established in 1876 by Georg Howaldt. It was one of the smallest of the six major private yards and like Germania, it struggled to remain financially solvent in the years before the naval expansion of the von Tirpitz era. In 1878–79 it built the twin screw steamers *Socrates* and *Diogenes* for the Peruvian navy, and in 1883 it produced two corvettes for the Chinese government. Its limited capacity forced it to specialize in the intermediate versions of the great commercial transatlantic steamers. Howaldt also built postal and passenger vessels and ships for colonial service.[15]

Along the southern rim of the Danzig Bight in the eastern Baltic, the city of Elbing was the site for one of the Howaldtswerke's largest and most diversified competitors. A successful machine works established in 1837 provided the base for the shipbuilding work begun there by Ferdinand Schichau in 1852. While acquiring a reputation as a first-class locomotive and machine company, Schichau built Germany's first steam dredger (1841) and Prussia's first propeller-driven ship (1855). By 1902 the firm's own factory produced better cast steel forms than some of Germany's best mills.[16]

Schichau's first contracts with the navy resulted in the production of three cannon boats. Although the RMA frequently balked at Schichau's high prices, the firm became the navy's primary supplier of small surface craft such as torpedo boats and was capable of building more sophisticated vessels. In 1891 it formally applied to the RMA for consideration in capital ship contracts and less than a year later acquired a shipyard in Danzig with sufficient depth to accommodate ships with a much greater draft than was available at Elbing. The depth of the Elbing dock facilities was 2.8 meters normally and 4 meters at high tide. The new Danzig facility, with a depth of 8.5 meters at the construction sites and a minimum depth of 7.3 meters on the way out to sea, put Schichau in the battleship business.[17] Schichau built six battleships for the RMA before World War I began.

From the beginning, this firm developed a reputation in the German shipbuilding industry for its success and diversity. Schichau not only excelled in shipbuilding and manufacturing but also created its own shipping business. It provided regularly scheduled freight service, mostly for grain and wood, between east Prussia and the manufacturing centers of the west.[18]

Considerably younger than Schichau, the Bremer Watjenschenwerft, established in 1843, became AG Weser in 1872 and began making the transition from its specialty of wooden construction to metal shipbuilding. Because of the early limitations of the Weser physical plant, it built primarily torpedo boats and light cruisers for the navy. Weser's first naval contracts included thirteen gunboats and eight torpedo boats.[19] The firm received few orders for battleships and built only two from 1890 to 1893: the SMS *Beowulf* and *Frithof*. Its next battleship contract, fourteen years after the *Frithof* joined the fleet, was for the SMS *Westfalen*. This construction pattern continued through World War I with Weser building only six battleships by 1918, compared with eighteen light cruisers and numerous torpedo boats and U-boats.[20]

Both because of Germany's unification and the incentive von Stosch's policies gave to shipbuilding, Blohm und Voss was established in Hamburg in 1872. It immediately won a contract to build a small oceangoing vessel for the Hamburg-American Line.[21] This firm's primary strength lay in the commercial area throughout the 1890–1914 period. It built 42,337 tons of ships in 1898 and exceeded that figure by 6,127 tons in 1899.[22] Between 1881 and 1890 it signed contracts for fourteen vessels over two thousand tons, and that figure rose to fifty for the next decade, or almost one-third of total German commercial production.

Blohm und Voss's willingness to adopt new technology and its ability to expand as the market demanded goes a long way toward explaining its success. In the 1890s the firm rebuilt part of its dock facilities to accommodate not only the increasing need for oceangoing liners and freighters but also the RMA's demand for battleships.[23] As a result, it could both service the huge, commercial Vulcan-built steamers such as the *Preussen, Bayern,* and *Sachsen* and build the largest capital ships the navy desired. In 1892 Blohm und Voss finished its first military vessel, the SMS *Condor,* during the expansion of construction facilities, and by 1897 the firm was ready for increased naval orders.[24]

Blohm und Voss built one battleship and three light cruisers for the RMA and in the process discovered its real naval specialty: heavy cruisers. Beginning with the SMS *Friedrich Karl* in 1903, Blohm und Voss provided the navy with eleven heavy battle cruisers, including the SMS *von der Tann, Seydlitz, Moltke, Goeben,* and *Derfflinger.* In 1916 these ships performed admirably against the British at Jutland.[25]

The last of the six major private shipyards, and, at the turn of the century the largest, was the Maschinenbau Aktiengesellschaft Vulcan of Stettin-Bredow. In 1857 Vulcan grew out of the firm of Fürchtenicht and Brock, a six-year-old Stettin shipyard.[26] Like many German shipbuilding firms, this joint-stock company diversified to pursue both marine engineering and machine construction.

Vulcan produced only 15,249 tons of ships for the commercial market in 1898, but by 1900 this figure had risen to 55,023. Between 1881 and 1890 Vulcan completed ten ships for Germany's merchant marine, including six large government-subsidized steamers for the North German Lloyd, one of Germany's premier shipping lines.[27] The following decade brought eighteen more contracts.

Vulcan's relations with the Imperial Navy commenced with the construction in Stettin of the first armored German ship ever produced, the corvette SMS *Preussen.* It was laid down in 1869 and completed well after Bismarck unified Germany. This was only the beginning of a very profitable association for both Vulcan and the navy. The Stettin firm eventually built nine battleships for the RMA, more than any other company. In addition, other contracts resulted in its building three heavy cruisers, eleven light cruisers, numerous torpedo boats, and, later, U-boats.[28]

Typically, any one of these privately owned shipyards performed a number of independent functions for a single project. It employed painters, skilled mechanics, boilermakers, and metalsmiths. It made fittings, valves, and different qualities of iron and steel. One yard engaged in repair work, others manufactured replacement parts, and all preserved the old carpenter's skills still very much in demand.

This diversification enabled some of the larger firms to produce other products or do piecework to keep them financially stable when naval contracts were scarce. Blohm und Voss's repair capability, Schichau's locomotive works, and Vulcan's machinery are all examples. For the smaller firms the erratic rhythm of commercial and naval contracts through 1898 and their inability to diversify created difficulties.

The three imperial yards, although physically similar to the private yards, served a variety of other functions for the RMA. Established in 1869 and located at Danzig and Kiel on the Baltic and at Wilhelmshaven on the North Sea, they functioned as centers for Prussian coastal defense in cooperation with Bismarck's North German Confederation.[29]

At Danzig, the site of the smallest of these imperial yards, the navy had three slipways, two stationary docks, several floating docks, and, later, facilities for U-boat construction as well.[30] Danzig and the Germaniawerft were the only shipyards in Germany engaged in U-boat research and development. This imperial yard produced twenty-seven of the sixty-two U-boats laid down before 1914; Krupp built twenty-eight, Weser six, and an Italian firm one.[31]

The Wilhelmshaven yard, the second largest among the three, specialized more in battleship construction than the other two. It also possessed extensive repair facilities because RMA policy was to execute repairs exclusively at the imperial yards. Wilhelmshaven had three large docks, two smaller ones, and a minimum of the required auxiliary facilities. In Kiel, at the largest of the three imperial yards, construction capabilities certainly equaled those of some of the better independent firms. The navy also had centers here for testing artillery and torpedoes as well as machine shops, materials testing laboratories, and considerable storage facilities. Besides nine slips for working on torpedo boats and three small construction docks, Kiel had six full-size docks for battleship and cruiser work.[32]

In the 1870s the imperial yards spearheaded official programs, performed administrative functions, and provided the RMA with greater freedom of decision. For example, although von Stosch encouraged the private shipyards to employ domestic materials and subcontractors, the imperial yards had to follow these naval directives as much as possible. Nearly two decades later, when von Tirpitz's ambitions for the fleet strained the entire industry to its limits, the capabilities of the imperial yards became one of his more effective tools in dealing with the private sector.

The RMA also employed the imperial yards to whittle down ship prices. When Schichau and Germaniawerft proposed bids that the RMA considered excessively high for the torpedo boats 90–101, it used the imperial yards to avoid paying a much higher price. Schichau bid 930,000 marks and Germania 1,075,000 marks for a project the RMA believed should cost around 770,000 marks. The RMA gave projects worth 560,000 marks to the imperial yards and awarded the rest to Schichau for 874,000 marks.[33] According to two British journalists who evaluated the imperial yards on the eve of World War I, they were "designed on the principle that they shall possess a sufficient power of output so as to prevent private yards from being in a position to fix the prices at which warships should be built, and they have shown themselves equal to the occasion, and are by no means behind private establishments."[34] Although serving as a price yardstick was not their original function, this became one of the major duties of the imperial yards after 1897.

Before von Tirpitz, the imperial yards fulfilled a financial and accounting role that the admiral expanded at the turn of the century. The administrative departments of all three imperial shipyards accounted for the expenditure not only of their own funds but also of those periodically released to the private yards to fulfill ship contracts.[35] They also controlled funds allotted for research and testing at all the yards.[36] The RMA Budget Department often authorized the imperial yards to issue vouchers which smaller contractors could present for payment at the Reichsbank.[37] Thus the already diverse responsibilities required of every shipyard were considerably broadened in the case of the imperial yards.

Though a solid industrial foundation existed for naval construction,

Germany still faced many related problems that would prove extremely difficult to solve. By 1899, German materials still amounted to only 2.7 percent of any given ship built at home. More than half of the materials used, and in a good many cases entire ships, still came from Britain or some other foreign source. Only 120,000 tons, or 1.9 percent of total German steel production, went to shipbuilding projects. Indeed, by the mid-1900s the percentage of German steel made for ships never exceeded 4.5 percent.

In 1900 the cost of shipbuilding materials in Germany exceeded that in Britain or France because of the lack of naval experience and difficulties within the industry. Germany's coal and iron ore prices, set largely by the Rhineland industrialists, were the highest in Europe. Long distances between the major shipyards on the Baltic and North seas and Germany's mines and inland industries created huge transport costs. A supply train had to travel 984 kilometers from the Krupp works in Essen to Elbing and 299 kilometers from Essen to Wilhelmshaven. Many small specialized firms could not pay the prohibitive transport costs and still show a profit. Thus large capital expenditures were deemed foolish.[38]

In the iron and steel industry innovation and corporate takeovers presented yet another problem. The Thomas-Gilchrist and Siemens-Martin processes for producing high-quality steel were still undergoing tests for naval use in the 1890s, and only a limited number of German firms could produce by these methods. Armor plate production techniques changed every five years or so, from the Ellis system developed in Britain in the 1880s, through the Wilson system, which first introduced steel into armor for resilience. Finally, by 1890, the Harvey Company of New Jersey devised a nickel-steel armor which Krupp almost immediately improved. Krupp had a virtual monopoly on armor in Germany and by the early 1890s was swiftly consuming competitors such as Gruson and the Bochumer Gussstahlfabrik and outcompeting others such as the Horder Verein.[39]

Furthermore, most iron, steel, or mineral firms in the Ruhr Valley formed cartels. The coal and coke suppliers of western Germany united in the Rhine-Westfalian Coal Syndicate and the Westfalian Coke Syndicate. Their east German counterparts later established two cartels centered in Berlin.[40] There were iron pipe, scrap iron, and conventional iron syndicates like the Grobblechverband, which was managed by Krupp's board of directors and united twenty firms producing steel plate from five to forty millimeters thick. The politically powerful iron and steel firms forced the suspension of many provincial tolls to facilitate cross-country transport of their product but rarely passed the savings on to consumers or the navy. They also had close ties with other cartels such as the Association of Ship Steel Producers and the Association of Cast Steel Producers.

On the positive side, the labor force was expanding. In 1895, according to the naval yearbook *Nauticus*, Germany had 1,130 ship construction or supply companies employing about 35,000 workers. Only 46 firms employed more than 50 workers, or 28,600 of the total. This was a modest increase from a work force of 23,000 employed by the industry in 1882, von Stosch's last full year at the Admiralty. By 1898, however, 11 of the largest shipyards employed 24,220 people out of a total related work force of 62,400 at a salary of approximately 67 million marks.[41] The expansion of the naval armaments industry to meet the new demands of von Tirpitz's RMA had already begun.

Von Tirpitz and the Naval Law of 1898

Alfred von Tirpitz is one of the most fascinating figures of modern German history. For the two decades after his appointment as RMA state secretary in 1897 he exerted absolute control over the development of the German navy. Evaluations of his ability and his effect on Germany's navy, domestic policy, and foreign affairs have been exhaustive. Conservatives Walther Hubatsch and Gerhard Ritter have portrayed him as a man with an essentially defensive policy, intent on protecting Germany's security and vulnerable international trade.[42] Many of the new socioeconomic historians, influenced by Eckart Kehr, however, believe that von Tirpitz advocated the High Seas Fleet to challenge Britain and neutralize the Reichstag's control over naval expenditures by means of a long-term commitment to shipbuilding.[43]

Here it is essential only to review the development of von Tirpitz's career and his theories on the purpose and eventual composition of the fleet. The consistency of these views and von Tirpitz's persistence in following them determined the types of ships added to the German navy in the years between 1898 and World War I.

Alfred von Tirpitz was born in 1849, entered the navy as a cadet sixteen years later, and passed through the naval academy between 1874 and 1876. His training as a torpedo specialist led to his first major commands as chief of the Torpedo Inspectorate and then chief of the Torpedo Flotillas. He later served as chief of staff, first to the commander of the Baltic Naval Station and then to the Supreme Command.[44]

In 1894, as chief of staff to the Supreme Command, von Tirpitz first calculated the essentials of his strategy for the future of the fleet in his "Service Memo IX." In it he proposed the risk theory, in which a vastly increased navy with an emphasis on battleships would challenge Great Britain. If Germany possessed a naval force large enough to inflict severe damage on its enemies, then any naval power, including Great Britain, would shrink from the risk of a surface battle because a victory would be too costly to contemplate. Von Tirpitz believed that only increased offensive potential could secure Germany's international ambitions without war.

The vogue in naval strategy during these years was the "Jeune Ecole," or "Young School," based on the *guerre de course* strategy of the French Admiral Théophile Aubé.[45] He proposed to challenge British naval supremacy by loosing a force of quick, powerful cruisers against her shipping lanes. This force would avoid the decisive battle, or *Entscheidungsschlacht*, with the Grand Fleet and attempt to strangle Britain economically. The interdependence of nations created by a large-scale industry, food scarcity, and rising populations lay at the foundation of this strategy. It was popular in Germany and was mentioned in the writings of Freiherr Kurt von Maltzahn and the U-boat partisan Vice-Admiral Karl Galster, and even the kaiser favored it for a short time.[46] Later, it formed the basis of many critiques of von Tirpitz, whose risk theory was the antithesis of the Young School.

Von Tirpitz embraced the risk theory to appear as the German foil to the French Young School. In this he reflected sentiments within naval circles stated more eloquently by the American Alfred T. Mahan.[47] The appearance of a dynamic German naval leader with an appealing strategy also proved a welcome change from the seeming aimlessness of Heusner and Hollmann.[48] Their ideas had perpetuated the navy's coastal defense role, a position that seemed outworn as German *Weltpolitik* developed during the reign of Wilhelm II. These factors worked to von Tirpitz's career advantage when he returned to Berlin from the Far East in 1897 as state secretary of the RMA.

With the appointment of von Tirpitz as state secretary, "Service Memo IX" became the bible of the new navy. Von Tirpitz's energetic drive to publicize, argue, organize, and otherwise impress his High Seas Fleet concept on Germany's leaders facilitated the passage of his naval construction bills of 1898 and 1900.[49] His reputation and credibility rested on his theory, and the entire construction program from 1898 until the war rested on his thought. As the program succeeded, his faith in these ideas deepened. Industrial and public support gave naval expansion a momentum that constantly reinforced his attachment to the risk theory in spite of significant changes on the international scene before 1914.

For von Tirpitz, the years 1897–98 were part of the strategic "danger zone," when Britain might launch a preventive attack before Germany completed its fleet.[50] Throughout this time he closely adhered to his policy both to see Germany out of the danger zone and to preserve the credibility gained earlier for himself and his ideas. He did not want a premature war with Great Britain, but if it came he was fully prepared to suggest using Germany's new naval strength to inflict severe damage upon the British as quickly as possible. He felt that a protracted war would be disastrous for Germany.

Some brother officers thought von Tirpitz, the shipbuilder and politician, ventured too far into strategic matters. Officially the Supreme Command formulated strategy because this arm of the navy would direct the fleet in wartime.[51] As SS/RMA (state secretary of the RMA), von Tirpitz consistently employed "Service Memo IX" as the blueprint of his construction program, but the Supreme Command did not adhere to it in matters of strategy. The two commands did not agree on fleet composition, location of the major naval bases, the use of the fleet in conflict, and the definition of exactly what constituted "favorable conditions" in a possible battle with the British. Thus instead of unity of purpose between these two vital branches of the Imperial Navy there was constant competition for the kaiser's favor. Von Tirpitz easily exploited the resulting confusion and indecision.

When he assumed the post of state secretary of the RMA, von Tirpitz envisioned the German fleet as consisting of nineteen battleships (plus two in reserve), eight armored coastal vessels, twelve heavy cruisers (plus three reserves for overseas duty), thirty light cruisers (plus three reserves for overseas duty), and twelve torpedo boat divisions.[52]

Although "Service Memo IX" gave a welcome direction and consistency to naval policy, this proposed fleet would cost a staggering 408 million marks spread over the years 1898 to 1905. In a cleverly conceived campaign to secure these funds from the Reichstag, von Tirpitz lowered his projected construction costs by 15 percent for both economic and political effect and proposed his naval program to the Reichstag not merely as part of the 1898 budget but as a new naval law. Parliamentary assent, therefore, would go far beyond the year's budget allocation, committing Germany to long-term naval development.

Von Tirpitz also mobilized his supporters and those who stood to gain from naval expansion. Led by Lieutenant Commander August von Heeringen, the RMA News Bureau, assisted by private industry, launched a propaganda crusade in support of the Naval Law. On 13 January, at the Kaiserhof in Berlin, the Central Association of German Industrialists and Hamburg's leading fleet proponent, Adolf Woermann, sponsored a meeting of the interested business community attended by 251 pro-naval individuals and groups, including seventy-eight Chamber of Commerce presidents. They agreed to coordinate their efforts to see the 1898 Naval Law through the Reichstag.

The parliamentary struggle over the Naval Law revealed von Tirpitz as an individual of considerable political talent. In a system governed by Bismarck's constitution, von Tirpitz was under no obligation to the parties that dominated the Reichstag. He answered to the kaiser alone. It was, however, "precisely because von Tirpitz behaved as if Germany had a parliamentary regime that he was so successful." He took the politicians seriously, talked, negotiated, and argued with them, and thus seemed to become one of them. This often seemed true to his naval colleagues as well for, as the scholar Samuel Huntington has pointed out, "he was generally viewed by the other admirals as an essentially political figure."[53]

Von Tirpitz could relate to people according to the demands of the moment. He was ruthless at eliminating rivals in the navy. He pushed Eduard von Knorr into the background and with him relegated the Supreme Command to a secondary position in naval affairs. He had Admiral Karl Galster censured for advocating quicker development of the U-boat because von Tirpitz felt it would challenge the primacy of the battleship.[54] He handled contacts in the Reichstag with seasoned grace, sending its leaders thorough memoranda to keep them well informed on naval affairs and frequently engaging them in personal conversations or encouraging his RMA subordinates Harald Dähnhardt (budget) and Eduard von Capelle (administration) to do so.[55] The RMA responded to all of their questions and even arranged tours of the imperial naval yards for some Reichstag deputies.[56]

Particularly important for parliamentary success was von Tirpitz's relationship with the Catholic Center party and its leader Ernst Lieber.[57] The Naval Law appealed to Lieber because of its potential for extracting political benefits for the party. Lieber looked beyond the religious and regional character of his party and fancied that the naval issue could make it the premier national party in Germany. He hoped that aiding von Tirpitz would help broaden the freedom and influence of the Catholic church and establish the Center as the arbiter in Reichstag disputes. But von Tirpitz, the prototype of the officer-politician, successfully sidestepped Lieber's efforts to place clearly defined limits on naval expenditures over the 1898–1905 period. He managed all this without losing the essential support of the Center party leader, who would help counter the opposition to the 1898 Naval Law from the progressive liberals and socialists.

If von Tirpitz obtained what he wanted from the Reichstag in 1898 it would truly indicate a great deal of political skill. Costs rose constantly, and politicians like Lieber sought economies and sharp definitions in every spending category. The SMS *Brandenburg*, built in 1890, had cost 9.3 million marks and costs for the SMS *Kurfürst Friedrich Wilhelm* also built in 1890, eventually went as high as 11.23 million marks.[58] No price was stable in the shipbuilding industry, especially now that the government contemplated spending in the billions.[59]

Only these high figures endangered the von Tirpitz–Lieber agreement on Center party support for the Naval Law. Could the Reichstag afford this measure without a new source of revenue? Proposed progressive income tax laws, designed to arrest the Reich's declining revenues, never got beyond debate and remained a specter that continued to haunt the Reichstag and the chancellorships of Hohenlohe and von Bülow well into the next decade.[60] Von Tirpitz overcame these handicaps with well-reasoned argument, brilliantly orchestrated propaganda, and an alliance of the right and center within the Reichstag.

The 1898 Naval Law passed the Reichstag on 26 March and received the kaiser's signature fifteen days later. Just before the law was voted on, August Bebel gave the final plea of the German Social Democratic Party (SPD) against the true nature and purpose of the legislation. In his analysis of that speech and the Reichstag's reaction to it, historian Jonathan Steinberg wondered whether von Tirpitz's cautious parliamentary tactics had been necessary. The house responded with "prolonged laughter" to Bebel's warning that Britain would crush Germany in a direct confrontation "even if (our fleet) is finished to the very last ship demanded in this law." Only one thing was sure: "What had been the closely guarded plan of an inner cabal in January of 1896 had become the wish of a substantial majority of the Reichstag by March 1898."[61]

Evolution of the Protocol System

As state secretary, von Tirpitz directly controlled every department and section of the RMA. But as naval affairs became more complex after 1898, he relied heavily on a group of very competent officers and civilian advisers to keep the RMA system running effectively. Communication between departments on matters of construction, budget, prices, research, and so forth, took place in *Sitzungen* or administrative conferences attended by representatives of all RMA departments.[62] Depending on the subject of the session, particular divisions of any given department or section would attend according to their specialty.

As Construction Department chief, von Eickstedt regularly attended these sessions. His department had four divisions to supervise the various stages of construction. KI was in charge of general ship construction matters, and KII conducted all relations with machine and motor firms. KIII supervised the shakedown cruises of capital ships, smaller vessels, and all related work. KIV regulated the correct methods of ship construction according to strict RMA guidelines.[63] Von Tirpitz kept himself abreast of the progress of the construction program through these meetings, remaining deeply involved but avoiding the headache of personally assuming every responsibility.

In the 1890s building capital ships required such a diversity of materials and skills that certain difficulties were inevitable, especially since the German shipbuilding industry was still growing and often lacked the skills or tools to keep up with the ambitious work schedules adopted by the RMA. The construction of the SMS *Kaiser Friedrich III*, *Victoria Louise*, and *Hertha* fell behind schedule in 1894 and 1895 because subcontractors often delivered flue pipes, boiler steel, armor, and other parts and tools to the shipyard rather than to the firms responsible for manufacturing the components.[64]

Inflation and artificially high prices also plagued the RMA in the early years of the construction program. Overruns in cost and weight became a chronic problem to the Construction Inspectorate, which reported every variation in cost or weight that deviated from contract specifications. Thus the construction files of all German ships are cluttered with cost and weight reports on everything from locks and hatches to armor plate.[65] The overruns ranged from insignificant sums to thousands of extra marks and kilograms. One inspection report from the imperial yard in Kiel informed the RMA that the parts inventories for two light cruisers averaged 3,300 marks above contract cost.[66] Three armored capital ships purchased by the RMA illustrate the dramatic rise in prices, which leaped from 4.5 million to 9.6 million marks over a five-year period.[67]

The RMA responded to such problems with a very effective system of regulations and protocol that began during the Hollmann period and was refined and perfected under von Tirpitz. The accounting functions of the imperial shipyards, the role of the Purchasing Office, and the resident inspector at every yard represented only a small part of the picture. This RMA protocol system involved firms in a labyrinth of requirements, tests, and screening that became the single most important lever the RMA possessed in its dealings with industry.

The roots of the RMA protocol system lay in the navy's first efforts to reach the level of technical expertise shared by its private contractors and the leading naval powers. Under the direction of Dietrich, chief of the RMA Construction Office from 1881 to 1898, the navy's experts attended most of the major international conferences dealing with topics essential to naval development. Most important among these were the international congresses on testing methods held in Zurich in 1895 and Stockholm in 1897. Here RMA officials accumulated valuable information regarding new construction methods, all manner of tests for materials, and procedures for shakedown cruises.[68] This free exchange of technical information enabled the RMA to take advantage of sophisticated procedures like the *Zerreissenprobe*, or breaking test, which strained such substances as Siemens-Martin cast iron and Schneider-Creuzot steel to their limits. The new techniques and information allowed Dietrich's people to judge more accurately the quality of the supplies they purchased and enabled the RMA to formulate a strict set of quality codes governing all naval purchases.

German naval attachés gathered information on foreign firms. Next to developments in Britain, the RMA found the United States most interesting because here also the theory of the superiority of battleships reigned supreme. The Americans and Germans were similar both in strategic theory and in their stage of naval growth. The RMA closely followed the U.S. Navy Department's relations with Carnegie and Bethlehem Steel on the armor issue.[69] It also studied American technical journals and amassed data on shakedown cruises. For example, a report on the first voyage of the light cruiser USS *Cincinnati* sent to the state secretary included data on boilers, steering mechanisms, and propulsion.[70] The naval office scrutinized American purchasing procedures as well as the engine systems of the battleships *Alabama* and *Kearsarge*.[71]

The RMA developed regulations to govern its interaction with industry. By 1894 general guidelines for naval projects were published. These regulations stipulated that routine inspections of construction sites must be conducted and technical specifications strictly adhered to as well as a weekly accounting of man-hours, work accomplished, and the amount and type of materials used. The yard or subcontractor took responsibility for safe working conditions and the purchase of construction tools and materials. The Construction Department received quarterly financial reports, and any requests for RMA assistance became part of the monthly reports submitted by the project directors. For certain projects the yard contractor was required to guarantee his workmanship for periods ranging from three months to one year.[72] In addition, every yard contracting with the RMA received specifications, called general construction guidelines, which varied for each ship.

All shipyards in Germany were subject to the same supervision and review regarding work for the RMA. The RMA Technical Department and Construction Inspectorate always had experts at the various naval yards whose duties included further inspection of sophisticated system components. In this function they were double-checking, in many instances, the tests performed by the Purchasing Office of the RMA, which restricted its work to the production sites of the various sub-contractors. If material was acceptable, the Technical Department people supervised and often assisted in its installation at the yard.

The ultimate authority over all phases of ship construction at the individual yards rested with the Construction Inspectorate. Usually one naval official functioned as supervising constructor for each project and reported directly to the RMA Construction Department in Berlin.

The supervising constructor ultimately determined the maximum number of hours and amount of output the RMA could expect from any yard's work force. It also fell to him to pinpoint and remedy any technical complications in construction to avoid falling behind schedule. Dietrich and his successors at the RMA Construction Department found it profitable to allow the inspectors as much independence and responsibility as possible. In that way the officials could quickly handle any problem confronting them without constantly contacting Berlin. The private shipyards sent all correspondence to the RMA via the resident inspector, who could comment on the contents of any communication and the RMA would immediately see both sides of an issue.[73] This procedure also confirmed the authority of the inspectorate and strengthened the RMA in its relationship with the private yards.

The most important element of the RMA protocol system was the *Lieferantenverzeichnis* or suppliers' list. Unless it appeared in this directory of approved naval contractors, a company could not participate in the RMA's construction program. Individual firms could apply for a listing for one or more products in a specific category or categories. Smaller firms usually had to be introduced to RMA officials by their Chambers of Commerce. Then a representative of the Construction Department would visit the firm to inspect its plant facilities and labor force and determine its capital and financial stability. If the RMA had no reservations, the company had to supply samples of its material or product at its own expense for tests at an official navy testing center according to established RMA standards. If the tests proved acceptable, the firm was added to the suppliers' list in the specific category for which it applied. A firm might fail to qualify with one of its products but have no difficulty with another. The suppliers' list became the ultimate screening procedure used by the RMA. If a firm once qualified and the Purchasing Office or Construction Inspectorate later felt that its products fell below standard, it was removed from the list. Unless it requalified, it would receive no further contracts from the RMA.[74]

When von Tirpitz took over in 1897 a good deal of the protocol system already existed. He expanded it as the needs of the fleet required and made it work effectively in a wide variety of situations. After he acquired ample parliamentary funding for naval construction in 1897, its expansion promised huge profits for German industry. If businesses wanted to work on naval projects, they had to follow the RMA's regulations. With the exception of certain technological innovations, this procedure assured the RMA of a strong position in its relations with industry.

Research and Development

Admiral von Tirpitz provided the shipbuilding industry with the consistency and direction it lacked before 1897, but his attitude toward new technical breakthroughs confounded industry. The admiral's loyalty to the battleship and slow, deliberate technological development led him to avoid any basic changes in naval hardware. In his memoirs, von Tirpitz discussed his painfully cautious attitude toward research and development. He believed that no innovation should be adopted before it was perfected in the private sector. Thus he restricted naval involvement in U-boat research and complained that wireless telegraphy was installed in warships too soon. He sought to avoid the avalanche of technical problems that usually accompanied hasty change but actually accomplished something quite different.[75]

Although the RMA encouraged some research and development, it left almost all of this work to the private sector, limiting its effort to testing materials and a very restricted U-boat program. Materials testing was done at the imperial shipyards, the Royal Prussian Testing Office, and the Technische Hochschule in Berlin-Charlottenberg. Naval U-boat research became the exclusive province of the Danzig Imperial Shipyard, but the resources employed and the extent of the navy's commitment in no way compared to that of Krupp at Germaniawerft in Kiel.[76] Following von Tirpitz's policy, the various naval departments merely kept themselves abreast of all current innovations in naval-related fields.

The importance of the RMA research and development policy under von Tirpitz is twofold. His technical personnel lacked experience in many areas of high technology and thus were often incapable of exercising effective control over vessels and weapons purchased by the RMA from private industry. In most instances they knew the theory behind certain innovations because the international flow of naval research information was still very free, but there was a considerable gap between theoretical knowledge and practical experience.[77]

More important, von Tirpitz's policy tended to shift the responsibility for research and development to firms whose financial stability and technical expertise could support such programs. Too often this resulted in a monopoly by a single firm or a select group of dominant firms expert in an area in which the RMA was weak. This is not to say that von Tirpitz should have possessed a clairvoyance that would have made him aware of how important inventions such as the U-boat would become. But a deeper interest, greater official involvement, and a measure of financial support could have substantially improved the RMA's position. The expertise thus obtained would have resulted in more informed judgments regarding new developments and greater control over their possible production by private industry.

A prime example of this problem is the length of time it took to place steam turbine engines in German warships. The navy carefully traced the development of the Parsons turbine in Britain after its invention in 1884. The experiments with the Parsons prototype, the HMS *Turbina*, occupied considerable space in reports from the German naval attaché in London.[78] Clearly, the RMA had no wish to depend on a foreign firm to supply this remarkably better form of naval propulsion, but German private enterprise could not match the advance.

The RMA saw possibilities in a turbine developed domestically by the engineer Adolf Müller, but he violated Charles Parsons's patents. The other options open to the navy, a system created by the American Curtiss Company in association with Allgemeine Electrizitäts Gesellschaft (AEG) and another of Swiss origin called the Zoelly system, could not compete with the tried and tested Parsons machine. Left with no option, the RMA eventually contracted with the Parsons Marine Steam Turbine Company to build the navy's first turbine-powered capital ship, the light cruiser SMS *Lübeck*, commissioned from the Vulcan-Stettin shipyard in 1903.[79]

Because no private German firm was sufficiently involved in turbine research to supply the navy with a Parsons-quality engine, the RMA found itself without recourse. It was dangerous to rely so completely on a foreign contractor for such an important breakthrough because a war could quickly interrupt the flow of parts and technical assistance. Navy officials felt obliged to approach Krupp through the kaiser in 1906, hoping that the Essen firm's substantial resources could successfully solve the problem. The effort was a failure. By 1911–12 the Parsons Company still controlled the market. It powered two of the four König class dreadnoughts with turbines manufactured by its subsidiary in Germany.[80]

The Armor Monopoly

Contrary to some historical interpretations, the German naval authorities did try to combat monopoly and price fixing,[81] but the RMA met with mixed results in this area. In 1897, for example, the Construction Department worried about the growing dominance of the Rheinische Metallwarrenfabrik of Düsseldorf in the production of boiler pipes. Concerted efforts brought about successful competition from Mannesmann and Phoenix. Thus the RMA developed a group of very capable firms, excellent products, and lower, more stable prices.[82]

It was not as easy to restrain Friedrich Krupp AG of Essen, the best-known land and sea arms manufacturer in the world. Anything related to high-grade iron and steel fell within the firm's area of expertise. Between 1890 and 1897 the RMA was fairly successful in finding a reasonable amount of competition for Krupp. Among others, Thyssen, the Bismarckhütte, Borsig, and the Pilsen firm of Skoda competed to some degree in all areas of naval steel save armor plate.[83]

In 1893, Krupp formed an alliance that would give it a virtual monopoly of armor plate. Its new partner was Dillinger Hüttenwerke, a company located in the Saar region, which had supplied the navy with modest amounts of armor plate from 1876 to 1890.[84] Both of these firms had mastered armor technology, but Krupp alone proved capable of producing the quantity the navy required. The RMA found this alliance nearly impossible to manage.

The RMA first invited Krupp to participate in armor production in 1890. Three years later, almost simultaneously, the firm purchased the company of Gruson-Magdeburg and entered into its alliance with Dillinger.[85] Their perfection of the 420 nickel-steel armor process in 1894 gave the alliance, now dominated by Krupp, a monopoly in the production of high-quality armor.[86] By 1898, when Krupp's German patent on the nickel-steel armor process expired, the firm made sure its patent was extended to restrict the possibility of new firms entering the market.[87]

Early in von Tirpitz's term at the RMA, he encouraged firms such as Skoda, Thyssen, and Röther Metallwerk in Düsseldorf to compete with Krupp and received from them small orders of armor plate, rivets, container coverings, and fasteners. Yet as naval expansion and more effective artillery required larger quantities of high-grade steel armor, the Krupp-Dillinger alliance could not be matched.[88] They constantly drove ship prices up and shared responsibility for contracts signed by one or the other with the RMA.[89]

A report by the Weapons Division of the RMA in 1899 blamed price fluctuations and the monopoly of the Krupp-Dillinger alliance on advanced technology.[90] Only a few firms successfully employed the new Harvey process of manufacturing nickel-steel armor: Krupp and Dillinger in Germany; Vickers and Armstrong in Britain; Schneider in France; and Carnegie, Bethlehem, and later Midvale in the United States. Antitrust groups in the United States made it difficult for American firms to ally or combine. No such legal or popular limitations prevailed in Germany.

The 1899 RMA report gave much attention to the United States, where the Congress and secretary of the navy, Hilary A. Herbert, had monitored the drastic rise in armor prices between 1893 and 1897. Herbert did not hide his suspicions and anger regarding perceived collusion in the steel industry,[91] and Congress explored both the possibility of a government-owned factory and the feasibility of legislating a lower fixed price of 1,200 marks ($300) per ton.

The latest figures for American naval armor purchased raised a few eyebrows at the RMA. In 1899 Bethlehem and Carnegie wanted 2,180 marks per ton for first-quality 4 percent nickel steel. Krupp, which sold its superior steel for 2,320 marks per ton in Germany, offered it to the U.S. Navy for 2,192 marks. The reduction of 128 marks only served to enrage the RMA administration and underscore their problems in dealing with the armor alliance.[92]

The RMA attacked Krupp's position whenever it felt there was a chance for success. But in this case, the odds seemed to go against the RMA. Krupp produced not only most of the navy's best armor but also naval steel for every other use and all of the heavy guns for von Tirpitz's battleships. Its shipyard facilities at Kiel were vital to the navy's growth. Von Tirpitz and his staff consequently found themselves in a dilemma. They had to make sure the firm received all the help the navy's resources could muster while seeking to draw new competitors into the armor field.[93]

When the RMA took the initiative and committed itself to research and development such as exploring ways to insulate battleship bulkheads, it discouraged monopoly and enhanced the navy's technical expertise. In this case, the problem was not a lack of subcontractors but the need to develop a specialized nonflammable, lightweight material. The RMA worked with many firms supplying asbestos, rubber, wood, cork, and various synthetics. It finally decided to employ several different materials to meet the requirements in various sections of the ship. In this area the RMA directed research and relegated the firms to a secondary role.[94]

The RMA became involved in materials research and kept pace with engineering advances and techniques, but quantum leaps in naval technology such as the turbine engine required extensive amounts of time, capital, and testing. In these cases von Tirpitz always waited and allowed private business to perfect the technology before the navy judged its fitness for military use.

This examination of conditions in the navy and industry when von Tirpitz came upon the scene should clarify several important points. Within the newly reorganized naval structure each of the officers in command of the three major divisions of the Imperial Navy tested the boundaries of his authority. In this contest, von Tirpitz proved the most aggressive and successful of all. He eventually elevated the RMA to the first among equals within the naval organization.

In choosing von Tirpitz as state secretary of the RMA, Kaiser Wilhelm indicated his preference for a new set of strategic ideas. Von Tirpitz religiously followed his strategic dogma as set down in "Service Memo IX" despite the objections of his colleagues. His beloved battleship strategy dictated the type of fleet he would build and the potential adversary he had in mind. Von Tirpitz was determined to fulfill Germany's ambitions, but according to his own design.

In 1897, the shipbuilding industry in Germany was still relatively primitive, but this disadvantage was largely negated because the German economy in general experienced a period of rapid growth and the prospect of huge profits from naval contracts was attractive. The firms already involved in naval-related fields increased their efforts, and new companies turned their attention to the navy's needs. The labor movement, lacking effective unions, posed no real threat to the RMA's expansion program, but a scarcity of skilled labor proved a source of anxiety for all naval purveyors. If von Tirpitz could guarantee continuous government appropriations after 1897, the German shipbuilding industry appeared able to progress beyond its primitive condition of the 1880s and 1890s.

The awarding of contracts required the armaments industry to conform to naval regulations, and the protocol system served as von Tirpitz's primary tool in dealing with industry. The accelerated pace of production after the navy's success in the Reichstag would severely test the effectiveness of the system. But industry no longer had to question the RMA's promises of possible profits, for the Naval Law of 1898 guaranteed them. Once his program gained the support of the kaiser and the Reichstag, von Tirpitz moved to impose his protocol system on industry.

During this period the naval authorities discovered certain areas that would present the greatest difficulties, such as the production of armor plate. Krupp and Dillinger forged a strong armor monopoly, and they charged the navy higher prices than their foreign customers paid, openly resisting any controls imposed by the RMA. In addition, the Construction Department had difficulty curbing massive cost and weight overruns on projects large and small. Von Tirpitz and his associates discovered very early the problems involved in large-scale expansion.

Other difficulties originated with the RMA. Von Tirpitz's cautious policy regarding research and innovation led him to question any development that clashed with his strategy or budgetary planning. This policy restricted the activities of the Technical and Construction departments of the RMA, which merely observed while the Parsons Company extended its lead in turbine development far beyond the scattered and unfocused efforts of German firms. The German U-boat programs experienced the same lack of support. The RMA was well aware of French, American, and domestic private research efforts with submersible vessels. The RMA, however, thought official involvement too expensive and an invasion of the private sector. Furthermore, the submarine did not seem to fit into the battleship strategy set down in von Tirpitz's "Service Memo IX."

2

Further Expansion and the Second Stage

1899 – 1901

Between 1899 and 1901, von Tirpitz maintained the momentum set by the fleet expansion program. As he began to push the second stage of his program through the Reichstag in the form of the 1900 Naval Law, the world situation seemed to bear out his political argument for increased naval expenditure. Germany's relations with Britain, France, and the United States deteriorated markedly, and von Tirpitz sought to convince the public that a lack of naval might was responsible for Germany's poor performance in various international crises.

There was no need to court industrial support for further expansion. German and foreign firms anxiously anticipated carving up von Tirpitz's substantial budget. The major difficulties von Tirpitz and his associates encountered in their early relations with industry, such as monopolies, continued, and in some cases the RMA had few options. In hope of breaking the armor monopoly, von Tirpitz tried to press Fritz Krupp officially and publicly, only to discover that the head of the House of Hohenzollern was the industrialist's trump card.

Although the efficient protocol system addressed overruns in cost and weight, the RMA had only limited success in arresting them. It imposed the strictest sanctions possible against these violations from the outset in a vain attempt to discover a comprehensive solution to the problem.

The state secretary's policy of limited research and development further heightened the RMA's difficulties. His technical personnel found themselves at an increasing disadvantage as recent products of high technology proved useful for naval purposes. Von Tirpitz's policies also increased the confusion in German efforts to develop a turbine on the Continent to rival the British Parsons machine. Only in the area of U-boat technology did the admiral's policy change. Submarines had already proved useful as part of the French navy, and the Americans showed interest in the vessel developed by John P. Holland. Both public opinion and pressure from the Reichstag forced a reluctant von Tirpitz to obtain a number of U-boats from the Germaniawerft and to extend the development efforts of the imperial shipyard in Danzig.

Political Background

In 1897, Bernhard von Bülow became foreign minister and, in 1900, chancellor.[1] His rise, along with von Tirpitz's appointment as state secretary, clearly signaled the adoption of the so-called new course toward *Weltpolitik*, for von Bülow shared the kaiser's ambitions. Only a formidable naval force could extend Germany's aspiration for world power beyond the borders of Europe to the far corners of the globe. Therefore, von Bülow never sought an alliance with Great Britain because he knew von Tirpitz's naval plans and the kaiser's attitudes. As historian Paul Kennedy has pointed out, the new foreign minister perceived the political and diplomatic realities in Germany's relations with Britain when "he himself told the Kaiser and von Tirpitz in 1897 that 'a really honest and trustworthy Anglo-German alliance' was irreconcilable with the intended naval expansion and 'more or less means the renunciation of it.' "[2] This was the source of lasting antagonism, which caused the Haldane negotiations eventually to falter in 1912.

Von Bülow and the kaiser interpreted every crisis in terms of how Germany would appear in contrast to other powers, and every tense situation seemed to echo the kaiser's plea for a vastly increased navy. From this point of view, the growth of American power in South America, the Far East, and the South Pacific seemed a direct threat to Germany's emergence on the world scene. Von Bülow and the kaiser insisted that Germany share in the carving up of Spain's Pacific empire and overreacted to American successes in the Spanish-American War. This attitude nearly led to a shooting confrontation between American forces under Commodore George Dewey and Vice-Admiral Otto von Diederichs's more powerful cruisers off Manila Bay in June 1898.[3]

In 1899, Bismarck's old settlement of the Samoan problem broke down. Faced with a full-scale civil war on the island, Germany, Britain, and the United States had to repair or replace the tripartite supervision of Samoa outlined in the Berlin Act of 1889. German preoccupation with securing national reputation, prestige, and possibly a few coaling stations further exacerbated already poor relations with the United States only one year after the Dewey-Diederichs confrontation and drew the English-speaking powers together. Germany became more isolated than ever.[4]

These setbacks reinforced popular German sentiments that the nation had fallen victim to superior naval power. Would the United States or Britain have dared act as they did if Germany's fleet matched theirs? They interpreted the rise of American power as an open political and military challenge and regarded Britain's performance in Samoa in the same light. When the English searched a German commercial ship in Delago Bay in 1899, the angry German press response was met with glee by naval expansionists. The seizure of the *Bundesrath* and other steamers on the suspicion that they were supplying contraband to the Boers seemed only one more in a succession of outrages. The kaiser and von Tirpitz returned to these themes repeatedly and, bolstered by economic and political pressure groups, argued for a larger fleet to relieve Germany's plight. As Wilhelm told von Bülow with his characteristic bravado in 1899, "After twenty years, when it is ready, I will adopt a different tone."[5] With von Tirpitz in charge of naval development, these words were significant.

The last step in the creation of the modern naval command structure came on 14 March 1899. The Supreme Command was replaced by the Admiralty Staff. In peacetime this new organization took charge of strategic planning, training officers in staff duties, and naval intelligence. During war it directed all naval operations with the kaiser's assent.[6]

The same year, the Construction Department also experienced a change. Dr. Dietrich had retired in 1898 after seventeen years as the director of naval construction, and von Tirpitz had to find someone to pilot the new construction program authorized by the Reichstag. On 10 November 1899 Captain Rudolf von Eickstedt was appointed head of naval construction, a post he held until his retirement as vice-admiral in 1906.[7]

The Progress of Construction

In the first Naval Law the Reichstag authorized an existing German fleet of twelve battleships, ten heavy cruisers, and twenty-three light cruisers in service or under construction by 1 April 1898. The goals set by this legislation for construction through 1903 included seven battleships, two heavy cruisers, and seven light cruisers, bringing the total in service and reserve to the legal limit of nineteen battleships and twelve heavy and thirty light cruisers.[8]

The first class of battleships laid down according to these regulations was the five-ship Wittelsbach Class (*Wittelsbach, Wettin, Zähringen, Mecklenburg*, and *Schwaben*). Built between 1899 and 1903, these ships cost an average of 22.3 million marks each and displaced 11,774 tons normal.[9] The main armament consisted of four guns of 25 centimeters, eighteen of 15 centimeters, and twelve of 8.8 centimeters. This class brandished one submerged torpedo tube more than the five the Kaiser Friedrich III Class possessed. The torpedoes used were of the 45-centimeter variety.[10] During this period advances in propulsion and gyroscopic guidance extended torpedo range to at least 1,600 meters.[11] Armor specialists and gun designers consequently had to strengthen belt armor at the waterline and extend the range of heavy guns.

The ships of the Wittelsbach Class had a maximum steaming range of 5,850 sea miles (at 10 knots) and a minimum of 3,150 sea miles (at 16 knots).[12] The power plant consisted of three triple expansion engines powered by six Schulz-Thornycroft and six cylindrical boilers.[13]

The bids entered for the Wittelsbach Class prompted the RMA to give the imperial shipyard two contracts and distribute three others to private firms. The Wilhelmshaven Imperial Shipyard built the SMS *Wittelsbach* and *Schwaben*, Schichau the *Wettin*, Germaniawerft the *Zähringen*, and Vulcan the *Mecklenburg*. Although the cost of the ships at the private yards varied very little, that was not the case for the Wilhelmshaven contracts. The 22.7 million marks paid for the *Wit-*

telsbach (built between 1899 and 1902) was the highest of the five by a slim 100,000 marks. The *Schwaben* (1900–1904), however, cost 21.7 million, or between 600,000 and 900,000 marks less than the cost at any private firm.[14] It seemed clear that if properly tooled and prepared for a particular ship design, the Wilhelmshaven Imperial Yard could save the RMA a great deal of money.

In the later Deutschland Class, the 24.25 million marks spent to build the SMS *Hannover* at Wilhelmshaven was the lowest compared with Germania, Vulcan, and Schichau. The imperial yard's first experience with a dreadnought, the SMS *Nassau* (1907–9), resulted in an expenditure of 37.39 million marks, making it the most expensive ship in the class after the SMS *Westfalen* (built by AG Weser, 1907–9). In the next dreadnought class, however, the price the RMA paid at Wilhelmshaven for the *Ostfriesland* (1908–11) was 43.5 million marks, the cheapest of the four in the Helgoland Class by 2.3 million marks.

The comparison between the *Wittelsbach* and *Schwaben* and the *Nassau* and *Ostfriesland* illustrates well the capability of the imperial shipyards to achieve sorely needed economies to the benefit of von Tirpitz's strained finances. Furthermore, the Wilhelmshaven yard proved, mark for mark, as good or better than the private shipyards in battleship building and a valuable alternative for the RMA when private bids seemed too high. Doubtless, von Tirpitz often wished that Wilhelmshaven could build more ships than its limited capacity allowed.

The *Schwaben* project saved enough for the entire Wittelsbach Class to remain within the appropriation. Based on the 1899 budget, for example, the Wilhelmshaven Imperial Shipyard saved the RMA 662,000 marks, which, along with Germaniawerft's saving of 214,000 marks, more than balanced out the cost overruns experienced by Vulcan, Schichau, and Wilhelmshaven's SMS *Wittelsbach* project.[15]

The imperial yard at Kiel built both of the heavy cruisers budgeted during this period. The SMS *Prince Heinrich* ultimately cost 16.6 million marks and weighed 8,887 tons normal. At a speed of 18 knots it had a range of 2,290 sea miles, which could be extended to 4,580 at 10 knots. This cruiser carried two 24-centimeter guns, ten each of 15 and 8.8 centimeters, and four 45-centimeter torpedo tubes.

All German heavy cruisers finished before 1905 had a similar offensive power. The SMS *Prince Adalbert*, laid down in 1900, had similar dimensions and the same armament as the *Prince Heinrich* but held more coal and oil and at a speed of 18 knots exceeded the *Prince Heinrich's* range by 690 sea miles. At 12 knots the *Prince Adalbert* was capable of 4,970 sea miles, a range the earlier cruiser could match only at 10 knots. The *Friedrich Karl, Roon,* and *Yorck* continued this trend of ever greater speed and steaming range for heavy cruisers through 1905.[16]

Only one of these two heavy cruisers exceeded the budget appropriated for it. In 1898, the *Prince Heinrich* went 1,329,000 marks over its yearly budget, but in 1900 the *Prince Adalbert* came in 1,258,000 marks under its projected cost. This deficit of 71,000 marks for von Tirpitz's first two cruisers in their initial budget years marked a beginning almost as favorable as that in the battleship program.[17]

Construction of the smaller vessels also accelerated. Six small cruisers were laid down between 1898 and 1900: three at AG Weser (*Niobe, Ariadne,* and *Medusa*), two at the Germaniawerft (*Nymphe* and *Amazone*), and one at the imperial yard at Danzig (*Thetis*). All but the *Niobe* and *Nymphe*, both begun in 1898, stayed within contract appropriation, and the cheapest of the six was the Danzig's *Thetis* at 4.5 million marks. The larger high-seas torpedo boats cost approximately 1 million marks each. Schichau had produced these boats exclusively since 1886, and this situation changed only slightly in 1900. The Elbing firm started eighteen new boats between 1898 and 1900, and the RMA awarded Germaniawerft contracts for six.[18]

The Protocol System

Along with its inspection system, the suppliers' list remained the strong point of RMA protocol vis-à-vis industry. Its revision was never final because the RMA deleted or added firms as it saw fit. In 1900 the RMA circulated versions of the suppliers' list among all the firms dealing with the navy. It recorded companies removed for financial instability, legal and military code violations,[19] or those deemed unreliable because of questionable business practices.[20] Firms could be readmitted to the list after their products passed standards set by the RMA.[21] Beyond these controls, the officials of the Purchasing Office and the Construction Department cleared naval purchases[22] and conducted on-site plant inspections of naval contractors.[23] The system proved surprisingly effective, limited only by its designers' abilities and the often considerable political and economic power of heavy industry.

Private industry often encouraged the RMA to expand the number of firms on the suppliers' list to keep the prices charged by subcontractors to a minimum.[24] But, if the RMA included many privately favored firms, the coercive power of that instrument would decline. Many industrialists regarded any efforts to use the list exclusively as too restrictive, and they occasionally accused the RMA of interfering with free competition. That accusation did not overly impress von Eickstedt or von Tirpitz in their struggle to get the best deal for the navy.

The RMA's system of awarding contracts to shipyards reflected the experience of other world naval powers. Much of the fine print in German naval contracts was taken from the standard British forms. For example, the RMA replaced the controller of British contract language with the inspector, who was directly responsible to von Tirpitz, via the Construction Department, for his project. These parallels with British policies also applied to product guarantees, pay schedules, work stoppages or slowdowns, patent matters, and cost and weight changes, among others.[25]

These contract specifications formed the structure within which the RMA and its primary suppliers operated, and exceptions were only occasionally granted. In one instance, Schichau successfully approached the Danzig Construction Inspectorate for permission to raise the price of a ship's coal bunker. As a result, the spending ceiling, spelled out in the contract, had to be adjusted.[26] Von Tirpitz, in consultation with von Eickstedt, kept exceptions to a minimum and strictly enforced contract restraints.[27]

Like the naval authorities of other nations, the RMA imposed financial penalties if a firm did not adhere to the construction schedule outlined in its contract. In one such instance, the RMA informed Germaniawerft that a 3.5 percent penalty would result if the firm departed from its construction schedule. This percentage pertained to the ship as a whole or any material Germania had agreed to supply within a specified time. The total price of the object multiplied by 3.5 percent and the length of the delay was deducted from the company's final bill.[28] This financial penalty system was similar but not identical to that of other navies. The United States, for example, charged a flat rate by the day for ships that fell behind schedule, stipulating a $300 penalty per day for the first month and $600 every day thereafter.[29]

Construction schedules proposed by the shipyards were an important consideration in the awarding of RMA contracts. The navy did not expect capital ship bids to vary greatly. For example, in the Braunschweig Class, the ultimate prices paid for the five ships fell between 23.8 and 24.3 million marks. The suggested pace of construction and the schedule of installment payments varied greatly, however. Every battleship was financed in four installments.[30] Blohm und Voss suggested that the second payment, bringing the SMS *Braunschweig* to half completion, would come after sixteen months and the final or fourth payment should come due in the twenty-third month.[31] Germania offered a somewhat tighter schedule. The second payment would come at the twenty-first month and the final installment in the twenty-fifth month. Vulcan's schedule called for the second payment at the twentieth month and the final payment at the twenty-seventh month.[32] As a result of the RMA's preference for Krupp's proposed payment scheme and its efficient construction schedule, Germaniawerft received the contract for the SMS *Braunschweig*, the first of its class.

The navy paid any monies owed to a subcontractor for armor, guns, spare electrical parts, and the like through the shipyards.[33] The only major concern was to keep the project on schedule and material quality up to par. If for any reason the construction inspector did not consider the subcontractor's obligation fulfilled, the firm's money would not be included in the installment paid to the shipyard.[34]

In response to questions from the new state secretary of the Imperial Treasury Office, Max Freiherr von Thielmann, von Tirpitz defended his disbursement of shipbuilding funds. He asserted that whether small contracts handled by the imperial yards or huge payments via installments to shipyards, the "current form of disbursement of shipbuilding funds is not only the cheapest but also politically the best." But he did not take all the credit, noting that the system's history recommended it: "As proof I declare that it had functioned faultlessly from 1887 to 1897."[35]

One of von Eickstedt's first efforts to address the more difficult problems of construction was directed to cost and weight control. Together the contract and the general guidelines dictated the RMA's expectations for time, weight, and cost at every stage of a project.[36] Unfortunately, these standards were not easily enforced. In the process of setting weight standards for an entire ship or class, the RMA found some of the yards less than cooperative.[37] Furthermore, because the increases in a ship's construction time, weight and cost added up slowly over time, resulting from small overruns on individual components, they were very hard to curb. The proper procedure in these cases required each contractor to clear up any cost, time, or weight overrun either with the construction inspector at the yard or the purchasing inspector and then report it to the RMA for final approval. The general guidelines stipulated that the RMA would pay for additional materials, labor, and supervision. In these cases, the RMA placed a 15 percent ceiling on the amount the yard could take as profit.[38]

Many cost, weight, and time overruns resulted from the failure of various industries and businesses to solve the problems posed by increasing demand. Sometimes a lack of cooperation between yards in sharing designs and technical information created expensive slowdowns.[39] Midstream design changes frequently revealed just how little the yards and subcontractors communicated, and this caused delays which often increased costs.[40] An RMA memo of 1899 also blamed slow and expensive plant expansion resulting from significantly greater naval needs and the problems of adaptation to von Tirpitz's plans.[41]

Growing pains were not entirely to blame. Schichau's work on the SMS *Wettin* of the Wittelsbach Class, plagued by cost and weight overruns, seemed to run consistently in the red. Difficulties arose with everything from turrets much heavier than anticipated, to a more expensive ventilation system, to technical problems with watertight doors.[42] The SMS *Wettin* was not the exception; it became the rule. Even though the RMA tightened its system of accounting and supervision and eliminated incompetent subcontractors by constantly revising the suppliers' list, the problem persisted. Even at the imperial yards, a combination of swift technical advance, profiteering by certain firms, and the practice of treating these cases individually rendered a satisfactory solution impossible.[43] In the long run, it seemed as if the RMA could minimize but not resolve the problem.

Industry and Monopoly: Armor and the Electrical Firms

In 1900 Germany produced 6.65 million tons of steel and iron. This represented 23.8 percent of the world's output as compared with Brit-

ain's 17.6 percent and the 38.5 percent produced by the United States
and Canada. The 101 independent firms that supplied materials for
shipbuilding assured the RMA of sufficient competition in most areas.
Twenty-one firms dealt in fine furnished steel plate and machine parts,
and twenty-two supplied lesser grades of steel. Only in the specialized
areas were the firms fewer in number. Eight companies produced special steel and parts for boilers, five for zinc-treated material, and only
two for armor plate.[44]

The Wilson process had first introduced nickel into armor for
strength and resilience. Krupp and Dillinger employed the superior
Tresidder-Harvey process in successfully establishing their monopoly
in Germany, and it enabled them to keep pace with the ever-growing
power of naval artillery between 1890 and 1901. In addition, Krupp's
influence with the kaiser and the firm's advanced research and development facilities gave it the edge in its occasionally uncomfortable
partnership with Dillinger.[45]

The most outstanding impression one gets from the early phases
of von Tirpitz's construction program is of the dominant position the
Krupp firm held in all phases of steel armor production, from questions
of ordnance,[46] to high-quality plate, to nickel-steel armor fasteners.[47]
Krupp's near monopoly in supplying armor was an accepted condition
of warship manufacture, although the Dillinger firm, based in the Saar,
produced armor of equal quality.[48] Krupp jealously guarded its techniques and asserted its primacy in the industry whenever possible, in
spite of its partnership with Dillinger.[49] This awkward situation sometimes created snags that delayed projects for months.[50]

Von Eickstedt obviously expected nearly equal quality and workmanship from both companies. In 1901, the RMA set armor requirements for the Wittelsbach Class at 7,353 tons. The contract awards for
the five battleships and one additional heavy cruiser distributed the
task of production between Krupp and Dillinger: 3,907 tons to 3,446
tons, respectively. The six ships were split between the two firms in an
effort to promote a smooth interchange of materials and technique. Dillinger was to outfit the SMS *Schwaben* and Krupp was to do the same
with the SMS *Zähringen* and heavy cruiser "B."[51]

The navy always hoped to lower armor prices without destroying
quality, but the Krupp-Dillinger relationship presented little opportunity to do so. The RMA could find no third competitor to provide an

alternative, nor did the Reichstag Budget Commission have any practical suggestions to offer.[52] The RMA needed to curb high prices, overruns, and waste, while encouraging industry to keep pace with the quality of foreign armor.[53] By 1901, however, Krupp's nickel-steel armor was recognized as the best in the world and the firm gladly sold its product but never its techniques.[54] The RMA found this shortage of competition disturbing.

Efforts in the early 1900s to reduce armor contracts to Krupp failed.[55] Since the navy's political good fortune contributed so much to Krupp's success in armor, the RMA had demanded reciprocal treatment, but Fritz Krupp answered by suggesting that he would close his armor plant rather than revise his business practices.[56] The RMA could not call his bluff because Krupp had the navy at a disadvantage. Von Tirpitz could not rely solely on Dillinger for the quantities needed, so Krupp demanded a steady stream of lucrative contracts to keep this dimension of his business profitable.[57]

The Imperial Treasury was equally annoyed with the Krupp firm. Its representative, Johann Jencke, argued, as did the navy, that given all its advantages, Krupp should seriously consider lowering the price for armor.[58] Fritz Krupp asserted in response that the firm should feel free to charge any price it wished.[59] This curt reply exposed tensions that were privately and publicly building over ever-increasing armor prices.

In February 1900 the German press accused Krupp and Dillinger of rampant profiteering. The liberal *Frankfurter Zeitung*, Eugen Richter's *Freisinnige Zeitung*, and many other publications printed basically the same story, accusing the two firms of collecting an unheard-of 176 million marks in armor profits from state contracts.[60]

In appearances before the Reichstag Budget Commission von Tirpitz had to explain the assertions in the press. Reichstag representatives Eugen Richter and Hermann Paasche argued that the armor manufacturing process that Krupp used was widely known. Why could no competition be found? Von Tirpitz presented the Budget Commission with many of the same reasons given by Krupp director Hanns Jencke to similar questions asked by the RMA: costly technology, higher wages, and increased overhead.[61] But the state secretary alarmed Krupp by openly supporting the necessity for new competition in this area. He related to Richter and his colleagues the navy's frustration and confusion at the willingness of foreign powers to buy Krupp armor, in spite of high prices, and, in some cases, viable competition.[62]

During February, March, and April of 1900, the press deliberately deemphasized the Stumm-owned Dillinger Hüttenwerke in its sensational accounts, most of which surely originated with the RMA News Bureau.[63] Clearly, Dillinger did not pose the same threat to the RMA that Krupp did so von Tirpitz directed his efforts at the Krupp side of the armor alliance. If he made headway against the Essen firm's high prices, Dillinger would surely follow Fritz Krupp's lead.[64]

At this juncture, Fritz Krupp, on holiday on Capri, told his director Hanns Jencke to arrange a meeting with the kaiser for early May through the latter's friend, August Graf zu Eulenburg.[65] The meeting actually took place later, in May, at Wiesbaden. There, Krupp spoke to Wilhelm and insisted that the pressure from the RMA would only drive him to turn the portion of his firm concerned with armor into a joint stock company. This suggestion and Krupp's agitation clearly disturbed the kaiser, prompting him to urge von Tirpitz to calm the situation.[66] In a later discussion with Krupp, the chief of the Naval Cabinet, Admiral Gustav von Senden-Bibran, expressed the feeling that von Tirpitz would not want the Essen firm's armor production independently incorporated. It probably never occurred to von Senden that the state secretary also preferred the existing composition of the Krupp firm because it remained vulnerable to future pressures in the person of Krupp himself. Von Tirpitz was hardly defeated, only put off.[67]

The state secretary, however, had a parting salvo. He advised Krupp to restrict his questions on naval matters to RMA headquarters on the Königin Augusta Strasse in Berlin before going to higher authorities.[68] In his price policy, von Tirpitz did not shrink from using the public pressure fomented by the press to strike a blow at a situation unfavorable to the navy, although he preferred encouraging contract competition, regulating the suppliers' list, and employing his political skill in the Reichstag.[69] All of these factors were at least partially responsible for a reduction in Krupp armor prices in 1901 from 2,300 to 1,900 marks per ton.[70]

Besides Krupp's eagerness to increase his profits, there were more fundamental reasons for the fluctuation of armor prices in Germany. Both rising raw material costs and advanced production techniques contributed to increased prices. Both the RMA and the Imperial Treasury recognized that metal ore costs had risen,[71] but they still jealously eyed the efforts of American congressmen to limit 4 percent nickel-steel armor to $300 (1,200 marks) per ton.[72]

Krupp's sale of armor to the United States at a lower price further aggravated German naval officials and prompted liberals in the Reichstag and press to call it outright robbery. In March 1901 the editors of the *Freisinnige Zeitung* said that if Krupp continued to sell in Germany at about 400 marks more than its current price in the United States, it would cost the German taxpayers 60 million marks over the duration of the 1900 construction program. They suggested the alternatives of securing armor abroad or building a government-owned foundry. Other publications, including the *Tagliche Rundschau*, agreed heartily.[73]

The Krupp firm called the figures in the newspapers overestimates and exaggerations. The price for armor at the factory was 28 marks cheaper than the press insisted, and the material delivered to Kiel and Wilhelmshaven barely exceeded 2,300 marks per ton. None of the firm's domestic prices went beyond 2,300 marks. Indeed, Krupp asserted that the difference in its prices for armor in the United States and Germany was actually only 222 marks per ton rather than the widely quoted 400 marks.[74] The firm's directors cited the RMA's "extraordinarily strict" inspection practices and the complicated technical and design problems in the production of modern warship armor as the reasons for high domestic prices. The Essen firm explained the lower U.S. prices by saying that the United States Navy would give it bulk orders for an entire class of ships in contrast to the RMA's ship-by-ship contracts.[75] Von Tirpitz presented this information to the Reichstag Budget Commission as the Krupp firm requested,[76] but few observers in the navy or the Reichstag were any less outraged by a difference of 222 marks than they were by 400 marks. Thus, with no alternative domestic source of armor available, the RMA paid dearly. In April 1901, Krupp collected 2.3 million marks for its portion of the payment for the SMS *Mecklenburg's* armor. Along with its share of the SMS *Wettin* and the armor for the heavy cruiser "B," Krupp collected 3.6 million marks in that month alone.[77]

The RMA could have driven a wedge between Krupp and Dillinger, and the volume of business it offered to each suggested a good starting point. The RMA was also in an ideal position for playing one side against the other—a powerful, self-justified Krupp versus an outraged press and Reichstag, all orchestrated by the state secretary himself, a man of considerable political talents.[78] But though Dillinger produced armor of equal quality, it could never have supplied all of the navy's needs if Krupp retaliated with a production slowdown. Furthermore, von Tirpitz and Admiral Rudolf von Eickstedt, head of the RMA Construction Department, risked alienating the firm responsible for all naval artillery and the owner of the Germania shipyard in Kiel. These considerations, as well as Krupp's political friends and royal connections, kept the RMA tied to a policy that redounded to Essen's benefit nearly every time.

The RMA's measures against emerging monopolies were occasionally successful, however. In one instance the imperial shipyard at Kiel informed the Technical Department that the firm of Schulz-Knaudt had increased its control over the supply of steel ships' flues. According to Kiel, "If this independence from a single supplier has, up to now, not led to major error, it appears still to lie in the interest of the navy to break the monopoly of Schulz-Knaudt and likewise to approach the productive competing firms about supplying flues."[79] The officials at Kiel suggested that the RMA might switch frequently from Firma Schulz-Knaudt to Duisberger Eisen- und Stahlwerke. Not only did this advice dilute the possible monopoly situation, but Duisberger's product quality guarantee turned out to be longer than that offered by Schulz-Knaudt and more appealing to the RMA.

The situation in the electrical industry was more favorable to the navy. Here the RMA had to deal with many companies, including the three giants, German General Electric (AEG) and the Siemens companies, but the diversity of smaller firms created adequate competition in this field.[80]

In 1847 Werner von Siemens and J. G. Halske formed the firm of Siemens and Halske. With the growing diversity of uses for electricity the company prospered and, by 1897, became a joint stock company with branches in England and Russia. In 1903, eleven years after the death of their father, Wilhelm von Siemens supported his brother Carl in establishing the Siemens-Schuckertwerke (SSW). Although united by family ties, Siemens and Halske remained separate from Siemens-Schuckert until 1970.[81]

The Siemens family were the premier German electrical contractors of their day. They participated in many phases of warship construction for the RMA, including wireless telegraphy, cables, wires, switches, and dynamos. Unlike the situation in the steel industry, this family had stiff competition that placed the RMA in a far better bargaining position. Emil Rathenau's AEG competed with both Siemens companies in nearly every field. In addition, the firm of Brown and Boveri, another formidable competitor, became the first German company to produce Parsons turbines under license as well as dynamos in competition with both SSW and AEG. Felton Guilleaume contributed an alternative source of wire and cable, and Voigt and Haffner switching systems were considered as good as or better than those of the Siemens firms. [82] This greater competition within the electrical industry caused a phenomenon that never occurred in the armor and artillery area: in 1900 Siemens and Halske guaranteed a 10 percent rebate on electrical systems and parts for the navy in return for an increased number of contracts. [83]

The contrast between the Krupp-Dillinger situation and that of the electrical firms is instructive. The latter had to respond to an ever-growing public market in electrical tools, appliances, streetcars, and gadgets of all kinds, and the widespread demand allowed room for a number of large companies and a host of small ones. Siemens and Halske's pioneering efforts in warship electrical systems opened up more new possibilities. [84] In addition, the widespread commercial market drew a large number of firms into research and development with the hope of ever-increasing profits. In contrast, the market did not attract many to the armor and artillery industry because its small size, dominant firms, and high risk required massive plant facilities and a long-term commitment to research and development. Besides, in the late nineteenth and early twentieth centuries the reputation and capabilities of firms like Krupp and Dillinger in Germany and Schneider-Creuzot in France would have presented a nearly impossible hurdle to newcomers. The electrical industry possessed no such long-standing giants, and at the turn of the century it showed considerable potential for expansion.

Research and Development

During this early period of naval growth the RMA occupied itself with broadening its technical expertise. An active correspondence was conducted between the Construction Department and inventors, from quacks to innovators of genius, and the RMA supported or created several research institutes devoted to naval-related fields.[85] The navy financed its own research center at Kiel, which was closely linked with another naval research institute at Marienfelde near Berlin. Private centers that worked with the navy included the Royal Research Institute for Shipbuilding and Hydrodynamics in a northwest suburb of Berlin and the facilities of the North German Lloyd in Bremerhaven.[86] Close cooperation between the navy and private shipping firms also facilitated the establishment of standards of quality. The construction experience and testing laboratories of Albert Ballin's Hamburg-America Line (HAPAG) and those of the North German Lloyd frequently benefited the navy in problems requiring expertise in physics, naval architecture, and engineering. The Lloyd provided aid in developing towing tests to determine the seakeeping qualities of new ship designs.[87]

In other cases von Tirpitz and von Eickstedt supported new research associations and explored those of other countries. In 1899 von Eickstedt played a personal role in the founding of the Society for Shipbuilding Technology. Along with other naval officers, he became one of its charter members, and by 1902 the society regularly provided the navy with the results of its research.[88] In addition, the Construction Department sent its people abroad to examine the latest research techniques at foreign institutes. One such trip produced suggestions for structural testing in imitation of standard practices at the British naval research centers in Dumbarton and Haslar.[89]

The shortage of personnel in the Construction Department prevented a significant broadening of the RMA's research efforts. Von Eickstedt constantly reminded the RMA's Central Section of this shortage, as the latter helped formulate the budget for the RMA. Cuts in the proposed budget frequently affected the numbers of qualified ship and machine building inspectors, whose expertise or lack thereof would reflect the RMA's commitment to research and education.[90] Von Eickstedt recognized that high technology was one of his department's weakest points vis-à-vis certain segments of industry and that cuts in the budget would exacerbate present shortcomings.

The education of RMA inspectors and the efforts of the navy to keep abreast of modern ship technology did not alter von Tirpitz's axiom that advanced research and development belonged to the private sphere.

Perhaps the best illustration of this view was the RMA's abdication of the initiative on development of the turbine to private industry. Brown and Boveri managed to obtain exclusive rights to the production of the new engine system in Germany,[91] but many on the Continent still contested Parsons's patent rights. Firms in France and Germany had similar engines under development, many based on the still imperfect systems of Laval (Swedish) and Rateau (French). In Germany, three private yards undertook to produce acceptable turbine-powered ships. Germaniawerft decided to build a torpedo boat (S-35) with its own turbine and a Schulz boiler system and poured more than 194,000 marks into this prototype.[92] Schichau followed along the same lines while the RMA urged Vulcan to cooperate with Brown and Boveri in producing a Parsons boat.[93]

RMA involvement in the situation might have provided some early uniformity and a later advantage for German industry, but the navy rejected any notion of an imperial yard entering into this process.[94] By insisting that naval ships employ the already tested Parsons system, the RMA could have brought turbine power to the navy earlier, forcing all of the yards to learn the same basic technology. Firms with research funds to spend, like Krupp, could have mastered and improved the system, later providing the RMA with a domestic, and perhaps better, variation of the original. A brief dependence on a foreign propulsion system could have given the Imperial Navy long-range dividends.

Instead, the situation degenerated into patent fights and ended with the Parsons Company retaining its dominance. The firm of John J. Thornycroft brought suit against the Schulz Company for violation of its boiler system patents, which retarded the efforts of Vulcan. Germaniawerft barely managed to avoid this problem by earlier signing an agreement with Thornycroft for exclusive use of its newest boilers in turbine research.[95] Domestic setbacks such as these became the rule in the application of turbine technology in the Imperial Navy.

Submarine technology also suffered from a lack of official direction. Von Tirpitz never believed that the U-boat might one day challenge the battleship, but he could hardly fail to appreciate the interest of other major naval powers in this invention. As early as 1899, the French had a good deal of success with the *Gustav Zédé*, and by 1900 the submarine became an integral part of their navy.[96] Late in 1899, the French authorities ordered twenty-six of the vessels, and twelve were nearly finished by February 1900.[97] The British experimented with two-man submarine prototypes late in the same year, and the American boats built by John P. Holland in Baltimore tested very well.[98] The RMA, however, maintained only a small-scale research effort at Danzig.[99] In Germany, Krupp alone proceeded full tilt with U-boat development at the Germaniawerft.[100]

Von Tirpitz thus paid attention to the U-boat only because he had little choice. When the liberal leader Eugen Richter confronted him in the Reichstag with the RMA's lack of interest in U-boats in spite of the French advances, the RMA chief begged the question by saying: "The U-boat is, at present, of no great value in war at sea."[101] He made similar statements before a Reichstag Budget Commission session in March 1901. In his marginalia to a report by the naval attaché in Paris, he commented on every imperfection in the French U-boats. Again he was exhibiting his policy that the navy should not become involved with technology still under development.[102] He noted, for example, that the French had yet to perfect a practical periscope. How could they attack submerged? Von Tirpitz never posed the possibility that German firms, with the RMA's assistance, might succeed where the French had not. The RMA rarely played the role of catalyst among its contractors, especially in the case of U-boats. Von Tirpitz also hesitated, no doubt, because the submarine had no part in his beloved risk theory.

The Naval Law of 1900 and Further Progress in Construction

In the wake of a barrage of RMA propaganda, the second Naval Law passed the Reichstag on 12 June 1900 by a vote of 201 to 103. Only nine months before, von Tirpitz had presented to the kaiser an ambitious plan to increase the navy to forty-five battleships and auxiliary vessels at a cost of 2,759.5 million marks.[103] This scheme projected RMA plans through 1917, and few observers believed that von Tirpitz intended to stop at these stated goals.

In his "Bitter Need Speech" of 18 October 1899, Wilhelm struck the first note for the state secretary's new proposals.[104] His main theme—the need to protect the empire against the British navy—became the basis of the RMA News Bureau's propaganda efforts. The British seizure of the mail steamer *Bundesrath* during the Boer War, the Boxer Rebellion in China, the embarrassing situation in Samoa, and the lessons learned from the Spanish-American War were cited to support Germany's need for a larger fleet to prosper in a world of far-flung empires.[105]

During the propaganda campaign for the 1900 Naval Law, the RMA became increasingly aware of the power held by private pro-naval groups. The German Naval League, the Pan-German League, the Colonial League, and the Liberal Association for Fleet Expansion all supported the Naval Law but conducted their affairs independent of RMA control.[106] In its drive for the passage of this law, the Naval League alone increased its private membership by more than 155,000 by 1900. It also added 176,881 organizations to its roster, and the circulation of its periodical, *Die Flotte*, grew by 175,000 copies in the fall of that year.[107] The RMA invested 222,035 marks in the propaganda campaign, but the Naval League more than doubled that figure, spending 760,000 marks on the cause. The contributions of other groups brought the total outlay to more than 1 million marks.[108]

The RMA directed its efforts at the German middle class and those who were politically centrist or slightly right of center. Although the large industrialists had everything to gain, the conservatives, whose privilege and economic security lay in agriculture, were not sure that this campaign served their best interest. Many feared that the mobilization of the middle and lower classes would upset the order of society and place their economic security at the mercy of the industrial Free Conservatives. It is in this atmosphere that the compromise proposed by the state secretary of the Prussian Finance Ministry, Johannes Miquel, christened *Sammlungspolitik* or coalition politics by historian Eckart Kehr, must be appreciated. Through this compromise the agrarian Prussians received tariff protection for their foodstuffs and heavy industry won its fight to broaden a potentially profitable naval construction plan. Above all, to the satisfaction of most agrarian and industrial conservatives, the successful cooperation between these two factions purchased a new lease on life for the existing social order in Germany.[109]

Von Tirpitz's determination combined with considerable industrial support allowed the 1900 Naval Law to gain Reichstag approval in the face of huge budget deficits.[110] Von Tirpitz did not overly concern himself about the Reich's debts, but his calculation of naval appropriations and careful spending always managed to create a surplus large enough to ensure continual construction in leaner times to come.[111]

The passage of the second Naval Law also allowed the Construction Department to continue its building plans. In 1901 and 1902 the RMA started construction on Braunschweig Class battleships at an average cost of 24 million marks per ship. Germaniawerft received both the *Braunschweig* and the *Hessen*, Schichau in Danzig the *Elsass* and the *Lothringen*, and Vulcan the *Preussen*.[112] These ships displaced about 13,200 tons and were powered by triple expansion engines and boilers on the Thornycroft system. The main armament consisted of two double 28-centimeter turrets, with a strong secondary battery of fourteen 17-centimeter and fourteen 8.65-centimeter guns.[113] They had a maximum range of 6,500 kilometers when steaming at ten knots and could manage 3,470 kilometers at a top speed of sixteen knots. When these ships were ready for service between 1904 and 1906, they finally gave the Imperial Navy a class that compared favorably with the ships of the Royal Navy.

Five other vessels made possible by this law were the heavy cruisers *Friedrich Karl*, *Yorck*, *Scharnhorst*, *Gneisenau*, and *Roon*. Blohm und Voss of Hamburg built the first three at prices between 15.6 and 20.3 million marks. AG Weser won the *Gneisenau*, and the imperial yard at Kiel built the *Roon* for the lowest price of the five, 15.3 million marks. They could steam at fourteen knots with a range of between 4,800 and 5,100 kilometers.[114]

The most ambitious expansion took place in the area of light cruisers. Von Tirpitz authorized twelve in all between 1901 and 1905. As was the case after the passage of the first Naval Law, Weser received most of the light cruiser contracts from the RMA. The imperial yard at Danzig qualified for two, Kiel one, Howaldtswerke one, Vulcan two, and Weser the remaining six.[115] The most expensive of these ships was Vulcan's *Lübeck*, which was the first German warship powered by a turbine.

Schichau and Vulcan also shared the three cannon-boat contracts awarded by the RMA. Vulcan built the *Eber* and Schichau both the *Tsingtau* and *Vaterland*. The *Eber* copied earlier models, such as *Panther* and *Luchs*; the two ships awarded to Schichau were much smaller.[116]

Turbine experimentation also took place with these smaller ships. In Schichau's S-125 (T-125), the Parsons system appeared for the first time in high-seas torpedo boats.[117] Schichau built all the boats in the 114 to 131 series, which cost approximately 1 million marks each. The S-125 was the exception at 1.27 million. Germaniawerft won a contract for five other torpedo boats at an average price of 1.18 to 1.20 million marks each.

The 1899–1901 period marks the beginning of the RMA's routine relationship with industry. During construction of the first ships made possible by the Naval Law of 1898 the strains placed on industry by sudden naval expansion became evident in intra-industry relationships as well as the difficulties between firms and the RMA.

In 1900, an RMA commission studying the shipbuilding industry made suggestions, all of which the navy pursued. Specialization in a single product or system was discouraged because the required investment seemed too great and the promise of profits too small. The navy needed a core group of reliable competing firms to supply high-quality products at the lowest possible prices to provide the stability that might become the RMA's best asset.

In areas in which only a few firms were at the navy's disposal, the commission suggested using the imperial yards and, when possible, the private yards to organize a front against any excessive prices proposed by subcontractors. In dealing with the private yards, secret sealed bids for whole ships would provide the navy with the best prices when awarding contracts. The shipyards could make bulk purchases to keep their costs as low as possible, and the navy could try to apply pressure on them or their subcontractors as it saw fit. Such pressure could be important in matters of price, building time, and prompt material delivery.[118] Above all, the commission encouraged consistency in the RMA's relationships with industry.

The RMA faced diverse problems during these years, and many could not be completely resolved. The RMA protocol system reduced but could not eliminate cost and weight overruns and construction delays. Firms like Krupp posed the greatest challenge because they appeared to survive and prosper, and occasionally monopolize, in spite of concerted attacks by the RMA. Von Tirpitz, von Capelle, von Eickstedt, and many other naval leaders never completely resigned themselves to this phenomenon, and frequent efforts against other would-be monopolists succeeded.

Their real failure came in the decision to leave major research and development efforts to the private sector. Although greater involvement in research and development would have absorbed a larger percentage of the RMA's annual budget, it would have placed the RMA in a better position to thwart monopolies based on the complexity and often prohibitive cost of the high technology.

In the cases of turbine development and perhaps of armor plate, deeper RMA involvement in research and development might have challenged Krupp's monopoly or paved the way for an even better engine than the Parsons. At least, these measures would have guaranteed a high degree of technical expertise among the naval inspectors and allowed the navy to disseminate an understanding of naval-related technology among interested firms, new and old.

In addition, during this period the U-boat became a reality for von Tirpitz. Whether he liked it or not, he could no longer ignore the vessel. Advances in submarine technology, actual sales by Krupp, and Reichstag pressures forced the state secretary to divert part of the funds won in 1900 to acquiring these weapons. But the RMA, by design, never clearly defined the extent of the navy's commitment to undersea warfare.

3

Business as Usual?

1902 – 1904

Just as naval-industrial relations settled down to business as usual, the changing international situation began to undermine von Tirpitz's risk theory. He ignored renewed British determination to maintain naval supremacy, however, and relied on public and industrial support to perpetuate the momentum of his fleet program in the face of growing opposition from the Imperial Treasury.

Political Background

Between 1902 and 1904, von Tirpitz's building program hit full stride, with two classes of battleships under construction and the Deutschland Class up for bids in 1904. It is sobering, however, to consider these events in the political context of the period. These three years witnessed the emergence of Great Britain from "splendid isolation" and the revelation of fatal flaws in the risk theory.

During this period Great Britain's world fortunes improved markedly. The naval treaty with the Japanese in 1902 stabilized the British position in the Far East and gave London greater freedom to become more involved in European politics. France suggested closer cooperation on Continental and colonial policy because of the successful stand made by Britain at Fashoda in 1898. Conflict with the United States seemed less likely than ever with the signing of the Hay-Pauncefote Treaty in 1901 and the Alaskan boundary settlement of 1903. The British government also shed the burden of protecting the Ottoman Empire in the East. By 1902–3 maintaining the status quo in the Dardenelles region was no longer a vital part of British foreign policy. Internally extensive army reforms were undertaken and the naval budgets of 1900 and 1903 were increased dramatically. Eventually ten new battleships and eighteen armored cruisers were built.[1]

The German service attachés in London sent back ominous reports regarding British press treatment of German naval expansion. An article in *Vanity Fair* recalled the 1807 "copenhagening" of the Danish fleet and suggested that the same technique used against the Germans would guarantee world peace for two generations. This idea hardly prompted the naval or military attachés in London to suggest scrapping von Tirpitz's plans, but Chancellor von Bülow's effort to calm the British press in a 1904 interview with Brashford of *Nineteenth Century* failed completely. The British mood was clearly changing, and the chancellor's claim that the fleet was for defensive purposes fell on deaf ears.[2] As historian Paul Kennedy had observed, Britain was "clearly looking very carefully at the expansion of the German fleet, which, due to the agitation of the *National Review, Spectator,* the *Times,* and other journals, had entered the 'danger zone' much earlier than von Tirpitz suggested was likely."[3]

By 1904 the political fortunes of Germany had taken a turn for the worse. Relations between Germany and the United States had not improved since the confrontation over the Philippines and Samoa. Indeed, the navy fully appreciated the ability of the United States to wage war.[4] In April 1904 the British and French eliminated one of their fundamental presumptions of German foreign policy by concluding the entente. With the appointment of Sir John Fisher as First Sea Lord (1904–10), the British also adopted a strategy greatly strengthening the Home Fleet at the expense of the Mediterranean forces. The entente with France made this possible, and the change of strategy showed Britain's determination to counter the new German threat. This more aggressive policy by the British rapidly rendered von Tirpitz's "danger zone" a permanent rather than a transitory situation.[5]

Von Tirpitz's desire to avoid a confrontation with Britain was seen by many as a lack of nerve or fighting spirit. At the German Foreign Office, Friedrich von Holstein concluded that von Tirpitz's disinclination to fight over Kiaochow in China or during the crisis surrounding the Boer War revealed an absence of *"kampfnerven."*[6] Given the primitive state of the fleet construction program, however, von Tirpitz's lack of nerve seems sensible rather than spineless. He was too busy trying to create a tool Germany could use effectively against Britain to allow any premature confrontation with the Royal Navy to destroy everything.

The admiral's attention focused on construction, extending the power and prestige of the RMA, and staying out of war. To these ends he strengthened the RMA by making it the channel through which all matters related to naval politics, finance, and construction found their way to the kaiser.[7] He raised von Eickstedt's Construction Division to the status of a full RMA department,[8] and the building program was so successful that a Second Battle Squadron was well on its way to completion by 1904.[9] Von Tirpitz never lacked *"kampfnerven."* He merely knew better than von Holstein that the German navy could not possibly confront the British successfully in the years between 1902 and 1904.

The RMA waged a constant fiscal war with the Imperial Treasury Office over expenditures and the budget. The preparation of the 1904 budget illustrates the relationship well. The sources of contention were the very headaches the RMA was trying to control: costly design changes, material and labor costs, expensive testing and research, and shipyard overhead. Discussions revealed a serious lack of communication between the Imperial Treasury and the navy. The Treasury, for example, insisted that the RMA inflated its budget estimates for battleship construction based on the mistaken belief that only two private yards could build these ships. This Treasury blunder caused considerable bewilderment at the Königin Augusta Strasse.

Hermann Freiherr von Stengel, state secretary of the Imperial Treasury from 1903 to 1908, insisted further that the imperial shipyards build battleships to keep RMA expenses down. Von Tirpitz had adopted this policy long ago, and the imperial yards already did this sort of construction. The recent decision to renovate them would increase their capability. Von Stengel also challenged the RMA's installment system of payment, as every RSA secretary seemed obliged to do. Forcing him to defend this system repeatedly did not endear the Treasury to Admiral von Tirpitz.[10] Von Stengel then suggested that no payment should be made until nine-tenths of the work specified in a contract was complete. The number of ships taken on by the six major private yards at any given time made this impossible. With the possible exception of the Germaniawerft, no yard could muster enough capital to absorb initially all but 10 percent of a battleship's total cost.[11]

Von Stengel's attitude reveals a lack of understanding of the shipbuilding industry and its relationship with the RMA. It also betrays von Tirpitz's propensity for isolating the RMA from interaction with the rest of the imperial government. All he desired was that the Treasury find a source for the appropriations he squeezed out of the Reichstag. The Treasury never felt that the state secretary of the RMA genuinely tried to get the best value for each mark spent and misunderstood the admiral's flaw as one of opulence and mismanagement. Von Tirpitz's hunger for ever-increasing funds arose from his self-imposed imperative to give Germany a tool that could truly challenge England. In the process he alienated some colleagues in the navy and left von Stengel with the problem of finding new sources of income for the Reich. This repeatedly raised the unsavory political issue of tax reform for the Reichstag and a harried Chancellor von Bülow.[12]

Although the appropriation was 10 million marks less than requested, the RMA budget rose in the fiscal year 1904–5 for the fifth consecutive time since 1899–1900. The Reichstag granted the 99.3 million marks requested for projects already under way but shaved 5.5 million from new construction and armaments and another 4.5 million from "special projects."[13]

During these years other nations found themselves unable or unwilling to maintain or increase current levels of construction expenditures. In German terms the French naval budget fell from a high of 265.4 million marks in 1901–2 to 250.3 million in 1904–5. The Russian budget fell a relatively modest 5 million marks between 1903 and 1905.[14] The 109.7 million spent on shipbuilding, however, remained constant to support the construction program Russia began in 1903.[15]

In the United States, primarily because of the efforts of President Theodore Roosevelt between 1901 and 1909, naval expenditures were second only to those of Great Britain.[16] Between 1899 and 1902, the American naval budget rose consistently to 351.1 million marks. After dipping slightly in 1902–3, it rose again to 404.6 million marks in 1905.[17]

Congress appropriated 122.6 million per year for shipbuilding between 1899 and 1905, but expenditures on new ships fluctuated constantly. Not until the threat of war confronted the Wilson administration did the building program of the U.S. Navy genuinely get under way.[18]

The German naval budget climbed 81.6 million marks between 1899 and 1905, averaged 185.5 million per year, and totaled 1,113.1 million marks for the whole period, but it still paled by comparison with other major powers. In 1902–3 the British naval budget was 637.6 million marks, 432.6 million more than the German allocation for that year. In the 1903–4 naval appropriations the British made a quantum leap for the reform and expansion of their navy of 91.2 million above the previous year. The Germans increased their spending by a mere 6 million.[19]

The Protocol System: Cost and Weight Problems and the Koch Case

In the struggle to make every mark count, the RMA pressed the Construction Department and inspectors to complete and publish the first full edition of the suppliers' list. The list finally appeared in 1902, and it provided the navy with a complete and easily revised handbook of all naval purveyors. It went through four editions between 1902 and the war, and the prewar system of supplements, called *Deckblätter*, appeared periodically, listing deletions and additions.[20] The *Deckblätter* included everything from a correction on the quoted diameter of some pipe supplied by Mannesmann to a response to a baking machine manufacturer's complaint that his firm was not listed.[21]

It was a measure of the list's importance that naval contractors responded promptly and accurately to any requests for information from the RMA. Many suggestions on format and possible use were forthcoming from RMA inspectors whose reputations often depended on the reliability of the firms admitted to the suppliers' list.[22] If their judgment failed one time too many, von Tirpitz would react strongly, as he did to von Eickstedt in 1903 regarding boilers, coal chutes, and ventilation systems.[23] Purveyors also notified the RMA very quickly if they were omitted from the list or listed inaccurately. Carl Flohr, for example, reminded the RMA in April 1903 that his firm manufactured cranes, munition conveyors, and small elevators. He wondered why the RMA failed to list it in these machinery categories.[24]

The smaller firms that were particularly dependent on RMA contracts also responded promptly. In most cases they took care to protect
their position on the suppliers' list by following the requirements and
specifications laid down in all RMA quality control publications.[25] In
1904, the Rheinisch-Westfälischen Copper Works tested the RMA system by failing to deliver sheet metal to the imperial yard at Kiel in time
or of the expected quality. The firm quickly found itself on probation,
and the Construction Inspectorate suggested an investigation.[26]

Of course, every institution occasionally ignores its own regulations.
In one case von Eickstedt went against the advice of his inspectors and
approved the admission of the Richard Gradenwitz Company to the
suppliers' list for pressure gauges or manometers. Later evaluations of
this firm's work prompted comments like "terrible" from the Torpedo
Inspectorate and the imperial yard in Kiel. Other firms, such as
Schaffer and Budenberg, gladly provided a high-quality alternative,
and Gradenwitz disappeared from the suppliers' list until its products
showed a marked improvement.[27]

Sometimes the organization of the suppliers' list created subtle problems that the RMA did not foresee. For example, of the five approved
vendors in competition for contracts in the list's category for electrical
gauges, three were privately owned companies in Frankfurt, Berlin,
and Hannover, and the other two were the biggest electrical firms in
Germany, Siemens-Schuckert and AEG. This was certainly unfair
competition, and the three smaller firms survived only because they
made products that required a high degree of technological expertise.[28]

In other cases a parent firm appeared in a single category along with
two or three of its subsidiary companies. Among eight companies supplying parts for heavy marine machinery, for example, Krupp and
three of its subsidiaries held half of the positions.[29] A closer examination of the firms in each category of the suppliers' list and more care in
distributing contracts could have increased the RMA's chances for getting the best prices in most product categories.

In many instances, divisions or departments within the RMA took
the variations in size and capability of the various shipyards more
closely into account. The RMA Construction Department always required a list of ship parts inventories so the navy could know each
yard's ability to manufacture, store, or stockpile goods related to ship
construction.[30] The private yards that were less able to gather very large

inventories before construction would need more capital from the RMA earlier in their contract agreement than other yards. Thus contract rate payments for the smaller private yards were scheduled to help them progress with construction without encountering a financial crisis.[31]

Besides the suppliers' list and the general construction guidelines, the Construction Department also published many technical handbooks for maritime firms to ensure their familiarity with naval practice. One such publication was the "Basic Guidelines for Electrical Systems" issued to Siemens-Schuckert, AEG, and any other firm involved in electrical work for warships.[32] Pamphlets such as these disseminated RMA technical expertise, regulations, and standards.

To guarantee that firms complied with its wishes, the Construction Department constantly tested the final products to ascertain their performance at the factory and value to the fleet. Predictably, most of the problems the RMA encountered in evaluating performance stemmed directly from the rapid pace of expansion. The multiple demands placed upon naval testing facilities and personnel made it extremely difficult to accommodate each firm as it produced needed materials. The RMA thus had to broaden its own inspection capabilities and employ the resources of private testing agencies with greater frequency. The North German Lloyd, for example, served the navy for many years as a research and development center by testing new ship prototypes.[33]

The RMA employed independent firms or allowed purveyors to use certain firms to augment the services of the Purchasing Office, which had to give its final approval before any product was shipped to the yards. The use of the Cassirer firm to test cables delivered to Schichau in 1902 is but one illustration of this practice.[34] In addition, RMA construction inspectors stationed at the shipyards supervised both the testing of materials fabricated at the yard [35] and products sent to it with Purchasing Office approval. By these various means, the guarantees of product quality demanded by the RMA regulations remained in force. If a private firm assumed the role of the Purchasing Office, as in the Cassirer case, the testing firm accepted the responsibility for guaranteeing the product, whereas if the RMA's inspectors supervised, obligation to guarantee the product rested with the producing firm.

The RMA Purchasing Office was composed of naval inspectors and approved independent engineers under contract to the navy, and its importance grew with the navy's ambitions. On-site inspections by purchasing officials became increasingly important because catching defects in naval equipment at the factory reduced expensive delivery and return costs as well as lost time.[36] To keep expenses down, by 1903 the RMA required many of the private yards to share the cost of the tests performed at their yards.[37]

The RMA evaluation and approval system usually met the navy's needs. The admission of a weak firm to the suppliers' list would occasionally reveal the system's limitations, but the Technical Department assured von Tirpitz in 1904 that the testing methods and rigorous inspections assured a minimum of flaws in naval building materials.[38] More important, the technical and administrative expertise of the RMA proved itself equal to the task von Tirpitz asked it to assume.

The RMA also evaluated materials, determined their relative suitability, and then demanded that industry abide by that decision. Boiler construction is an example. Up to 1902 the most common material used in the construction of ships' boilers was crucible steel. This form of tool steel, first developed in 1740, had a high chromium and low silicon content. A century later, crucible steel was the standard material used by Krupp on many navy and army contracts, although resmelting was often required to obtain the desired quality.[39] In 1902, the RMA decided to use steel made by the Siemens-Martin process for boilers because with this material finer quality control provided a far more desirable product. In spite of Krupp's argument that insufficient quantities of the new steel would make construction more difficult, the RMA ordered a changeover and Krupp abided by its decision.

Krupp's facilities already produced large quantities of crucible steel, and the RMA's request obliged it to change to the Siemens-Martin process for boiler material, rendering large quantities of the firm's crucible steel unsuitable for future RMA boilers.[40] In this case, a sufficient number of firms were willing to supply the type of steel desired if Krupp refused, so even the most powerful of Germany's steel firms had to cooperate.

The RMA subjected all vessels already in naval service to a constant series of standard tests. The Königin Augusta Strasse received a perpetual flow of reports on every aspect of a vessel's routine performance.[41] In this way the RMA ironed out flaws from faulty boat cranes to the rudder vibration problems that briefly plagued the ships of the Braunschweig Class.[42]

By 1902, the RMA realized the true complexity of having ten new battleships under construction at once. Those of the Wittelsbach Class neared completion, and work on the Braunschweig Class had just commenced. In addition, heavy cruisers and a multiplicity of smaller vessels were being built. As many more companies flocked to obtain their share of lucrative navy contracts, administrative problems strained the RMA's abilities to the limit.

The virtual avalanche of cost and weight excesses received by the Construction Department offices in Berlin determined the most vulnerable point in the entire building program, with the possible exception of the armor monopoly. Von Eickstedt's staff had to verify and evaluate each and every additional cost report, which took great amounts of time and money. [43] Since the construction of modern warships required precise unity and integration of materials and systems, solving one problem of cost and weight might cause many others. These problems occurred mostly in the private sector, as Krupp's late deliveries during the construction of the SMS *Kaiser Friedrich III* illustrate. Inquiries by the kaiser as to the reasons for the delay obtained almost immediate results. [44] Essen blamed RMA design changes, its own production errors, and early RMA delivery deadlines for the problem. [45] Krupp's suggestions for improvement involved increasing the competence of the firm's technical personnel and fostering closer cooperation between the shipyard, the RMA, and the subcontractors. [46]

Evaluating every overrun became a great burden for the RMA. The very nature of this process, including the large number of firms involved and the variety of reasons proposed for the increases and excesses, diffused its ability to act effectively. This inescapable consequence of a very ambitious building program represented a vulnerable point which the kaiser's intercession could not solve.

One typical case involved the manufacture of drinking water containers for the Braunschweig Class. These seemingly insignificant items increased the ship's weight by more than 100 kilograms and cost between 330 and 449 marks more than the contract allowed. The RMA had to approve an additional 2,000 marks for these battleships. [47] An accumulation of small cases like this could create a financial crisis for the RMA, threatening the entire program.

These headaches had many causes. Sometimes contractors or yards overextended themselves by accepting too many projects. Usually the

RMA avoided this situation by examining a firm's commitments before signing a contract, but when a firm became overextended the result would often be production flaws, a decline in quality, and disrupted schedules. Problems of this sort arose between the RMA and Krupp over the latter's diverse commitments to the Deutschland Class.[48]

Other causes included the failure of designs to arrive at the factory on time, the late delivery of parts, and damage to a ship's vital systems in transit or when malfunctions occurred during performance tests. All of these irregularities resulted in extra spending, lost time, and often increased weight. Siemens-Schuckert's late installation of a radio telegraphy system delayed the construction of the cruisers *Prince Adalbert* and *Hamburg*.[49] Vulcan complained that Krupp took far too long to make the cannon mountings for the SMS *Mecklenburg*, and Schichau appealed to the RMA to exert pressure on the SMS *Wettin* subcontractors to keep them on schedule.[50]

In one particularly grievous case, Krupp's efforts to economize damaged the foundations of the 15-centimeter turrets on the cruiser SMS *Prince Heinrich*. The bolts used to anchor the turret housing at various deck levels were spaced too far apart so fewer would be required. The resulting lack of stability caused damage to the turrets, and the RMA had to call on the imperial yard at Kiel to repair the damage.[51] When the builders of the SMS *Wilhelm der Grosse* employed the same turret design, the RMA had considerable difficulty in getting Krupp to change the plans.[52]

Other flawed designs presented fewer difficulties, but their number made them just as expensive. A change in specifications for the stern galley in the SMS *Wettin* eventually cost 1,655 marks extra and added another 436 kilograms to the ship's weight.[53] Extra work needed to strengthen the cannon mountings on board the SMS *Wettin* and *Zähringen* cost 8,172 marks and 2,787 marks, respectively.[54] Both the Braunschweig and Deutschland classes had problems with excessive vibrations in the steering system and rudder. The firm of Haniel and Lueg in Düsseldorf installed systems with similar defects in both the SMS *Hannover* and *Pommern*.[55] Schichau received similarly flawed designs for the SMS *Lothringen*, and rudder alterations made on the SMS *Braunschweig* at the imperial yard at Kiel cost an extra 6,850 marks.[56] Eight new watertight doors for the SMS *Wittelsbach* came in 400 kilograms and 1,600 marks over projections, and the chains for the SMS

Braunschweig added 1,612 kilograms and 7,104 marks to that ship's contract weight and cost.[57] These few examples show only a small part of the problem.

The cost of alterations or repairs to Krupp projects presented the most trouble for the RMA. Reinforcing the SMS *Preussen*'s 15-centimeter turrets cost 41,282 marks.[58] Alterations to the 15-centimeter turrets of the SMS *Zähringen, Wettin,* and *Mecklenburg* involved a total of 43,885 marks.[59] Krupp absorbed none of these costs, and the RMA had to pay the firm or have the work done at one of the imperial yards. As a result, the navy lost substantial amounts of money and time. Krupp usually completed most of its heavy guns and turrets on time, but if delays occurred, the construction schedule had to be altered. In one case, the delivery of 10.5-centimeter cannon for the light cruiser SMS *Merkur* came six months late because of a minor design change that Krupp deemed necessary. In these situations, the RMA could not turn to a competitor and had to absorb the losses.[60]

Admiral von Eickstedt used the RMA cost accounting system to cope with these overruns in an orderly fashion. The firm or yard claiming the overrun had to submit a strict spending breakdown, using quarterly spending control reports compiled by the imperial shipyards for all projects. The RMA could then evaluate the various weight and cost changes for each ship, determine their overall effect, and plan official action.[61] To make the process more effective, von Tirpitz gave the Construction Inspectorate discretion to release funds for work it felt met RMA standards. Krupp protested this policy as unwarranted interference by the RMA in business affairs, especially between the private yards and subcontractors.[62] Nevertheless, von Tirpitz and von Eickstedt insisted on the measure and closer cooperation between the yard, subcontractor, and RMA to strengthen the position of the latter.[63]

The shipyards also felt the impact of steady expansion. The RMA evidently expected some yards and subcontractors to feel the strain and ordered the imperial yards to extend credit or determine some disbursement schedules according to the financial need of the more reliable naval purveyors.[64] The yards at Wilhelmshaven and Kiel were responsible for most payments on capital ship projects, and the one at Danzig dealt mostly in smaller craft and U-boats.[65]

An interesting clash over contract payments took place between an imperial yard and a private subcontractor in 1904. Although the case of the imperial shipyard at Danzig versus the Stettin firm of Bruno Koch was atypical of shipyard-subcontractor relationships, it does illustrate the power of an imperial shipyard in its function as RMA bursar and the ability of the naval authorities to support their subordinates in some situations.

In September 1904 the Koch firm extended the RMA's shipyard facilities at Danzig to include a large breakwater, a new 67,000-cubic-meter dock, and pilings to stabilize the dock's shoreline foundation. Koch's engineers suggested using many more pilings than originally estimated.[66] The imperial yard decided that since the Koch firm had not cleared the additional work and departure from the contract with Berlin, the 3,300-mark cost overrun was not a legitimate expenditure, and it refused to pay the firm for those costs.

In the prolonged legal battle that followed, Koch brought suit against the RMA for violating the contract. He contended in court that the work at Danzig was well done, only 5 percent over contract cost, and justified according to conditions at the construction site. He struggled "not against a person, but against a system," which he thought was far too restraining.[67] In this instance, the RMA focused its authority and influence on a breach of naval-industrial protocol. It supported Danzig's arguments against Koch. The case dragged on until 1921, when the navy handed it over to the civilian government and washed its hands of the affair.[68] By that time his claim against the Danzig yard was all Koch had left, for his firm went bankrupt before 1914.

The Koch case was the result of a long overdue RMA plan to renovate the imperial yards. The private shipyards used their own resources to expand their facilities, but the imperial yards usually degenerated out of sheer neglect, as the head of the RMA Shipyard Department, von Ahlefeld, often complained.[69] How could he keep official prices below those of private shipyards?[70] Only consistent and increased capital expenditure to expand and improve the facilities at each imperial yard could fulfill the RMA's expectations.

Krupp: The Vulcan Scheme and the Armor Monopoly

A firm the RMA could never conquer as it did Koch now tried to broaden its shipyard holdings. In 1903 the Krupp firm's directors approved a plan to begin a takeover of the Vulcan shipyard at Stettin. The initial plan was to negotiate a gentleman's agreement with the Stettin firm for close cooperation, similar to the alliance with Dillinger. When Vulcan rejected these approaches, the director of Krupp, Max Rötger, ordered the slow but steady purchasing of the shipyard's stock.[71] Vulcan's stockholders received a two-part appeal to help quicken the pace of the annexation. Essen guaranteed a consistent 4 percent dividend on Vulcan shares and minimum changes and experimentation for thirty years to assure Vulcan's stability after the takeover.[72] Vulcan was particularly vulnerable to this attack because it did not get enough contracts from the RMA to keep its entire work force employed on a continuous basis. In 1902 it received contracts for a light cruiser and a cannon boat, followed by another cruiser in 1903 and a battleship in 1904. It finished the lighter vessels in less than twenty-four months and released many highly specialized workers at various stages of construction because it could not provide alternative work. Before the acquisition of its larger Hamburg facility in 1906, Vulcan could not accommodate many capital ships simultaneously. The Hamburg site would later enable a vastly increased capacity, but the firm's employees needed work immediately.[73]

Krupp made it difficult for Vulcan's directors to oppose the takeover by slowing down armor and cannon deliveries, thereby endangering Vulcan's position with the RMA. This could affect both Vulcan's reputation with the navy and the status of Vulcan stock on the exchange.[74]

Krupp's aim was to possess shipyards on both the North Sea and the Baltic. Effectively controlling or owning Vulcan would double the value of the Germaniawerft to the RMA and reduce the Krupp shipyard's competition.[75] This effort continued until 1914, as the Vulcan directorate under Justus Flohr barely kept Krupp at bay.

During the 1902–4 period the Krupp firm continued to dominate German armor plate production. It managed to keep this and its lucrative business in high percent nickel-steel products beyond the reach of the Association of Steel Works.[76] Otherwise, Krupp, as one of the association's larger companies, observed its quotas governing steel production and profits in the Ruhr.[77] Essen benefited both in and out of cartel organizations.

Krupp was not the only steel producer employed by the navy, although it often seemed so. Many firms turned out a variety of special steel products, and not all were as well known or as powerful as Krupp,

Dillinger, Thyssen, and Stinnes. Furthermore, many of the shipyards deliberately used a variety of steel firms in an effort to reduce overhead, among other reasons. The Schichau shipyard in Elbing, for example, frequently purchased nickel steel from Borsig, Hörder, or the Bismarckhütte rather than Krupp.[78] The Vulcan yard (Hamburg and Stettin) also contracted with Hörder in Westphalia on the SMS *Preussen* contract and preferred Dillinger to Krupp for armor when possible.[79] Given Krupp's efforts to take over this company between 1903 and 1906, it comes as no surprise that Vulcan refused to rely too heavily on Essen for anything.[80] Vulcan also contracted with the Panzer firm in Wolgast for small quantities of armor plate.[81] These other companies did not present much of a threat to Krupp, but these cases clearly illustrate that neither the shipyards nor the RMA were content with Krupp's dominant position in the steel industry.

The RMA had to endure Krupp's prices for armor and artillery. In a discussion of this matter during October 1902, Rudloff of the Construction Department stated his belief that Krupp did not seize all possible opportunities to cut costs. He referred Admiral von Capelle of the RMA Administrative Department to one case in which an 80,000-mark saving on armor costs might have been possible. Von Capelle replied that if he pressed the issue with Krupp, "the entire armor plate question would again unravel," and the admiral was all too aware of von Tirpitz's failure to alter that situation.[82] In the time between Fritz Krupp's death in Essen on 22 November 1902 and the marriage of his daughter Bertha to Gustav von Bohlen und Halbach in 1906, the situation began to change.[83] The firm's grant of a 2.5 percent rebate on all naval orders in April 1903 was interpreted as a hopeful sign, but nobody at the RMA was rejoicing too loudly because the rebate would not alter the prices dramatically.[84]

Research and Development: The Turbine Engine and U-Boat

Discussions among RMA staff officers determined the areas of research and development in which the navy took particular interest. By 1902, for example, a consensus among RMA leaders directed artillery research toward larger weapons with a much greater muzzle velocity.[85] The 28-centimeter guns that would arm Germany's first dreadnoughts as well as a new ship design capable of 19.5 knots originated in RMA planning sessions.[86]

Events abroad heavily influenced the decisions of these *Sitzungen* or planning sessions. The RMA received a constant flow of technical information from its naval attachés which it shared with the private shipyards and firms.[87] Another important foreign source was Lieutenant von Löwenfeld, who observed the Battle of Tsushima between the Russians and the Japanese in late 1904 from the battleship *Tsarevitch*. His report emphasized Japan's effective use of torpedoes against the Russian battleships. Torpedoes became a topic of intense debate within the RMA, as the German navy was well acquainted with these weapons.[88] But any hope of using the torpedo in conjunction with the U-boat perished in tactical discussions and evaluations of battleship performance. In a fourteen-page memo entitled "Reflections on the *Tsarevitch*," Vice-Admiral Kurt von Prittwitz, chief of the Cruiser Squadron, concluded that torpedo nets had justified themselves by keeping damage to Russian ships to a minimum.[89] Twelve years later, the navy discarded these defensive nets after evaluating the Battle of Jutland (Skaggarak). Nonetheless, observations of an actual war were considered to have provided invaluable opportunities to improve the quality of decisions mapping the future of a navy. With few exceptions, however, the lessons learned from the Russo-Japanese War reinforced already predominant points of view rather than provoking experimentation.

One result of research and development, the Parsons turbine, complemented well the current strategic viewpoint. In the spring of 1902, von Tirpitz sent a naval commission to Great Britain to examine firsthand the performance of the Parsons engine and advise the Construction Department on its suitability for use in the Imperial Navy. The group returned enthusiastic about the engine's possibilities, with only one reservation. They were not sure how this high-powered system would work as part of an on-board electrical dynamo.[90]

German industry took the navy's generally favorable evaluation as the go-ahead signal. Up to 1902, only Brown and Boveri was licensed to manufacture the Parsons engine in Germany. In that year, however, the British Parsons Company opened its own German branch, the "Turbina," Deutsche Parsons Marine AG, named after the first successful British turbine ship prototype.[91] Thus Brown and Boveri suddenly fell to the status of a Turbina affiliate for the Parsons system.

The rest of the German electrical industry did not stand still while these developments took place. The North German Lloyd, Krupp,

Siemens-Schuckert, and MAN all explored the Swiss Zoelly turbine system, and the *Berliner Tageblatt* reported the imminent formation of a huge combine among these firms. No such combine was formed, however, for Krupp was investigating propulsion systems of its own and would commit to no single engine design. AEG and Vulcan began joint research, while Siemens and Halske continued to deal with Parsons through Brown and Boveri.[92] Nevertheless, the Parsons remained the only engine that had been designed, tested, and proven effective. It soon became recognized around the world as the most advanced form of reliable marine propulsion. Jay Gould and J. P. Morgan jointly paid £100,000 in 1902 for the American rights to the Parsons patent to power five fast transatlantic steamers with 50,000-horsepower Parsons turbines.[93]

Although the British lead in turbine technology presented a problem, it indicated to von Tirpitz that Germany had reached the stage of self-sufficiency that Stosch had hoped for thirty years earlier. The navy needed only home-based firms and yards to fulfill von Tirpitz's naval ambitions. Even in the case of the turbine, the position of the RMA did not seem nearly as tenuous after 1902. Almost every German electrical firm and even a few shipyards desperately scrambled to upset Parsons's dominance.[94] With the foundation of a Parsons affiliate in Germany, it was unlikely that the RMA would find itself cut off from vital technical information in case of war. Domestic engineering expertise, coupled with the facilities of Turbina and Brown and Boveri, would ensure independence in cases of extreme necessity.[95]

The RMA's other problems with the electrical industry seemed small by comparison. Occasionally the minor design modifications required by poorly engineered electrical hardware upset some naval officials. Too often lamps, lanterns, and lighting fixtures failed to fulfill their function, and on-board electrical dynamos, powered by small turbines, presented problems of space and stability.[96] In addition, the Construction Department feared the growing market share of the Siemens companies in wireless telegraphy, but at this point the RMA still thought there was sufficient competition in the industry.[97] Between 1902 and 1904, it outfitted some forty-one new and old ships with the latest in wireless telegraphy for about 1,500 to 2,000 marks per ship.[98] In every case the navy insisted upon strict adherence to the suppliers' list and the official guidelines for electrical equipment and wireless apparatus.[99]

By 1904, when the Germaniawerft began construction on the first U-boat ordered by the RMA, the Imperial Navy found itself far behind Germany's three top naval rivals in this area of weapons technology. In 1903, the French submarine *Forelle* successfully completed a three-nautical-mile test cruise during which the sixteen-ton vessel simulated a submerged attack and returned to base. About three months later, the kaiser saw the boat in action and later his brother Admiral Prince Heinrich became the first German officer to ride in a U-boat.[100]

The French led submarine development in 1904 with forty-six U-boats in service or under construction, financed by a budget of 1,337,858 francs. The Americans did not lag far behind in research and development, but it took World War I to push the U.S. Navy into finding a place for the new vessels in its strategic planning. The design perfected by John P. Holland went into production by 1896, and his efforts placed nine successful boats in service before the end of 1901, at an average cost of $700,000 per boat. When the British approached the American inventor in 1902 with an eye toward producing the new American submarine in England under license, the Admiralty had already completed four submarines at state shipyards and five others at Vickers' Sons and Maxim.[101] In Germany, only Krupp's work at the Germaniawerft made any genuine progress, but, according to a 1904 memorandum, the RMA did not indicate any official interest in full-scale development and deployment of U-boats.[102]

Krupp launched the first U-boat prototype at Kiel under the supervision of the French expert Raymondo Lorenzo d'Equevilley in 1902 and officially entered the U-boat market by applying for a German patent to construct diesel-electric submarines in 1904. Krupp immediately encountered vigorous international competition.[103] The American-based Lake Torpedo Boat Company of Bridgeport, Connecticut, peddled its Protector class submarines in St. Petersburg, London, and Berlin. Initially, the Krupp firm approached this challenge the same way it had dealt earlier with Dillinger steel and the Vulcan shipyard. Krupp director Max Rötger and his colleagues tried to initiate negotiations with the Lake Company in hopes of cooperating in U-boat sales to the tsar's navy. They were prepared for head-to-head competition if Lake did not respond favorably.[104] Krupp had purchased a Holland submarine of a similar type for research purposes and knew the potential of some American designs.[105] The approach to Lake, however, was no more successful than the attempt to annex Vulcan. Although Germaniawerft foreign sales proved disappointing, Krupp knew he could rely on a near monopoly at home now that von Tirpitz had begun to bow to foreign and domestic presssure and seriously accepted the need to examine this new weapon. Between 1904 and the end of World War I, the Germania-werft would build 101 U-boats, of which the RMA bought 86.[106]

With the beginning of construction on the U-1, the RMA chief quickly saw the need to educate his engineers and inspectors for work with this new vessel. In 1904 von Tirpitz ordered the Technical Department to recruit engineers and to subject some of its younger personnel, on a volunteer basis, to an intense course in the niceties of U-boat construction.

Progress in Construction

Between 1903 and 1905 work began on the last pre-dreadnought class of German battleships. The Deutschland Class included the *Hannover, Pommern, Schlesien, Deutschland*, and *Schleswig-Holsten*.[107] The first and last ships were built by Germaniawerft, the third and fourth, by Vulcan and Schichau, respectively. The imperial yard at Wilhelmshaven received the contract for the SMS *Hannover* at 24.2 million marks, the lowest price of the class by 130,000 marks. The five ships averaged about 14,000 tons and had a top speed of between eighteen and nineteen knots. Their main armament consisted of two twin 28-centimeter turrets and fourteen 17-centimeter guns along with a number of smaller quick-firing cannons. The final type of vessel built under the financial auspices of the 1900 Naval Law was the U-1. The RMA spent 1.9 million marks on this boat, which joined the fleet in 1906. It had a submerged range of 1,400 sea miles at five knots.

By the time the U-1 was half complete, the RMA was working on supplementing the 1900 Naval Law. The 1906 Supplementary Naval Law was the first of three prewar bills of its kind successfully presented to the Reichstag. Von Tirpitz's continued good fortune with the legislature gave him both the means to respond to Britain's HMS *Dreadnought* and the money to perpetuate the new U-boat program.

Between 1902 and 1904 an active and aggressive British response to RMA ambitions destroyed the foundations of the risk theory. Von Tirpitz's position continued strong, however, because the battleship remained master of the seas and contemporary analyses of the Russo-Japanese War confirmed this dictum. Outside the military establishment, public opinion and the business community still supported the notion that an imperial policy and a strong navy went hand in hand as part of the image of a great power.

It is difficult to credit the reasoning behind von Tirpitz's absolutely consistent policy during this period. He was politically astute and realistic, and he was aware of British determination to meet Germany's naval challenge. But his decision to explore the possibilities of the U-boat represented less an admission of the vessel's potential as a weapon against British numerical superiority than a stopgap measure to ensure German technological parity. His belief in the continued predominance of capital ships, an inner imperative to challenge Britain, and the dependence of his professional position and reputation on the risk theory prevented him from reacting to changes in world events.

Relations between the RMA and industry were characterized by an increasingly accepted routine during these three years. The navy was still expanding at a rapid pace, and the protocol system and testing procedures were firmly established. Industry knew the standards it had to meet and the extent to which the RMA would go to ensure compliance. In some instances, the RMA even sought to regulate not only its contractors but also their relationships with their subcontractors. It became clear that the RMA regarded any industrial activity involving naval construction as its province. Yet von Tirpitz's refusal to allow the RMA actively to direct and promote research and development prevented the effective growth and extension of naval authority through technical expertise and did little to prevent both wasteful duplication in turbine development and near monopoly in the U-boat industry.

4

Criticism, Continuity, and Legislative Success

1905 – 1908

Between 1905 and 1908, von Tirpitz began an uphill battle against criticism from energetic opponents who took him to task for his relentless devotion to the risk theory and the battleship. In spite of scathing attacks by Captain Lothar Persius and Admiral Karl Galster, among others, the admiral kept to his course and struck back at his detractors. His success in guiding two supplements to the 1900 Naval Law through the Reichstag in 1906 and 1908 testified to his continued strength and resilience in the face of open challenges to his strategy and building plans. He also persisted in his aversion to the U-boat, despite the growing popularity of the weapon in naval circles. Thus RMA policies were characterized by continuity over these four years, and the admiral's position remained as strong as ever.

Admiral Rollmann became chief of the Construction Department upon von Eickstedt's retirement in 1907. He faced basically the same problems as his predecessor. The armor monopoly consumed ever-increasing amounts of RMA money and contributed to overruns beyond contract cost and weight limits. The Parsons Turbina Company still controlled the turbine industry in spite of challenges by Siemens, AEG, Krupp, and others. Furthermore, as the cost of building the fleet rose dramatically, von Tirpitz became conscious of a need to give every advantage possible to the imperial shipyards as the navy's only alternative to private industry. In the face of a 20 to 25 percent rise in the wholesale price index after 1905 and the usual industrial price gouging, the RMA needed every advantage it could muster.

Political Background

By 1906, the British had resolved to adjust their naval policy in response to developments elsewhere. The director of British Naval Intelligence commented that Germany would soon surpass Russia as the principal Baltic naval power. He was certain that the Admiralty would shift the focus of the two-power standard to France and Germany, rather than France and Russia.[1] Thus Ambassador Metternich's 1905 comment that "no reasonable man here [Great Britain] thinks of war against Germany" soon required amendment.[2] The Royal Navy planned to match and perhaps surpass any further German naval expansion. The British did not want war any more than von Tirpitz did, but they refused to play blind man while the state secretary guided his fleet program through the "danger zone." The change in the British political climate between 1902 and 1904 destroyed the international foundations of the risk theory and propelled Germany into a full-scale arms race before von Tirpitz expected or realized it.

Why did von Tirpitz continue as planned? Surely his strongest motive was that his reputation and position rested on the risk theory, but there were other reasons. Von Tirpitz came from a strategic, offensive school of naval thought that found a commerce war or *guerre de course* repulsive. He felt that Germany would face a challenge from Britain sooner or later in the imperial and economic arenas. Only winning the Royal Navy's respect in battle could ensure Germany's right to compete economically. Therefore, von Tirpitz would wage a war against British commerce only as a last resort, after losing the decisive battle. The best he felt a commerce war strategy could accomplish in a contest against Britain was "a favorable peace," and he believed Germany required more than that.[3]

Nonetheless, he had no shortage of strategic challengers. In 1907, the commercial war theories of the newly retired U-boat advocate Vice-Admiral Galster were endorsed by ever more high-ranking officers in the German navy.[4] Other officers argued that a battleship strategy could succeed against Britain only in certain clearly defined circumstances and locations such as the restricted waters in the belts north of Kiel and east of Denmark. Both of these points of view had flaws which von Tirpitz considered fatal, and therefore he felt secure in retaining his adopted strategy. He never regarded the U-boat as an important primary weapon and hence dismissed Galster. The belts strategy depended on the occupation of Denmark to secure the fleet's western flank for offensive operations. In the event of war, von Tirpitz knew that the Army General Staff would probably resist committing troops in Denmark. It was also doubtful whether the British could be drawn out of the North Sea and into the belts region.[5] Instead, the High Seas Fleet would have to challenge the Royal Navy on the open sea. This was the path to achieving the status of a true world power.

Therefore, the state secretary did not occupy himself with Galster's theories but concentrated on new, all big-gun battleship designs. Besides, the British introduction of the *Dreadnought* in 1906 provided von Tirpitz with both the challenge he welcomed and a comfortable reaffirmation of the battleship's future dominance in warfare. Between 1904 and 1906 the RMA produced three designs for a ship of the dreadnought type. Project 10A (1904) displaced 14,000 tons and carried all heavy guns, but of two calibers. In 1905, Project C weighed 17,000 tons with eight heavy guns of a single caliber. The true forerunner of the Nassau Class dreadnoughts was Project G76, an 18,000-ton vessel with twelve heavy guns, drawn up in 1906.[6]

Other influences besides technical and strategic considerations pushed von Tirpitz to continue the fleet program unchanged. In spite of both public and private doubts voiced by people such as Albert Ballin and Friedrich von Holstein, popular support for fleet expansion grew.[7] By 1906 membership in the German Naval League rose to 330,044 individuals and the participation of 621,778 organizations,[8] and the RMA News Bureau produced more fleet propaganda than ever in preparation for the presentation of the 1906 Supplementary Naval Law to the Reichstag.[9]

The shipbuilding industry also wanted von Tirpitz's construction plan to continue. The expansion of the shipyards and new capital investments made by firms in hope of reaping considerable profits were a direct result of von Tirpitz's projections of naval needs. The entire industry would experience a setback if these estimates fell. The RMA's relationship with industry developed a momentum of its own that encouraged the admiral to continue his past policies and played a role in limiting the scope of German diplomacy during these years.[10]

Without increased funds, von Tirpitz's future plans as well as important technological and design developments would come to nought. To thwart this possibility, he had decided before the launching of the *Dreadnought* to present two revisions of the 1900 Naval Law to the Reichstag. The first of these would come in 1906, the second in 1908. Since the Naval Laws of 1898 and 1900 did not stipulate a standard pace of growth, he designed the supplementary laws of 1906 and 1908 to require the replacement of battleships in twenty years rather than twenty-five and to give his proposed construction schedule the force of law.[11] Although he focused on getting the fleet through the danger zone, von Tirpitz relied politically on the power of the industrial and agrarian right-wing coalition, a major force both for the fleet and for the preservation of the existing political and social order in Imperial Germany.[12]

In both 1906 and 1908 von Tirpitz entered the Reichstag on a wave of RMA-inspired Naval League propaganda and his own detailed projections of naval needs. In his desire for these 1906 and 1908 supplementary laws, however, he rarely showed any willingness to understand the financial pressures bearing down on the Reichstag and the Imperial Treasury Office. Rather, the RMA became a ruthless competitor for appropriations, and von Tirpitz always felt, to the regret of Chancellor von Bülow and Treasury Secretaries von Stengel and von Sydow,[13] that the government should find enough money to meet its obligations to the RMA.[14]

As usual, von Tirpitz employed a personal touch in parliamentary relations as he promoted naval power as a vital element in Germany's political and economic growth. In 1902 he had a large Reichstag contingent brought to England to witness, with Germany's military representatives, the naval review for the coronation of King Edward VII. He always notified the Reichstag deputies of impressive signs of naval power at home and abroad.

During the debate over the 1908 supplementary law, he provided tours for some of the wavering deputies to naval bases, shipyards, and even some of the newer capital ships.[15] For example, the RMA took the Reichstag Budget Commission on a tour of the Schichau shipyard in

Danzig to evaluate plant facilities, materials, labor, and working conditions. The Budget Commission thus obtained firsthand estimates of increasing costs at one of the larger private yards.[16]

Prices were rising rapidly, and further increases in size, artillery, caliber, and necessary armor for dreadnoughts formed a vital part of the 1908 debate. Between 1905 and 1909 the cost of a battleship rose nearly 96 percent and the price of heavy cruisers 107 percent. Part of this escalation is attributed to the general rise in German prices during this period, but increased production costs and profiteering were also responsible. A battleship that cost 24 million marks in 1905 cost 47 million by the time debate began on the 1908 Supplementary Naval Law.[17] A look at the RMA's first installment payment on the Nassau (1907) and the Helgoland (1908) classes further illustrates this dilemma. AG Weser received an opening payment of 12.02 million marks for the SMS *Westfalen* in 1907. One year later the SMS *Thuringen's* first installment topped that figure by 2,681,000 marks, and the same shipyard built both vessels.[18] In 1905 the considerable expense for artillery and armor set by the Krupp-Dillinger alliance alone made up 30 to 40 percent of the cost of a capital ship.[19]

The modernization of the imperial naval yards absorbed the navy's attention as a second major priority after shipbuilding. By 1905 the RMA expanded these facilities, and future plans emphasized the increased specialization of each yard. Every imperial shipyard had its coal and oil storage capacity increased as well as its facilities for stockpiling explosives, supplies, and ship parts. The imperial shipyard at Danzig built U-boats and repaired light cruisers. Kiel provided a central base for all torpedo work, and new slips augmented its ability to handle capital ships by 1908. The property owned by the navy at Brunsbüttel, adjacent to the Kiel Canal, now became part of the yard. Wilhelmshaven, as before, remained the primary location for battleship construction, and, like the others, its capacity for fuel and explosives was increased.[20] Sustained improvement would require large yearly appropriations over the entire prewar period.[21]

Von Tirpitz exploited every possible theme in his efforts to secure the passage of both fleet law supplements. The RMA publicly pinpointed England as the main adversary abroad, and von Tirpitz argued that the danger zone and the fear of "copenhagening" would disappear only if the navy adopted a policy of building three ships per year. He targeted the opposition of the Progressives and the SPD for propaganda attacks in the press[22] and once again argued so convincingly in political debate that the Reichstag passed the Supplementary Naval Laws on 5 June 1906 and 6 April 1908.[23]

The 1906 law increased the Foreign Service Fleet by five heavy cruisers and the Reserve Fleet by one. The more important of the two laws, however, was the 1908 supplement, which established both the policy of three ships per year and a twenty-year service life for every ship. In effect, this meant construction of four ships per year including new projects and replacements.[24] Von Tirpitz's building program peaked with the passage of this law. Between 1906 and 1912 the bulk of Germany's most effective capital ships joined the fleet.

Research and Development: The Dreadnought Revolution and the U-Boat Alternative

The revolution in ship design wrought by the appearance of the HMS *Dreadnought* in 1906 caused the RMA to reevaluate naval architecture, gunnery, and propulsion.[25] Von Eickstedt shared the determination of his chief that the navy should have practical and effective weapons at minimal cost. They accelerated research on new vessel designs at the Kiel Technical Institute, where the navy made stress tests on hull designs and cooperated with such firms as Zeiss Optical and Siemens on development of special instruments and gauges.

The RMA also planned to locate a new research institute at Berlin Marienfelde and another for materials testing in Stuttgart.[26] The latter would complement those at Charlottenberg, the Berlin Technische Hochschule, and the Purchasing Department offices in Düsseldorf, Essen, and Berlin.[27] RMA technical personnel were required to visit these centers and the facilities of private companies to improve their skills in the increasingly complex fields related to ship construction.[28] At the imperial yards the RMA kept lists of independent commercial and private research projects of possible interest to the navy.[29]

In their joint research and experimentation, industry and the RMA encountered few of the difficulties that plagued them during standard construction projects because the results of the research at Kiel, Berlin, and Danzig not only benefited the navy but also provided new directions and opportunities for the firms involved. Thus in this realm the navy experienced little of the tension usually found in government, military, and business relationships. Furthermore, naval research efforts frequently aroused the interest of other divisions of the German government. The Ministry of Public Works, for example, provided significant support for certain aspects of the work done by the Research Center for Shipbuilding in Berlin.[30] This relative harmony served the navy well in support of development and construction during these formative years.

The RMA knew the difficulty of keeping new ship designs secret. Obviously, the appearance of the *Dreadnought* would oblige every naval power to emulate the British. The RMA did not intend to copy the British but rather to create a ship that would best fit German needs vis-à-vis the Royal Navy in the North Sea and the Baltic. Thus the designs that ultimately resulted in the Nassau and Helgoland classes and the battlecruiser SMS *von der Tann* were different enough to require more secrecy than ever before. Von Tirpitz solicited designs from private firms, and the navy developed its own.[31] In a note to Germaniawerft and Vulcan on this matter, the RMA reminded these firms, which might become involved in the construction of new designs, "to maintain the greatest discretion regarding everything pertaining to our ships of the line."[32] As the development of new designs progressed, the same secrecy was applied in the preparation of the publications that spelled out the design specifications and RMA construction requirements to each shipyard and purveyor.[33]

Initially the RMA departed from the British preference in its choice of heavy guns for the Nassau Class. The HMS *Dreadnought* carried 30.5-centimeter guns, but the German navy at first favored a smaller-caliber gun. In 1905 and 1906, the RMA thoroughly investigated the potential of 21-, 24-, and 28-centimeter guns[34] and decided, not unexpectedly, to move away from the old midrange 21- and 24-centimeter weapons in favor of a uniform big-gun design but not the 30.5-centimeter main weapon used by the British.[35] The new Krupp 28-centimeter, 45-caliber model not only performed as well as the 30.5 but was also lighter and cheaper to produce.[36] Thus although the British presented the threat, the response was entirely an RMA creation.

A wide variety of improvements now went into capital ship designs. Max Krause, the director of the Borsig Mining and Foundry Company, presented a new plan for the mounting of torpedo nets on the sides of the ship that reduced the possibility of tangles, slack, rust, and other problems occurring during deployment.[37] The RMA also received a favorable consensus from the private shipyards on a new method of hull construction which combined an oblique alignment of steel plate on the surface with double wall construction. Both of these measures provided better defense against torpedoes.[38] Every aspect of naval architecture and every sort of ship system now came under scrutiny as part of the general revolution in battleship design.[39]

In 1905, many of the most important shipyards could not build the projected dreadnought types because their slips were not wide enough. All six of the major private yards began a crash program to alter their facilities. In spite of some efforts to claim certain wide-berth construction techniques as patented private property, all of the firms effected the improvements.[40] By early 1906 Vulcan had acquired its new Hamburg facility, and the other five private firms upgraded their yards to accommodate ships with berths from 20 to 41 meters. Weser was the smallest of the six with a 20- to 30-meter capacity and Vulcan the largest, covering up to 41 meters.[41]

The increased specialization of the imperial yards evolved in part as an effort to compete effectively with the private sector for certain ship types. Thus Wilhelmshaven built every battleship assigned to an imperial yard through 1914 save for the SMS *Kaiser,* and the RMA limited both Danzig and Kiel to U-boats and midsized vessels.

Thanks to the success of the 1906 and 1908 Supplementary Naval Laws, the pace of the U-boat program quickened. Eleven boats were laid down during this period, and money for research and development became more plentiful, 1.5 million marks each year in 1905 and 1906. For the next two years the figure rose by 1 million marks per year, finally leaping to 5 million marks in 1909.[42] In his statements at the time, and by the array of technical faults he later attributed to the first U-boats in his memoirs, von Tirpitz showed a consistently negative attitude toward them. In spite of the good performance achieved by the U-1 and foreign boats, he restricted the RMA's investment in the weapon: "I refused to throw away money on submarines so long as they could only cruise in home waters, and therefore would be of no use to us; as soon as seagoing boats were built, however, I was the first to encourage them on a large scale, and, in spite of the financial restrictions imposed upon me, I went as far as the limits of our technical production would permit."[43]

Von Tirpitz was not beyond stretching the truth, and the needs of his battleships always defined the limits of the RMA commitment to the U-boat.

During his tenure as state secretary, von Tirpitz made no secret that he found the U-boat potentially useful only as a possible auxiliary to the battleship. In a Reichstag session in January 1908, von Tirpitz listened to Progressive representative Leonhart's favorable evaluation of a pamphlet on the U-boat and commerce war by retired Vice-Admiral Galster and responded that he was not going to convert to the gospel according to Galster: "If the honorable representative believes that, then he is badly misled."[44]

Indeed, von Tirpitz treated the opponents of his strategies ruthlessly. He classified officers such as Vice-Admiral Galster, Kurt von Maltzahn, and Lothar Persius as enemies of the navy and had their writings banned while they remained in the service.[45] After his retirement, Lothar Persius became a formidable foe. His series of books and articles praising the possibilities of the U-boat in a commercial war persistently took von Tirpitz to task. When the state secretary's theories fell from favor during the war and he reluctantly retired, Persius administered a journalistic coup de grace. In a book entitled *Die Tirpitz Legende*, Persius indicted the admiral's strategic dogma and blamed him for Germany's lack of preparedness to fight a U-boat war in 1914.[46] But when Persius began writing and the first U-boats appeared, von Tirpitz still stood among the world's great naval leaders and the battleship ruled the seas.

Of the boats built before 1908, the imperial yard at Danzig received the U-2, 3, 4, and 9 through 12. The Germaniawerft and its U-boat chief, Hans Techel, received boats 5 through 8 after completing the U-1 in 1906. Krupp charged 1.9 million marks for the U-1, and the more sophisticated 5–8 series cost an average of 2.57 million each. As a rule, Danzig's boats were substantially cheaper. The U-2 cost 1.5 million, the U-3 and 4 about 300,000 more, and the 9–12 series, 2.2 million. All of these boats displaced between 200 and 500 tons, and the cruising radius, even in the later models, varied very little. The U-1 was capable of 1,400 sea miles at 10 knots on the surface. Its successors reached 1,600 to 1,900 sea miles at a maximum of 12 to 14 knots. The electric motors of the U-1 through 4 could propel these boats submerged for 50 to 55 sea miles at 4.5 or 5 knots. The better electrical systems on the U-5 through 12 increased the submerged radius to 80 sea miles at a standard 5-knot speed.[47]

At the same time, the RMA initiated work on many U-boat-related projects and facilities. In 1906, when the fortification of Helgoland began in earnest, the navy built dock facilities to accommodate ninety torpedo boats and eighteen U-boats along with considerable shore batteries to protect the installation.[48] The RMA also purchased more time for U-boat research at the Research Center for Shipbuilding in Berlin,[49] but von Tirpitz refused to employ an independent firm to increase the output of U-boat torpedoes. He found the quality and workmanship at the navy's torpedo work station in Friedrichsort far superior to the best private manufacturer, Schwartzkopf. Thus Friedrichsort became the beneficiary of increased RMA funding, and it supplied all of the navy's torpedoes until the outbreak of the war.[50]

In 1904, Germany trailed its major naval rivals in the number of U-boats in service or on order. The international U-boat situation was summarized by the British that year as follows:

	Completed	Under construction
Britain	8	11
France	26	13
Germany	1*	0
Russia	1	14
Italy	1	2
United States	8	0
Japan	0	0

*The U-1 was actually still under construction.[51]

Although all the major naval powers now began in varying degrees to consider the need for U-boats, France alone cast the new underwater weapon in a major strategic role and adjusted the composition of its fleet accordingly. In 1906, French naval experts submitted to the Senate the following projections of naval needs through 1919: 34 battleships and 36 cruisers, 109 torpedo boats for defense and 170 more for offensive operations, and 49 defensive and 82 offensive U-boats.[52]

The French obviously agreed with those in the German navy who saw value in the strategic doctrines of Karl Galster and Lothar Persius.

Though von Tirpitz's views did not go unopposed, they showed little sign of succumbing to those of the U-boat advocates.

Revisions in the Protocol System: A Plague of Overruns in Time, Cost, and Weight

The substantial increases in construction between 1905 and 1908 necessitated revision of the protocol system to streamline inspection procedures and supervisory methods. The modification of publications governing construction and product quality often caused difficulties for the yards because some specifications changed during the building process. Although Weser, the Germaniawerft, and the imperial yard at Danzig voiced their dissatisfaction to the RMA, the latter depended on the continued excellence of materials that the revised regulations booklets guaranteed.[53] In spite of occasional delays, the quality of naval goods made the regulations seem worthwhile.

The general construction guidelines also underwent revision during these years for the first time since 1898 and the first Naval Law. The RMA solicited suggestions from the imperial yards, naval inspectors, and private firms.[54] According to the Construction Department, "The revisions of the construction manuals, weight specifications, etc., will strive for clarity, lucidity, and an ability to exert control."[55]

New editions of the suppliers' list appeared in 1905 and 1907.[56] Some firms such as Postler Chemical of Dresden did not appear thanks to information from the regional government that it had engaged in illegal business practices.[57] The firm of Wilhelm Meyerholz was found guilty of false representation—it was an approved company acting as a clearinghouse for firms not on the suppliers' list.[58] This information came to the RMA courtesy of the Hannover Chamber of Commerce.

In many instances, a better product was achieved in each category of the list by limiting concerns to their areas of expertise.[59] Purging as many inadequate firms as possible from each category enabled contractors and the RMA to focus on the best ones in any given field. Knowing their suppliers also enabled RMA officials to pick out new areas in which certain firms might be useful in the future. The editing process even addressed the problem of unfair competition within the list's categories, but the RMA never found a completely satisfactory solution to that problem.[60]

The imperial yards frequently received a special advantage by the way the RMA employed the suppliers' list. Blohm und Voss once complained about having its electrical contractor for the battlecruiser SMS *von der Tann* selected by the RMA. The Hamburg shipyard angrily observed that the imperial yards could choose from AEG, Siemens-Schuckert Werke (SSW), Felton and Guilleaume, or any other firm on the suppliers' list. The RMA replied that it restricted Blohm und Voss because with Siemens-Schuckert doing most of the ship's electrical work the yard could achieve a uniformity impossible if it used two or three contractors. Of course, the RMA knew that this decision also offered the imperial shipyards a wider selection of vendors and an excellent opportunity to reduce their overhead.

The imperial shipyards always had complete freedom to choose the best purveyor at the cheapest price.[61] They also received first notification of any new addition to the suppliers' list and early results of product tests.[62] As public institutions in an economic system that supplied every possible freedom to the private sector, the imperial yards needed artificially created advantages to keep pace. The RMA obliged, and, as well as expanding the facilities at the imperial yards, it gave them a safety valve against higher prices.

German business leaders often felt confined by these protocol controls. Mix and Genest Company protested that not only did suppliers to the imperial yards receive preferential treatment but the navy took far too long to test finished products ready for shipment to Mix and Genest. Von Tirpitz insisted on the tests and urged the directors of Mix and Genest to notify the Purchasing Office as early as possible that a product was nearing completion.[63] Because every product had to be tested, the RMA frequently asked firms to build an extra ten days to two weeks into their construction schedules to avoid delays and possible late delivery.[64] Many firms, like Krupp, continued to balk, but to no avail.[65] A 1908 memorandum from the Construction Inspectorate in Hamburg, although a bit effusive in its praise for the protocol system, nonetheless made an essential point: in the majority of cases the system worked well for the RMA, keeping a tight rein on the navy's business relationships.[66]

German private business leaders expected government to ensure their privacy, to support them against the demands of labor, and not to meddle in their affairs, but the RMA found it difficult to grant them so much independence. The industrialists involved in shipbuilding found the naval construction program's promise of substantial profits attractive, but they resisted official interference. In rare instances, industry and the state found themselves playing the same role because both the state and private coal mines in Prussia belonged to the Rheinisch-Westfälischen Coal Syndicate.[67] Most of the time, however, the private sector preferred that the government remain at arm's length. Industrialist and mine owner Emil Kirdorf wrote a scathing letter to Chancellor von Bülow in 1905, when there was labor unrest in the Ruhr, accusing him not only of interfering but of actions less than friendly to industry.[68] Most industrialists expected support and encouragement from the government but not daily involvement in their business affairs.

Just before his retirement as head of the RMA Construction Department in 1907, Vice-Admiral von Eickstedt declared that the RMA could never take a neutral stand in business matters directly relating to naval projects.[69] Although the industry often protested bitterly, von Tirpitz and von Eickstedt placed the RMA in the role of partner in every business transaction involving contracts granted by the navy. Rear Admiral Rollmann, von Eickstedt's successor, justified such interference because it was naive to think that industry would place the interests of the navy first.[70] Rear Admiral Guido von Usedom, the director of the imperial yard at Kiel, asserted in a memo to the Construction Department in 1906 that patriotism and service came second to profit for the private sector in any naval project.[71]

Thus, in spite of the business community's opposition to its involvement, the RMA did not play either ally or bystander. Von Tirpitz and his associates cast the RMA as an "interested party" in every business transaction with full authority to intervene if the navy was not properly served. It took time for the navy to decide to take this role. To do so in 1898 might have hurt von Tirpitz's chances of pushing the first Naval Law through the Reichstag. Furthermore, his policy of noninterference in technological development encouraged industry to expect the freedom Emil Kirdorf demanded in his 1905 letter to Chancellor von Bülow. Only between 1905 and 1908 did the RMA have the chance to define clearly its relationship with the private sector without damaging the progress of the construction program. Both sides had committed themselves beyond recall.

The RMA Administrative Department coordinated all of the scattered branches of the naval construction program because it alone had the authority to settle disagreements among officers, technical experts, and industry which might disrupt construction schedules.[72] The RMA's policies indicated that time was of the essence and the longer it took to build each ship the greater the risk of confronting Britain before von Tirpitz felt the fleet was ready.

Neither France nor Germany could build a capital ship as fast as the British. Work that took the French between fifty and sixty months to accomplish took thirty-six months in Germany and only twenty-four months in Britain. Rollmann concluded that the French shipyards had too little money, excessively complex designs, and subcontractors who were slow with deliveries. They also suffered from a problem the RMA frequently encountered—personnel shortages. Rollmann knew all of these difficulties well and responded by giving the Construction Inspectorate and the various technical inspectors on each project greater freedom to deal with daily problems.[73]

Both Rollmann and von Tirpitz sought to match the construction times achieved by British yards. In 1906, the German shipyards still took thirty-three to forty-nine months to build battleships and heavy cruisers. The year before, the Devonport yard in Britain built the HMS *Montague* in thirty-nine months and the Brown Company finished the HMS *Hindustan* in thirty-two months. Both of these represented the maximum times usually invested in British ships.[74] Von Tirpitz judged that faster construction would offer economies as well as political and diplomatic advantage, but some of the private yards argued that a quicker pace could drive costs up rather than down.[75] The RMA chief firmly believed, however, that the advantage of speed was worth the risk.

The manufacture of artillery and armor was the most time-consuming part of any naval construction project. In 1905 the Weapons Division optimistically informed the state secretary that more efficient construction techniques could save at least two months in building any given ship. Furthermore, improvement in material delivery times and shakedown procedures might save from thirty-six to twenty-four months and have a ship in service, complete with shakedown, before the thirty-third month.[76] Officials at the Weapons Division felt that with quick action these improvements could take effect by 1907. Krupp, however, still projected six to eight months for ordnance and armor installation during this period, pushing the optimistic project estimates to at least twenty-seven months, sometimes thirty-two, after which the ship still had to make its shakedown cruise.[77]

Krupp and Dillinger often slowed construction schedules by making late deliveries. Dillinger retarded the SMS *Pommern* project at Vulcan to such an extent that the latter complained to the RMA, and the incident was mentioned in a report to the kaiser.[78] The Construction Department addressed this problem by ordering that the yards alter their construction techniques to allow armor installation to begin earlier in the building process.[79]

The success of any time-saving measure was most dependent on punctual delivery by the firms and cooperation between them. In the case of the SMS *Schlesien*, Dillinger cooperated closely with Schichau.[80] The opposite was more typically the case, as happened with the Krupp portion of the SMS *Schlesien*'s armor. Schichau director Karl Ziese told two Reichstag representatives on a fact-finding tour of the Elbing yard that he would need only twenty-two months to complete a capital ship if Krupp would meet its armor deadlines.[81] In this case the RMA could only apply the few pressures within its power and hope for a favorable result.

The RMA also found it hard to keep projects assigned to private subcontractors on schedule, and it was not always the fault of the private sector. Firms often pointed to the time wasted while waiting for quality tests by the Purchasing Office, Construction Inspectorate, or other naval agencies. A shortage of Purchasing Office personnel exacerbated this problem for the RMA. Rollmann approved of the work done by the Purchasing Office, but he needed more qualified people.[82] This problem reduced the office's promptness and flawed the protocol system.[83]

More frequently, defective products caused the inspection slowdowns and a series of tests had to be conducted to discover the exact nature of the problem and its solution.[84] The RMA sought to remedy these difficulties by requesting more technical personnel and using the suppliers' list to eliminate substandard products.

Cost and weight overruns also continued but fell in number and consumed smaller amounts of time, money, and weight because of better RMA controls, but this problem still defied a comprehensive solution. In some instances the RMA forced the private yards to absorb extra costs, but not without resistance. The Germaniawerft agreed to pay an extra 200 marks on a small overrun incurred on the SMS *Deutschland*, but that was the extent of Krupp's cooperation on this project.[85] The RMA paid 17,900 marks for alterations to the command bridge of the ship.[86]

Yet the RMA rejected some overrun claims. In the case of the SMS *Preussen*, for example, it refused to accept overruns of 3,972 marks and 1,400 kilograms beyond the agreed contract terms for the crew's clothing, hammocks, and living supplies.[87] These signs of progress, however, were accompanied by overruns that still added up to a disturbingly large total. For example, the auxiliary boats placed aboard the SMS *Braunschweig*, *Elsass*, and *Lothringen* in 1905 added an average of 4,447 kilograms overweight, with 4,594 marks of excess cost per ship.[88]

Other costly imperfections emerged during sea trials. Fundamental design flaws, like the steering system difficulties with the Braunschweig Class, required repairs to the steering mechanism, bulkheads, deckplates, and other parts damaged by excessive vibration.[89] Though not as serious as a poor design, most post-shakedown work threatened to consume significant additional hours and marks. Alterations to the *Deutschland*'s command bridge, for example, came to almost 27,000 marks,[90] and the SMS *Preussen*'s torpedo tubes required modifications, as did the ventilation system of the *Braunschweig*.[91] The RMA patiently dealt with these challenges as well as the necessary minor repairs that might be expected in a rapidly expanding program, such as damage to a ship's internal system of communications piping.[92] Only the consistently high quality of the finished products partially compensated for the financial problems these overruns created.

The Armor Monopoly

Krupp's monopoly in armor and artillery made it difficult for the navy to conserve time, money, or weight, and the RMA's protests had no results.[93] One Krupp overrun on the small guns for the SMS *Pommern*, for example, totaled 4,200 marks with an extra 2,960 kilograms over contract weight.[94] In March 1906, when the Construction Department took exception to Krupp's 2,300-mark price to cover an artillery range finder with nickel-steel armor, the low-nickel-content, soft-steel alternative costing 1,950 marks offered neither adequate protection nor substantial savings.[95] Such situations drove the RMA to search constantly for alternatives to Krupp.

As the building program progressed, the low price of Krupp products abroad and the ability of the Americans to produce cheaper steel of similar quality became a major source of frustration for the RMA. American competition finally forced Krupp to reduce his armor prices. When the American Midvale Company lowered its price to 1,650 marks per ton in 1903 and the highest amount paid in the United States was 1,900 marks, exactly Essen's rate, Krupp had to respond. Midvale had already penetrated the European market, in Italy, so the growing, innovative, and competitive American armor industry suddenly became a threat in Europe as well as North America. In 1905 the Essen firm dropped its price from 1,900 marks to 1,780 marks per ton, about midway between the low Midvale rate and the higher price charged by the American Bethlehem and Carnegie firms.[96] The RMA had little influence over these events, however, and von Eickstedt gave voice to the Construction Department's helplessness when he commented that "the Krupp firm will do everything in its own interest to deliver good things."[97]

Krupp exercised awesome financial power and technical expertise. Besides its monopoly of armor and gun supply, the technicians of the Krupp firm were the only ones in Germany who could properly assemble and install heavy guns on naval vessels.[98] Its research facilities regularly produced breakthroughs in steel strength and resilience, as in the case of Siemens-Martin special steel.[99]

The firm also expended a great deal of its financial strength buying up raw materials deposits abroad to augment its domestic resources. In one case, the F. F. King Real Estate Company of Denver, Colorado, offered to sell seven tracts of land rich in tungsten to the RMA for ten thousand dollars in gold. King informed Admiral von Tirpitz that Krupp and an English syndicate already had extensive holdings in the area.[100] Von Tirpitz must have found this offer tempting. To have a private source for these raw materials would secure a great advantage for the navy. Krupp used tungsten to harden its steel for the artillery and armor that represented nearly one-third of the cost of every ship the RMA built.[101] Unfortunately, the navy had neither the resources nor the authority to make such purchases. In most instances, it could only appeal to the Krupp directors for more reasonable prices in view of current budget difficulties,[102] and it rarely received a response.

Krupp's towering position in the industry often prompted other naval officials to join von Tirpitz in his efforts to make some progress against the firm. Rear Admiral Goetz of the Weapons Division voiced an appeal very common among von Tirpitz's subordinates when he insisted that competition for Krupp, in any form, was absolutely necessary.[103] Goetz dealt with Krupp in nearly every weapons contract and realized the firm's power better than most. Heinrich Ehrhardt's Rheinische Metallwaren-und Maschinenfabriken in Düsseldorf manufactured gun barrels that came close to Essen's standards, but no other firm matched Krupp in the quality and quantity of armor produced for battleship protection.[104]

In other areas, however, Krupp occasionally took second place to other companies. The Mülheim firm of Thyssen and Company had entered the nickel-steel armor market in a small way by 1908,[105] as had Phoenix, Duisberger Eisen und Stahlwerke, and the Friedrichshütte,[106] all of which became involved in research on various new types of ship steel. Thus it seemed likely that any further inroads against Krupp would come by exploiting the firm's few limitations and the willingness of other companies to provide competition. When new contracts kept the Krupp facilities occupied in the spring of 1908, the Thyssen firm was awarded some armor orders for the deck of the SMS *Westfalen*.[107] Other companies, such as the Bismarckhütte and Borsig, also periodically filled in for Krupp after they perfected the techniques required to produce nickel steel.[108] Thus by 1908 many smaller firms finally had the technology and skill to fabricate and cast nickel-steel armor, but the Krupp-Dillinger collaboration kept them fighting for contracts and the naval crumbs falling from the boardroom tables at Essen and Dillingen.

Electrical Firms and the Turbine Engine

The RMA faced yet another challenge in monitoring developments and enforcing controls in the ever-changing electrical industry. As with the general construction guidelines, the basic guidelines for electrical systems had been revised by 1908, and although it provided a sound basis for RMA supervision, the occasional disturbing surprise or omission did occur.[109]

In one instance a Krupp complaint to the RMA about two faulty AEG 60-kilowatt generators slated for use in a 28-centimeter gun turret turned into a classic example of naval frustration with the Essen firm.[110] In the course of dealing with this difficulty, the RMA discovered in the *Journal of the American Society of Naval Engineers* that Krupp had nearly perfected an economical 25-kilowatt system for 28- and 30.5-centimeter turrets.[111] Krupp protested that the system was incomplete and denied inspiring the publication.[112] This did not quell the outburst of anger from both the Construction Department and Weapons Division. They found it hard to believe that Krupp had no knowledge of the article, especially when it discussed the possible use of the new system in the 30.5-centimeter turrets of the USS *Louisiana*.[113] Once again Krupp's premier position in artillery manufacture made effective action impossible so the RMA officials issued their reprimand and the matter died.

Not all the RMA's experiences with electrical firms caused as much frustration. The case of switches for the various ship control panels and backup systems offers an illustration. The RMA showed its dissatisfaction with the quality of the automatic switches produced by both Siemens-Schuckert and AEG[114] by turning to Voight and Haffner for this device, with the wholehearted support of the imperial yard at Wilhelmshaven and other shipyards.[115] Siemens-Schuckert and AEG did not vanish from the suppliers' list as a consequence. To maintain competition and ensure a better-quality product, the RMA simply issued a reprimand demanding improved standards.

In yet another instance, the RMA confronted a less clearly defined problem. By 1904 it feared that Siemens and Halske would soon monopolize the manufacture and installation of wireless telegraphy systems and asked Wireless Telegraphy, Ltd., to provide competition. The navy quickly discovered the limits of a smaller, less diverse company. Whereas Siemens and Halske produced most of the required parts for a wireless, the newer and smaller company relied on a host of subcontractors and its own marginal research and development efforts. Initially abandoning the standard electrical transformers for wireless systems made by SSW for a model of its own, Wireless Telegraphy soon discovered major technical flaws in its device and had to fall back on an approved RMA purveyor, Felton Guilleaume.[116] Admiral von Usedom of the Kiel Imperial Shipyard actually welcomed the cost and weight overrun caused by the heavier Felton transformers when they enabled the contractor to finish the job, allowing the yard to get back on schedule.[117] Similar annoying technical difficulties beset the design and construction of the wireless rooms aboard many ships,[118] but the RMA refused to suffer even the possibility of a Siemens and Halske monopoly. Von Tirpitz and the Construction Department had no desire to repeat the armor-artillery stalemate in the vital area of communications. In the dynamic electrical industry, new organizations always moved in to challenge the old, providing plenty of competition. Therefore, the RMA saw no reason to take a risk, even with a usually dependable contractor.

The RMA also encouraged turbine development within Germany.[119] The success of the Parsons system in large German transatlantic commercial ships showed the great promise of this style of propulsion. The HAPAG liner *Kaiser* was put through tests at the Kiel Imperial Shipyard as a favor to the navy from the line's director, Albert Ballin. These tests and the trial results of the 30,000-ton British liner *Carmania*, built by John Brown and Company, proved the turbine well suited for larger vessels designed to obtain higher speeds.[120]

Von Tirpitz rejected an offer from Turbina to sell licenses to the imperial yards for turbine construction.[121] The deal would have cost the RMA 300,000 marks for a fifteen-year period. Von Eickstedt, like von Tirpitz, preferred to keep turbine work in the private sphere to avoid permanently tying the navy to Parsons while some German companies continued to explore other systems. Furthermore, von Eickstedt felt that Parsons's German branch did not give the RMA its best effort because the performance of German vessels powered by Parsons turbines did not measure up to current British test results. When he said as much to the directors of Turbina, they categorically denied national favoritism and accused the RMA of suspicion, excessively rigid rules, and denying the company access to information vital to its work.

The RMA did not hide this distrust because von Eickstedt had a reason for his suspicions.[122] The tests on the light cruiser SMS *Lübeck* met expected performance standards. Why, then, could the SMS *Hamburg*, its sister ship, accelerate and stop faster without turbines in identical trial runs? The *Daily Telegraph* captured the RMA's attitude when it paraphrased von Eickstedt's November 1906 speech before the Society for the Study of Shipbuilding: "The German Admiralty was not convinced that the Parsons system was the best, and they would be glad to consider any system which claimed to have eliminated the drawbacks at present apparent."[123]

In this case, the RMA's impatience with the poor performance of the Parsons machinery masked an earnest desire for development of a reliable turbine of German design. The acceleration and stopping problems certainly should be solved, given the vast increase in speed and the lighter weight of the turbine. A virtual Parsons monopoly naturally made the RMA uncomfortable, and Admiral von Müller of the Naval Cabinet reported to von Tirpitz that Kaiser Wilhelm had approached Krupp with this problem while visiting Villa Hügel.

Gustav Krupp indicated that his firm had decided to work with the Zoelly system and might ask Emil Rathenau of AEG for aid.[124] In fact, Krupp belonged to a syndicate that was bent on using the Zoelly system to challenge Parsons. Other participants included Escher Wyss and Company, MAN, and the North German Machine and Armature Company of Bremen.[125] This syndicate ended up competing rather than cooperating with AEG. Rathenau had already signed a contract with the Curtis Marine Turbine Company of West Virginia and felt certain its system was better than the Zoelly.[126] Vulcan allied itself with AEG to use the Curtis machine in capital ships.[127] Later, this combination led to use of an AEG-Curtis engine for the Vulcan-built battleship SMS *Friedrich der Grosse*, one of the Kaiser Class begun in 1910. Two other private yards committed themselves to turbine deals as well. AG Weser decided to invest research time and money in a system developed by Schultz, a retired propulsion engineer.[128] Both Schichau and the Bergmann Company, a division of Electrical Industries, Ltd., produced their own engines. A Schichau model went into the dreadnought SMS *König Albert* and a Bergmann system powered the SMS *Markgraf* (1911) of the König Class.

Nevertheless, by 1911 German turbines drove only a handful of the navy's ships. Parsons supplied most of the engines that the RMA eventually purchased, including those in the battlecruiser *von der Tann* and in the Moltke and Sachsen classes. German industry started late in this field, and the navy failed to require an early concentration of industrial resources that might have provided more reliable alternatives to Parsons.

———

For the RMA, the years between 1905 and 1908 were ones of continuity rather than change. Von Tirpitz found his basic faith in the risk theory and the superiority of battleships reinforced by the sheer momentum of public and industrial support. Thus assured, he stepped up his program by increasing construction and achieved a building schedule of four ships per year by means of supplementary legislation in 1906 and 1908. Eight new dreadnought battleships were built in those years.[129]

Its successes in receiving appropriations from the Reichstag enabled the RMA to deepen its involvement with the U-boat for the sole purpose of keeping pace with international naval technology and quieting internal criticism of the state secretary's policies. Von Tirpitz never responded kindly to his critics. Vice-Admiral Galster's 1907 pamphlet entitled "Which Type of Naval Armament Does Germany Need?" started a battle with the RMA that lasted for five years.[130] Galster's defense of the *kleinkrieg* or commercial war strategy, with emphasis on the U-boat, led the RMA to harass him in many ways, including intense adverse publicity and investigations of the admiral-turned-publicist by the Berlin police.[131]

Lothar Persius, always far more relentless than Galster, added criticisms of von Tirpitz's ever-rising budget demands to the list of his objections to the admiral's administration of naval construction. Persius suggested that Germany could avoid a direct confrontation with Britain if its naval budget were reduced. As compensation, he suggested encouraging a naval buildup by Austria-Hungary that would strengthen the alliance as a whole vis-à-vis the Triple Entente.[132] As a reward, he received the same treatment as Galster, including threats of arrest from the Berlin police.[133]

Continuity in dependability and leadership was exhibited in von Tirpitz's choice of a successor for von Eickstedt as head of the Construction Department. Rear Admiral Rollmann, described by a colleague as a "distinguished, somewhat professorial, splendid character," was an excellent administrator and ran the department according to von Tirpitz's directives. He provided reliable leadership through the outbreak of the war in 1914.[134]

During these four years, the RMA's problems with industry did not change. The Krupp-Dillinger alliance remained a frustration, and both firms collected profits from inflated domestic prices. The RMA handled cost and weight overruns, often a direct result of steel and armor prices, more effectively during this period than before, but a comprehensive solution eluded the state secretary, and his ships still carried excess weight, straining engines and burning not only extra fuel but time and money as well.

Von Tirpitz also found himself adjusting his policies toward the shipyards to the advantage of the imperial yards. To keep them serving as a safety valve against high prices at the private yards, they received additional benefits to help them keep costs down. The German economy gave extraordinary freedom to private business to expand, combine, monopolize, and profit. The RMA needed to keep the imperial yards economically healthy and technologically sound so as to preserve a financial bargaining tool and to maintain a delicate balance with the private concerns that were vital to the navy's growth.

Von Tirpitz's policy regarding research and development redounded to the benefit of the Parsons Company. Although a handful of German companies scrambled to displace Turbina in the forefront of the turbine business, the RMA remained dependent on the British-based firm as the only proven purveyor in the market. The AEG-Curtis, Schichau, and Bergmann systems were the earliest home-grown alternatives. If the RMA had involved itself in this matter sooner by focusing industrial efforts and conducting research of its own, a German turbine might have appeared much earlier.

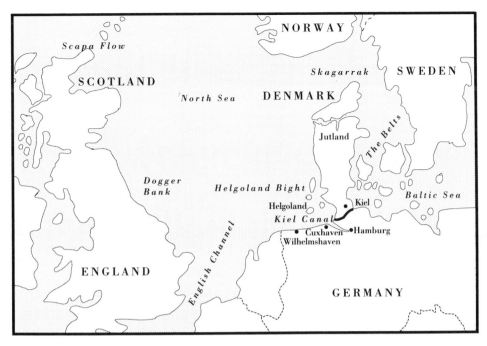

The North Sea and Home Waters, 1914–1918

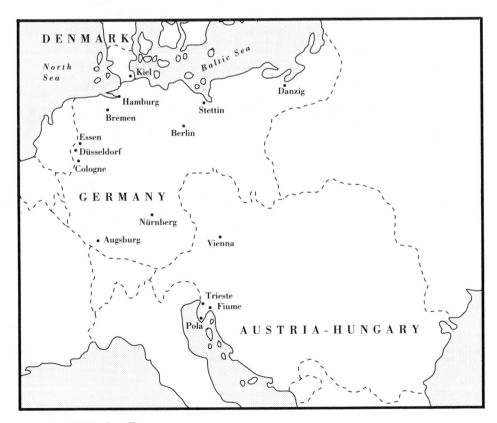

World War I in Europe

This view of the Vulcan Shipyard in Stettin was originally painted by the Berlin artist Carl Hochhaus in 1886. He depicted the fitting out of the battleship SMS *Oldenburg*. (NAVAL HISTORICAL CENTER)

A portrait photograph of Friedrich Alfred Krupp, 1890. (HISTORISCHES ARCHIV FRIED. KRUPP)

A portrait photograph of Dr. Gustav Krupp von Bohlen und Halbach, 1911. (HISTORISCHES ARCHIV FRIED. KRUPP)

The final pre-Dreadnought battlecruiser SMS *Blücher*, which was lost at Dogger Bank in 1915, is pictured here shortly after completion in 1909. (NAVAL HISTORICAL CENTER)

An excellent contrast to the SMS *Blücher* is the more modern post-Dreadnought battlecruiser SMS *Seydlitz*, completed at Blohm und Voss just before the war. This photo was taken shortly before the fleet was interned at Scapa Flow in November 1918. (NAVAL HISTORICAL CENTER)

A battleship of the Braunschweig class dominates this panorama of the Germaniawerft in 1904. (HISTORISCHES ARCHIV FRIED. KRUPP)

An interior view of the shipbuilding shed at the Germaniawerft in 1906. (HISTORISCHES ARCHIV FRIED. KRUPP)

A Germaniawerft dock crane lifts a portion of the battleship SMS *Deutschland*'s triple expansion steam propulsion plant in this picture of the yard's outfitting dock circa 1905–06. (HISTORISCHES ARCHIV FRIED. KRUPP)

The battleship SMS *Schleswig-Holstein* shortly after launching at the Germaniawerft in Kiel on 17 December 1906. (HISTORISCHES ARCHIV FRIED. KRUPP)

The first German warship powered by turbine propulsion, the light cruiser SMS *Lübeck* was outfitted by the Vulcan Shipyard in Stettin with 14,000-horsepower Parsons steam turbines. The Office of Naval Intelligence added the black stripe to the two forward funnels after the picture was received to reflect the ship's appearance in 1908. (NAVAL HISTORICAL CENTER)

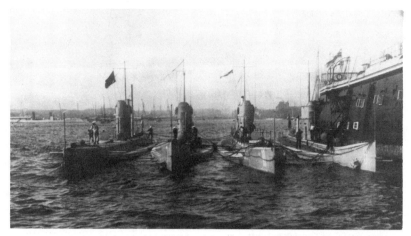

Four early German U-boats are pictured in port in 1913. From left to right they are the U-12, U-7, U-10, and U-6. The U-6 and U-7 were of the U-5 class, built by Krupp at the Germaniawerft. The other two vessels were of the U-9 class, products of the Danzig Imperial Shipyard. (NAVAL HISTORICAL CENTER)

The first major German warship powered by turbine propulsion, the SMS *von der Tann* is shown here in 1910. This battlecruiser was capable of a top speed of 27 knots. (NAVAL HISTORICAL CENTER)

A panorama of the Gusstahlfabrik as it appeared in 1912. (HISTORISCHES ARCHIV FRIED. KRUPP)

A German S-7 Class torpedo boat performed picket duty for three Helgoland-class battleships at sea in 1915. The torpedo net defense on the battleship hulls was removed in 1917. (NAVAL HISTORICAL CENTER)

5

The Money Runs Out

1909 – 1912

Never before in his program did von Tirpitz experience sharper contrasts in success and failure than he did after 1909. He finally discovered a way to change the price policies of the Krupp-Dillinger armor monopoly. But his good fortune ended with the inroads made during this period against the armor monopoly. The SPD election victory in 1912 gave hope to the trade unions in the shipbuilding industry and support to those who believed the navy was an expensive luxury. The fleet's negative effect on Germany's international relations and financial condition dismayed Chancellor Theobald von Bethmann-Hollweg and led him to question the wisdom of the RMA's long-term plans. Furthermore, von Bethmann found an ally in the Treasury Office, which, in 1912, told the Reichstag to choose increased appropriations for either the army or the navy because the Reich's financial situation would not allow additional spending for both services. On top of this, a scandal broke in the press in 1909 revealing that certain private vendors had defrauded the imperial shipyard in Kiel. Even the state secretary's political agility could not counter the growing feeling among the Reich leadership that the nation's financial resources would be more secure if the balance of official investment tipped toward the army. Thus the state secretary looked on while his building tempo declined and the navy once again took a back seat to the army.

Political Background

As 1912 approached, military and political thought regarding the fleet became more confused than ever. As usual, only von Tirpitz seemed secure in perpetuating past policy. The new naval attaché in London, Erich Müller, urged that an attempt be made to reach an understanding with Britain. He witnessed at close range the determination of the British government not to allow the German challenge to progress further. Rear Admiral Harald Dähnhardt, chief of von Tirpitz's Budget Department, rejected the idea that victory over Britain could be achieved based on the risk theory; he believed that Germany would find it difficult to wage an adequate defensive war against the Royal Navy.[1] The debate intensified when von Capelle of the RMA Administrative Department indicated his agreement with von Tirpitz. Naively, he believed that Britain would have to seek an agreement with Germany at the expense of France because of the threat presented by the High Seas Fleet. "We hold the trump cards," he asserted, "not England. All we need to do is wait patiently until our present naval act [1912] has been fulfilled."[2]

The kaiser wavered between full-fledged support for von Tirpitz and fear of a confrontation with England. His secretary of the Naval Cabinet, Admiral Karl Alexander von Müller, cautiously argued against precipitating a war but did not want to settle for more modest construction goals in exchange for a stable agreement with the British. Neither did he fully agree with von Tirpitz's building program. Relying exclusively on a battleship strategy seemed risky, but he did not come forth with any viable alternatives.[3] In all of this debate only two characters were consistent: Lothar Persius in his scathing public critiques of von Tirpitz and von Tirpitz in his relentless efforts to carry out his plans.[4]

The state secretary believed the fleet could easily destroy Britain's hope of maintaining a two-to-one battleship ratio during this period.[5] The RMA needed time to finish the construction program so von Tirpitz advised the kaiser against any offensive that would oblige the British to react.[6] This same goal prompted him to take a hard line in conversations with the kaiser and Lord Haldane on naval arms reduction in February 1912. Von Tirpitz's refusal to enter into any sort of rapprochement during the Haldane mission angered the kaiser, but the admiral stood his ground. He refused to pay for an Anglo-German understanding with a marked reduction in the construction plans outlined in the 1912 Supplementary Naval Law. He felt vindicated in his resistance when a later discussion between Albert Ballin and Winston Churchill, First Sea Lord, offered little hope of British neutrality in the event of German involvement in a Continental war.[7] Von Tirpitz still believed that he could bring the navy through the danger zone without precipitating war along the way. By 1904, however, political realities had prompted Britain to discard her splendid isolation in order to meet von Tirpitz's challenge.

The policy of the British government toward German naval growth appeared moderate when compared with statements by the public and press. Naval intelligence in Britain had carefully monitored German raw materials imports and the capability of the shipbuilding industry as a whole. The Admiralty felt that the German yards had reached a capacity equal to Britain's, erasing an advantage that had provided the Royal Navy with a one- or two-year lead in ship construction. According to historian Arthur Marder, the British drew the "most alarming conclusion" that the Germans would have seventeen dreadnoughts to their twenty-one by the spring of 1912.[8] London began to believe that it would be hard-pressed to maintain even a 5:4 ratio in dreadnoughts with Germany.

This situation and the reaction of the press produced the British Naval Scare of 1909. At the height of this public outburst, the liberal Asquith government presented its 1909–10 naval budget to the Commons. It proposed the construction of four new dreadnoughts immediately and four more the next year on proof of their necessity. Although the official naval sources in Britain felt a total of six ships would restore a favorable balance, Conservative MPs and their allies in the press demanded all eight immediately. Eventually the latter position prevailed.[9]

Actually, neither nation fully appreciated the position of the other. The Germans wanted the assurance of British neutrality in a European war if Germany were attacked. In effect, this would damage the foundation of the Triple Entente system. In return the British argued for a real reduction, not a slowdown, in the German construction program for

1909–12. As Marder put it, "The British never appreciated that the French entente was for Germany a potential threat to their safety, but no more did the Germans ever realize that in a world of armament races, *Realpolitik* and imperialistic rivalries, naval supremacy was vital to Britain's safety."[10]

The 1909 scare obliged the British government and navy to respond over and above the pledge of eight new battleships. The dominions were asked to help, and New Zealand and Australia each promised to contribute a battleship to the Royal Navy. The latter offered two if the need appeared great enough. As anti-German feeling reached a new high in Britain, all MPs save a few radical Liberals saw limiting naval arms as politically and militarily suicidal. The political ramifications of the 1909 scare also contributed to Admiral Fisher's retirement as First Sea Lord in January 1910.

The British overestimated both the capability of the German shipyards and the time it would take them to place new dreadnoughts in service, but they did not exaggerate von Tirpitz's determination. Haldane experienced von Tirpitz's determination firsthand in 1912, and it soured his originally optimistic assessment of a possible understanding with the Germans.[11]

The breakdown in Anglo-German relations dismayed the kaiser. On 8 December 1912, in a meeting with von Tirpitz, von Müller, and General Helmuth von Moltke, chief of the Army General Staff, he expressed his fears for the future and the need to take some steps to prepare for war. Burdened by British loyalty to its entente allies and the failure of the Haldane mission, Wilhelm found himself bombarded by conflicting opinions from his military advisers. Von Moltke advised action as soon as possible to give the army an advantage. Von Tirpitz argued for a delay of up to eighteen months to ready the fleet and continue construction. For the moment, von Tirpitz prevailed because Wilhelm seemed very concerned about the state of U-boat readiness and the still partially completed naval base on Helgoland, and he still viewed a war with Great Britain as involving offensive naval operations and not a Continental land war.[12]

Characteristically, Wilhelm did not invite any civilians to these discussions in part because few of his political advisers agreed with von Tirpitz or von Moltke. In 1909 von Bülow's government fell and Theobald von Bethmann-Hollweg became chancellor. He did not support further drastic increases for the navy and instantly clashed with von Tirpitz. The new chancellor perceived the contradictions of government policy regarding the navy and had to endure endless infighting and differences of opinion. Both Prince Metternich, the ambassador in London, and Richard von Kühlmann, an influential member of his staff and foreign minister in 1917–18, suggested that an offensive role for the navy would now be diplomatically counterproductive and risked destroying a potentially profitable friendship with Britain.[13] Von Bethmann agreed, adding that "the policy of working for English friendship while demanding new ships from the Reichstag is a fiasco." At one point he asserted that the pro-naval policy of the Reich alienated both potential allies and the army, Germany's first line of defense.[14] Von Tirpitz defended his position against the new chancellor so fiercely that at one point the latter's friend and adviser Kurt Riezler was convinced the admiral wanted the chancellorship for himself: "However he can't do it, because no one will trust him."[15] Nevertheless, before the war von Tirpitz's position was strong enough to force a stalemate.

In spite of questions raised by the effect fleet expansion would have on relations with Great Britain, von Tirpitz pushed continuation of the policy of building three battleships per year in the Reichstag. His assurances of success had less effect than before because of a number of new influences.[16] After its 1912 election victory, the SPD was the largest party in the Reichstag. The left wing of the SPD opposed von Tirpitz, while moderate socialists pushed for the coexistence with Britain that the naval program, in its pure form, made impossible.[17] The SPD as a whole constantly attacked von Tirpitz, the arms manufacturers, and the industrial combinations that reaped huge profits from Reichstag appropriations.[18]

Between 1898 and 1911, according to the RMA's publication *Nauticus*, the Reichstag pumped 1.31 billion marks into the naval shipbuilding industry. Over half of the figure went to ship construction and another third to pay for armor and heavy guns.[19] Even the Kaiser Wilhelm Canal required alterations to accommodate the dreadnoughts.[20] These financial and political factors, combined with the opposition of the SPD, von Bethmann, and some officers within the navy itself, placed the future of the building program in doubt two years before the world war began.

During November 1909, a scandal broke in the German press that further endangered the plans of the RMA. The firm of Frankenthal, among others, was discovered defrauding the imperial shipyard at Kiel. The directors of the imperial yard paid transport costs that were never earned and accepted old steel sold for new and bronze when brass was called for. The final bill totaled in the millions, and newspapers of every political persuasion criticized von Tirpitz and the RMA administration in their editorial columns.[21] *Der Tag* predicted a severe political backlash. *Die Post* reported that the Reichstag waited for an explanation while von Tirpitz hid behind a wall of technical jargon, a smoke screen to reduce public perception of the navy's problems. Even though the courts convicted the businessmen involved of fraud and meted out stiff jail sentences, the public outcry refused to die down. The *Vossische Zeitung* suggested that there was more to the problem than the conviction of felons: "Mr. Tirpitz must answer for faults and mistakes."[22]

When the Reichstag interpellated von Tirpitz as a minister of the von Bethmann-Hollweg government in December, he defended the RMA administration in the German parliament by claiming that the matter had been resolved. While the civilian defendants endured their trial, the navy cleaned house at Kiel. Unfortunately, the Reichstag committee of inquiry would not tolerate what it perceived as a naval cover-up. After one session in the Reichstag the *Vossische Zeitung* reported that von Tirpitz wanted to pass the affair off as experience when wholesale internal reform was necessary. The liberal *Freisinnige Zeitung* joined in the call for naval reform. It supported the suggestions made by the Reichstag progressive Dr. Leonhart that there should be more civilian technical and business people in the administration of the naval construction program. The state secretary did not altogether oppose some reform measures. As the *Vossische Zeitung* of 7 December reported after von Tirpitz's hour-long defense of naval measures taken during the crisis, "Mr. von Tirpitz made assurances that he has swept with an iron broom: he has ordered all kinds of reforms and placed others within view." But he did not relinquish naval control over the imperial shipyards as was suggested by many of the Reichstag representatives. Civilian penetration of the construction program administration would greatly increase public influence in a heretofore purely military sphere. Indeed, on 7 December, Dr. Leonhart called for von Tirpitz's removal and a complete reform of the naval hierarchy.[23]

The 1909 Kiel scandal revealed much more than the need for reform within certain parts of the RMA administration and the protocol system. It showed just how precarious von Tirpitz's political base in the Reichstag had become. The conservatives remained curiously quiet in all of this, and the intensity of the barrage fired by the radical liberals and the socialists was unprecedented. Von Tirpitz managed to weather the storm, but the odds seemed against him in the long run. His Reichstag opponents sought his recall, and his naval associates questioned his definition of the navy's needs. Even von Bülow, whose imperial policies relied on German naval might, parted company with the state secretary over the long-range consequences of German naval growth without some sort of understanding with Britain.[24] With the accession of von Bülow's successor, von Bethmann-Hollweg, these disagreements became permanent. The public and official reaction to the Kiel scandal was symptomatic of a political climate increasingly unfavorable to von Tirpitz's vision of the naval construction program.

Research and Development and the U-Boat

The RMA continued its research and development efforts but with a greater eye toward economy. The General Naval Department received a memo from the naval attaché in London, who suggested that many existing ship designs wasted RMA funds. He then betrayed, perhaps unconsciously, the growing conflict between the navy's battleship strategy and both economic and political reality. U-boats, torpedo boats, and destroyers, he wrote, were easy and relatively cheap to build but limited in their capability. A navy composed entirely of big-gun battleships was still the answer. Speed, reduced size, and maximum fire power should be the goal of naval architecture. In the process, the RMA administrators could build ships that were better prepared for war, but at a lower cost.[25] He did not ask, however, whether the cost would fall low enough to allow the von Tirpitz Program to continue unaltered. Furthermore, the state secretary himself never paused to consider seriously the economic and political consequences of an arms race with Britain if his plans remained unchanged.

The modest RMA research and development effort still relied heavily on the facilities of private companies. Discussions regarding turret designs always included Krupp, for only at the facilities of the Gusstahlfabrik could industry execute plans drawn up by the firm and the RMA.[26] Krupp's facilities initially included two laboratories, one devoted to metals research that had been established in 1863, the other for materials testing, set up in 1895. Between 1907 and 1909, 2 million marks were invested in a newer, more comprehensive facility in Essen.[27] These laboratories enabled the company to conduct studies on ship design for the RMA, concentrating on battleships of reduced size and weight. One such research effort completed in 1911 lasted nearly four years, costing the RMA 33,075 marks.[28]

The North German Lloyd and HAPAG continued to aid the RMA. HAPAG worked on an improved water cooling system for capital ship turbines in 1911, and the North German Lloyd cooperated with the Deutsche Seewarte on highly sophisticated navigation techniques and compass testing.[29]

In 1910, the RMA considerably expanded the facilities of the Naval Research Center at Marienfelde to include a model basin to test new ship designs,[30] necessitating an intensified search for technical personnel to staff the center. In one case the navy promised a skilled mechanic and fitter a good salary with a yearly raise schedule, in addition to paying for his family's transport and his first month's rent.[31] Financial limitations prevented such expenditures on a broad scale. Paying good employees was as hard as finding them, and the situation would worsen before long because von Tirpitz did not place this item high on his list of budgetary priorities.

One of the subjects high on the admiral's list became the subject of a Reichstag session in early 1909. The legislators asked von Tirpitz to verify statements by the British press that German yards were now building ships faster than those of the Royal Navy. The press reports placed German construction time at between twenty-six and thirty months for capital ships. Although he probably would have enjoyed asserting the truth of this statement, he could not. Without the time allotted for the shakedown cruise, private yards took thirty-six months and the imperial yards an average of forty.[32] Reports on this same topic reached the kaiser through the Naval Cabinet. His marginal notes to an article from the British publication *Shipping World* showed a great deal of frustration and impatience: "24 months against 34 months in Germany, sometimes 36–40!" After visiting the Weser shipyard in March 1910 and seeing a ship still under construction which was begun just before his last tour of the yard the previous year, Wilhelm added to the above notes: "It should have been launched in 9 months!"[33] Von Tirpitz would have agreed with the kaiser's remarks on the Naval Cabinet's annual report on the international situation in 1909: "We build too slow! A light cruiser takes 39 months! No English ship of the line takes that long, and 20 months longer than an English heavy cruiser of the same type! Unheard of."[34] Unfortunately, the kaiser's outrage did von Tirpitz little good at the shipyards. Late deliveries, parts that did not pass purchasing tests, late inspections, and other now well-known problems kept these construction times at the existing levels until the demands of war forced a change.[35]

The seagoing adversary to the fast battleship, the U-boat, had achieved recognition as a useful naval weapon, but discussion persisted as to its exact strategic use. In a 1909 memo, a Technical Department official expressed optimism about the submarine's future. He felt that the U-boat was ready for minelaying and harbor defense, with offensive operations not far off. He favored dropping one or two capital ships from the budget in order to accelerate submarine research and production, advising that "we should build more U-boats and fewer capital ships."[36]

Von Tirpitz strongly disagreed, but he did express interest in deploying the new submarines awaiting assignment at Wilhelmshaven to the best possible advantage.[37] Eventually, he envisioned three stations for a force of thirty-six boats. Twelve would operate within a thirty-sea-mile radius of Helgoland, with about five sea miles between each boat. Another dozen would soon go to the Kiel Bight. Of these, four would take up position in the belts area, four in the harbor approaches, and the rest in reserve. Von Tirpitz saved the last dozen for offensive action in the case of a British North Sea blockade of Germany.[38] Clearly, he still strongly doubted the U-boat's offensive capability. The entire force was slated for defense or for desperate action in the event the Imperial Navy lost the decisive battle that still lay at the core of his strategy.

Although most submarine work met with considerable success, the RMA's U-boat construction was not without tragedies. In 1911, the U-3 was unable to surface after submerged tests in Kiel. When a floating crane pulled the boat up by the bow, twenty-nine men escaped through the torpedo tubes after twenty-five hours underwater. The rest of the crew, including the captain, asphyxiated in the other compartments before the boat was completely raised. Tragic lessons like this one prompted standardized safety measures, more salvaging equipment, and further research into on-board ventilation systems.[39]

The RMA's U-boat testing and construction effort could not be as independent and comprehensive as that of the private firms, which could fall back on a diversified heavy industry developed in the lean years of the pre–von Tirpitz era. Krupp, for example, did most of his own work because the Germaniawerft needed to subcontract only for electrical propulsion systems. Other firms, like AG Weser, not only refined their U-boat designs but proposed new ones and built prototypes at their own facilities.[40] Unlike Krupp, the RMA was utterly dependent on subcontractors in nearly every phase of U-boat construction.[41]

Although the process of building U-boats at the Germaniawerft was more self-contained than at Danzig, both yards pursued standards set by the RMA protocol system and employed only those purveyors appearing in the suppliers' list. The RMA published the guidelines for U-boat construction in a special edition of the general construction guidelines in 1908,[42] and by 1912, U-boat construction settled into a smooth routine similar to that of the capital ships in 1904–5.

Germaniawerft forecast an average construction time of at least eighteen months per boat. Depending on the number of vessels in any given contract, it could deliver up to four boats in twenty-four months.[43] Two RMA departments governed similar projects for the RMA on location at the imperial shipyard in Danzig. Matters pertaining to electrical systems, propulsion, and weaponry were handled by the yard's Technical Bureau. The U-boat Inspectorate directed submarine construction and repair, the submarine school, and research efforts.[44]

Occasionally, minor problems beyond the RMA's control caused annoying slowdowns.[45] Krupp's difficulties in developing diesel engines are an illustration, and only assistance from Körting, Daimler, and MAN prevented extraordinary delays.[46] If the alternative purveyors proved less able than MAN or Körting, or if no other option existed, it was feared that progress would slow to a crawl.

Eventually U-boat construction became an expensive proposition. It increased the RMA's dependence on the imperial yard at Danzig because Krupp offered the only alternative, and prices at the Germaniawerft drew regular complaints from the RMA.[47] Rising prices, however, were less attributable to Krupp's propensity to overcharge than to the high cost of modern technology. Krupp's profits on early models were very small compared with its capital ship work. It also lost about 4 million marks in its protracted efforts to perfect a U-boat diesel engine to render the firm independent of MAN or Körting.[48] The percentage of the total cost for newly developed technical components of submarines and the salaries of specially trained personnel nearly matched that of the Kaiser Class battleships.[49]

The Armor Monopoly

As the first decade of the new century ended, the RMA's relations with the Krupp firm had assumed a character of coexistence based on profits and naval necessities. Krupp prices, occasional production errors, and frequent late deliveries frustrated von Tirpitz and his associates.[50] The Krupp-Dillinger combine still dominated the armor plate industry, although their prices on other steel products often differed.[51] The RMA took no consolation from the rare differences between Essen and Dillinger on rivet prices and their charges for particular parts custom built with nickel steel.[52] Moreover, artillery remained the special province of the Krupp firm, and the bills increased as the caliber and number of guns required by the dreadnoughts grew. The first installment paid to Essen in 1911 for the SMS *Kaiserin*'s guns, for example, came to over 7.9 million marks, a full 17 percent of the total cost for the battleship.[53] The RMA did not have enough coercive power to force a reduction in Krupp's prices, primarily because of its monopoly in gun production.

By 1909, however, new developments gave the RMA its best opportunity against the Krupp-Dillinger armor plate alliance. Earlier, international competition from the American Midvale Company had helped drive Krupp prices down to 1,780 marks per ton. In 1906 fierce competition with U.S. Steel and Bethlehem in the United States had produced a record low price of 1,450 marks for Midvale armor.[54] Taking advantage of the international pressure this reduced price placed on Krupp, the RMA had asked Midvale in November 1906 to provide the Imperial Navy with samples of its armor for tests. The same month the RMA offered its support to Fritz Thyssen if he would enter the armor market against Krupp-Dillinger.[55]

The momentary pressure provided by Midvale gave the RMA the opportunity to use Thyssen (Mülheim), the best of the smaller arms-producing firms, to explore any vulnerable points in the armor monopoly. Von Tirpitz earnestly desired to reduce the monopoly's power, especially when Schichau asserted that the RMA could build ships 20 to 25 percent cheaper if British firms supplied the armor and artillery.[56] Discussions with the Mülheim firm began in 1906 and continued well into the next year.

Even though American prices bounced back to 1,750 marks in late 1906, the RMA maintained its interest in the Midvale product, while Krupp complained of the difficulty in equaling the prices that resulted from intense American competition. By this time, however, the Krupp-Dillinger price was also down to 1,750 marks. As the talks with Thyssen continued, Krupp and Dillinger enacted two further reductions, to 1,680 marks in May 1907 and then to 1,630 marks in June. Krupp and Dillinger offered to keep their armor at this low level only if the RMA agreed to a long-term contract extending to 1915. By August 1907 the price was down to 1,600 marks, and Krupp then agreed not to object to any competition the navy might promote. The two dominant firms assured the navy that they could produce armor at least 5 percent cheaper than any competitor.[57] At last the RMA was making progress against the monopoly.

The negotiations with Thyssen soured in June 1907 because the firm was unsure whether it should risk competing in the world of Midvale and Krupp. In 1909, however, it returned to the discussions with the RMA at the request of Reichstag member Graf von Oppersdorff. During the Budget Commission hearings over the Krupp-Dillinger armor contracts, von Oppersdorff launched a political attack against the monopoly. He appealed to Thyssen and corresponded with the American Secretary of the Navy Truman H. Newberry regarding Washington's policy toward armor producers. He then drew the Ehrhardt artillery firm into the talks with the navy as well.[58]

In a twenty-page memorandum to von Tirpitz, von Oppersdorff criticized past RMA policies, noted the dangers of monopoly, and presented some possible solutions. He thought the navy might find ways to circumvent the difficulty posed by Krupp and Dillinger by lengthening the duration of its contracts past the usual three years to coax new firms into the field. It could also provide competition either by supporting a state-owned armor factory or by giving every possible advantage to a third firm. He believed it was essential to keep Krupp and Dillinger from bearing full responsibility for Germany's armor. The Reichstag coffers had limits, and in case of war, both Essen and Dillingen were too close to the French border for comfort.[59]

In April 1909, the RMA once again entered discussions with Thyssen's technical representative, but the negotiations faltered over the substantial guarantees Thyssen demanded to make the risk worthwhile. By January 1910, Thyssen explained that it wanted at least one-third of all navy armor contracts for the next ten years. The firm would provide the RMA with a low price that could exert further pressure on the Krupp-Dillinger monopoly until 1915. Thereafter, Thyssen would feel free to charge the same price as the alliance. If the navy decided to participate in the creation of a state armor factory, the provisions of this agreement would stand unchanged. Arguing that this risky venture could ruin the firm, Thyssen refused to assume any responsibility for changes in material and labor costs that might eventually increase the price of the finished product.[60]

The atmosphere created by possible American competition, debates in the Reichstag, and talks with Thyssen drove the Krupp-Dillinger price down to 1,550 marks per ton by early 1909.[61] Nonetheless, von Tirpitz faced accusations in the Reichstag during February 1910 that the navy was not doing enough to lower armor prices.[62] Indeed, in June 1911 Center party representative Matthias Erzberger joined von Oppersdorff in encouraging Thyssen to enter the armor field against the monopoly, and the political pressure on the RMA to employ an alternative source of armor increased.[63] Ironically, Krupp's lower price and Thyssen's demands for a guarantee made von Tirpitz less willing to pursue an alternative than ever before.

During these proceedings, a number of RMA department chiefs expressed their views on the alternatives open to the navy. Rollmann of the Construction Department believed that since the Krupp-Dillinger prices were already down to a reasonably low level, the navy should continue to deal with these two firms. A state factory would not produce better or cheaper armor and might take as much as ten years to compete with Krupp.[64] Rollmann had doubts about Thyssen's capacity to function as an alternative source. Von Capelle of the Administrative Department shared these opinions. The current Krupp price was good, the alliance could deliver immediately, and Thyssen's contract demands far exceeded those ever suggested by Krupp or Dillinger. Von Capelle also thought a state factory would be far too expensive to consider. Besides, there was no guarantee that it could ever outproduce or undersell a private armor company, and Krupp had already agreed to keep his prices down even if a state-owned factory entered the field. No such guarantee came from Mülheim. Von Capelle stressed that Essen and Dillingen wanted an early arrangement with the RMA on a long-range contract under more favorable conditions than ever before. He advised the state secretary to stay with the alliance.[65]

Rear Admiral Harald Dähnhardt of the RMA Budget Department agreed completely with his two colleagues. He quickly rejected any suggestion from the political arena that the RMA did not truly desire competition for Krupp and Dillinger. Nonetheless, the RMA's current alternatives to the armor alliance did not impress him. A state armor factory would not justify the navy's investment. Another alternative suggested by Graf von Oppersdorff was a compromise between a *Staatswerke* and a private effort, a partnership in which the state would partially finance a privately directed effort. Dahnhardt strongly advised against this as well because it would have all the disadvantages plaguing military-industrial relations with no guaranteed advantages. The military could never exert the control in a mixed enterprise that was the primary reason for wanting a public one. Besides, said Dahnhardt, "This theory has never been realized in practice, there are *Staatswerke*, but absolutely no mixed enterprises."[66] The new lower prices, the stability of the Krupp-Dillinger alliance, and the reliability of their products now appealed to him far more than any alternative.

The RMA enjoyed lower armor prices between 1908 and 1912 more as a by-product of foreign competition than as a direct result of its own efforts. The price war in the United States and Midvale's penetration of the foreign market forced Krupp to respond. Von Tirpitz openly explored the possibility of using Midvale products to challenge Krupp's position at home. Although the state secretary could never permanently depend on foreign sources for armor, he kept up RMA contacts with U.S. Steel, Bethlehem, and Midvale through 1913.[67] The long-term negotiations with Thyssen and the serious consideration given to Graf von Oppersdorff's suggestions showed that the RMA never merely endured the armor monopoly if a viable alternative presented itself.

The renewed negotiations with the RMA and the energetic support of von Oppersdorff convinced Thyssen that it was in a strong bargaining position. Furthermore, von Oppersdorff and his Reichstag associates probably felt vindicated in their antimonopoly efforts by the drastic reduction of Krupp-Dillinger prices between 1900 and 1909. If the alliance could reduce its price to 1,600 marks per ton and still turn a handsome profit, why had it not done so long ago? Could prices not decline even further? The specter of Thyssen's possible success and continued Reichstag assaults on armor prices pushed a worried Krupp to stabilize the situation by suggesting a long-term contract with the RMA at 1,550 marks for battleship armor.

Unfortunately for Thyssen, the guarantees it demanded destroyed its chances of capturing a portion of Krupp's armor profits. Although Thyssen did risk a great deal in this joint venture to shake Krupp's hold on the armor market, the alliance's prices had fallen sharply so that its current contract proposals were appealing. The unanimous approval of these proposals by Rollmann, von Capelle, and Dähnhardt leaves little doubt that this feeling predominated within the RMA. The resulting long-term agreement with Krupp and Dillinger lasted until the outbreak of war in 1914.

Thus, in the final reckoning, von Tirpitz's effective handling of political and economic forces both inside and outside Germany eventually produced the best armor prices the RMA had procured in many years.

The Protocol System, Labor, and Overruns

By 1909, the RMA Purchasing Office was experiencing severe personnel shortages. The existing Purchasing Office inspectors were too few and could not work quickly enough to keep construction on schedule. In one instance, the Bismarckhütte waited nearly three months for purchasing tests required for its steel by RMA protocol.[68] These cases prompted many naval officials to push for more personnel in spite of budget restrictions. Von Goecke of the imperial yard at Wilhelmshaven argued that if the Prussian railroad alone could have ninety-six inspectors the navy should be able to increase its number.[69]

Some naval suppliers resorted to independent engineers or firms to perform tests required by the Purchasing Office. The Zeiss Company did this in 1913 to have cables approved for a U-boat periscope system.[70] Most firms employed this alternative reluctantly. If the Purchasing Office did the job, the firm paid only for the tests and not the personal expenses of the naval officials. Hiring a private testing agency meant accepting all of the additional costs. Furthermore, this practice, although not forbidden, was not encouraged by the RMA.

In hopes of resolving these difficulties, the Construction Department proposed that hard-pressed independent suppliers should seek permission to transport their products to the private and imperial yards, where shipyard workers could assume some of the tasks usually done by the Purchasing Office. RMA officials discussed this idea for at least two years, between 1910 and 1912, but the imperial yards and some chief inspectors strongly opposed it. They argued that it was counterproductive because the additional transport costs to send defective equipment back to the factories would be far greater than increased appropriations for personnel.[71] Thus this issue remained a nagging problem well into the war years, primarily because von Tirpitz would not reduce his construction spending to allow for an increased personnel budget.[72] By 1912 most purchase tests were still performed at the factory.[73]

Germany's naval competitors faced similar dilemmas and decisions. The Austrians also limited purchasing tests to the production site and then allowed delivery and installation under naval supervision at the shipyard. They demanded the very same guarantees required by the RMA and left their Construction Inspectorate in ultimate control of decisions at the construction site.[74] Naval officials in Vienna managed to avoid delays at the end of a ship's construction period by convincing their yards to increase the number of naval technical personnel on board at the time of launching and shakedown. This would guarantee quick acceptance of the product by the navy and a much shorter, more efficient trial period. While the RMA had a great deal of trouble carrying out this same measure, the Austrians cut their shakedown time to less than three weeks.[75] The RMA endured constant debates with industry over who should pay the costs for the on-board personnel during these trial runs, which lasted a month or more.[76] Afterward the vessel still had to face final approval by the Ship Testing Commission.[77]

The RMA frequently found itself defining the boundaries of responsibility and spending for industry. The private yards often argued that the navy should pay much of the cost for tests on machines, boilers, and other apparatus. The RMA retorted that the well of construction funds had its limits. It would bear the cost of docking and maintenance, some research projects, and a percentage of the work on the submerged parts of the ship, but not standard product testing. [78] As was the case with adhering to the suppliers' list and obtaining permission to employ some patents, the individual firms bore the responsibility for providing the navy with well-constructed and tested products. [79] If a firm encountered difficulties, as it might over a patent, it could count on the RMA to provide assistance, [80] but the ultimate responsibility lay with industry.

In its search for suppliers or information about firms applying for a place on the suppliers' list, the RMA became closely associated with scores of local *Handelskammern* or chambers of commerce. The RMA regularly checked out every firm that desired to work for the navy, and much of this information came from the chambers. [81] In 1910, the Hamburg Chamber of Commerce revealed that the Henry P. Newman Company had sold the navy some corkboard ship insulation not produced in Germany. The RMA later assured itself that the material it bought from Newman was manufactured in Germany. [82] Nonetheless, providing such information assured some chambers of a great deal of influence at the Köningin Augusta Strasse. Others merely supplied details on a firm's financial stability and fixed capital. The Frankfurt a.M. chamber gave the RMA facts on the Gummiwerke Frankfurt AG that revealed the firm's capital and distribution of shares, as well as information on its dividends and founders. [83]

It was the function of a chamber of commerce to promote the fortunes of business in its locality. By reporting accurately on the best and the very worst of firms, many trusted chambers successfully sponsored small firms in their ambition to work for the navy. [84] These chambers of commerce actually assumed the role of minor pressure or lobbying groups for companies that otherwise might have had a difficult time obtaining naval consideration. In January 1910 the Düsseldorf chamber appealed to the RMA not to go abroad for an insulation material called polypyrit. The navy investigated the product manufactured by the R. G. von Kokeritz Company in New York City, but the chamber made an excellent argument for staying at home by proposing a capable Düsseldorf firm as a domestic alternative. [85]

In other cases, chambers of commerce acted on behalf of groups of small firms with as few as fifty workers each or banded together with other chambers to introduce a single firm to navy work. In one instance the Plauen and Zittau chambers joined to sponsor the bid of the Otto Büttner firm in Bautzen for a place on the suppliers' list.[86] More characteristic of this facet of the RMA's relations with industry were letters from Berlin, Hannover, Dresden, and Hamburg. This symbiotic relationship provided influence for the smaller businesses in the highest circles and vastly expanded the number of firms from which the RMA could choose.

Von Tirpitz also had to enforce greater security measures, primarily because of complaints from some of the private yards. The RMA had become very security conscious regarding foreign vessels under construction at the private yards and required the yards to give the navy any information it requested on these vessels.[87] But RMA procedures did not take into account possible security problems with foreign workers employed at the private yards. Both Schichau and Vulcan complained about less than stringent security measures against foreigners working for Blohm und Voss in Hamburg. Although these accusations were probably a by-product of competition, the RMA nonetheless rewrote its paragraph in the general construction guidelines in 1913 to avoid any further danger, real or imaginary, posed by non-Germans working on naval projects.[88] At the same time it tightened security on the exchange of private or patented technical systems and methods. It seems that RMA engineers and inspectors too freely disseminated information that private yards often wished to keep to themselves.[89]

As the RMA prepared for the 1912 naval budget, it gave more consideration to expanding the imperial yards and lending greater financial support to the services they performed for the RMA. By this time construction was only one facet of the work at the imperial shipyards. They also served as fleet repair bases, dock facilities, centers for training technical personnel, and competition for the private yards. They assisted in research and the accounting and disbursement of construction funds.[90] Every yard and subcontractor had to give the imperial yards at least thirty days' notice of any cost, weight, and design changes to ensure accurate quarterly financial reports.[91] Thus the RMA knew whether the construction funds for a particular project were adequate or overdrawn and just how much each vendor should receive. No imperial yard did the cost accounting for its own projects. Rather, one of its sister yards assisted in the role of naval auditor and bursar.[92]

At various times during the year the fleet entered the imperial yards to undergo repairs.[93] In 1912 Wilhelmshaven could dock forty ships of various sizes and types and the Kiel yard provided thirty-two more places. But because of the size and continuous growth of the fleet, these two primary imperial yards needed even better facilities. The navy slated 16 million marks in the budget proposals of May 1912 to enlarge both Wilhelmshaven and Kiel for capital ship and U-boat work.[94]

Even with the promise of expanded facilities, the RMA found it more and more difficult to build at cost in the imperial shipyards and keep expenditures within reasonable limits. The rising price of materials and labor, long construction schedules, the ambitions of private firms for maximum profits, and lengthy repair work in the imperial yards all contributed to von Tirpitz's financial dilemma.[95]

Von Tirpitz did possess some effective weapons in his efforts to cut costs. The RMA had very reliable accounting procedures, the protocol system offered a series of legal and bureaucratic advantages, and more companies were forced to abide by their contracts and absorb excess costs than ever before.[96] In the fall of 1911 the RMA took action to lower its transport costs by reducing the weight of the heavy metal containers for the bulk delivery of rivets.[97] Moreover, it insisted that despite their reluctance, firms should assume any transport costs from the factory to shipyard as stipulated in their contracts.[98]

Sometimes a technological breakthrough helped the chronic budget problems. Schichau and Blohm und Voss initially deemed a new system for reducing the number of steel ribs supporting a ship's hull too risky and expensive. In 1909, tests at the Vulcan shipyard proved this new construction method more reliable than first imagined. It promised to reduce markedly the weight of light cruisers at a cost of less than 75 percent of the figure first predicted.[99] Unfortunately, the large number of overruns still outweighed these successes. Revisions of a battleship's rudder system at the imperial yard in Wilhelmshaven in 1911 cost over 1,600 marks, including labor.[100] The regularity of these cases continued unabated into the war years.

The Money Runs Out: The 1912 Supplementary Naval Law

Von Tirpitz probably faced the greatest challenge of his career in the debate over the 1912 Supplementary Naval Law. The technical and strategic demands posed by his goals for the fleet had become financially oppressive.[101] He came under attack by both the Reichstag and the Imperial Treasury Office. By now, managing the former had become second nature to von Tirpitz. The Treasury presented quite another problem. In the state secretary of the Treasury Office, Adolf Wermuth, von Tirpitz met his match. Historian Peter-Christian Witt has characterized the relationship between Wermuth and von Tirpitz as an "extremely bitter, small scale war." The head of the Treasury saw the 1912 Supplementary Naval Law as symptomatic of a general "egotistical department policy" that characterized both the army and the navy. In his confrontation with von Tirpitz, however, Wermuth brandished some traditionally formidable weapons. The conservatives' antipathy to an inheritance tax and their traditional ties to the army, coupled with the political clout he and von Bethmann could muster, made the Treasury a considerable threat.[102]

Supported by Chancellor von Bethmann-Hollweg, Wermuth launched a crusade to redraw the budget priorities of the Reich in 1912. He wanted a broader fiscal foundation for the country, which meant resurrecting the old tax question that had plagued the Reichstag throughout the years of naval development. Without a modern tax law, most of the programs desired by the armed forces would depend upon traditional sources of revenue, augmented by increased taxes on consumer products. Furthermore, he agreed with the chancellor that Germany's true power lay with the army, and the best possible public investment in defense would reflect this fact. Ever since the outset of von Tirpitz's construction program, the navy's rate of growth had far outstripped that of the army. In spite of a budget three to five times larger, the army had virtually marked time while the navy had grown twice as fast in the short period since Wermuth had taken office in 1909.[103]

In this political environment, the state secretary of the RMA clung to his battleship strategy and capital ship construction plans with a dogged determination. He used RMA-inspired reports from the London naval attaché to convince Wilhelm that the British expected a further German naval buildup and were resigned to it.[104] He argued that in spite of what the British might say publicly, they would not place their navy above every other consideration and go into a building frenzy. Thus he defended and promoted his current building plans, his reliance on the capital ship, and the strategic deployment of the fleet in the Baltic and North seas.[105]

For the first time since 1897, however, he dreaded the debate over the naval supplement and the issue of tighter financial conditions within the Reich. Privately, he expressed doubts to his RMA colleagues about pushing much further beyond the 1911 spending levels. Inflation, the colossal cost of the newer dreadnoughts, and the high price of technology dried up his reserves and made success in the Reichstag less certain than ever before.[106]

In the debates over the 1912 Supplementary Naval Law in the Budget Commission hearings and then in the regular sessions of the Reichstag, von Tirpitz pounded away at his old themes. Britain posed a great threat to Germany which required a two-to-three ratio in capital ships in the near future. He asked the Reichstag to discount British vows to outbuild Germany at any cost as inflammatory propaganda designed to intimidate rather than expressing reality.[107] Actually, the members of the Reichstag seemed less concerned with Great Britain than with the Reich's financial condition. The challenges von Tirpitz faced in the Reichstag focused on high prices, efficiency of the imperial yards, monopoly, and cases of cheaper shipbuilding abroad.[108] Reichstag representatives of every persuasion took a greater interest in serious shipyard fact-finding tours, not the show tours of the 1898–1900 period, and they now criticized RMA budget proposals from a much more informed and concerned position.[109] After the intense debates over the naval supplement concluded, the Reichstag established an Armaments Committee to examine more closely the financial aspects of military arms purchases.[110] It became increasingly obvious that the days of rapid growth and rich appropriations had come to an end.

When the 1912 Supplementary Naval Law passed the Reichstag on 14 June, the vote signaled the conclusion of fourteen years of political success for the state secretary. On the surface, it seemed that von Tirpitz had achieved his ends. His construction funds increased and the active fleet received a third squadron, but naval reserves in home waters were tapped to form the third squadron. All of the battleships and cruisers of the regular fleet and one-quarter of those in reserve now remained permanently on active duty. Thus the active fleet was increased by four battleships, four heavy, and four light cruisers. The Reserve Fleet flagship was also activated, and new funds completed the third squadron by providing for three more battleships and two light cruisers.[111]

Personnel no longer took a back seat in the RMA's construction program. As historian Gerhard Ritter explains: "Clearly, the rate of construction had far outstripped the facilities for procuring trained personnel, especially officers."[112] In 1912, however, in response to requests by the chief of the High Seas Fleet, Admiral Henning von Holtzendorff, the Reichstag diverted a greater amount of money to the acquisition and training of personnel to man the fleet. Support for this measure also came from some of von Tirpitz's associates in the RMA. Rollmann of the Construction Department had already increased personnel spending on his own initiative as far back as 1909.[113]

Although the addition of the reserves to the active fleet momentarily obscured it, von Tirpitz's precious building rate fell markedly. From 1908 through 1911 the state secretary built at a tempo of four capital ships per year: three battleships and a heavy cruiser. Now, reduced resources allowed only one of each type for the 1912 budget year, and the Supplementary Naval Law funds increased this by only one battleship in 1913[114] (see Appendix A, Table 4).

A variety of forces acted on the naval construction program during the 1909–12 period. Von Tirpitz turned a blind eye to political and military realities such as the British unwillingness to allow the German challenge to go unanswered. He chose to disregard the British threat when it called for a reduction in German shipbuilding because this did not further his goals or satisfy his imperative to complete the fleet required by the risk theory. By this time, however, his vanity and the momentum gained by fleet expansion, fueled by both public and industrial support, had pushed the navy toward the international confrontation the state secretary repeatedly said he wished to avoid.

In spite of a limited capacity for self-deception, von Tirpitz fully appreciated the opportunity presented by American competition in the steel industry. He used this situation very effectively to force the Krupp-Dillinger alliance into concessions the RMA had sought since 1897. Always perceptive in this respect, von Tirpitz quickly recognized a strategy that might further his aims, such as the pressure he placed on Krupp-Dillinger by using Midvale, Thyssen, and von Oppersdorff.

In 1912, domestic political and economic forces also handed von Tirpitz his first legislative defeat in fourteen years. The more modest increase in construction funds and slower building tempo authorized by the Reichstag indicated that von Tirpitz's construction program had reached its zenith. The opposition of von Bethmann-Hollweg and Wermuth proved as politically decisive as the public exhibition of the navy's vulnerability during the Frankenthal-Kiel scandal. This combination was too formidable even for a man with the state secretary's considerable political talents. In addition, strikes became more frequent if not more effective, and the SPD's election victory in 1912 ensured that they would have a great political and economic effect in the future.

6

The Tables Begin to Turn

1913 – 1914

The financial condition of the Reich in 1912 finally slowed the development of von Tirpitz's navy. The RMA was now caught between the renewed priority of the army's financial needs and the complex tax issue that plagued the Reichstag. The large portion of imperial revenues spent on armaments seemed to be justified by the political instability of the time. The Balkan crisis aroused the specter of war among the Great Powers, and the army seemed the safest shield against possible conflict.

The country was also in need of increased revenues, but private property owners and special interests were determined to keep their tax burden light.[1] Therefore, it became financially impossible for von Tirpitz's naval expansion to continue at the rate it had so far maintained.

The central task of this chapter is to examine the last months of peace and the adjustments forced upon the navy and industry by mobilization. What was the policy of the RMA after the setbacks of 1912 and what was in the future of naval-industrial relations now that money was less plentiful? These questions bring into sharp focus the issues and challenges that faced von Tirpitz and his colleagues at the RMA in 1913.

War, Politics, and the RMA

The coming of war in August 1914 brought with it some rude shocks for industry and the military. As historian Gerald Feldman has described, the army initially found itself without a comprehensive plan for mobilization.[2] When the illusion of a short, glorious clash between nations began to dissipate, the true demands of war became apparent. Civilian businessmen such as Karl Helfferich and Walter Rathenau called for a rationally organized system of raw materials distribution and effective interaction with the industries supplying the armed forces. Although both the army and navy were dependent on the War Ministry for their weapons and supplies, the RMA in no way relied on its sister service in matters of procurement.[3] Neither was the navy caught up in the frantic activity that characterized the army and War Ministry during mobilization. The construction of the High Seas Fleet and seventeen years of von Tirpitz's determined leadership came as close to a practical drill for mobilization as one could imagine. Both the navy and industry had already reached and sustained a degree of readiness normally achieved only during wartime because the RMA and von Tirpitz relentlessly pursued the best possible product to enable an effective challenge to the Royal Navy. Therefore, the events of August and September 1914 did not require the RMA and its suppliers to take drastic measures to prepare for the coming conflict. Essentially, they were already mobilized. Indeed, when the War Office assumed the authority of the War Ministry in the area of military-industrial relations in 1916, the navy's independence received an overdue commendation. It was exempted from the authority of the Waffen und Munitions Beschaffungsamt (WUMBA), the War Office's agency for controlling weapons and munitions procurement. This was official ex post facto recognition that since August 1914 the RMA had executed its responsibility to the war effort independently and effectively with very little outside assistance.

The power and influence of the RMA went far beyond its ability to control its suppliers. It developed a departmental independence which, like that of the Prussian War Ministry, frequently helped form or confuse official policy, initially giving von Tirpitz a great deal of political clout.[4] Unfortunately, his influence had a detrimental effect on Reich policy, especially with regard to conflict with England and the international effect of further arms expenditures.

When the growth of the fleet slowed in 1912, von Tirpitz continued to lobby for increased naval spending. Indeed, his political activities were still so successful that Kurt Riezler, the chancellor's confidant, expressed doubts as to whether von Bethmann-Hollweg could conduct foreign policy with even a modicum of support from the press if he dared propose further naval budget cutbacks.[5] Riezler called von Tirpitz "the father of lies" and accused the admiral of placing Germany in danger of war with England and her allies merely to reap glory later as a national savior.[6]

What were the admiral's real intentions? Albert Ballin, director of the powerful HAPAG shipping line, who had old ties to the RMA, felt that von Tirpitz wanted peace and insisted that the state secretary feared the consequences of a war against France, Russia, and Great Britain. Ballin submitted that von Tirpitz's hostility to the policies of the Wilhelmstrasse stemmed from civilian efforts after 1912 to limit the growth of the fleet.[7]

Here we see the essential flaw in the admiral's policy. He wanted to create a weapon that would make Germany a world power and confront Britain with the ultimate risk. Yet he and many of his supporters chose to believe that Britain could not or would not act to prevent the inevitable change in the naval balance of power if the High Seas Fleet grew to the desired strength. This apparent naïveté probably caused Riezler to believe that von Tirpitz was a liar, or perhaps a coward, who would back down if the chancellor called his bluff.

Would von Tirpitz actually use the fleet against Britain if his plans precipitated a war?[8] If von Tirpitz responded positively, Riezler would have called it bravado. In reality, the admiral intended to do just that from the earliest days of naval expansion. In May 1914 von Tirpitz confided to von Müller, chief of the Naval Cabinet, that the fleet would need another six to eight years to prepare for war.[9] Von Tirpitz was nothing if not consistent in his strategy. If war came, he wanted to strike against England with the weapons at hand, even if the fleet was still incomplete. Von Tirpitz felt that the Great Powers understood and respected only naval readiness and the threat of force.

Von Tirpitz's greatest challenge, however, came not from an opposing naval force but from his political adversaries in the Reichstag. Matthias Erzberger of the Center party publicly questioned the propriety of retired naval officers joining private concerns currently working for the

RMA. He implied that a conflict of interest existed and companies with close ties to the RMA received an unfair advantage through these retirees. Some former officers even proposed themselves as candidates for Reichstag seats with the support of heavy industry. Erzberger mentioned one case in which a retired army lieutenant general ran against a Centrist candidate. He clearly feared that former RMA officers would do the same.[10]

Erzberger did not strive to restrict industry to the same extent as did the socialists. The Center party leader opposed both underhanded business practices by private industry and extensive public involvement in arms manufacturing. He felt that national security required only controls and restraints applied through a modest measure of state participation. Erzberger cited the imperial shipyard at Wilhelmshaven as a case in point[11] because he believed that as a government facility it provided an important and necessary alternative to private industry. Such endeavors protected Germany and made official authority stronger without imposing severe restrictions on private firms.

A former member of the Thyssen board of directors, Erzberger strongly supported von Tirpitz's risk theory before the war and frequently attacked the power of the Krupp-Dillinger armor monopoly to the RMA's benefit. Unfortunately, neither he nor von Tirpitz recognized that the British would interpret the construction of the fleet as the ultimate challenge to their national welfare. Once the war began, however, he perceived long before Germany's naval leaders did that neither the fleet nor the U-boat would assure a German victory.[12]

In contrast, Gustav Noske of the SPD spoke acidly of heavy industry to a Reichstag much more receptive to leftist points of view after the 1912 elections. Rarely missing an opportunity to subject naval-industrial relations to careful public scrutiny, Noske took great pains to inform the Reichstag in early 1914 about a trial in which a direct link between the RMA and Krupp was found in the person of Essen's man inside the RMA, Brand. There was also a scandal involving bribery to cover up poor workmanship in a Magdeburg factory contracting with the RMA. In this case 1,500 marks were paid to silence a master craftsman. Noske also exposed the existence of an organization designed to help subcontractors win lucrative naval contracts in return for a kickback amounting to 10 percent of the contract's total value.[13]

Both the SPD and Center parties insisted upon basic policy changes affecting the fleet. Erzberger denied that the existing battleship ratio with Great Britain was sixteen to ten. He publicly suggested that it was closer to twenty-five to ten, a deficit that Germany could not make up in the foreseeable future. Erzberger and the Center proposed a compromise accepting a sixteen-to-ten ratio as a future goal, after a one-year naval construction holiday eased the international tensions created by the naval competition between Germany and Britain. These suggestions, however, took second place to the solution the Center party desired most—an eventual negotiated settlement with the British.[14]

The platform of the SPD and Center intersected only with the proposal of a naval holiday. The SPD wanted to go far beyond the mild proposals of Erzberger and his associates, insisting upon further naval spending cuts designed to reduce tensions with the British. The SPD wanted to bring the attack directly to the arms manufacturers, condemning their monopoly and kickback practices as well as their affiliation with and support of various politically extreme associations. The socialists linked these groups with the expansionist policies that provoked conflict, increased military appropriations, and promised substantial profits for the arms merchants.[15]

The Center and left raised questions that piqued the curiosity of many regarding the strategy pursued by the RMA since 1897. In July 1913, the legislature created a committee to probe irregularities in the arms industry, and the RMA nervously monitored the activities of this group through Admiral Dähnhardt's Budget Department.[16]

In response to these challenges, von Tirpitz clung to his position more tenaciously than ever and defended RMA policies, insisting that the protocol system and traditional controls could correct current problems and adapt to future challenges. Punitive cutbacks in the naval budget would, he argued, deprive the imperial shipyards of essential operating funds. In addition, if the Reichstag reduced appropriations, the deputies could not stop the private yards from signing more contracts with foreign governments to compensate for lost domestic business.[17] The weapons and systems seized by the German government in 1914 before they could supplement the armed forces of other powers testified to the prewar international diversity of the German shipbuilding business. Krupp alone had coastal defense guns for the Spanish, Chileans, and Brazilians near completion when mobilization began,[18] and a light cruiser for Russia was confiscated while still under construction at Schichau.[19] In this case the naval industries supported von Tirpitz's arguments. Business profits hung in the balance and only future contracts from whatever sources would keep a skilled work force employed.

Von Tirpitz's arguments and defensive rhetoric have a disturbingly contemporary and familiar sound. If national security depended in part on the navy, and the armaments industry formed an important component of national defense, the Reichstag had to honor the financial commitment begun with the 1898 and 1900 naval laws. Furthermore, since thousands of laborers, skilled and unskilled, relied on the industry for their jobs, additional budget cuts seemed not only a national security risk but a real danger to the national economy as well. Therefore, von Tirpitz could expect some success in his efforts against further cutbacks. He could always find new foreign "enemies" to inspire further fleet construction or the economic need, whether real or imagined, to support greater government spending in the naval sphere.[20]

The kaiser's determination not to lose his capital ships in a premature battle with the British also presented von Tirpitz with a formidable threat to his political and professional position. Wilhelm would allow the fleet only brief probing sorties against the enemy, nothing more than exaggerated reconnaissance patrols. More careful officers such as Admiral Franz von Hipper momentarily agreed with these tactics in opposition to the RMA chief, who persisted in his desire to explore favorable conditions for engaging the British fleet. Von Hipper did not take von Tirpitz seriously for he was fully aware that many officers rejected the admiral's strategy as that of a schemer and politician, and his stance further undermined the state secretary's professional support in the last few months before the war.[21]

Not only did the kaiser's fears restrict the use of the fleet, but the early successes of the U-boat operations against Britain after September 1914 called into question the navy's decisions in the types of ships it chose to build, the validity of current naval strategy, and the future of von Tirpitz's construction program. Kurt Riezler's diary chronicles the kaiser's increasingly favorable attitude toward submarines in 1914. He went so far as to urge a shift in construction priorities to increase their numbers.[22] Still, the day after the U-boat blockade of Britain was declared on 8 November 1914, von Tirpitz argued against a U-boat-based strategy until sufficient numbers were available.[23] As in the past, he never sought adequate funding for the additional boats, continuing to prefer the construction of battleships. By January 1915, however, von Tirpitz changed his mind about U-boat warfare. He had little choice. The man who had never attempted to promote full-scale U-boat research and development now found himself forced by events to contradict his own strategy and past policies.[24] With this turn of events, the admiral's star began to wane.

The Essential Factors: Raw Materials and Labor

The most dramatic adjustment for the RMA during the 1913–14 period was the nationwide problem of allocating raw materials for war production. In August 1914, Walter Rathenau of Allgemeine Elektricitäts Gesellschaft (AEG) took it upon himself to assist the government in creating an agency, affiliated with the War Ministry, to transact business with private firms supplying the war effort. This new arm of the bureaucracy became known as the War Materials Office (KRA), and it functioned under Rathenau's direction until his resignation on 1 April 1915.[25]

The importance of this development was twofold. First, because the Reich had no regulatory authority of this type in late summer 1914, the War Ministry responded by creating the KRA. Second, the KRA participated with private industry in the creation of independent monopoly companies designed to regulate production, allocation, and prices in virtually every major sector of the economy. These alphabetically designated monopolies administered everything from cloth and towels to chemicals and metals. They were all linked to the War Ministry through the KRA. The roster of these companies reads like a list of American New Deal agencies during the 1930s: Kawo, KCA, KGT, Klag, KMA, and VDW among others.[26]

The KMA or War Metals Company (Kriegsmetall AG) was of the greatest concern to the RMA. Created on 1 September 1914, it had twenty-two member firms and capital resources of about 6 million marks. Director Peierls of AEG chaired the KMA board, and most of the member firms were in the electrical industry or minor foundries and factories.[27] Although the steel giants like Krupp participated in the KMA, the agency sought to guarantee the rights of smaller firms to a share of the scarce raw materials and thereby a fair portion of the profit promised by the war. The War Ministry made this a priority. Need governed distribution, and the KMA allocated the limited raw materials among firms placing their orders with the KRA at the War Ministry.

Any policy allowing the civilian businessmen who controlled these monopolies to procure and distribute raw materials during wartime had an obvious flaw. The temptation to raise profits and favor one's own concern proved too great in many instances. In addition, the giant postwar German trusts that plagued the Weimar Republic with their political influence became a major by-product of the wartime monopoly system. I.G. Farben, the mammoth chemical trust, traced its roots to the wartime KCA or Kriegschemikalien AG.[28]

The shortage of labor posed one of the more difficult problems that Germany faced during the war.[29] The initial mobilization severely displaced the prewar labor force. In 1914, the military raised the sectors of the economy considered nonessential for wartime production from 3 percent to 22 percent, leaving thousands unemployed. The armed forces immediately claimed most of these displaced workers, and many others had to wait for the economy to readjust itself to war, creating jobs elsewhere. After this disruption the labor market did not begin to approach prewar conditions until 1915, after which a widespread labor scarcity persisted through the battle of the Somme in 1916.[30]

The RMA tried to control the movement of labor between the shipyards and factories according to the priorities of its projects. In 1914 the navy limited the number of workers allowed to change jobs so as to maintain continuity, quality, and efficiency in production. These practices only partially offset the movement and eventual shortage of skilled labor. All of these decisions fell to the General Naval Department of the RMA, in conjunction with the Dockyard and Construction departments.[31]

Mobilization exacerbated the tendency of many highly skilled technicians either to change their naval jobs or to transfer to private industry in search of better pay. Continuing a widespread prewar pattern, these people would gain training and experience in the navy and then join private firms or other naval departments. In one instance, the Construction Department complained of an overabundance of electricians at the Dockyard Department while other divisions of the RMA went shorthanded because of the unimpeded crossover of skilled workers. In another case, the imperial yard at Wilhelmshaven needed five skilled electrical technicians but could not afford to accept crossovers from industry who demanded the higher wages available in the private sector. These people would probably return to the private sector as soon as a higher-paying opportunity arose. Wilhelmshaven desperately needed naval employees who would stay on the job.[32]

The military draft partially solved this problem of labor scarcity and movement. Skilled workers and their employers were required to justify all exemptions from military service, which significantly slowed the practice of crossing over. A worker's job could keep him off the front lines or out of the army altogether if his services were important enough to the war effort.[33]

The war also dramatically affected every German laborer's standard of living. Between the founding of the Reich and 1913, real earnings, or actual weekly buying power, increased considerably. Although statistics varied in each industry, buying power rose 18 percent from 1890 to 1900 and another 10 percent from 1900 to 1913. Taxes offset these increases, however, as did social welfare insurance and a reduction in the length of the workweek from seventy-one hours in 1871 to forty-eight hours in 1919. Although available statistics indicate that take-home pay tripled in Germany between 1871 and 1919 and buying power doubled, disposable net earnings never increased more than one-third in the entire 1871 to 1944 period. With the rise in prices caused by the wartime scarcity of consumer goods, coal, and oil, the buying power of the average worker declined markedly. Weekly buying power dropped every year of the war, reaching a low of 35 percent below 1913 levels by 1918.[34]

In 1913, the wages paid by the navy were competitive with those in the private sector. A lathe operator, for example, made between 40 and 53 pfennigs per hour working for the navy while his counterpart in private industry earned from 41 to 54 pfennigs. Machine- and shipbuilders earned more in the private market. If they worked for the navy they would fall within the wage scale for the lathe operator, whereas an independent firm would pay between 41 and 58 pfennigs per hour.[35] Mobilization and war ended the near parity of naval and private pay rates for many workers. At the end of 1914 the daily average wage at the Krupp Gusstahlfabrik in Essen jumped 46 pfennigs from 5.44 to 5.90 marks.[36] Private industry expected substantial profits from the war and therefore willingly retrained skilled labor at a slightly higher cost.

The imperial yards could not satisfy the demands of skilled workers in the same way. Pay for carpenters is an example. In 1906, the imperial shipyard at Wilhelmshaven paid its carpenters 50 pfennigs per hour. By 1914, the navy offered 70 pfennigs, but the workers could often ask and get more elsewhere. In December 1914 the navy received a request from master carpenter Wilhelm Speckmann for 90 pfennigs per hour retroactive to the beginning of mobilization.[37] Perhaps industry could meet such demands, but the RMA could not.

Wartime pressures quickly revealed flaws in the general mobilization plan, but few were the fault of the RMA. The logistical planners, for example, did not fully consider the probability of disastrous rail traffic congestion when their work began in 1914. By the second week of August, the Borsig firm was already having trouble transporting its goods to the imperial yards and complained loudly to one of von Tirpitz's construction supervisors.[38] The full extent of the problem would not become apparent until 1916, when the Hindenburg Program hurled a still inadequate railroad system into the first attempt at total mobilization. Gerald Feldman's research shows that steel, manufactured in the Ruhr, often went first to eastern Germany for conversion into shells and then west again to receive high-explosive charges before shipment to the army and navy.[39] The railroads could barely handle the enormous strain placed upon them in 1914, and by 1916 the burden became impossible.

Excessive transport costs obliged the authorities at the Wilhelmshaven Imperial Shipyard to place stricter controls on truck transport charges. New naval regulations permitted only a 20 percent rise in rates above peacetime levels.[40]

Other difficulties seemed both predictable and normal for wartime conditions. Shakedown cruises for ships nearly ready for service, such as the SMS *Grosser Kurfürst*, the SMS *König*, and others, were accelerated to prepare them for active service on short notice.[41] As a result of this haste, an abnormal number of malfunctions and mechanical problems occurred during the early months of the war.[42] Communication and transport problems often caused delays in delivering plans and specifications.[43] The shipyards also recognized the need for greater security. The RMA supported requests in this area by closely supervising the activities of non-Germans working on naval projects.[44]

The U-Boats

The exact role of the U-boat was still a strategic mystery in the last
year before the war, but the job of building and arming these boats
began to require a greater amount of naval time and money. In December
1913, the kaiser ordered changes in the administration of U-boat
affairs. He created two distinct offices to manage undersea warfare.
One would govern the manufacture of torpedoes, and the second,
dubbed the U-Boat Inspectorate, directed everything related to submarines.
In addition, it managed the U-boat school, developed new prototypes,
prepared for mobilization, and supplied the daily needs of related naval and civilian personnel.[45] Construction matters were left to
the inspectorate's technical bureau under the leadership of Marinebaurath Reitz.[46]

In 1912, the RMA made very little money available for U-boat work.
The navy planned a total of six new boats for 1913–14 and allocated 7.2
million marks to cover the construction expense. At the same time the
legislature voted 99 million more for maintenance. Future projections
did not appreciably increase these figures. The RMA's schedule called
for four boats in 1915 and twelve during the 1916–19 period. The navy's
commitment did not seem to extend further because the projected 18-
million-mark U-boat budget for 1918–19 sank by 13 million in the budget estimates for the next fiscal year.[47] In spite of Admiralty Chief Hugo
von Pohl's support for U-boat operations, von Tirpitz did not increase
the RMA's outlay in time and money. Von Pohl suggested that the
U-boats could reduce the numbers of attacking capital ships to a
strength favorable to the High Seas Fleet in a surface battle.[48] Statements by the chief of the RMA at this time tended to make little of both
the offensive capability of the U-boat and von Pohl's professional
evaluation.

Building the U-boats presented less of a headache for the RMA than
did battleships. With the aid of the U-boat Inspectorate, von Tirpitz
and Rollmann kept prices down and cost and weight overruns to a bare
minimum. Final costs for the U-boats tended to be extremely close to
those specified in the contracts.[49]

In 1913 only the Germania Shipyard (Krupp) in Kiel and the imperial yard at Danzig built U-boats. The latter kept its costs down with
RMA assistance, but it was frequently difficult to come to agreement

with Krupp on costs. This pressure decreased somewhat with the beginning of the war.[50] The entrance of Vulcan and AG Weser into U-boat construction in 1914 reduced the necessity to buy boats from Krupp.

When the war began, Germany had twenty-eight U-boats in service and nineteen under construction. Immediately after mobilization, the RMA ordered another eighteen boats of varying types, and other orders quickly followed.[51] The U46–50 went to the Danzig Imperial Shipyard in August 1914. The yard's efficient management and freedom from the many ancillary projects that often characterized private business promised quick results. Krupp, for example, had to delay production on the U31–41 series just as mobilization began because it had not been able to develop its own two-stroke diesel engine for these boats.[52] In 1913–14 alone, the firm lost 4 million marks in its effort to rival the leading German diesel manufacturers, MAN and Körting.[53] When Germania received the contract for the first six Ms-boats (U51–56) on 23 August 1914, the RMA specified that it use a four-stroke MAN diesel engine and not the flawed Krupp engine. Weser received the contract for the next six Ms-boats in November 1914 (U57–62) mainly because it built them faster than the imperial yard, cutting one and a half years off the projected construction time for the series.[54]

The UB-boat also appeared during 1914. This brainchild of the U-boat Inspectorate had excellent seakeeping qualities and a short construction time, which made it very attractive in 1914. It would protect the Baltic flank of the army in Belgium and the Low Countries by operating in the intricate coastal waters to the north. The RMA approved the design on 28 September 1914; contracts for the first fifteen boats went to Germania and Weser on 5 October. The Weser yard also received approval to build the UB16 and 17 in November 1914. Germania completed the first boat of this type in one hundred days, nearly three weeks ahead of schedule. The UB17 came off the slipway in May 1915.[55]

Between 17 October 1914 and the end of February 1915, the RMA awarded contracts for a larger form of the UB which was primarily for laying mines. This UC boat had six tubes capable of holding two mines each. Contracts for the UC1–10 went to Vulcan and the UC11–15 to Weser. Germany loaned many of both the UC and UB types to Austria-Hungary for operations in the Mediterranean.[56]

The greater demand on the firms and plant facilities for increased

U-boat production created slowdowns and enlarged every problem in
the eyes of anxious naval administrators. A characteristically heated
exchange took place in 1914 between Captain Hermann Nordmann-
Bergau, chief of the U-boat Inspectorate, and Krupp over late deliveries. The former, aware of the navy's needs and under pressure to accelerate construction, accused Krupp of profiteering and excessively
late deliveries, vowing to tighten supervision at Germania. Krupp re-
buffed all accusations, blaming delays on the call-up of his workers to
the military and problems with the diesel engine program. Krupp's
profits were considerable, but so were the pressures of mobilization on
the inspectorate.[57]

The U-boat became more important in naval strategic thinking because the realities of war showed that the fleet built by von Tirpitz and
the RMA could not effectively challenge the British in a surface battle.
Unfortunately, the German U-boat force was not large enough to fight
the commercial war for which the submarine was so well suited. The
legacy of von Tirpitz's prewar U-boat policy became disturbingly clear
and a source of considerable anxiety.

Iron and Steel

By 1913–14 the governing circles of Britain, France, and the United
States clamored for increased competition in the production of high-
grade steel armor. Giving long-term contracts to the clique of international steel firms dubbed the "armor ring" by Winston Churchill
plagued the politicians because in so doing they seemed to support
publicly the formation of cartels and the practice of profiteering. Frequent criticism of this policy arose in the British Parliament. In the
United States, Secretary of the Navy Josephus Daniels established a
publicly owned armor factory by 1916.[58] During a Sunday evening session of the German Reichstag in March 1913, the representative from
Bromberg complained about Germany's excessive dependence on a
small group of armor firms. His speech was no doubt inspired by prices
the RMA still considered excessive.[59] In one of many complaints to the
RMA, the resident naval inspector at Vulcan noted some of the problems involved with using Krupp armor. If Vulcan had purchased armor
from the American Bethlehem Steel Company for a cruiser then under
construction for Greece (the *Salamis*) it would have cost 11.4 million

marks. From Krupp armor and steel products cost 14.1 million, an extra expenditure of 2.7 million marks.[60]

The problem went far beyond Germany's borders. The navy needed to promote competition, but who would provide it, given the entrenched position of companies like Krupp and Dillinger? The RMA knew Germany's options all too well after the agreement with Krupp and Dillinger in 1910: Thyssen, a host of smaller German firms, and Midvale, the American alternative. Even after settling for a long-term contract with the armor alliance, von Tirpitz investigated new ways to lower prices. To this end, he formed close ties in 1914 with the director of Dillinger, Weinlig, recording the essence of their numerous meetings in his RMA war diary. He made a concerted effort to gain influence with the director and to increase Dillinger's share of the naval armor contracts.[61] The admiral hoped both to encourage further output from Dillinger and to lure it away from its alliance with Krupp. Earlier in 1914, a Budget Department report to the Reichstag Armaments Commission exhibited this same determination to increase competition in the war industries.[62] Publicly and privately the state secretary never lost an opportunity to encourage competition or change the status quo to the navy's favor.

The mercurial character of the American armor market remained one of von Tirpitz's old tools in the war on prices. The unpredictable element in the American steel industry was Charles Harrah's Midvale Steel. He unwittingly provided von Tirpitz with a weapon against Krupp during the 1906–10 period and frequently surprised his American competitors as well. Midvale undercut both Bethlehem and U.S. Steel by $54 a ton in 1914 to win a huge battleship armor contract from the Wilson administration.[63] When the war started in Europe, Midvale maintained its position as one of the big three American armor companies. Initially, Harrah decided for family reasons not to do business in war materials with either England or Germany. One of his daughters was married to an Englishman, the other to a German. But Harrah sold his interest in the company for $10 million in 1915, and before the end of that year Midvale's new directors were doing business with Great Britain. In 1916 they produced field guns for the British and very often gave Entente orders priority over American.[64] Thus in spite of its wartime sympathy for the Entente, Midvale may still have considered overtures from the RMA before 1917.

Besides the financial power of the individual German iron and steel firms, the navy faced a handful of cartels and lobbying organizations all determined to make the greatest profit possible from the war. The most influential industrialists manipulated prices and production both privately and through the war monopolies. In private groups like the Kriegsausschuss der Deutschen Industrie (War Committee on German Industry), they coordinated industrial and financial efforts to supply the war effort. Formed in August 1914, this committee combined the clout of the CVDI (Central Association of German Industrialists) and the Bund der Industrellen (Association of Industrialists). Most of the committee's more influential members were directors, entrepreneurs, and financiers directly tied to the iron and steel industry.[65]

Regardless of their private affiliation, most of these firms formed part of the KMA, which served throughout the war as the major source of metal supply for naval contractors.[66] The KMA often maximized profits at the expense of nonaffiliated firms or the government to maintain prearranged quotas for its member firms. It managed to increase trade in many metals during the first three years of the war, overcoming the initial shock and dislocation of mobilization. Copper sales, for example, went from 135,552 tons in 1914–15, down to 68,094 in 1915–16, and then rose to 139,782 in 1916–17. The sales in aluminum were about the same, tin much less, and zinc many times greater.[67]

The most significant problems in the metals industry lay with iron and steel because of the extraordinary rise in prices. The RMA put strict limits on the price it would pay for certain items and tried to exert pressure to keep prices down, and the War Ministry published its accepted price limits.[68] Ultimately, however, the government could do little. A Krupp report on the rising price of raw materials for high-quality steel reflected the pressures of scarcity and increased wartime demand. In early 1914 chrome ore sold at 51 marks per ton. By November 1916, it had risen 784 percent, leveling off at 400 marks. Domestic manganese went up 107 percent, and phosphates from outside Germany exceeded 76 marks per ton, a rise of approximately 216 percent.[69] Every grade of steel was in short supply by 1916, and much of it used in the 1914–18 conflict came from Sweden.[70] German private firms frequently used Sweden as a secondary supplier during the war.[71] Industries requiring brass and other metals felt the same constraint and also sought alternative suppliers. Consequently, many firms found it difficult to restrict their purchases of raw materials to any single source, domestic or foreign.

A few companies justifiably blamed the war for late deliveries, broken deadlines, and high prices.[72] But the high prices charged by the iron and steel manufacturers certainly helped them endure the disruption of mobilization. An interoffice Construction Department memo dated September 1914 reflected the frustration felt by the RMA at the extreme variation between maximum and minimum steel prices.[73] The industry clearly had the upper hand, and in one of its evening editions in 1916 the *Frankfurter Zeitung* noted that the 594-million-mark profit enjoyed by the domestic iron and steel industry that year exceeded the 1913 figures by 209 million.[74] The navy paid what the iron and steel industry asked for its services, as did every other branch of the military, for the armed services could exert only modest control over wartime prices.[75]

The Protocol System, Purchasing, and the War

The need for greater security precipitated by the war intensified the enforcement of naval regulations, especially as they applied to the use and dissemination of the suppliers' list. This list was readily available and a matter of public record before the war, but after August 1914 only approved firms received it, and it was confiscated from those companies struck from the list by the Construction and Budget departments of the RMA.[76] Furthermore, businesses found it equally as difficult to appear on the list in 1914 as they did before the war. It remained one of the central controls vital to the protocol system, and the RMA intended to keep its standards high, particularly during the critical activity surrounding mobilization.[77] It even sought to extend the advantages the navy gained from the suppliers' list by seeking out firms willing to compete with cartels or monopoly companies. The Firma Eisenwerk Kraft (Abteilung Niederrheinische Hütte) of Duisburg-Hockfeld, for example, appeared on the list after the customary product inspection and received an unusually warm welcome because it was willing to compete with the members of the Steel Shipbuilding Association.[78]

At the outset, the RMA and the firms that supported it depended on the authority of the War Ministry to coordinate all procurement activities as part of the general mobilization effort. Firms supplying weapons, aircraft, ammunition, vehicles, and all other war materials had to be cleared by the War Ministry.[79] A firm under contract to the RMA would make a formal application to the Metal Supply Section (Metall Meldestelle) of the KRA at the War Ministry via the War Metals Company (KMA). In the case of a subcontractor, the request first passed through the shipyard and then went to the RMA. The Allotment Office of the Metal Supply Section would then approve all or part of the materials requested, releasing them in the exact amount to the firm in question. The War Ministry transmitted its decisions to the RMA's purveyors through the office of the state secretary.[80]

For matters exclusively within the navy's jurisdiction, von Tirpitz's prewar system of checks and restraints remained the reliable foundation of the RMA's advantageous relationship with industry. The navy strictly bound companies to their contract agreements, always conscious that the success and timing of mobilization depended on the reliability of the firms involved in each project.

In many cases the navy kept up its practice of predetermining the subcontractors hired by private firms to complete certain projects. In the case of the SMS *Bayern*, the manufacturers of the primary turbines and on-board diesel engines were named in the contract—Brown and Boveri and Benz, respectively.[81] In patent matters, contracts stipulated that individual firms should forgo collecting their royalties for the duration of the war when in the service of the Imperial Navy.[82]

Even before the war erupted, the RMA continued its strict policies, and on 5 May 1914, it reminded its staff and contractors that a treason charge awaited anyone found in violation of construction and procurement rules. With the advent of war, the RMA once again investigated foreigners working on naval projects and discouraged the further employment of non-Germans. It also tightened security with regard to models, designs, and blueprints. Various departments received a list of regional police authorities in case of a violation or need for a security check.[83]

Enforcement of the protocol system regulations fell to the Purchasing Office and the RMA's Technical and Construction departments, which had the expertise to judge the final quality of workmanship.[84] Many firms disappeared from the suppliers' list between July and December 1914 in an RMA effort to leave the navy with the absolute best industrial support possible. Some firms fell from the list because of financial instability, some at the suggestion of the War Ministry for violations of legal and military codes, and others because of business practices not approved by the RMA.[85] Still others, like Delta Metall Gesellschaft of Düsseldorf, vanished from the list when their products began to decline in quality.[86]

Of the three RMA divisions, the Purchasing Office had the greatest difficulty coping with mobilization. By 1913 this office had already begun to encounter serious delays in inspecting and approving naval orders at the factory because of a chronic personnel shortage,[87] and the coming of war further complicated this profound handicap. As the deluge of requests received at the RMA to accelerate on-site purchasing inspections accumulated, some firms began notifying individual purchasing inspectors as well as the RMA far in advance of the pending completion of a contract. They hoped that doing so might streamline the inspection schedule,[88] but the Purchasing Office continued to receive scores of impatient inquiries asking the reasons for persistent and chronic delays. Virtually every aspect of RMA business was affected, from appeals to inspect a Wieland brass tubing order in Ulm to a shipment of Flexilis Steel in Berlin overdue for delivery to MAN.[89] Firms wished to fulfill their contracts and avoid a late penalty that could be as high as 15 percent,[90] but the Purchasing Office was hard-pressed to accommodate them.

In December 1914, Krupp advised von Tirpitz of its dissatisfaction with this situation, and these complaints made a great deal of sense. Even if a firm reported the impending completion of a naval order, too much time elapsed between production and shipment to the yards. As the months progressed and the RMA's priorities shifted away from the huge capital ships to U-boat production, the Purchasing Office recovered a bit of its lost time. The smaller boats consumed fewer hours during inspection tours.[91] The problem remained a continuing source of concern for the RMA, however, because of the paucity of qualified technical personnel available to conduct these tours.

Although the responsibility for prompt and efficient inspection of equipment and weaponry lay squarely with the RMA, von Tirpitz and his colleagues faced a nearly impossible situation at the Purchasing Office. The peacetime scarcity of highly skilled technical inspectors did not change just because of the imperatives of war.[92]

Occasionally the RMA publicly exaggerated the extent of its control over industry, with very expensive results. In February 1914 the Budget Department asked that the Construction Department respond to a newspaper report claiming that the Siemens-Schuckertwerke was selling electrical products to the Japanese for 30 to 50 percent less than it charged the German navy. Construction overreacted and claimed that because of protocol inspection methods the products received from Siemens-Schuckertwerke were the best that could be obtained. In this case, the department felt that quality justified the high price and dismissed the press criticism. Clearly, the results here did not serve the navy's best interests.[93]

In formulating official policy, von Tirpitz did not display the same naïveté. The Construction Department no doubt tried to keep its price problems and debates within the confines of its office so as not to reveal flaws to its colleagues or the public. Von Tirpitz knew that many cartels and individual firms excessively overcharged the RMA. As we have seen, he acted when he felt success was possible.[94] The state secretary also instructed his personnel working with various vendors not to establish too close a relationship with the private sector. Any hint of corruption might retard the RMA's efforts to obtain the best price and workmanship.[95] Even von Tirpitz, in his constant vigilance, did not always succeed. Retiring officers tended to attach themselves to the naval armaments companies. Retired Vice-Admiral Hans Sack became a member of the Krupp Board of Governors, and in 1907 the future state secretary of the RMA, Ernst Ritter von Mann, expressed a desire to retire into the service of the same firm.[96]

Many companies chafed under RMA restraints. In December 1913 four major private shipyards asserted in a letter to the RMA that restrictions pertaining to construction regulations, contracts, security, and foreign business far exceeded naval authority. Blohm und Voss, Krupp, Weser, and Schichau insisted that their positive responses to the RMA's wishes met with unfair treatment in return. The state secretary did not offer his sympathy, and the RMA continued enforcing its policies and regulations without change.[97]

The events of the summer of 1914 did not catch the RMA unprepared. Unlike the army, indeed the Reich in general, the RMA did not need to create any special offices to handle the challenges of mobilization. The RMA organization in 1914 was a tested system for turning legislative appropriations into naval hardware. Of all the offices and departments in von Tirpitz's organization during the first year of war only the Purchasing Office had great difficulty keeping pace with stepped-up production.

Some influences on the RMA's performance lay beyond von Tirpitz's direct control. The most important of these, raw materials procurement, placed the navy at the mercy of intensified competition between army and navy contractors. The smaller firms had the greatest trouble competing with heavy industry for basic resources. The manufacturing and finishing firms did not have the influence at the War Ministry and the KRA enjoyed by Krupp, Haniel, Thyssen, and other major industrialists. The participation of the smaller contractors in the war monopoly companies like the KMA only partially compensated for their disadvantages.

In addition, mobilization caused a general and prolonged dislocation of both labor and rail transport. The exemption of workers vital to the war industries occurred slowly and very haphazardly until the total mobilization of 1916 further streamlined the process. When these workers began to produce at markedly increased levels, the German railroad and trucking systems were totally unprepared for increased freight traffic.

Another particularly aggravating effect of mobilization and increased war production was the dramatic increase in price for virtually everything the navy required. Von Tirpitz and the RMA struggled both to enforce price controls and to curb artificially inflated prices, but the war ended any expectation that the admiral might repeat his early success against such powerful firms as Krupp and Dillinger. Von Tirpitz no longer had time and competition on his side.

Although the navy built submarines quickly and usually within budget estimates, von Tirpitz still placed the vessel in a minor auxiliary role. As the first few months of war passed, the success and popularity of this weapon forced the state secretary to reconsider his basic strategy and give greater attention to the U-boat. Germania and the imperial shipyard at Danzig were joined by Weser and Vulcan in U-boat construction. Three new types of boats went into production in late 1914 and the early months of 1915. This not only increased the number and function of the available boats but also encouraged further competition within the industry.

7

The End of the von Tirpitz Era

1915 – 1916

The realities of war gave rise once more to the traditional conflict within the navy regarding strategy. Early U-boat successes supplied the advocates of a commercial war with ammunition for a new assault on von Tirpitz's battleship strategy and in so doing challenged the indecisive kaiser to resolve the eighteen-year-old debate.[1]

Much more was at stake now than the validity of the risk theory. The construction program and the credibility of the state secretary of the RMA were called into question, as well as the de facto leadership of the German navy. In 1915, von Tirpitz and his RMA still held the prime position in naval affairs, but the initial successes of the U-boats and the relative inactivity of the surface fleet brought a new threat to the primacy of the RMA in naval circles. One prominent battleship captain boldly asserted that true authority in the navy was misplaced and that the Admiralty should lead the navy in wartime because the skills needed to fight a war were found there, not in the RMA.[2]

In three position papers written in the summer of 1915 for circulation within the navy, Lieutenant Commander Wolfgang Wegener dissected the risk theory and questioned the value of the decisive battle which formed the core of von Tirpitz's strategic dogma. Wegener, a staff officer

142

to Vice Admiral Wilhelm von Lans, commander of the Second Squadron, rejected the idea that any single victory over the Royal Navy would prove decisive. Seeking to establish a broader strategic framework, Wegener insisted that the Imperial Navy turn its attention to Britain's communications and her vital sea lanes. To accomplish this end, the navy required not only von Tirpitz's High Seas Fleet but also the geographic advantage which occupying the Kattegat, Skaggerak, and Faeroe islands would provide. The key to mounting a challenge to Britain lay with fleet and position. It could be accomplished in no other way.[3]

The changes in the naval command during the course of 1915–16 reflected these fairly widespread doubts about von Tirpitz's leadership. In the crisis of February 1915 involving unrestricted submarine warfare, a von Tirpitz partisan, Gustav Bachmann, briefly replaced Admiral Hugo von Pohl as head of the Admiralty, but this extension of RMA influence into the upper reaches of the Admiralty was short-lived. The kaiser soon replaced Bachmann by calling Admiral von Holtzendorff out of retirement.[4] The new man at the Admiralty intensely disliked von Tirpitz and refused to accept a role secondary to the state secretary of the RMA.

The U-boat issue finally forced the conflict over authority and strategy to a climax. After his sudden advocacy of the unrestricted use of submarines in 1914, von Tirpitz was perceived more than ever as a political opportunist. For the doctrinaire advocate of the battleship suddenly to reverse the passion of a lifetime severely damaged his credibility. Wegener's penetrating criticism of von Tirpitz's strategic concept spilled over to include the types of ships the RMA had added to the fleet. According to historian Carl-Axel Gemzell: "Wegener also maintains that German war preparations had concentrated quite one-sidedly on the battle in the Helgoland Bight. . . . The consequences of this had affected the dislocation of our naval forces and even the construction of our ships."[5] The sinking of the *Lusitania* in May 1915 focused even greater attention on von Tirpitz's long-term wisdom and the composition of the fleet. At that point it seemed as if the U-boat, the unwanted stepchild of the von Tirpitz era, had become the only effective offensive weapon the Imperial Navy possessed.

In the two years following March 1916, the RMA would build eighty-three large Ms submarines, U-cruisers, and minelayers, each displacing a thousand tons or more. By then, however, construction was no longer von Tirpitz's responsibility. On 30 August 1915 the state secretary lost both his position on the General Headquarters Staff and his advisory post at the Admiralty. Twenty-four hours later, Bachmann surrendered his position at the Admiralty to von Holtzendorff, who retained it until August 1918.[6] Although von Tirpitz continued to defend his policies, the tide had clearly turned against him. The kaiser accepted his resignation on 17 March 1916.

His successor at the RMA, Admiral Eduard von Capelle, defended his predecessor's ideas and actions both in the navy and before the Reichstag, but to no avail.[7] The government of von Bethmann-Hollweg and many of the state secretary's naval colleagues did not miss him. The chancellor's confidant Kurt Riezler characterized the risk theory in his diary on 19 March as a suspension of reality. He now described the former state secretary's private attacks on the chancellor as "delirium."[8] In a memoir, Admiral Paul Behncke noted the quick political decline of the RMA after von Tirpitz departed: "The opinions of the state secretary hold no weight among the people. In the navy, the position of the RMA has become purely administrative, it no longer plays a leading role."[9] The focus of naval authority now returned to the Admiralty, which would give birth in August 1918 to Admiral Reinhard Scheer's centralized Naval High Command or Seekriegsleitung (SKL).

Politically, Admiral von Holtzendorff's presence at the Admiralty only partially filled the uneasy vacuum within the navy during the long hiatus between the resignation of von Tirpitz and the creation of Scheer's SKL. He pushed for the unrestricted use of the U-boat in spite of von Bethmann-Hollweg's stated policy, but the situation remained static until the army leadership won the political debate over unrestricted U-boat warfare at the end of 1916.[10]

With the office of state secretary of the RMA in a position of secondary political importance, von Capelle concentrated on his administrative role within the RMA. He naturally focused on building more U-boats, but not at the expense of the RMA's future plans regarding capital ships, which called for a force of forty heavy and forty light cruisers built at the rate of two per year.[11] Von Capelle proposed this new cruiser series in 1916 hoping it would complement the commercial war strategy carried out by his submarines.

In spite of plans to increase its numbers, the U-boat arm was not prepared for the role it was now asked to play. Von Tirpitz asserted self-servingly in his memoirs that enough submarines existed during this period to attain the ambitious goals of the unrestricted U-boat warfare advocates,[12] but German naval power still essentially depended upon capital ships and torpedo boats. As we have seen, naval priorities did not include U-boats until late 1914. Although submarine production increased substantially and made good progress in 1915, it would take many months to approach the numbers desired by the Admiralty, even though the Imperial Navy had 165 boats under construction or in commission by January 1916. These early vessels of the Ms, UB, and UC series were all primarily designed for short-range operations and had a surface displacement of approximately 900 tons or less.[13]

After von Tirpitz's dismissal in 1916, Chancellor von Bethmann-Hollweg severely curtailed the extent to which the navy's limited U-boat force could hunt in the war zone around Britain. Von Holtzendorff received permission to attack British ships but not those of the United States or other strategically important neutrals such as Norway, Denmark, and Sweden.[14]

As long as the political leadership restrained the undersea offensive, the RMA could realistically hope to meet the Admiralty's call for both new U-boats and surface vessels. After the Allies prevailed at the Somme in 1916 and the team of General Paul von Hindenburg and General Erich Ludendorff replaced General Erich von Falkenhayn, however, Germany's military leadership tossed restraint aside and launched the Hindenburg Program. This first attempt at total mobilization, initiated on 31 August, overshadowed the RMA's latest plans. The autocratic Army High Command or Oberste Heeresleitung (OHL) decided to double the nation's munitions output and triple machine gun and artillery production without consulting the war minister, Wild von Hohenborn. Gerald Feldman aptly described this program as a triumph of fantasy over the true limits of Germany's economic potential to wage war.[15]

State Secretary von Capelle found himself obliged to respond to the drive for total mobilization by pushing naval armament firms far beyond previous production levels. In response to questioning by the Progressive-Liberal Reichstag representative Gothein, von Capelle argued that the RMA already encouraged firms to produce as many U-boats as possible because "we could never have enough."[16] In contracts with Krupp alone, the RMA's orders for materials and ammunition nearly doubled between the 1915–16 and 1916–17 fiscal years.[17] Thus, in mid-1916, the navy joined the army in its struggle to meet the awesome demands of total mobilization.

U-Boats

In 1915 there were still many unanswered questions about the U-boat. For example, to what extent should the weapon be used? Only the fears and doubts of people like Chancellor von Bethmann-Hollweg and Interior Minister Karl Helfferich withstood RMA pressure and von Holtzendorff's earnest desire for unrestricted use of this weapon. Helfferich, in particular, feared a war with the United States if the U-boats' attacks on shipping were not restrained,[18] and he managed to influence the kaiser in support of the chancellor's policies restricting their activity. Thus he significantly contributed to von Tirpitz's demise and von Holtzendorff's temporary frustration.

Were there enough U-boats in 1916 to test all the positive assertions made about the untapped potential of this weapon? The answer, of course, was no, and the RMA's public statements about the U-boat program were deliberately vague.[19] In April 1916, von Capelle told a session of the Reichstag Budget Commission that 650 firms now appeared on the U-boat suppliers' list. He felt that this would quiet the navy's critics and illustrate the high priority given to the Admiralty's U-boat requirements.[20] In fact, the RMA had just begun to produce high-quality boats in the desired numbers.

During the spring of 1915 the U-Boat Inspectorate formulated plans systematically to increase the number of submarines joining the fleet through July 1916. These boats varied in type and purpose. The new UE boats were minelayers and much larger in size than the UB or UC. The RMA awarded contracts for the UE 75–80 to Vulcan on 27 February 1915. The UBII and UCII, a second generation of each type with increased capacity and size, went into production in the spring and summer of 1915. The UCII carried eighteen mines and had six torpedo tubes in the bow as well as three tubes for 5-centimeter torpedoes. Initially, MAN produced its diesels, joined later by Körting and Daimler.[21] Even though it took eight months to produce a UCII, the RMA leadership felt enthusiastic about their operational potential.

In April 1916, projects 42, 44, and 45 called for an increase in the UB and UC types. These larger boats would satisfy the Admiralty's desire for new 900-ton U-boats and submarine minelayers capable of operations off Britain's west coast at surface speeds exceeding 15 knots. The RMA planned to build a total of 46 boats at an estimated cost of 172.4 million marks.[22] This plan formed part of a general scheme conceived in January 1916 setting 350 new boats as the minimum number needed to patrol the Atlantic, North Sea, English Channel, and Mediterranean.[23]

The RMA's attempt to fulfill the Admiralty's expectations in 1915 and 1916 revealed the essential accuracy of Gerald Feldman's analysis of the Hindenburg Program. It was a gamble at best to think the RMA could suddenly make up for almost a decade of strategically ignoring the U-boat in less than two years.[24] Before the war, von Tirpitz had refused to entertain the possibility of a commercial raiding strategy, much less one in which the U-boat played the leading part. Thus the RMA and its suppliers undertook a task of monumental proportions, handicapped by a shortage of time, labor, and materials.

With rare exceptions, the RMA awarded contracts for between two and five submarines to any given firm. By 1916 German industry required only four to seven months to produce the boats awarded under a single contract.[25] The shipyards managed to quicken this pace by the end of the year, although the drain of skilled labor to the front occasionally forced production slowdowns. As early as 1915 some private yards requested time extensions of between two and five months.[26] In one case, Blohm und Voss informed the U-Boat Inspectorate that it needed approximately two hundred workers, skilled and unskilled, to complete each boat. When there were not enough workers, the Hamburg-based firm complained that it could not meet its deadlines. The RMA always insisted that the workers could be found and demanded that the firms meet their delivery dates.[27]

By 1915, the navy drafted additional shipyards to fill the pressing need for more boats, but acceleration began to take its toll. Reiherstieg and Bremer Vulcan joined Weser, Vulcan, Schichau, Blohm und Voss, Howaldtswerke, Germaniawerft, and the Danzig Imperial Shipyard in the production effort. Because these companies manufactured no less than six different types of U-boats on a tight schedule, the significance of any production difficulty increased according to time pressures.[28] In one case complications slowed the adoption of a new oil bunker necessary for submarine minelayers. The RMA also had to consider that Weser, Blohm und Voss, and Schichau were also constructing surface ships. In addition, Howaldtswerke's conversion of a portion of its torpedo boat plant to the manufacture of U-boats took far longer than the RMA anticipated. Occasionally transportation and delivery errors consumed even more precious time. In one instance, two MAN diesels destined for the imperial yard at Danzig ended up in Austria.[29] In yet another tangle, MAN's perfection of a four-stroke, 1,200-horsepower diesel engine was delayed until April 1916, further limiting production capability before that date.[30] A possible electric motor storage battery monopoly by MAN came under discussion during Reichstag Budget Commission hearings that same month. The RMA and its suppliers operated with surprising efficiency despite numerous handicaps. Monthly reports from the RMA Purchasing Office reflected general satisfaction with the finished products in spite of the significant problems caused by accelerated production.[31]

Portents of a critical domestic raw material shortage during this period led German business to seek an answer in submarine technology. The idea of using commercial transport U-boats to circumvent the British blockade originated with a prominent Bremen businessman, Alfred Lohmann. He received 2 million marks in initial financial backing from the Deutsche Bank and the North German Lloyd before communicating with the RMA in October 1915. Ten months later, the Krupp firm received a contract to build three submarine freighters, often called U-cruisers. Germaniawerft delivered all three, designated the U-139 to 141, in six months, qualifying to build six more. Krupp took the initial contract because it offered the RMA a deal that Essen's prime competitor, AG Weser, could not match. Krupp feared the growing shortages of certain metals used in the production of its armor, especially nickel. In exchange for a guarantee from the navy that priority would be given to Krupp orders for nickel and other vital metals, the Germaniawerft produced the first three U-cruisers at no cost to the navy.[32] In 1916, the two successful voyages to North America by the first of these vessels, the *Deutschland* (later called the U-155), brought the Imperial Navy a great deal of popular acclaim as well as modest amounts of raw materials. Krupp also had a minor form of insurance against a total absence of certain essential metals as long as these commercial U-boats remained successful.[33]

As it turned out, the historic transatlantic commercial operations of the *Deutschland* and her sister the *Bremen* did not provide the anti-blockade insurance sought by Germany's military and industrial leaders. The first of the *Deutschland*'s two trips to the United States placed her in Baltimore on 10 July. The *Bremen* was less fortunate. She vanished at sea on her maiden voyage without any indication of the cause.[34] This disaster and the limited capacity of these vessels combined to retard the commercial career of the U-boat during World War I. In all, seven of these boats saw service in the Imperial Navy. When it became clear that their commercial value was limited, the RMA converted them for offensive operations, and they served as the U-151 to 157 in the unrestricted submarine campaign.

The cost of producing these different types of submarines increased dramatically during the war. According to a report by Admiral Harald Dähnhardt's RMA Budget Department, U-boat prices rose 20 to 23 percent between 1912–13 and 1915. The admiral listed manifold reasons for this leap. When the demand for these boats increased, the yards initiated twenty-four-hour shifts as well as work on Sunday, prompting a call for higher wages, which did not reduce the cost of construction. The RMA also noted the scarcity of raw materials, and Dahnhardt assumed that most naval vendors would insist upon maximum profits.[35] He fully expected prices to go higher as the war exacerbated these shortages as well as conflicts between labor and management.

The scarcity of labor first became a major issue in the spring of 1915, when the army drafted approximately 10,000 skilled naval workers. The effect of this loss of men varied from firm to firm. In one case, Blohm und Voss lost only 100 U-boat workers, but the Germaniawerft and AG Weser lost 600 skilled workers at about the same time.[36] At the time of the acceleration of U-boat production at the beginning of 1916 and the introduction of the Hindenburg Program in August, however, the Blohm und Voss U-boat work force dropped sharply to 690. The ill-considered policy of randomly drafting shipyard workers reflected the high priority given to the army and a poor appreciation by the OHL leadership that these people were vital to the navy's war effort. Von Hindenburg and Ludendorff wanted the U-boat war at sea to complement their total effort on land but failed to address the critical labor problem at the shipyards.

The detrimental effect of these actions by the army became immediately apparent when firms were unable to meet their contract dead-

lines. Many subcontractors operated with 22 to 32 percent fewer
workers than normal.[37] The managers of MAN seriously questioned
whether they could reduce the time required to produce diesels for the
navy's U-boats in 1915 because of the shortage of skilled craftsmen.[38]
According to the Körting firm, the primary liability hampering quicker
production of its U-boat engines was labor: "We reiterate that the completion of U-boat motors is, for us, a question of personnel.[39]

This dilemma led to an agreement between the RMA and the command of the Ninth Army Corps that brought skilled workers back to the
yards and factories. The RMA gave as the primary reason for its request the customary annual period of major capital ship repairs. When
the army leadership acceded to the navy's plan, the RMA managed to
retrieve a good many of its U-boat workers while also improving the
general quality of the labor it received in terms of youth and fitness.
Unfortunately, the navy could not hand-pick the men returned from the
front so their technical skills did not improve with their numbers.
Moreover, the workers were available for only a short period of time.
The army usually insisted on their return by the end of August each
year.

Fortunately for the RMA, a further compromise allowed the men to
return to the front in stages. Between September and December 1916,
for example, the army expected the return of seven thousand men in
four stages. Many of these men escaped immediate reassignment when
the RMA construction inspectors at the shipyards judiciously delayed
the process of their reclamation. By postponing official approval of certain repair projects, the inspectors could keep a worker at his shipyard
or factory for extra weeks. These delays reduced the backward flow of
workers to a mere 50 to 100 men per week rather than the planned 250.
According to Hermann Blohm (Blohm und Voss) and Director Wall-
ritz (Vulcan), these schemes barely made their contract deadlines
possible.[40]

About one-third of the total U-boat work force, numbering forty-one
thousand by the spring of 1916, returned from the front by this special
arrangement. The RMA already had the rest of the workers in place,
supplemented by one thousand British, French, and Russian prisoners
of war and another thousand neutral or sympathetic foreigners, along
with thirty-two hundred women. Permanent transfers from the army
were occasionally made possible by emergency circumstances, but this

was done only for the imperial yards (for example, Wilhelmshaven had a 59 percent increase in number of personnel), the Torpedowerkstatte (47 percent increase), and a few private firms such as Blohm und Voss and Schichau.[41]

When the army penetrated into Belgium, the navy's U-boat construction program took advantage of labor and facilities beyond Germany's borders. The RMA and its vendors moved into industrial plants seized in the initially successful Schlieffen Plan and quickly classified Brugge and Ostende in Flanders as imperial shipyards with responsibility for assembling, testing, and repairing submarines.[42] A note written by Admiral Albert Hopman of the RMA mentioned the assembly of at least six and perhaps as many as nine UB boats as an early goal for the Flanders area.[43] The RMA also planned to station a U-boat purchasing office there, as well as a home base for submarine shakedown cruises. In addition, Antwerp acquired the title of imperial shipyard in RMA correspondence by early spring of 1915,[44] and the navy earmarked a full U-boat flotilla for occupied Belgium in January 1915.[45]

Private industry also exploited foreign resources in the process of building U-boats during the war. Krupp approached firms in both occupied Holland and neutral Sweden, as had Blohm und Voss and AG Weser. Weser designs went into production under license at Malmo and Karlsruhe in Sweden, and Vulcan of Hamburg later became active in Holland. Although Krupp had little success in Sweden, where it hoped to imitate Weser, the Maatschappig voer ships in Werkturgbouw "Tejenoord" in Rotterdam did cooperate in building fast cruisers.[46] Krupp also worked with the Turks at the behest of State Secretary von Capelle. Germaniawerft contracted to build twelve torpedo boats and twelve U-boats for the Ottoman Empire, and von Capelle felt confident that this eleven-month project would not significantly interfere with production for the German fleet.[47]

Krupp also benefited considerably from RMA efforts to support Germany's primary ally, Austria-Hungary. The Germaniawerft worked with the AG Danubius Stabilimento Tecnico on U-boat designs and production. This yard manufactured Krupp U-boats in cooperation with the Imperial and Royal Navy. Buschfeld, the director of Danubius, and Arthur Krupp, the owner of the Berndorfer Metallwarenfabrik and a nephew of Alfred Krupp, together directed this branch of Essen's U-boat activities.[48]

The Protocol System

The RMA now clung tighter than ever to the system for production that had served it so well in the past, neither changing nor relaxing the regulations. If anything, its supervision and control tightened in certain areas. The RMA leaders felt that regulations and experience had clearly defined the navy's financial responsibilities to wartime contractors. In a typical case pertaining to torpedo boats in 1916, Admiral Dähnhardt's RMA Budget Department restricted its financial obligations on any project to the price of labor and materials, 100 percent of the administrative and technical supervisory costs, plus 10 percent for marginal profit. [49] Naval leaders felt that the clear conditions governing their relationship with industry had become a formidable ally.

At other important points in the system the RMA reiterated its prewar policies. The construction inspector had ultimate authority at the yard. He composed the official estimates regarding labor needs, work time, and the capacity of each shipyard. This brought moans from the private yards over both scarce labor and contract deadlines. The firms contended, sometimes correctly, that the optimistic RMA inspectors tended to underestimate industrial needs in order to satisfy the RMA's expectations in the face of limited resources. The RMA kept well informed in every case because the protocol system obliged each yard inspector to transmit industrial concerns to naval headquarters in Berlin. Von Tirpitz felt that even with the effect of the draft on the work force, each yard could take realistic emergency measures to maintain production at three-fourths of the prewar level. [50] This policy frequently forced the RMA to defend its administrators against recalcitrant firms. [51]

The RMA rarely granted exceptions to the shipyards in cases of conflict with protocol system regulations. Only firms appearing on the suppliers' list were used for wartime construction. Thus removal from the list had an even greater effect as a control device for the RMA after August 1914 because no company wanted to risk losing the profits promised by the war.

Early in the construction of the SMS *Bayern* in 1916, a Construction Department officer praised the RMA on-site inspection system for finding defects in the ship's electrical system. [52] Early detection of flaws through careful inspection and skillful use of the suppliers' list ensured that the quality control desired by the officers under von Capelle's command remained a vital asset in the RMA's supervision of the building process.[53] Firms were either denied a place on the suppliers' list if their products were substandard or were investigated and risked losing their listing if the quality of their merchandise declined. In a familiar scenario, Howaldtswerke sought an alternative vendor for heating and ventilation on the SMS *Bayern* because its preferred supplier, C. August Schmidt and Son of Hamburg, no longer appeared on the list for the services in question.[54]

Unfortunately for business, the RMA's wartime regulations threatened to curtail the exploitation of foreign markets by naval contractors. With rare exceptions, the navy demanded that its firms use domestic subcontractors. These restrictions prohibited deals with companies based in neutral countries.[55] Submarines, however, qualified as one of the rare exceptions because of their high priority. In nearly every other case the RMA investigated German companies that relied on unauthorized foreign resources in any way.[56]

The worst consequence of this policy was the loss of prewar world markets to foreign competition. In 1915, for example, MAN complained to von Tirpitz when it could not install diesels in U-boats purchased by the Dutch, even though these engines predated the wartime business restrictions announced on 29 December 1914. When naval regulations caused private firms to violate their contracts, their international business could be permanently damaged. In the case of MAN, the RMA later permitted the installation of these diesels because the transaction took place before the December decree, but only after MAN gave assurances that the Dutch construction inspector was not a spy.[57]

Industrial grievances usually took the form of letters arguing against the frequently shifting construction priorities. The RMA felt that the war dictated its priorities, and industry insisted that shifting from capital ships to much smaller vessels often required more time than the RMA allowed. Patent problems and design changes continued to cause similar difficulties, and many of these grew worse as the RMA followed the army's lead toward total mobilization and the volume of orders rose while allotted production time fell.[58]

The Protocol System and the Purchasing Office

The RMA Abnahmeamt (ABA, the KII section of the RMA) or Purchasing Office and its functions remain a virtually unexplored area in studies of naval mobilization in World War I. If accelerated production presented other naval departments with unwelcome adjustment problems, the ABA nearly perished in the avalanche of requests to test and approve items manufactured for the navy after August 1914. From its central offices at Graf Adolfstrasse 531 in Düsseldorf, the ABA assumed responsibility for the integrity and reliability of all goods ordered by the RMA from private firms.

It went about fulfilling this task in a variety of ways. Some central locations became testing centers for certain types of marine equipment. The Research Center for Shipbuilding in Berlin served the RMA in this capacity for many years before the war began.[59] Occasionally this private facility also provided a testing ground for German private industry and the Swedish navy, as well as the commercial vessels and warships of the Italian fleet. Central testing centers at Kiel and Wilhelmshaven served basically the same purpose. Kiel became a second headquarters for the ABA, and the RMA used the facilities of the imperial yard at Wilhelmshaven to do minor tests, especially on some wartime U-boat prototypes.[60]

In most cases, however, testing took place at the contractor's facilities and the ABA inspectors traveled all over the Reich to observe these tests and judge the quality of naval material. During the war there developed an acute shortage of engineers, university professors, and technical experts to do this work. By 1916 the RMA Construction Department began relying more on its resident shipyard construction inspector to supervise some of the testing so as to alleviate the intense pressure placed on the small cadre at the ABA.[61] The Dockyard Department soon complained that the task required more highly qualified personnel. The Construction Department agreed but in a marginal comment on one memo rhetorically asked where these qualified personnel might be found.[62]

The ABA had little to offer the technically skilled professional who might find this work appealing. Low wages provided no incentive, and moving from site to site occupied a great deal of time. One inspector, Professor Wagenbach, complained of the time spent in transit. He mentioned one jaunt that took thirty-eight days and another of twenty-eight days just working in the vicinity of Berlin. In a plea for increased wages, he asserted that he made 60 marks more at one time working in Berlin itself without the difficulties of constantly moving about.[63]

Unfortunately, the pay, the required travel, and the high technical skills needed to perform this job efficiently kept the ABA purchasing and testing officials small in number.[64] Therefore, the authority and responsibility demanded of the individual inspector proved an extraordinary burden. Inspector Grauert, for example, took charge of the RMA work given to Siemens and Halske and some of the cable firms. His colleague Francke worked with Maffei, AEG, and Cassirer. Master naval constructor Schulthis concentrated on cable and turbine work at AEG, Siemens-Schuckertwerke, and Schiffsunion (Berlin). Paul and Ruppel also labored among the electrical contractors. These men had to test and approve the massive amount of electrical hardware produced by these firms.[65] Their colleagues all over Germany found themselves in a similar quandary.

Because the RMA insisted on thorough testing and most industrialists rushed to meet their mobilization deadlines, the ABA was caught in a tug-of-war between them. Its meager force, obliged to perform the tests required by the RMA, chafed under criticism from the industrial sector when they inevitably fell behind schedule. But because of this strict policy the material received by the RMA during the war performed well in nearly every instance.

The ABA's basic testing procedures did not change after August 1914.[66] Each purchasing inspector filed a monthly report with the ABA, which quickly fowarded the test results to the RMA in Berlin.[67] The firms usually notified the ABA when each project approached completion so the naval officials could plan their inspection tours to conserve traveling time and money. In many instances both the contractor and the shipyard requiring the product joined in requesting that the ABA expedite inspection to avoid disrupting a ship's construction schedule.[68]

Attempts to circumvent ABA procedure to save time brought a mixed reaction from the navy. In one case, AEG shipped electrical equipment directly to the yard without the required tests. The ABA inspector, Professor Francke, asked the Construction Department's KII section for clarification of the regulations in this case. He was about to journey to the Siemens-Schuckertwerke and wanted assurances that the trip had a purpose. The Construction Department replied to both Francke and Siemens-Schuckert that the AEG's action violated RMA regulations. If a shipyard requested quick shipment, the yard became the testing site and the ABA would fulfill its obligations there, but the firm had to apply for permission to take this route. KII section refused to regard this situation as normal operating procedure.[69] In rare instances the ABA allowed the resident construction inspector at the shipyard to receive materials and conduct approval tests.[70] Otherwise the ABA strictly enforced RMA regulations and repeatedly reaffirmed the importance of inspections by ABA personnel at the production site.[71]

The RMA constantly received requests to waive these regulations. As the war progressed, shipyard testing with RMA approval became more frequent to help relieve the ABA's hectic on-site inspection schedule.[72] Official pressure to produce U-boats quicker and in greater numbers presented further complications. Some firms constructing U-boats concluded that the navy's need for more boats implied the partial or total suspension of normal RMA inspection and purchasing procedures. The ABA received support from von Tirpitz and Admiral Rollmann of the Construction Department in requesting that vendors strictly adhere to the RMA protocol system.[73] Suppliers still asked for exceptions but could usually expect the same answer. Whether firms requested that they be allowed to do their own testing, ship to the yard early, or hire an independent engineering firm to examine their naval merchandise, the RMA insisted that the contract was not fulfilled until the products were approved by the ABA.[74]

The RMA's extensive records regarding major delays in ABA testing indicate that the agency was nearly overwhelmed by its many commitments. In a note sent to von Tirpitz via the resident construction inspector in October 1915, the Schichau firm succinctly summarized the problems resulting from the shortage of ABA personnel and wartime demands. Focusing on the construction of Ms-type U-boats, Schichau complained of three launching delays and hundreds of idle yard workers all wasting time, space, and money.[75]

Production costs also rose because Schichau's subcontractor had to abide by standards made stricter by the war. For example, in April 1915, the yard's pipe supplier had to meet revised galvanizing standards set after the fabrication of its product when a delayed ABA inspection postponed delivery beyond the effective date for the new requirements. The yard saw this situation as particularly odd because it earnestly wanted to stay on schedule.[76] Another company, Mix and Genest, accused the RMA of giving preferential treatment to the imperial shipyards and their vendors.[77] As we have seen, this practice was RMA policy long before the war, but in this context it precipitated revealing expressions of the wartime pressure and frustration felt by private firms.

By the fall of 1916, the ABA stepped up the pace of its inspection tours by allowing purchasing officials to transmit their reports by telephone. At one point the average wait for a visit from an ABA inspector fell to between one and two weeks.[78] Just when it appeared as if the surge of demand created by mobilization had slowed, the introduction of the Hindenburg Program foiled the Purchasing Office's attempts to keep pace with the navy's suppliers.

Raw Materials Distribution: Iron and Steel

On 1 November 1916 a royal decree granted the War Office, under the direction of Lieutenant General Wilhelm Groener, the authority to absorb all official procurement and disbursement agencies governing war materials and labor. Formerly a part of the old Prussian War Ministry, the War Office immediately drew the Section for Exemption Questions (Abteilung für Zurückstellungswesen or AZS), KRA, and WUMBA into a single unified administration under the control of the OHL.[79] The War Office also controlled the Clothing Procurement Agency (BBA), Imports and Exports Section (A8), and Food Section (B6) and eventually centralized every aspect of procurement and distribution until the political downfall of General Groener on 16 August 1917.[80]

Metal shortages gave the RMA its greatest difficulties in wartime materials procurement. Kriegsmetall AG (KMA) represented the entire metals industry with particular emphasis on the rights of the smaller private producers, whereas Eisenzentrale GmbH directed the interests of a few industrial giants. Both of these organizations exercised considerable influence over iron and steel imports as well as the regulation of domestic production. Neither presented the RMA with any true insurance against a scarcity of iron, nickel, steel, tin, or copper. Fischer, Eisenzentrale's director, and its more influential members, Emil Kirdorf, Peter Klöckner, Gustav Krupp von Bohlen und Halbach, Carl Röchling, Hugo Stinnes, and Fritz Thyssen, had always given the RMA considerable trouble in dealing with the metals industry. With a new national investment of 470 million marks to promote the exploitation of raw materials during the Hindenburg Program,[81] and in spite of the army's control over this effort, success depended more than ever on the goodwill of these leading industrialists and their interest groups. The military was completely dependent on them.

The RMA's directives regarding metal purchasing during the critical year 1916 offered a variety of procurement options for industry. In April of that year the navy encouraged its vendors to apply very early to the Prussian War Ministry for bulk orders to sustain their efforts for one or two months,[82] only to change course in October and direct suppliers to support the KMA and the customary procurement methods. They had to use an M36 form, filed three months in advance, to get the needed materials.[83]

Germany's need for metals to wage war and its landlocked, blockaded condition led to critical shortages and delivery delays by the spring of 1916. Schichau pleaded with the RMA in March 1916 to use its influence on behalf of C. G. Haubold, Jr., GmbH (Chemnitz) for the release of 3,500 kilograms of copper needed to finish an ammunition room cooling system on the SMS *Baden*.[84] In another case, Krupp used untested metals in turbine steel because of a lack of nickel, and the diminished operational safety margin precipitated a storm of protest from the yards.[85]

Scarcity forced the War Office to ration certain metals by mid-1916.[86] This move prompted Krupp to build U-cruisers without payment if the RMA would use these vessels to import nickel for him from abroad.[87] The metal shortage even induced the RMA to allow vendors already on the suppliers' list to expand their services to the navy in other categories within a very short time frame if this would alleviate the emergency condition.[88]

The leaders of the armed forces shielded the U-boat program from the full force of the metal shortage, hoping that the submarine would favorably affect the course of the war, but the torpedo boat and cruiser programs did not emerge unscathed.[89] A lack of nickel for deck armor and a paucity of copper and tin pushed construction deadlines further back, while intense and widespread demand complicated and slowed disbursement.[90]

The RMA resorted to the very few extraordinary measures available to combat the shortages. A wholesale search commenced for any metal (*Sparmetall*) that might substitute for some of the scarcer varieties. Indeed, official requisition forms demanded a thorough investigation into the availability of alternative metals before any allocation was granted.[91] The exploitation of any foreign markets and investments still open to Germany provided the navy's only other option. The RMA seized ships and parts previously committed to foreign construction projects once the war commenced.[92] It also tried to get neutral countries such as Switzerland and the United States to reduce their metal sales to the Entente powers, but these efforts met with little success.[93] Sweden's decision to grant Germany credits to purchase iron ore constituted the only star in the RMA's foreign constellation. Between 1915 and 1918, the German war effort consumed 17,005,428 tons of Swedish ore, which helped the RMA support its U-boat program and fulfill its few commitments to builders of surface craft.[94]

Wartime Prices

The desire to profit from the war had a dramatic effect on prices. The cost of all wages and materials rose, even for the private commercial ship companies like HAPAG and North German Lloyd. Between the beginning of the war and the end of 1916 steel prices climbed 10 to 15 percent. Nickel prices leaped 8 percent in 1914 and then rose another 42 percent by June 1915. Firearms, powder, and torpedoes (produced by Schwartzkopf [Berlin] and Whitehead & Co. [Fiume]) increased 10 to 20 percent. Many naval essentials followed suit, including telegraphic systems (15 percent), gasoline (100 percent), lubricating oil (19 to 45 percent), nautical instruments (6 to 30 percent), and optical instruments produced by Zeiss (10 percent). Costs in shipyard operations rose correspondingly, with Schichau, for example, reporting a general 5 percent increase in 1916. But even though doing business with the RMA became more expensive, the larger vendors still showed an average profit of 10 percent. Thus in most cases the prices the navy paid offset the increased overhead.[95]

The RMA warned its vendors in August 1914 that peacetime prices should prevail, but it had little practical control because of wartime imperatives.[96] The Kriegsmetall and Eisenzentrale organizations set fixed prices for various grades of metal in every variety (see Appendix A, Table 5).[97] The navy found this practice nearly impossible to curb. During 1915 and 1916, for example, Krupp collaborated without RMA approval in setting prices for MAN diesel engines installed at the Germania shipyard in Kiel. At times, private firms even determined the price of replacement parts.[98]

The pressing need and lack of sufficient authority or influence often forced the navy to pay progressively higher prices, compounding the effect of the wartime currency inflation. Indeed, on 12 July 1917, Captain Richard Merton of General Wilhelm Groener's War Office Staff released a report entitled "Memorandum on the Necessity of State Intervention to Regulate Profits and Wages." Merton echoed the feelings of his superior by suggesting that pure avarice on the part of industry and labor promoted a wage-price spiral that tended to retard an effective war effort.

Merton had also observed that domestic raw materials producers took advantage of predictable shortages to extract the highest price Germany's wartime market could bear, and their industrial customers, in turn, passed on increased costs to the army and navy. Groener's support of Merton's memo played a large part in the general's dismissal from the War Office. When he brought Merton's ideas to the attention of an unreceptive Chancellor Georg Michaelis, the latter marked the memo for no action and buried it in his files.[99] Less than one month later, in August 1917, Groener lost both his OHL support and his position at the War Office.

Regardless of these conditions and events, the RMA did not disapprove of every aspect of the price situation during the war. The cost of protective armor for the ever-increasing number of U-boats remained stable at 1,600 marks per ton for Dillinger 420 nickel steel (1,400 marks for Krupp-Germaniawerft projects) and 625 marks for low percent nickel steel (600 marks at Krupp).[100] These levels persisted while international steel prices in general rose to 240 percent over prewar levels by December 1916, with an additional 120 percent yet to come over the next seven months.[101]

The RMA, Labor, and Wages

The draft ravaged the skilled and unskilled manpower resources at both the yards and independent vendors, causing a conflict between the needs of the army for soldiers at the front and the requirements of an industrial sector faced with ever-increasing demands. Initially all of the yards suffered acute labor shortages directly attributable to conscription. The imperial yard at Wilhelmshaven declined in personnel from a 1914 high of 14,284 down to 6,749 by 6 June 1915.[102] As a result, the yard had to withdraw from or delay 641 contract obligations for naval parts and supplies. At Kiel, the Torpedo Inspectorate reported only 6,744 workers available for U-boat construction in January 1916, and of these more than 3,000 were of draftable age. Along with the potential draftees, this total work force included disabled men, laborers under eighteen years of age, foreigners, women, and prisoners of war.[103]

These basic problems of the shortage, distribution, and fluctuation of the labor force plagued the entire industry. The Howaldtswerke in Kiel fell fifty electricians short on the SMS *Bayern* project.[104] Schwartzkopff and Julius Pintsch failed to deliver torpedo parts on time because of a paucity of skilled workers. Krupp made an application to bid for skilled Austrian and Swiss craftsmen to make up the labor shortage at Germaniawerft in Kiel. The Kiel Imperial Shipyard argued in January 1915 that any shipbuilding projects required a bare minimum of 1,155 skilled workers of all sorts, and Schichau pleaded with the army to return 1,010 of its workers on 26 January to help the yard fulfill a pressing deadline. An RMA officer, reading his copy of this last request, merely placed an exclamation point next to Schichau's labor figure. Apparently, he was not sure that the firm had any prospect of success.[105]

Only those firms involved in vital U-boat work experienced any relief from this industrywide malady. In a telegram to the Admiralty Staff, General Ludendorff made it clear that the normal army draft regulations did not apply to U-boat workers.[106] The War Ministry further facilitated U-boat production by initiating a list of firms vital to the war effort at sea, which meant involvement in submarine work. Among those appearing on the list, Germania, Schichau, and six others built the boats and firms such as MAN, Körting, Benz und Cie, Westfälische

Stahlwerke, and Daimler Motoren-Gesellschaft manufactured engines and parts in a supporting role.[107]

In spite of Ludendorff's concession to the U-boats and the efforts of the War Ministry and the War Office, the labor shortage evolved into a perpetual tug-of-war between the army and industry with the workers and the RMA caught in the middle. By early 1916, firms began resorting to extreme measures to keep their people on the job. Although obligated to return repatriated workers periodically to army service, Krupp Germania began to hold some of these men against the army's wishes, supplementing them with prisoners of war, recuperating wounded, and naval personnel to fulfill contracts on time.[108] The Vulcan shipyard went so far as to invoke paragraph nine of the Auxiliary Service Law, which threatened a worker with front-line service if he sought higher pay or a position change. The War Office ignored some of these unsavory techniques because they helped increase U-boat output and brought a small degree of stability to the shipbuilding work force.[109]

By 1915 each army corps had organized a Fabrikenabteilung, or Factories Department, which supplied industry with labor from the front on the approval of the War Ministry and in response to specific requests from the RMA or individual companies. The men released by the army corps received the title *Dispositionsurlaüber* and returned to their jobs for a specific period of time. In one typical case the Ninth Army Corps released men for service at the Germania shipyard between 30 June and 31 August 1915.[110]

The main criteria used by the army in these situations centered around need, the value of the firm's output to the war effort, and the likelihood of industrial cooperation. Of course, no firms could obtain *Dispositionsurlaüber* for private projects not related to war production. The army combined a company's past record of product quality and reliability with the opinions of the resident naval inspectors at the shipyards to make decisions on labor rationing.[111] Only a critical need for labor would bring emergency replacements, and then they usually came from garrison troops and not the front line.

After acquiring soldiers on loan, each yard had to account not only for the presence of each man but for his work hours, the cost of his residence and food, and his pay per hour. The shipyard inspectors sent the workers' total pay figures to the RMA.[112] Even with these constrictions most firms managed to keep enough people to complete their tasks. But the shortage placed a severe strain on German industry and its labor force. Both those at the front line and the repatriated workers were uncertain as to their disposition from month to month.

By 1915, the RMA's two construction divisions solved part of the war's labor scarcity problem. These divisions consisted of recalled skilled workers and naval personnel who could quickly fill a pressing labor need at one of the factories or shipyards. Each of these divisions consisted of twelve companies of 250 men each. The imperial yards at Kiel and Wilhelmshaven housed and fed these 6,000 men, who could barely keep pace with the demands placed on their time. This concept emanated from RMA–War Ministry cooperation with the aid of the resident yard inspectors.[113] Over half of the construction divisions' personnel filled vacancies in the labor force of the private shipyards by March 1915. Two months later another 177 of their personnel were working on U-boat projects in occupied Antwerp.

Naturally, the already formidable demands on meager labor resources intensified in spite of this welcome aid. A report compiled in spring 1915 by the General Administrative Division of the RMA stated that of all the yards, only the imperial shipyard at Wilhelmshaven and the Torpedowerkstatt in Friedrichsort had surplus labor: 4 extra men at the former, 16 at the latter. A select number of yards and firms cited in the report needed another 2,489 workers to make up a required skilled work force of 11,610. These figures covered only some of the companies involved with final vessel assembly, never touching the needs of those firms appearing on the remaining pages of the wartime naval suppliers' list.[114] As the war progressed, the effort to meet and satisfy the need for skilled labor at many different locations and in ever-changing quantities began to seem like trying to cope with an old leaking roof during a torrential rain. Once one leak was plugged, another opened, and there was no relief in sight.

Shortages of labor and raw materials threatened the firms' effective performance. AG Weser's work force fell considerably below 6,000 in 1915 as compared with nearly 7,000 before the war began.[115] From Essen, Gustav Krupp von Bohlen und Halbach wrote to von Tirpitz on 8 June 1915 in near panic. After pleading for relief from a drop in raw materials supplies estimated at between 30 and 50 percent, he asked von Tirpitz to intercede with the OHL to release greater numbers of workers from the front. Krupp sought to restore his firm to the estimated 750,000 workers needed at Essen and Kiel to fulfill his contracts with the army and RMA.[116]

German industry now began calling upon women to help in the war labor emergency. Their numbers were still small, but it became increasingly obvious that the war would interrupt the traditional domestic life of the German female. In 1915, the Siemens-Schuckertwerke employed 216 women out of 1,237 workers on its U-boat projects.[117] Only 83 out of 1,272 workers at the Durener Metallwerken were women, but the Army Logistics Office in Berlin expected this number, along with prisoner of war volunteers, to rise in the days ahead.[118] Many more women appeared at the imperial shipyards, and their numbers increased rapidly. RMA Budget Office statistics for 1916 clearly show a dramatic increase in female labor in the war effort (see Appendix A, Table 6).[119]

At the same time, the RMA sought volunteers from the ranks of the war prisoners and encouraged its suppliers to look there for willing laborers.[120] AG Weser openly recruited prisoners for its payroll by July 1915, and prisoners appeared at the facilities of Vulcan, Germania, and Howaldtswerke by October.[121] Depending on the number of prisoners employed by the factory or yard the hourly pay ranged from 1.30 marks to 1.50 marks. The firm paid 25 percent of the salary, the state the rest.[122] Initially these laborers were not allowed to work on sensitive projects such as the U-boat, but when clearance for them to do so came in September 1915, the small number of volunteer prisoners never fulfilled even a fraction of the navy's expectations. There were too many skills to replace in too short a time. No quick answer was found for a perpetual problem that nearly defied solution.[123]

Although wages increased in various war industries, for the most part a worker either preserved prewar standards of comfort or saw them decline. Many unions and workers' associations agreed to support the war by joining the spirit of the Burgfrieden (Truce of the Fortress), but by 1915 this political truce to facilitate patriotic unity had decayed.[124] The men and women worked under terrific wartime pressures and demands with a bare minimum of leisure time and an increasing shortage of food and provisions.[125] In July 1915, a Berlin doctor protested the absence of vacations and sufficient rest, and workers in Essen held a massive street parade to complain about food scarcity.[126] The roots of the strikes and unrest that occurred in 1917 existed a full two years before the actual walkouts.

As death and destruction became rampant during 1915 and 1916, a frantic need to keep pace with the war's demands descended upon the RMA and its industrial support. With the decision to employ the U-boat to assault Britain, planning priorities shifted quickly away from capital ships to the submarine. Unfortunately, the RMA unrealistically expected to atone for a decade of virtually ignoring this weapon in less than two years.

In addition, the inflated expectations of the army's Hindenburg Program placed the navy and the armaments industry in an impossible position. The RMA could not provide the U-boats necessary to blockade Great Britain, challenge the Grand Fleet, and satisfy the army's new armaments goals. Although Admiral Eduard von Capelle essentially discarded von Tirpitz's shipbuilding program and shifted his priorities to the U-boat, he initially refused to terminate capital ship construction. In the face of a nearly exclusive demand for submarines from influential political and military leaders, the RMA's resources were momentarily split among U-boats, battleships, and cruisers in the name of a better-balanced force.

The debilitating shortage of labor during this period reflected the realities of war. Von Hindenburg and Ludendorff did not realistically evaluate the labor problem at the shipyards and factories which slowed the navy's response to the fantastic demands of the OHL's mobilization program. Only the RMA's machinations and tenuous temporary arrangements with the army for the release of workers from the front allowed the naval armaments firms to attempt on-time delivery. Then, when the ships and parts lay finished and ready for inspection by the RMA Purchasing Office, the shortage of qualified inspectors created frustrating delays for both the navy and private industry.

Indeed, the war created great strains for German industry. Only a few companies could exert some control over essential raw materials without depending completely upon the KMA and the War Office, yet the substantial profit promised by wartime demand inexorably drew industry into this uncertain market. As Gerald Feldman has pointed out, "Shortages and high demand placed a premium on maximum production and insured high prices."[127] Thus, in spite of the high overhead and considerable risk, the prices commanded by German industry allowed the alluring profits to continue flowing. Furthermore, the opportunity created by the need for more submarines encouraged German private industry to extend its activities into the occupied Low

Countries in cooperation with local shipbuilding firms. In spite of the possible advantages, however, even the monopoly companies and the large industrial associations could not comfortably control resources and prices in this environment. War was costly, hectic, demanding, and full of anxiety, but immensely profitable.

8

The Unexpected End

1917 – 1918

In 1917, all appearance of reality and rationality seemed to disappear. One by one, the last few German leaders who kept a tenuous grip on the progress of the war fell by the wayside, defeated by the ambition of excessive nationalism and blind hope.

The political machinations of both the government and the military reflected this sense of unreality throughout 1917–18. In the wake of the decision on 1 February 1917 to restore the policy of unrestricted submarine warfare, the OHL managed to force Chancellor von Bethmann-Hollweg from office on 13 July. General Groener's advocacy of effective wage and price controls lost him his position in the War Office on 16 August. As Gerald Feldman has indicated, both von Bethmann-Hollweg and Groener "were victims of the OHL" because they opposed de facto military control of German policy and the wanton exploitation of vital manpower and natural resources for profit by business leaders.[1]

In contrast, the believers in final victory flourished. Admiral von Tirpitz shot journalistic and vocal barbs at the departing von Bethmann-Hollweg government from the relative safety of retirement and the comfortable political environment of the Fatherland party, with the assistance of press organs dominated by heavy industry.[2] The RMA, under von Capelle, Behncke, and Ritter von Mann supported the old state secretary by trying its best to censor his critics, especially Galster and Persius.[3] In this effort, the RMA met with mixed success, especially in the case of Lothar Persius. He continued to contribute articles critical of von Tirpitz and his legacy to the *Berliner Tageblatt* and published his caustic *Tirpitz Legende* in the spring of 1918.[4]

A far more important force that the RMA could not control was the Centrist leader Matthias Erzberger. During July 1917 he launched an attack on the navy's unrestricted U-boat policy as a preliminary to his eventually successful campaign for a Reichstag Peace Resolution.[5] Naturally, the ideas expressed by Erzberger in the Reichstag and through the press, especially in the Centrist vehicle *Germania*, greatly disturbed the RMA.[6] State Secretary von Capelle vigorously rejected Erzberger's suggestion that the German war effort was deteriorating rapidly. He also feared that initiating far-reaching reforms to address the serious food shortage and equal suffrage issues raised by the political center and left would only facilitate the radicalization of the workers who were so valuable to the war effort. Thus von Capelle saw Erzberger as a threat and suggested that the Imperial Justice Office initiate proceedings against him. Possible charges suggested by the state secretary included treason or violations of war secrets because of the details regarding the U-boat fleet revealed in the Reichstag debates.[7] When no official action materialized, von Capelle charged Captain Karl Boy-Ed of the RMA News Bureau with keeping Erzberger's journalistic exploits under surveillance and reporting the general sense of his articles to the appropriate RMA departments.[8]

The Scheer Program

In September 1918 the Seekriegsleitung, or Naval High Command, embarked on a program characterized by Admiral Reinhard Scheer as "a twelfth hour attempt to save everything."[9] This effort was an expression of the German Imperial Navy's new, post-Jutland strategic formula and an ambitious experiment in the total mobilization of the submarine industry.

The Scheer Program, formulated by Admiral Scheer, head of the SKL, Vice-Admiral Ernst Ritter von Mann, director of the U-Boat Office of the Naval High Command, and industrialist Hugo Stinnes, called for a substantial increase in U-boat production. Commencing in October 1918 with a twelve- to fourteen-month takeoff phase, Scheer's plans envisioned an increase in average monthly production from 16 boats at the end of the fourth quarter of 1918 to 36 by December 1919. The program's designers anticipated the construction of up to 450 U-boats of various types. [10]

This scheme had a dubious quality about it. It would seem unlikely that after four years of war and near military and economic exhaustion, any German leader would seriously propose such an ambitious program. These fantastic plans and the importance placed by the SKL on their psychological effect have led historians such as Bernd Stegemann, Wilhelm Deist, and Holger Herwig to insist that the SKL never expected the program to succeed. Rather, fully aware of the problems involved, the navy proceeded in hopes of lifting morale in the Officer Corps, while impressing friends at home and enemies abroad with the SKL's determination to continue the struggle against the Entente. [11]

Stegemann believes that the psychological lift provided by the program was the key to its role in the SKL's planning as the war drew to a close. Herwig essentially agrees, paying particular attention to the time and place chosen by the SKL for announcing its plans. Making the Scheer Program public in Cologne would enlist the aid of the known Allied spy ring in that city to attract the attention of the Entente powers. Deist goes slightly beyond the thesis offered by Stegemann and Herwig, viewing the program as a function of the reorganization of the naval leadership that created the SKL. In Deist's view, the Scheer Program allowed the navy's leaders to appear dynamic and determined, but the plan itself was mere propaganda with no basis in reality. [12]

Indeed, a determined effort to improve Germany's position, or at the very least to mislead its adversaries, would certainly give the officers of the German Imperial Navy the feeling that hard work and perseverance could make a difference, even at the twelfth hour. [13] A closer examination of the plans laid by industry and the navy between August and October 1918, however, suggests that the program went far beyond a simple psychological boost. The authors of the Scheer Program sincerely sought to build a submarine fleet that would bring Britain to its knees and the Triple Entente to the bargaining table. Never intended solely as a professional placebo, it would certainly lift morale while it concentrated Germany's remaining naval resources in one last attempt to demonstrate the effectiveness of the Imperial Navy.

Furthermore, the program had its beginning long before that critical autumn of 1918. It evolved from a process of redefining naval strategy made necessary when the conduct of the war at sea graphically demonstrated the error of Admiral Alfred von Tirpitz's prewar strategic dogma. The Battle of Jutland forced a change in basic strategy and provided a charismatic leader to fill the vacuum left by von Tirpitz's departure in 1916. Scheer's tactical success at Jutland resulted from both his own experience with commands at sea and the high quality of his officers, such as Vice-Admiral Franz Ritter von Hipper, who commanded the cruiser scouting force that first encountered Admiral Sir David Beatty's battle cruisers at 4:48 P.M. on 31 May 1916.[14] More important, Scheer's experience with this battle convinced him that a change of strategy was necessary. The navy could not continue paying the price in men and matériel required by battles like Jutland. He told the kaiser in his postbattle report that the U-boat would have to play the decisive role in humbling the British.[15]

Coming from the "victor of Jutland," this statement had deep significance for the future of both the navy and the war. For the first time since von Tirpitz's professional demise, the navy had someone who both commanded universal respect and spoke with an air of authority once attributed only to the former state secretary of the RMA. Scheer's call for a strategy based on undersea warfare did not fall on deaf ears.

Unrestricted U-boat warfare had ceased on 20 April 1916 in reaction to American outrage when the UB-29 sank the British liner *Arabic*, with a loss of American lives. Indeed, Scheer recalled his long-range patrol submarines because he questioned the value of remaining on station with a restricted hunting license. After June 1916, however, resuming U-boat warfare and accelerating construction took on a new importance.

As far back as the spring of 1915, the RMA had planned systematically to increase the number of U-boats joining the fleet. Now it was obliged to accommodate both the Admiralty's interest in greater numbers and the awesome demands of the army's Hindenburg Program. The navy's post-Jutland construction plans were based on the scheme first conceived in January 1916, which set 350 new U-boats as the minimum number needed to patrol adequately the Atlantic approaches, the English Channel, the North Sea, and the Mediterranean. As a first step, the RMA had allocated 172.4 million marks for 46 boats of various types, including the next generation of UC submarine mine-layers and the UB type, noted for its exceptional seakeeping qualities on the surface.[16]

The Admiralty complemented accelerated submarine production with a resumption of unrestricted U-boat warfare on 1 February 1917 after Scheer's advocacy of the weapon and von Holtzendorff's political efforts finally obtained the kaiser's approval for a renewed offensive to cut Britain's food imports. Thus the commercial war strategy of the Young School, executed now by the submarine rather than the cruiser, returned to help the Imperial Navy address the reality first experienced by von Pohl in 1914 and then by Scheer at Jutland.

Imitating the centralized power entrusted to the Army High Command, or OHL, a new and younger group of naval officers, driven by the tireless planning and political machinations of Rear Admiral Adolf von Trotha, chief of staff of the High Seas Fleet, now forced the reorganization of the naval leadership on the OHL model. With Scheer's blessing, this group convinced the kaiser of the need for new, more dynamic leadership. In August 1918, Admiralty Chief Henning von Holtzendorff stepped aside at the kaiser's request, State Secretary of the RMA von Capelle offered to do the same, and the promise of resignation was extorted from Admiral Karl Alexander von Müller, head of the Naval Cabinet. On 11 August, Scheer took over at the Admiralty and the next day assumed command of the new consolidated Naval High Command, or SKL. Vice-Admiral Paul Behncke became Eduard von Capelle's deputy at the RMA, and von Trotha remained in his position as chief of staff until von Müller's resignation was finally secured in November. The U-Boat Office formed the last piece of von Trotha's now completed puzzle. Created within the RMA in December 1917 to coordinate all submarine matters and led by yet another Scheer protégé, Rear Admiral Ernst Ritter von Mann, it complemented well the fact and spirit of the navy's new concentrated command structure. By 12 August 1918, Scheer had accomplished what von Tirpitz had always coveted in vain—complete control over strategy, operations, and construction.[17]

Scheer determined that the SKL's first venture should provide the navy with a sufficient number of U-boats to carry out a true undersea offensive against Britain. Although the course of the war gave Scheer's plans an unprecedented urgency, his idea was hardly revolutionary. As far back as May 1914, an adjutant in the U-Boat Inspectorate, Lieutenant Ulrich-Eberhard Blum, prepared a report for State Secretary von Tirpitz proposing the construction of 222 U-boats for a commercial war against Great Britain. Captain Andreas Michelsen, future commander of submarines, and Lieutenant Commander Herman Bauer, the High Seas Fleet's leader of submarines, strongly supported Blum, but the state secretary had not sufficiently changed his views to see such a program as a valuable new course.[18]

Indeed, the minutes of a meeting held on 3 September 1917 between State Secretary of the RMA von Capelle, Vice-Admiral Kraft of the RMA Budget Department, and Anton von Rieppel, director of MAN, suggest that behind their request to increase U-boat diesel production lay a plan to double the number of available U-boats a full year before the Scheer Program began.[19] Thus the ambition that gave birth to the 1918 submarine construction proposals had deep roots in various quarters of the navy and industry long before the circle around Scheer actually tried to implement such a plan.

In August 1918, Scheer had no lack of proposals to review for the acceleration of U-boat production. Both the Admiralty and the RMA's U-Boat Office offered similar programs. The Admiralty's evaluation of the problem, in the form of a memorandum penned by Lieutenant Commander Scheibe, engaged in an intricate analysis of Allied tonnage sunk by the navy's submarines to date. Based on an average sinking ratio per boat and projections of the amount of lost tonnage needed to endanger Britain's vital supplies, a figure of 257 new boats emerged from the mathematics as the program's goal. The U-Boat Office, following a much less complicated process, suggested that 238 new boats would suffice and presented its program as an official proposal on 15 August, entitled the "Great Construction Program."

Scheer and the SKL quickly realized that the Admiralty statistics describing the effectiveness of each submarine against the British would have little impact on the war if industry could not make the boats a reality. Therefore, the same day the great construction program was proposed, the SKL assigned the project to the RMA as the navy's traditional construction division. Then, as soon as the SKL set up shop at the kaiser's general headquarters in Spa, Belgium, on 10 September, Scheer arranged a meeting for the twelfth with coal mine owner and industrialist Hugo Stinnes.

The understanding reached at this meeting set the official pace of construction for the Scheer Program. Feeling the pressure of lost time, the navy planned to raise production in the final quarter of 1918 from 12.7 boats per month to 16. Thereafter, regular quarterly increases would place monthly production at 20 by the first quarter of 1919, 25 by the second quarter, and 30 by the third. Peak production of 36 boats per month would be reached by the fourth quarter of 1919, and the RMA was expected to sustain this level well into 1920. Scheer expected the chief of the U-Boat Office, with the close support of the state secretary of the RMA, to overcome the hurdles of scarce labor, supply, and resources involved in achieving these ambitions (see Appendix A, Table 7).[20]

Seven days later, Admiral Behncke of the RMA called a meeting in Berlin of representatives from the navy and industry to discuss the possibilities and problems of accelerating U-boat construction. Among those in attendance on 19 September were Hugo Stinnes, Anton von Rieppel, and Vice Admiral Ernst Ritter von Mann of the U-Boat Office.

The shortage of manpower quickly emerged from these discussions as the primary problem. The shipyards needed twenty to twenty-five thousand skilled U-boat workers and laborers to achieve the production goals of the Scheer Program. If the navy and industry could overcome the labor problem, the next most important task required the SKL and industry to focus on a small number of standard boat types to minimize cost, limit building time, and simplify construction. In addition, von Mann felt that industry should try to maximize its output and improve the current rate of repair. Although the industrial representatives present echoed the admiral's observations, he nervously questioned whether the shipbuilding firms and their subcontractors could stand the strain of an accelerated building program after nearly four years of war.[21]

None of the comments at this meeting surprised Admiral Paul Behncke. In his preconference notes, penned on 14 September, he pinpointed labor as the primary problem. Behncke seriously doubted whether the army would release the necessary workers, which he estimated at fifty thousand and which was considerably higher than the figure discussed on 19 September. Another vital aspect of this labor scarcity was the specific shortage of engineers. Behncke knew that the acceleration of U-boat construction required and would not succeed without these highly skilled people.[22]

At the end of the Berlin meeting, Admiral Scheer addressed the assembled naval and industrial leaders on the necessity of throwing their remaining resources and effort into the revitalized submarine program. Although his major emphasis was on taking the offensive against Britain, Scheer also stressed the need for peace and the role a new U-boat fleet could play as a possible trump card in negotiation with the Entente. As a goal he suggested that at least 127 new boats be constructed by the end of 1919.[23]

In spite of the odds against success, industrialists met with representatives of the RMA and the U-Boat Inspectorate at the Blohm und Voss shipyard on 24 September to begin implementing the Scheer Program. For some the program served as a morale booster, for others it brought Germany precious time and bargaining power, and for others it offered the possibility of huge profit. Present were spokesmen from the navy, notably Ritter von Mann, and representatives from Weser, Neptune, Atlas Works, Blohm und Voss, Bremer Vulcan, Germaniawerft (Krupp), Schichau, Seebeck, Tecklenborg, Vulcan, and the Danzig Imperial Shipyard. The estimated number of laborers needed for the construction program as projected at this conference seemed to confirm Behncke's early September estimates. The yard directors agreed on the necessity of 46,500 workers, 6,500 of which were currently in the work force. Forty thousand men would have to come from the army. After comments made by General Ludendorff and Colonel Max Bauer of the OHL on 20 September, however, Ritter von Mann knew they could expect only half this number, supplemented by monthly increases so as to avoid any major disruption in the front lines.

Beyond these guarantees, Ritter von Mann and the RMA placed the burden of executing the Scheer Program squarely on the shoulders of private industry. The challenge of finding and paying new laborers and negotiating with the unions, as well as coping with the varying quality of the workers returned from the front by the OHL, became the property of Germany's shipyards and subcontractors.[24] The RMA was initially encouraged by the increasing number of firms signing up to assume this responsibility in September and early October 1918, but the demand for scarce workers and materials persisted and threatened to overturn the best-laid plans.[25]

At a meeting at the Hotel Excelsior in Cologne on 1 October, the labor needed for the Scheer Program claimed center stage once again.

In a discussion with SKL staff officers and Colonel Max Bauer of the OHL, Scheer, Flohr (Vulcan), Zetzmann (Germaniawerft), and Nawatski (Bremer Vulcan) now projected that sixty-nine thousand workers could execute the program, and only fifteen to twenty thousand would be needed in 1918–19. Bauer stated that the OHL expected to scale down war operations by mid-November so the navy could soon expect the first installment of the workers required for the opening phase of the program.[26]

While the industry and the SKL grappled with labor scarcity, the RMA assumed responsibility for further expanding public and private facilities to satisfy Scheer's expectations. Domestically, plans for new shipyard and repair facilities met with mixed results. Earlier, in July 1918, a joint effort by Lubecker Maschinenfabrik, the Henry Koch Shipyard, and the Hanseatic Siemens-Schuckertwerke to establish a U-boat repair station came to fruition.[27] Another joint venture, this time by Guthoffnungshutte, AEG, and the Hamburg-Amerika Line, created Deutsche Werft AG in Hamburg-Finkenwarder in the same month as the Lubeck venture. Almost immediately, however, the Deutsche Werft faltered, a victim of the chronic labor shortage. Only direct entreaties by the U-Boat Office reopened the facility in the face of complaints that its staffing drew needed workers from the imperial yards and other private companies.[28]

The RMA also looked to the Austro-Hungarian shipbuilding industry to provide labor and physical plant space for the program. Austrian yards often supported German submarines patrolling the Mediterranean by providing repair and overhauling services. In October 1918, for example, a Vienna-based company overhauled the German submarine minelayer UC-53 in Trieste.[29] Other Austrian firms, such as Ganz and Company (Danubius), already worked with German firms such as Krupp to acquire spare parts or engines to keep imperial and royal U-boats in operation.[30]

Formal plans sealing the cooperation of Austrian shipbuilding companies in meeting the goals of the Scheer Program materialized in October 1918. Following a proposal made by Scheer in September, the SKL drafted three Austrian yards into the effort, matching them with German firms to assure a technically sound product. The Danubius yard (Ganz and Company) in Fiume had just expanded to a fifteen-boat capacity. Because of its frequent contact with Krupp, these two were paired. Danubius added 1,500 workers out of a peacetime force of 2,000 to the Scheer Program effort and fully expected an increase to 4,200 if it could get the labor to support its plant expansion. The yard's directors accepted the German navy's pledge to provide both technical assistance and additional skilled labor.

In Trieste, the Austria shipyard's work force of 1,030 men, depleted from 2,400 in 1914, received AG Weser's assistance, bolstered by its own dock expansion project. In addition to an affiliate engine factory in Linz producing MAN diesels under license, Austria's extant facilities allowed the simultaneous construction of four boats.

The third facility slated to participate in the program, Cantiere Navale Monfalcone, had ten boats overdue for delivery to the Imperial and Royal Navy because of damaged plant facilities. Thus the SKL quickly diverted valuable Weser technical aid originally intended for Cantiere Navale Monfalcone to the Austria yard. In addition, the Germans looked for other possible sources of assistance, including the San Rocco Shipyard in Trieste, Danubius affiliates in Pola and Fiume, and the Austro-Hungarian imperial shipyard in Pola, as well as other facilities further north in occupied Flanders. [31]

When Admiral von Capelle retired as state secretary of the RMA in October 1918, the SKL forced his deputy, Paul Behncke, to leave as well because of his conservative and occasionally skeptical attitude toward the Scheer Program. Ritter von Mann took their place at the RMA and immediately implemented economy measures to cut down the number of standard U-boat types to six, limiting each shipyard to two in an effort to streamline production as the program began. [32]

After much debate, the U-Boat Office decided to build a combination of standard types and newly developed models. The Ms, or mobilization boats, which formed the bulk of the Imperial Navy's wartime submarine fleet, would appear in two forms. The navy assigned 27 large Ms boats with a surface displacement of 1,347 tons to Blohm und Voss, AG Weser, and the imperial yard at Danzig. These boats could make eighteen knots on the surface, nine submerged, and had four torpedo tubes forward and two aft. They could carry sixteen 50-centimeter torpedoes when fully armed. The smaller Ms boats displaced between 800 and 1,000 tons and moved through the water at sixteen knots on the surface, eight or nine submerged. Later models of the smaller Ms carried from twelve to fifteen 50-centimeter torpedoes.

Contracts to build seventy-five of these vessels went to Germaniawerft, Schichau, and Bremer Vulcan.

Submarine minelayers appeared in the U-Boat Office's plans in two forms. The new, larger minelayer, project 45, carried forty-two mines of the UC200 type with thirty more in deck-mounted containers. The smaller UCIII minelayers displaced about one-third of project 45 boat's 1,175 tons, carried eighteen UC200 mines, and had one stern and two forward torpedo tubes for its seven torpedoes. Vulcan was supposed to build fifteen of the larger minelayers and AG Weser took responsibility for sixty-nine UCIIIs.

The two remaining U-boat types displayed small size, excellent handling, and a powerful punch for defensive coastal work off France, Flanders, and Germany. Vulcan and Weser collaborated on forty-three planned UBIII submarines. These vessels displaced between five and seven hundred tons and did 13.6 knots on the surface and 8 below. Four bow and one stern tube serviced ten 50-centimeter torpedoes.

The UGI, although designed slightly heavier than the average UBIII, could make 14.5 knots on the surface with its 950-horsepower diesels. The most attractive aspects of the UG type were its ability to dive to one hundred meters and its main armament of four bow and two stern tubes for twelve torpedoes. Vulcan and the smaller yards such as Tecklenborg, Neptune, and Atlas were assigned to build 101 UGs.[33]

In spite of the many formidable challenges the program presented, Ritter von Mann's task was the toughest. He had to defend the Scheer Program before the Reichstag as state secretary of the RMA and then ask for the necessary credits. Particularly since von Tirpitz's resignation and the resumption of unrestricted submarine warfare, the members of the legislature questioned the prewar naval wisdom, which had allowed Germany to build a fleet of capital ships without a significant U-boat force. In 1916 and early 1917, more of them realized the value of the submarine and the shortsightedness of von Tirpitz's prewar policies regarding U-boat technology and severely criticized and questioned the RMA chief and his successors.[34] This "historical guilt," as Wilhelm Struve (SPD, Kiel) put it, weakened the credibility of the navy and haunted Ritter von Mann when he asked the Reichstag to fund a new and ambitious project in the midst of the suffering caused by a fourth year of war.[35]

The September–October 1918 appropriations debates in the Reichstag once again revealed the Achilles' heel of the navy's proposal. Ritter von Mann valiantly defended the program and asked for funds to pay a forty- to fifty-thousand-man work force that he knew he might never find. Nonetheless, he set a four- to six-week deadline for all bids and contract awards, displaying both the determination to launch the program and his resolve to force the Reichstag to act as quickly as possible on the funding measure.

Although officially confident and optimistic, Ritter von Mann privately admitted the desperate nature of the Scheer Program, expressing some of his doubts at the Blohm und Voss meeting on 24 September. To him and many other naval officers, it was no longer a matter of winning but of surviving. To the politicians in the legislature Ritter von Mann said, "The question of whether the boats come to be before the end of 1919 plays no part now. I must build them without reminding myself that the war may end."[36] He certainly feared that the Imperial Navy's final and most decisive battle would be fought in the Reichstag chamber rather than on the North Sea.

In that confused and desperate fall of 1918, the specter of defeat touched the navy far earlier than even Ritter von Mann had expected. Chancellor Prince Max von Baden had already made peace overtures to President Woodrow Wilson on 5 October, only sixteen days after the Berlin meeting had officially launched the Scheer Program. Subsequent diplomatic negotiations, the naval mutiny in Kiel on 5 November, and revolutionary activity in Germany's major urban areas brought preparations to a sudden halt. The reality of Germany's military and economic limitations and the intense desire to end the war stifled the navy's final hope of playing a more significant role in the last days of the conflict.

Construction Outside the U-Boat Program

The demands of war brought about complete reversal of the navy's prewar construction priorities. Instead of consuming the energies of Germany's shipbuilding industry, there was barely enough labor, plant space, and funds to meet the fleet's replacement and repair needs for battleships and other surface craft. By 1917–18, what labor and money there were belonged to the U-boat, creating a shortage of appropriations and materials as well as slower construction times and higher

costs for capital ships.[37] New types were designed to shorten construction time and reduce expenditures without necessarily forsaking
speed, power, or armor protection. In a January 1918 conference with
Scheer, von Capelle, von Holtzendorff, and the construction engineer
Burkner, Kaiser Wilhelm unveiled the vessel he felt best suited the
navy's present needs and resources. This "large battleship type L 20e"
should be fast but of similiar dimensions to current types. It should
have only three 42-centimeter turrets, stronger armor in the super-
structure and deck, but no underwater broadside armor. The question
of bow and side torpedo tubes was left open. The key factor in construction was rapid completion and operational surface speed.[38] The naval
leaders desired to reduce the time between keel laying and shakedown
cruise by avoiding the expensive and time-consuming process of in-
stalling broadside armor. They hoped a ship's speed would make up for
the resulting vulnerability to torpedo attack.

Efforts by the RMA's General Naval Department to encourage Krupp
to build the experimental 42-centimeter turret advocated by the kaiser
immediately brought battleship work into conflict with U-boat priorities. When Krupp made it clear that the turret would have to wait,
von Capelle did not object too strenuously.[39] An RMA report dated
1 February 1918 indicated that capital ship work had virtually ground to
a halt. Projects under way were accelerated only to free the labor and
plant facilities for U-boat work, and the RMA delayed building of new
capital ships to focus all available resources on submarines.[40] The latter received the utmost priority in these matters because only the submarine brought the navy regular victories against the Allies.

The only large public or private expenditures made for capital ships
were for shipyard improvement and repair facilities. Admiral von Capelle asked the Reichstag in April 1917 for appropriations to alter the
three entrances to the imperial yard at Wilhelmshaven to permit modern, larger ships to pass without difficulty. At present, only one entrance was suitable. Von Capelle further proposed opening a fourth
entrance in a year or two.[41] Tecklenborg AG in Bremerhaven expanded
its facilities for repair work, as did many of the smaller yards, to include light cruisers and torpedo boats, as well as U-boats.[42]

In the navy's concerted effort to employ all the shipbuilding space
available, the smaller companies carried the extra burdens the larger
firms found impossible to bear. In March 1917, the Reiherstieg Ship-

yard (Hamburg), Oder Works (Stettin), Stulken and Son (Hamburg), and Unterweser (Bremerhaven) joined the RMA war effort. Like their Austro-Hungarian counterparts, they were paired with the major yards to gain valuable technical expertise that would allow them to increase their production quickly.[43]

Both the private and public sectors saw the need for newer, more modern shipbuilding facilities. In March 1917, the RMA began planning a massive postwar renovation and expansion of the imperial shipyards at Kiel and Wilhelmshaven and a more modest effort at Danzig. In all, it expected to spend between 40 and 50 million marks.[44] To keep in step with German ambitions abroad, Krupp and Blohm und Voss collaborated in the construction of a Turkish shipyard capable of producing dreadnoughts. The proposed construction time for the project, begun in mid-1915, was two and a half years. By completion time, a consortium of Blohm und Voss, Vulcan, Weser, Germania, and Schichau owned the facility, called the Deutsch-Osmanische Werftengesellschaft mbH., or DOW. By mutual agreement, Blohm und Voss managed the yard when it opened in 1918.[45]

As in the past, cost and weight overruns plagued construction of surface ships. The labor and material shortages caused by the war merely exacerbated a traditional prewar management dilemma.[46] Only the reduced number of capital ships under construction partially alleviated this nagging problem. With the increased pressure to build more U-boats, keeping costs down remained as difficult as it was during the von Tirpitz era.[47]

Labor, Wages, Unions, and Strikes

In 1917 the labor shortage reached epidemic proportions. The Hindenburg Program forced companies to compete for workers, not only within the private sector but with the navy as well. According to Holger Herwig, "Technicians, engineers, and shipyard labourers were being absorbed at an alarming rate by munitions and weapons factories, thereby depriving the navy of skilled personnel so desperately needed for the increased submarine production required after February 1917."[48]

In written remarks intended for the chiefs of the Naval Cabinet and Admiralty Staff, State Secretary von Capelle strongly suggested that the army had sufficient cannon fodder and that experienced technical personnel were of greater use working for the navy.[49] He knew that workers, anxious to retain their jobs at some of the smaller yards and firms, occasionally faced unemployment because an insufficient supply of specialized labor often caused production delays or the loss of a contract.[50] Thus the demands of the Scheer Program in 1918 forced the navy and the private sector to search painstakingly for any and all available labor, very often without satisfactory results.[51]

On 3 September 1917 MAN voiced its displeasure when obliged to delay diesel deliveries to AG Weser by three to four weeks because of a depleted labor force.[52] This was yet another example of the chain reaction that might ensue if those responsible for the flow of labor to the front did not consider the effect of their decisions on the naval construction industry. The RMA even employed emergency funding to initiate construction of small surface vessels at select yards with the sole purpose of keeping workers on the job and out of the army. Naval managers called these projects *pufferobjekte* or *pufferarbeit* (buffer objects or buffer work). The RMA could ill afford to lose any of its labor force from either public or private facilities. Since the buffer projects had marginal budgets and, most important, no set completion dates, these workers remained securely at their positions. Momentarily, the army could not touch them, but neither could the workers easily transfer to factories farther from the coast or in other regions of the country.[53]

In a report to the Reichstag dated 16 February 1917, the Budget Department of the RMA urged an emergency recall of technical experts from the other war services for naval use. It went on to suggest that the desperate labor situation might require special legislation.[54] Feeling the pressure of the same emergency, the War Office resorted to existing legislation to exert greater control over the movement of skilled labor. It severely limited the number of exemptions allowing a job transfer under paragraph nine of the Auxiliary Service Law. Workers who tried to leave their positions without obtaining the proper clearance ran the risk of going to the front.[55]

Even the high-priority U-boat projects confronted delays caused by labor shortages. The U-cruisers U-145 through 147, on the slipways at Vulcan, were delayed for five and six months before they saw war service.[56] Germany's leaders had finally reached the limits of their country's physical and material strength though they did not recognize that truth.

The most potent pressure to meet Germany's wartime industrial goals fell upon the workers and the unions as their representatives. They replied to this pressure with a series of strikes between January and March 1917. The iron and steel plants of the Ruhr experienced walkouts precipitated by inadequate food supplies and the inequitable distribution of available provisions. The coal mines of the same region added poor wages to the roll call of major issues. In addition, the policy of drafting dissenting workers into the army at the request of the plant owners raised the question of job security in this already dangerous occupation.

When the Berlin munition workers went on strike for increased wages and reduced hours, the significance of these events impressed General Groener at the War Office. He realized that without union support it would be impossible to control the labor force through the Auxiliary Service Law. He therefore sought and successfully obtained a rapprochement with organized labor in 1917. With War Office recognition, union membership rose dramatically. The population of the Free Trade Unions alone increased from 967,000 in 1916 to 1,107,000 in 1917.[57] But Groener's independent actions addressed only part of the problem. For example, between 1914 and 1918 take-home pay in Germany doubled while real earnings dropped by one-third.[58] The German labor force needed the government to address wages, working conditions, food, and the necessities of living. Having one man recognize the crisis did not set the country on its way toward a solution.

The general's cooperation with the unions revealed his basic understanding of wartime labor management. Other important government agencies and industrial concerns, however, reacted to the necessities of the moment rather than in concert to address fundamental problems. Immediate needs and the influence of particular industrial interests won the day. Thus the German government formed the habit of reacting to events rather than formulating realistic policies to address the underlying causes.[59]

The RMA also came under fire for not fully appreciating the financial plight of the workers as well as for alleged mismanagement, as Reichstag representative Weinhausen of the Progressive People's party pointed out during a general session of the Reichstag on 9 May 1917. He and Brandes (SPD, Halberstadt) made it clear that they appreciated labor's dilemma. Wartime wages rose only about one-half as rapidly as the cost of living, skilled workers were in short supply, and no effective wage policy existed.[60] But although they blamed the RMA for poor administration, they along with most of Germany's other political and military leaders failed to realize that even if they formulated a concerted policy to combat wage and labor problems, Germany's nearly exhausted resources placed limits on what they could accomplish. More efficient management would eliminate neither the acute shortages of labor and resources nor the detrimental industrial particularism stemming from self-interest. The RMA's hardly unique problems did not necessarily indicate mismanagement. The history of the RMA's construction program would suggest just the opposite. By this time Germany's most fundamental problem went deeper than management. As long as bringing the war to a victorious conclusion remained the government's first priority, recognition of the nation's exhaustion was unlikely, and little would change.

Predictably, the RMA's position in this naval-industrial malaise did not improve, even when the Scheer Program attempted to rationalize, streamline, and expand U-boat production at the expense of all other construction. Both Germania and the Howaldtswerke yards reported short strikes during the first two weeks of November 1918. These actions failed to improve the situation for the labor force at the yards, though, and they painfully illustrated that a solution was still quite a long way off.

In the midst of all the revolutionary turmoil of late 1918 and the kaiser's abdication on 9 November, the Howaldtswerke sent a note to the state secretary of the RMA, Ritter von Mann, informing him that the firm would pay only a much reduced token penalty rate for any days missed during the strike.[61] This tone of business as usual uncomfortably belied the political, economic, and social turmoil taking place in early November. It arouses the suspicion that many within the arms industry neither fully appreciated Germany's state of exhaustion at this point nor concerned themselves about anything beyond their own survival. Three days after the kaiser's abdication was announced, Blohm und Voss sent a telegram to the U-Boat Office in Berlin suggesting adjustments both in hourly wages and in the length of the workweek at the yards. To this firm the end of the war meant an eight-hour day and 2.30 marks per hour for all male and female workers over seventeen years of age, with no overtime and no individual contract arrangements.[62]

The Protocol System

In spite of challenges from the Reichstag, labor shortages, and often delayed U-boat construction deadlines, the RMA preserved, to a remarkable degree, its effective authority over most naval purveyors. In a special report to the RMA Construction Department, penned in February 1918, Purchasing Office Inspector Ruppel admonished the RMA never to allow its standards to falter, even with the end of the war: "It seems important to me that a demand be made from the RMA's point of view for painstaking and strict control through a dependable expert at the firm."[63] Ruppel's position was secure, for the RMA did this and much more. It still enforced 5 percent profit margins on most contracts until November 1918.[64]

A new Ship Artillery Inspectorate arose out of a perceived need to consolidate and streamline testing and inspection at all artillery centers, imperial and private.[65] The RMA even continued to exhibit its administrative agility by sidestepping a near monopoly in some areas of naval hardware during 1917 and 1918 by awarding Brown and Boveri and AEG contracts for electrical systems which habitually fell to Siemens-Schuckert.[66] The RMA also monitored relations between its two primary gun barrel manufacturers, Ehrhardt and Krupp. A vigorous prewar competition between Ehrhardt's Rheinische Metallwaren und Maschinenfabrik AG (Düsseldorf) and Krupp had ended by 1917 and their prices soon coincided, with cooperation the order of the day. Gustav Noske of the SPD urged the navy to monitor this situation, apparently unaware that the RMA always observed Krupp's activity carefully. Rear Admiral Maximilian Rogge reported to the Reichstag committee reviewing war suppliers that the two firms had thus far satisfied the navy's needs without collusion.[67]

The RMA also continued to use the suppliers' list as a potent weapon when the need arose.[68] Firms supplying substandard products, such as the condenser pipe manufactured in 1917 by Aders in Magdeburg, quickly disappeared from the list and lost substantial revenues.[69] The RMA used great care in editing the list by thoroughly screening new additions. In this way the RMA preserved not only its power of discretion in accepting or banishing companies but also a great freedom of action in regulating the business activities of the firms admitted to the list.[70]

As the war concluded, the RMA made its authority felt in matters vital to naval interests both at home and abroad. In 1917, Blohm und Voss reported that the German Steel Association (Deutsche Stahlbund, Düsseldorf) contemplated supplying gas pipelines to Swiss customers. The shipyard needed pipes of this sort to finish its light cruisers and U-boats. The RMA stepped in and blocked the deal.[71] It had broad powers in this area but not as great as those exercised, for example, by the United States Navy. If a contract or price arrangement on vital war materials did not emerge from negotiations, the Americans could appropriate the items in question for 75 percent of the appraised value. The firm could only take up its case for compensation in court.[72]

Although it could not appropriate materials, the RMA's subtle powers of coercion had usually elicited the necessary cooperation from most contractors, and it could oblige firms to conform to certain prescribed practices because of wartime necessity. In December 1917, MAN chose to challenge the contract cancellation clause in its diesel engine agreements with the RMA. Von Capelle informed MAN that under no circumstances, not even peace, could the firm, at its own discretion, stop building a navy diesel already in progess. He gave the same warning to Körting. Both vendors knew from past experience that the RMA would enforce naval regulations.[73]

The RMA's authority even extended to the sensitive issue of patent rights and obligations. In 1918, the MAN U-boat diesel engine surpassed all others. When the navy's plans to accelerate U-boat production began to take shape in mid-1918, MAN's ability to keep up with the pace of hull production came into question. The U-Boat Inspectorate (UI) decided to ensure increased diesel production by making MAN engine designs available to new companies entering the field. This action seemed sound because the best machinery available was needed for scores of new U-boats. MAN, however, disputed the RMA's authority to allow the UI to ignore private patent rights. After discussing the matter with Krupp, MAN issued a preliminary protest to the UI in March and again in May 1918.[74] Germania's director, Regenbogen, supported these protests by his counterpart at MAN, Lauster, in a note to the UI. Regenbogen recited a litany of difficulties facing Germania and MAN, including the issues most pertinent to this case, metal shortages and the sharpness and severity of the UI's demands. He felt that the armaments industry could not produce boats any faster, and violating patents to accelerate production would not help.[75] Privately, MAN and Germania did not place great expectations in their joint protest. Furthermore, Körting confirmed Lauster's suspicion that the UI would stand fast on this issue. In a letter to Regenbogen, Lauster wrote: "The Körting firm believes, as Herr Kritzler has commented to me, that the struggle against the UI on this point cannot lead to the desired ends, so it must be abandoned."[76]

The observations made by director Kritzler of Körting proved to be a good evaluation of the RMA's power and authority, especially regarding U-boat production in 1918. The UI appreciated MAN's dilemma, but operational necessity made it impossible to honor the diesel patent. If it was any consolation, the UI assured the firms that the same standards applied to all of the companies engaged in war work.[77] Ultimately, MAN and the UI met in conference at Kiel on 4 July 1918 to clarify the situation. MAN requested that if it could not deliver the desired number of diesels, it should be consulted when the UI chose an alternative firm and transferred patented information.[78] The UI rejected this request, affirming its total authority over the production of naval vessels and components.

The challenge to the RMA's authority posed by MAN and Germania seemed hopeless, not only because of the war but also because of the extreme importance of the submarine. Because the U-boat played the most vital role in Germany's war at sea, the UI's authority rose to new heights along with the importance of its particular seagoing responsibility. Even General Ludendorff, in a February 1918 memo to the staff at the General Headquarters, gave the transport of U-boat parts to the yards a higher priority than aircraft, motorized vehicles, and rolling stock containing powder and munitions.[79] The U-boats had completely turned the tables on von Tirpitz's vaunted battleships.

If the firms and the workers felt the strain of war by 1917, so did the inspectors of the RMA's Purchasing Office, who had to test and approve every job done for the RMA by shipyards and subcontractors. According to the minutes of the Purchasing Office meetings on 3 March 1917 and 17 July 1918, the building code standards covering every aspect of construction remained consistent and individual inspectors had to enforce them.[80] Exceptions to the code were rare. Between March and May 1918, for example, inspectors discovered that Brown and Boveri of Manheim had shipped electric motors to shipyards and other purveyors without proper clearance. The firm showed certain motors to the purchasing inspectors and then shipped large numbers of similar ones once the few received approval. In spite of pressure from Brown and Boveri, the RMA did not grant an exception, and all the motors had to pass inspection individually. Such cases occurred frequently, and each received the same treatment.[81] If the firms supplied technical information and on-site assistance without trying to escape the required testing, the inspectors could do more faster. When a test done by Paul resulted in a damaged engine, however, he lamented that if he had received more assistance from a company expert, he might have discovered the flawed air cooling system before the engine trial began.[82] Instead, both the RMA and its purveyor faced delays waiting for a replacement and further testing.

Throughout the war, a shortage of qualified personnel plagued the Purchasing Office. A great deal of hiring took place in 1917 and 1918,[83] but not nearly enough to keep up with the huge number of pressing wartime orders. The corps of inspectors who served through the war tried to cover for one another in an effort to satisfy all of the companies requesting shipping clearance. In rare cases an inspector's schedule kept him in a certain region, but most of the time ABA personnel traveled across Germany to conduct inspections or to cover for their hard-pressed colleagues from the Düsseldorf office.[84]

As the war progressed, the inspectors discovered that support and information from many firms became less and less trustworthy. Consequently, the RMA advised its ABA personnel and the resident supervisors at the shipyards not to depend on industrial representatives when performing their duties. Most of the inspectors thus found themselves in an isolated and difficult position.[85]

Obviously, this branch of the RMA, through no fault of its own, could not handle the avalanche of demands placed upon it. In his report for the month of December 1917, Paul pleaded for more time to do a thorough job, to avoid overlooking the particulars that often made the difference between substandard and quality.[86] These conditions disrupted the ABA's performance and morale over the next eleven months, and only the modest hiring program gave Paul a reason for hope.

The RMA supported the decisions made by these men on their endless rail trips and hundreds of inspection stops.[87] The only hint of discord was the occasional clash of authority between the resident shipyard inspectors and the traveling Purchasing Office personnel.[88] At times the yard inspectors exhibited loyalty to the firm, to their immediate superior in the person of the state secretary of the RMA, or to other organizations. In one case the Purchasing Office clashed with a construction consultant who, besides his duties for the RMA, took great care to protect the interests of the German Steel Association, of which he was a member.[89] But such confrontations were few and did not significantly affect the performance of the inspectors.

Disrupted construction schedules and work delays resulted when inspectors arrived late, or the testing process took too long, or the reports from the ABA were overdue at the RMA.[90] In an attempt to alleviate some of these difficulties, in June 1917 the ABA obliged all firms contracting with the navy to have at their facilities the machinery and instruments necessary to test their products properly.[91] Producers not able to provide the required instruments received instructions to ship their wares to a better-equipped factory or to the shipyard, where the testing would take place. This improved ABA efficiency and streamlined scheduling, but nothing short of peace could lighten the load.[92]

In spite of the RMA's sustained wartime authority via the protocol system and the indefatigable efforts of its personnel, Germany's resources could no longer satisfy the navy's needs. At a general meeting of the Purchasing Office on 2 July 1918, chief construction consultant Schulz recited a list of critically scarce raw materials, including, among others, copper, tin, nickel, rubber, and asbestos. He thought some help would come from new Russian and Ukranian sources, but not nearly enough.[93] Although pipe manufacture continued relatively uninterrupted,[94] the yards suffered a shortage of rubber for the U-boats, and the armor and electrical firms had almost become accustomed to critical metal shortages.[95] Both Krupp and Dillinger frequently made this problem very clear in notes to the RMA in Berlin.[96]

Heating and fuel oil prices rose by leaps and the RMA searched both at home and abroad for new sources. Germany drew oil from Austrian, Romanian, Belgian, and Russian stores as well as those still available at home.[97] Heating oil prices doubled between 1917 and 1918, and fuel costs increased with each passing month.[98] Foreign coal, also used for heating and for oil extraction, came to Germany from Sweden throughout the war at the rate of about 250,000 tons per year. Approximately 80,000 tons of it passed through Rotterdam. In 1917 and 1918 this

Dutch route suffered from the tightening British blockade. The Swedes felt obliged to avoid possible losses from British warships and mines and threatened to cut off the coal supplies if the Germans could not guarantee the saftey of these shipping lanes.[99]

When firms applied to the KRA for raw materials at this late date, they could hope for only partial satisfaction. The *Belegscheine*, or raw materials ration permits, issued by the KRA now rarely fulfilled a company's needs.[100] It became increasingly apparent that the war had consumed nearly everything so the RMA decided to close nonessential companies as a conservation measure.[101] Some purveyors had their material supplies cut off because the navy considered them expendable. Essential firms felt the austerity program to only a small extent and received what resources the RMA could find.[102] These resources often included workers and other factors of production stripped from unfortunate concerns that were far down on the list of priorities. The RMA also approached groups such as the Shipbuilding Steel Exchange in Essen and the German Steel Association of Düsseldorf to determine if the navy's search for useful materials had exhausted every avenue of investigation.[103]

The RMA's strict policies and the critical labor and raw materials shortages now frequently disturbed naval-industrial relations. Production difficulties increased, intensified by a mad scramble among purveyors for the available resources. The ABA inspectors and the RMA continued to expect prewar quality but in greater quantity.[104] As each day passed, lamented MAN director Lauster, production became more difficult and the RMA's enforcement of contract provisions more exacting.[105]

Demobilization

When the events of October and November 1918 brought the desperate rush of events to a halt, a very different task remained for the RMA. The transfer of the High Seas Fleet and the U-boat force to the Allies, though certainly humiliating, could not match the task of dismantling Germany's naval-industrial war machine. Others have eloquently related the former story elsewhere. This short concluding section will focus on some basic problems in coming to terms with peace.

The navy's policy during the months of demobilization rested on a single goal: survival. The German navy sought to sustain not only itself but also the industry and the shipyards it would need to rearm. Some officers immediately and characteristically began planning a "less expensive but first class" future fleet.[106] All, however, realized that only the naval armaments industry could ensure their future. Therefore, a well-managed effort to keep the naval armaments industry alive during the transition between war and peace assumed a high priority during these trying months.

To this end, a naval and private review of the shipyards took place during 1919. When the navy finished, it felt that the yards had enough work to keep them active for nearly five months past the armistice in spite of the cancellation of the Scheer Program between November 1918 and February 1919. In November, 240 out of 439 contracts were canceled. The RMA tried to occupy a minimal work force at the imperial and private shipyards with repair work and some commercial construction.[107] Although the head of the Imperial Office of Economic Demobilization technically had authority over the labor and materials as well as the yard activities, the RMA wished to ensure the navy's future by taking the initiative in these areas.[108]

In a private study, a committee of shipyard owners and administrators chaired by Georg Howaldt came to many of the same conclusions as their naval counterparts. They wanted to minimize unemployment and guarantee some work to each facility so the yards could survive financially.[109]

Some firms, however, rarely needed to worry. In 1919, Germania and Vulcan had already agreed to sell U-cruisers (type U-142) and U-boat minelayers (type U-117) to Japan. To this end, Krupp's U-boat expert, Hans Techel, left Germany and worked with the Japanese at the Kawasaki Shipyard at Kobe.[110]

Public agencies handled most of the administrative work in demobilizing the navy. The Verwertungsamt, a branch of the Treasury, became the center for settling all outstanding government debts to industry.[111] The Reich negotiated final payment and settlements between the shipyards and subcontractors after the war as well as any outstanding debts of the former imperial government to the firms employed by the navy. These settlements, once accepted, ended all obligations to the purveyors.[112]

The Imperial Office for Economic Demobilization found itself in charge of nearly every other aspect of industrial adjustment, from the disposition of surplus phosphorus imported from Sweden in the last days of the war to certain labor matters. Under Josef Köth, formerly of the KRA, it took responsibility for easing Germany's transition to a peacetime economy.[113]

The war's end completed the cycle of the RMA's rise and fall. Reaching its peak of authority under von Tirpitz in 1912, the office declined in influence under von Capelle, until the creation of the SKL pushed it into political obscurity. When the former head of the U-Boat Office, Ritter von Mann, assumed control in October 1918, it marked the final triumph of the U-boat over the battleship in German naval strategy, as well as a political victory for the Admiralty Staff over the RMA. These new circumstances, however, did not have the impact they once might have had. When Vice-Admiral Maximilian Rogge replaced Ritter von Mann and took over the remains of von Tirpitz's once-powerful office in December 1918 as leader of the RMA, the authority and prestige of the state secretary had already left Germany along with the fleeing kaiser.

The RMA overextended itself to meet wartime demands in 1917 and 1918. Creative ideas for expanding production led to new shipyards and closer integration among international firms and facilities, but the RMA could barely fulfill its inspection and administrative duties. It maintained a high standard of quality and a remarkably large output, but by 1918 even these attainments soured in the hectic and ruthless competition for scarce labor and materials. In spite of the RMA's effort and experience, the last two years of the war form a disconcerting picture of intense planning, eventually frustrated; of constant sacrifice, with only a remote hope of effect; and of selfish bargaining and infighting, all in the name of nationalism, service reputation, and corporate survival.

Conclusion

The First Phase, 1890–1914

The key to naval-industrial relations in Germany between 1890 and 1914 is Admiral Alfred von Tirpitz. He was a man of intense determination, political talent, and personal ambition. Spurred on in his construction program by the support of the kaiser and industry, von Tirpitz came to believe that his strategic viewpoint was Germany's only path to world power. He perceived officers, publicists, and politicians as friends or enemies of the navy by the degree of support or opposition they rendered.

In addition to the political triumphs of the 1898 and 1900 Naval Laws, which provided the foundation for expanding the fleet, von Tirpitz's confidence in his chosen policy was reinforced in other ways. Industry provided a great deal of support, not only because von Tirpitz commanded professional respect but also for the huge profits promised by his political and administrative talents. Wilhelm Deist's analysis of the enthusiastic response of the Naval League and other right-wing organizations clearly indicates the political energy these civilian groups generated for von Tirpitz's cause. Although the RMA frequently felt

uncomfortable with the awkward, politically clumsy activities of such organizations, they increased the state secretary's confidence in his policies.

Some of the more unpleasant aspects of von Tirpitz's behavior, however, manifested themselves in his treatment of those who offered alternatives to his ideas. The RMA chief drove von Maltzahn, Galster, and
Persius into professional obscurity because they opposed him. Later,
when the admiral's power began to falter, Galster reemerged as the theoretical mentor of von Tirpitz's strategic opponents. Only Lothar Persius consistently struck back at von Tirpitz. In 1918 he took particular
satisfaction in publishing a public condemnation of von Tirpitz's strategic ideas and his total loyalty to the battleship.

For the navy and industry, the plans initiated by von Tirpitz in the
1897–1900 period soon revealed the liabilities inherent in a new, ambitious program. The problems created by sudden acceleration of the
fleet-building program were most obvious in the hardships encountered by the Purchasing Office in its efforts to complete its technical
review of naval projects on schedule. One problem frequently caused a
multitude of others, expanding like a chain reaction, wasting time,
increasing construction costs, and often delaying the installation of
turbines, armor, and ordnance.

The protocol system became von Tirpitz's most effective weapon
in managing this process. This labyrinth of rules and regulations
governed the RMA's relationship with industry remarkably well. Von
Tirpitz did not create the system, but he broadened and perfected it,
using as his foundation the general construction guidelines and various
other regulatory devices that obliged most of the naval armaments
industry to cater to the RMA. Although not unique or ingenious, the
protocol system did provide the RMA with a way of asserting itself in
industrial relations through determination, persistence, and expert
management.

The protocol system offered the RMA many opportunities, especially through the suppliers' list, to enforce its wishes on industry.
Through its own inspectors and assisted by regional chambers of commerce, the RMA became thoroughly familiar with every company that
applied for naval work. It then had the opportunity to test all the materials and products destined for use at the shipyards, withholding approval until standards were met.

The suppliers' list did have some basic flaws. The RMA could have shown more care in grouping the firms in each category to avoid creating unfair competition. Greater discretion in assembling the list's categories and a clear indication of the relationships between companies and their affiliates would have placed the private yards in a better position to select qualified subcontractors at an advantageous price. This would have reduced direct supervision by the RMA and perhaps resulted in fewer accusations from industry about unwanted interference. Yet, ultimately, the suppliers' list proved an effective tool in an efficient system of industrial regulations.

In his supervision of the construction program, von Tirpitz allowed von Eickstedt and Rollmann a great deal of freedom to pick their own people and employ their own style. They exhibited considerable administrative talent and effectively employed the protocol system to achieve von Tirpitz's aims. This freedom also extended to those who supervised shipbuilding at the yards. The supervising constructor attached to each yard made most decisions and seldom had to contact Berlin for consultation or orders. All business correspondence with the Königin Augusta Strasse regarding a given project crossed the constructor's desk for his commentary. In this way, the RMA could evaluate the performance of the firms, the supervising constructor, and relations with industry in general.

The imperial yards played a particularly important role in von Tirpitz's system. They supplied the RMA with an alternative to excessively high bids from the private yards. These three facilities assumed a leading position in naval growth as far back as General von Stosch's call for the development of a strong domestic shipbuilding industry, and they fulfilled a variety of functions defined by von Tirpitz as the pace of the navy's growth quickened. For example, U-boat research at the Danzig Imperial Shipyard gave the RMA a great deal of technical expertise that von Tirpitz never used to full advantage. His policy throughout this period both left the development of major technological innovations entirely in the hands of private enterprise and discounted the usefulness of the U-boat. Thus, though von Tirpitz had a facility in Danzig to keep the navy officially involved in U-boat research and development, he did not allow it to become the strong alternative to Krupp's Germaniawerft that the navy needed and careful precaution dictated.

The admiral sought to keep as much of the building program within the precincts of the navy as possible. The protocol system and the imperial yards often allowed von Tirpitz to limit his dependence on private industry. He also tried to keep the Reich's political and financial leaders at arm's length. The less naval influence the Reichstag, chancellor, and Treasury Office wielded, the better von Tirpitz liked it. By 1909, however, this effort had failed. The state secretary was unable to stop the determination of von Bethmann-Hollweg to moderate the navy's negative impact on both the domestic economy and Germany's relations with Great Britain.

Neither the protocol system nor the imperial yards could ever fully resolve persistent overruns in cost and weight, which were a disagreeable, unavoidable part of building sophisticated weaponry. Every design revision, every price change, and every small production delay resulted in cost and weight variations. The RMA found that it could minimize but never fully solve this expensive dilemma.

Transport and labor also caused extra costs. The RMA and its suppliers constantly debated the ultimate responsibility for transport costs from the factory to the shipyard. In most cases the RMA coerced the suppliers into arranging transport and paying the cost. There were no major shipbuilders' strikes through 1912, and the socialist and independent labor unions failed to force any dramatic changes in hours, pay, or working conditions. They experienced only a minor degree of success in helping the shipyard workers and those working in the mines and foundries of the Ruhr. Between 1910 and 1912, however, isolated work stoppages became more frequent. With the political success of the SPD in the 1912 elections, the future of union influence in Germany looked promising.

A major exception to the RMA's relative success in keeping the upper hand with its vendors was the Krupp-Dillinger alliance. In the spring of 1900, von Tirpitz's clash with Fritz Krupp over armor prices caused the latter to employ his relationship with the kaiser as trump. The incident did nothing to enhance the RMA's relationship with the Essen firm, and von Capelle and the other RMA leaders thereafter hesitated to bring up the subject of armor prices lest the scene be replayed. Even von Tirpitz himself avoided another confrontation until favorable external forces changed his mind.

Only Krupp and Dillinger could produce nickel-steel armor in the quality and quantity the navy required. Although private competition among steel suppliers seemed rigorous, there was no breaking the armor alliance. Not only did the industry present a united front to the navy in business matters, but it also seemed dangerous to attack Krupp-Dillinger. Von Tirpitz needed the armor, he had no alternative source, and the threat of retaliation was too great to challenge the monopoly. A production slowdown at Essen would have caused a major setback in the naval construction program. Besides, Krupp owned the Germaniawerft and nearly monopolized ship artillery production. To attack Essen without the expectation of certain success would be to invite disaster. Von Tirpitz knew this, and it colored his relationship with the firm. Von Eickstedt and his successor at the RMA Construction Department, Rollmann, felt the same restraint and counseled von Tirpitz against attacking Krupp or Dillinger.

Krupp was the most powerful and independent of all the naval contractors, and the navy had little control over the firm's tendency to consume its competitors. The annexation of Gruson Magdeburg and the alliance with Dillinger gave Krupp its preeminent position in armor production. The firm's nearly successful takeover of the Vulcan shipyard in Stettin-Bredow failed more because of Vulcan's strong corporate leadership than any intervention by the RMA. By 1906, the addition of its new Hamburg facility guaranteed Vulcan more capital ship contracts from the RMA and continuity for its workers, bringing both greater profits and new strength against a possible takeover.

As Krupp's successful alliance with Dillinger in armor plate showed, the proper combination could assure complete control of a market. Dillinger had to enter this arrangement or suffer retaliation from Krupp, which might take the form of exclusion from the market or an annexation attempt. From Essen's perspective, either of these options might cause a price war, redounding to the benefit of the military and squandering possible profits. Furthermore, the armed services could support Dillinger as an effective competitor against Essen. Thus for Fritz Krupp, the alliance assured a monopoly and kept Dillinger from becoming an effective competitor in the future.

Krupp's failure to draw the American Lake Torpedo Boat Company into an alliance gave an indication of things to come. The submarines Lake sold in Europe competed well with Germaniawerft products. Furthermore, many American firms would not embrace Krupp's comfortable alliance proposals if they thought they could successfully compete with Essen. Ironically, Krupp's inability to extend its alliance and combination practices to the international scene later gave the RMA its first real chance to reduce armor prices.

The activities of the American Midvale Company in Europe and its amazingly low armor price of 1,450 marks per ton in 1906 provided a source of competition the alliance could not control. Von Tirpitz skillfully combined early overtures to Midvale and serious negotiations with Thyssen with the opportune attacks on the alliance by von Oppersdorff later in 1909 to pressure Krupp into lowering prices. Thyssen also became a threat because the Reichstag and RMA could give it advantages that would endanger the alliance's hold over the armor market. At the very least, Krupp perceived this combination as a threat, and that was exactly what von Tirpitz needed. Domestic German armor prices dropped more in the period between 1906 and 1910 than in the entire history of naval expansion to that time. Thus competitive forces outside Germany made possible the armor contract signed with Krupp-Dillinger in 1910 at 1,550 marks per ton. Von Tirpitz's ability to perceive the advantage allowed the RMA to exploit a favorable situation to the fullest.

Yet, von Tirpitz did not exploit the advantages of the U-boat because he did not consider it an integral part of the fleet program. RMA U-boat construction from 1906 to 1914 illustrates von Tirpitz's pragmatic reaction to a successive series of stimuli provided by a number of individuals and pressure groups. The Foreign Office provided the RMA with many reports on French and American progress with this technology, and some of the state secretary's colleagues in the navy and many in the Reichstag frequently wondered why the navy did not more fully investigate and exploit the possibilities of the U-boat. Von Tirpitz felt the political necessity of responding to foreign and domestic pressures and thus involved the RMA in enough U-boat development to satisfy most critics, departing as little as possible from his original plans for the High Seas Fleet.

Von Tirpitz's dogmatism rendered him blind to the possibilities of the U-boat. He classified the submarine as a defensive weapon and a minor auxiliary to the battleship. Spending more time and money on these vessels would detract from the capital ships which formed the backbone of his fleet and his strategy. The Germaniawerft was thus in a strong position when von Tirpitz reluctantly allowed U-boats to become part of the Imperial Navy in 1904 and Krupp was the only private manufacturer available. On one hand, the Germaniawerft's extensive research and development facilities showed the diversity of German industry and its ability to appreciate new technology. On the other lay the possibility of a domestic Krupp U-boat monopoly, which was only narrowly averted by the Danzig Imperial Shipyard's modest advances in the field. On the whole, U-boat production was a lost opportunity for the German shipbuilding industry before 1904 and remained the province of Krupp, and to a much lesser extent Danzig, until 1914, when AG Weser first expanded into the area, closely followed by Vulcan.

Von Tirpitz's research and development policies also proved a handicap in meeting the RMA's electrical needs. In this industry, the navy could take advantage of the intense competition, the high demand for products, and the resulting ability of smaller firms to survive.

In the case of the turbine, however, diversity and intensity were a disadvantage. German shipbuilding and electrical firms diluted their efforts to produce a domestic turbine by experimenting with many different types in various business syndicates and alliances. Though his need for turbine-powered ships might have motivated him to guide or channel private firms and their resources in a concerted effort to rival Parsons, von Tirpitz insisted that research and development remain exclusively in the private sector. As a result, the building program reached its peak in 1912 without a German turbine to compete with the Parsons system.

By employing the options open to him, especially through the protocol system and the suppliers' list, von Tirpitz could have avoided much of this wasted effort. Had RMA purveyors been limited to the Parsons system at the outset and research and development into new variations and improvements been encouraged, the results might have been much better. Von Tirpitz had never hesitated to interfere in business affairs in the past, and greater RMA involvement in turbine development might have focused the powers of industry to a higher degree. In this case, von Tirpitz's policy of not adopting major technological innovations until they were perfected encouraged too much competition. Parsons's early prominence should have quickly given way to a German variation. Instead, the British firm dominated this form of propulsion through its German subsidiary until the war.

The final questions regarding the RMA's prewar relationship with the shipbuilding industry are twofold. First, did the navy achieve its goals within the strict boundaries set by von Tirpitz? Second, was von Tirpitz himself an asset or a liability to the RMA's industrial relations in the long run?

Within the limits stipulated by von Tirpitz, the RMA succeeded in purchasing high-quality naval hardware and keeping the upper hand in its relations with industry. The RMA dealt with a multitude of diverse vendors and shipyards, coordinated, with a few notable exceptions, by the protocol system. Even the power of the Krupp-Dillinger alliance eventually succumbed to RMA pressure. Furthermore, there is little question that the ships built by von Tirpitz performed well in combat. The British confronted the practical result of the RMA's efforts at Jutland, only two months after von Tirpitz resigned as state secretary in 1916.

The construction program promoted the growth and financial well-being of German business, and von Tirpitz's clearly defined ambitions brought the shipbuilding industry to maturity more quickly than General von Stosch would have thought possible. The consistent and dependable funding, the diversity of skills, and the technological expertise needed to create the High Seas Fleet provided the incentive needed for Krupp, Siemens, MAN, Körting, and others to rise to the occasion.

Throughout the fleet expansion program, von Tirpitz's outstanding political and administrative abilities shone forth. He began with an extremely primitive navy and gave it purpose and direction. Von Tirpitz persuaded the Reichstag to commit itself to his considerable ambitions for the navy less then two years after it had spurned Admiral Hollmann's meager requests. He did all this while mobilizing the industrial strength needed to build the fleet and preserving for the navy an advantage in its relationship with industry.

But the admiral's theories of naval warfare placed artificial limits on what the navy could build. Although he designed the fleet construction program as the opening shot of the decisive battle with the British, he made the mistake of trying to defeat the British at their own game. Instead of focusing on the vulnerability of Britain's geographic position and the promise of a hit-and-run war against commerce, he advocated a direct confrontation between capital ships. The British, given their naval tradition and their numerical head start, naturally relied on their battleship strength. Germany possessed neither the numbers nor such ancient traditions, but it had considerable industrial potential. If von

Tirpitz had worked for a commercial war strategy as hard as he did for his risk theory, the danger to Great Britain would have been far greater. The U-boat might have become a major part of the German navy sooner and in greater numbers. The building program to fulfill such a strategy would have equally benefited industry. A large force of fast cruisers and hundreds of smaller craft, including the U-boat, also promised industrial challenges and profits.

Von Tirpitz showed an amazing ability to adapt politically and to sense an advantage that would further his goals. He used these talents effectively in the Reichstag and among the industrialists and manufacturers under contract to the navy. Yet his dogmas prevented him from transferring this adaptability to the areas of strategy and technological innovation.

Under von Tirpitz, the fleet program certainly satisfied both the RMA and industry but not the Admiralty Staff. Without von Tirpitz's dogmatic views, the fleet might have played a greater role in the war, for it was the ultimate contradiction to have the political and technological wing of the navy dictating strategy to the operational leadership. But the RMA's decisions on fleet composition did exactly that, without the consent of those who would direct the navy in wartime. If as an administrator and politician von Tirpitz was necessary for the success of the 1898–1914 naval expansion program, as a strategist he proved a liability, playing into his chosen enemy's strength and reducing the options open to the Admiralty Staff. Only the kaiser could have resolved this curious impasse between naval authorities, but he chose not to do so. Therefore, von Tirpitz proceeded to create a fleet of his own design, from his own political and military motives, not only satisfying the kaiser but also accurately reflecting the chaotic political and social system of which he and Wilhelm were only one part.

The Unwelcome War, 1914–1918

For the RMA, the transition from peace to war did not require the earthshaking measures forced upon the unprepared army. After seventeen years of von Tirpitz's strict direction and the dramatic expansion of the fleet, the RMA was well prepared for mobilization. During the opening months of the war, the admiral's battleship strategy clashed with reality. As he had feared, the conflict came far too soon and his own principles required him to advocate engaging the British fleet as soon as a favorable opportunity presented itself.

Instead of an opportunity, he encountered yet another challenge. The kaiser did not wish to lose his precious ships, and careful officers like Admiral von Hipper, not tied to a strategic dogma by reputation and political commitments, considered an early surface battle with the Royal Navy suicidal. When in 1914, the U-boat successfully launched the naval offensive von Tirpitz had long reserved for the battleships, his past policies and building priorities for the fleet were openly challenged. When he supported measures to increase the undersea offensive, his naval colleagues seriously, and in increasing numbers, began to question the state secretary's long-term wisdom.

Von Tirpitz remained loyal to his strategic viewpoint, and he was doggedly consistent. Though he publicly applauded the U-boat's success, von Tirpitz took no extraordinary measures to find the necessary funds to build the boats called for by the submarine partisans. As the U-boat gradually proved itself a viable alternative to the battleship, the legacy of von Tirpitz's risk theory became an impossible burden for the Admiralty Staff. Germany could not risk losing an incomplete fleet in a pitched battle with vastly superior British numbers, but neither could it remain inactive. The principles that guided the RMA made no provision for a strategy other than the risk theory, and the fleet did not possess sufficient strength in 1914 to pose a true risk to the British. Thus the Admiralty Staff had von Tirpitz to thank for a fleet that was ill equipped to execute the strategic and tactical options still open to Germany. A pitifully small U-boat force was the country's sole practical offensive instrument. When the navy awakened to this state of affairs, the admiral's credibility and reputation were shaken to their foundations, and he resigned under fire on 17 March 1916.

Instead of preparing Germany for war or effectively enhancing its offensive capability, the risk theory increased Germany's vulnerability. Von Tirpitz failed to exploit his enemy's weaknesses and satisfied his own vanity and that of his sovereign by challenging Britain's strength. In 1914, von Tirpitz knew full well that his plans for the fleet could not be completed for another decade. That he expected to have the time to do this in the face of the challenge it would pose to the British reveals a great deal about the power of an idea. He should not have assumed either that Britain would stand idly by watching the High Seas Fleet reach equality with the Grand Fleet or that unlimited funds would be available to build the ships necessary to achieve his grand design. Furthermore, virtually ignoring the U-boat as a promising alternative to surface weapons when many of his potential foreign rivals made earlier and deeper commitments to explore its possibilities revealed the static nature of his strategic and technical thought. No weapons system, least of all the battleship, could claim the distinction of being perfect. Technology grows with demand and necessity and adapts to circumstances. To ignore this fact is to court disaster. Although one can understand von Tirpitz's loyalty to a set of ideas which brought him success, his lack of flexibility and his self-serving evaluation of both the international situation and the observations of his professional critics placed Germany in a very vulnerable position in 1914.

Thus it became clear early in the war that the navy's major offensive threat lay with the U-boat. Even before the admiral's departure in 1916, the navy accelerated production of the submarine. This process required retooling, designing, testing, and allocating labor and materials, all while a war raged full tilt. During peacetime a complete change of priority in naval construction posed sufficient difficulty, but to carry out these plans while mobilizing and fighting came close to asking the impossible.

As the war continued into 1915, the RMA chose to diversify both the task of the U-boats and their types. The Ms boat took the war to the Entente while the UBs and UCs patrolled or scattered mines in the English Channel and North Sea. The number of shipyards building U-boats increased from two to seven by 1916. Time, however, worked against the RMA's plans. Construction on surface ships progressed slowly, and conversion of plant space to U-boat work took longer than expected, as did the transport and delivery of parts. In addition, the commencement of the Hindenburg Program on 31 August 1916 intensified the demands on the shipbuilding industry beyond its capability. The Admiralty needed hundreds of boats to pursue a commerce war against the British, and the RMA had made virtually no strategic plan before the war for the industrial sector to address such a need. Thus it is remarkable that the German U-boat force grew to such proportions and proved so effective during the war. It achieved success in spite of von Tirpitz rather than because of him.

Confronted nearly unprepared by a demand to increase dramatically the navy's U-boat fleet, both von Tirpitz and his successor von Capelle joined the ruthless competition in wartime Germany for scarce labor and raw materials and found themselves at a distinct disadvantage. In spite of regulation by the War Ministry and later by the War Office under General Wilhelm Groener, the raw materials available in Germany dwindled as rapidly as their prices rose. Neither foreign sources like Sweden nor innovations like the U-boat freighters *Deutschland* and *Bremen* could disguise the limits of Germany's resources.

The labor situation also illustrated the scarcity of Germany's resources and was the source of considerable conflict. The RMA and its suppliers waged a constant tug-of-war with the army over the priority given to materials for the front versus the necessity of properly manning the factories. At the beginning of the war an erratic draft policy made deep cuts into the work force of some companies while hardly affecting others. Ironically, the selection for war production of firms most valuable to the war effort initially left thousands of men unemployed, released by nonessential firms no longer able to pay the current wage. Many of these displaced laborers went into the army, and the rest found new work as the economy adjusted to the war. The momentary abundance of manpower ended when front-line attrition and the demand for increased production made labor a truly scarce commodity. By late 1915, when the army began to allow the limited repatriation of workers, the RMA's yards and purveyors used every ruse available to keep as many as possible beyond the agreed time limits.

The use of foreign plants and personnel in the occupied areas also helped alleviate the labor problem to a limited extent. The RMA built U-boats at Brugge, Ostend, Antwerp, and Rotterdam. A small number of volunteers from among the prisoners of war held in Germany and a significant contribution made by a few thousand German women doing office and factory work quickly brought the RMA to the end of its options.

Only the projects with the highest priority received sufficient labor. Predictably, these usually included the various U-boat projects. In many cases the extra emergency labor took the form of construction divisions created by the navy to keep high-priority construction from falling behind. The labor scarcity consumed the services of even these professional naval craftsmen as quickly as the divisions assembled.

As one of the more unfortunate by-products of the labor and materials scarcity, the RMA could exert virtually no control over wages and prices during the war, a significant departure from its prewar relationship with industry. Because factors of production were universally scarce, price controls worked only under unusually favorable conditions. Thus metal prices doubled and tripled, while the labor force dwindled with each battle, and contract deadlines obliged firms to pay the highest price for those workers they could keep out of the army. In these circumstances, the navy was at the mercy of both the market and the army.

To retain as much of its prewar authority as possible, the RMA continued its strict enforcement of the protocol system. Before the conflict began, this in-house system of checks and balances served the RMA well. The war changed this as it did everything else because the domestic situation had changed dramatically. The navy's strict regulations often hurt smaller firms caught in the wartime vise between contract obligations and the scarcity of labor and raw materials. Although many of the larger companies complained about the RMA's uncompromising attitude, their corporate relationships and internal resources sustained them through the difficult times in a very profitable war. Smaller firms, however, faced high prices for scarce resources, difficult transport and delivery deadlines, and a shrinking labor force. Not every company could strike a bargain with the government, as Krupp did, to build U-cruisers without remuneration in exchange for preferential treatment to offset the firm's depleted metals store.

Resource management and labor difficulties burdened the RMA as well as industry. During the war the RMA assumed two responsibilities that tested the talents of the organization to its limits. First, it needed to create from almost nothing a submarine force that could fulfill the Admiralty Staff's needs in the naval war with Britain. In this endeavor the RMA came remarkably close to success in the 1916–18 period, recovering well from von Tirpitz's prewar policies. Second, the RMA had to help carry out the total mobilization of the Hindenburg Program, which not only put great pressure on the private sector but also demanded constant vigilance and exceptional managerial skills from the military personnel overseeing construction and procurement. In meeting these challenges the protocol system functioned well as a tool in the RMA's struggle to fulfill its wartime obligations to the navy and remained its most important means of keeping pressure on naval contractors.

The RMA reluctantly found it necessary to bend the rules of the protocol system when the demands of the war effort required it. For example, the restrictions against foreign workers participating in U-boat projects fell by the wayside when the navy moved into Belgium and Flanders to expand plant capacity for submarine construction. The scarcity of skilled technicians and the pace of construction mandated by the goals of the Hindenburg Program took a toll on the Purchasing Office inspectors. The standard, on-site factory inspections required by the protocol system before a product went to the shipyard fell before accelerated production schedules. In the last two years of the war most inspections still took place at the factory, but the resident shipyard inspectors assumed an increasing number of these tasks when parts and materials arrived at the yard in order to complete projects on time. This help from the naval personnel at the yards allowed the RMA to limit the Purchasing Office inspectors to certain regions and reduce the time they spent in travel. But the RMA's still considerable power in this area enabled it both to resist many other compromises and to maintain the product quality the navy expected.

Perhaps the most remarkable facet of naval-industrial affairs during World War I was the Scheer Program. Most analyses of this attempt to increase dramatically the size and power of the German submarine fleet stress the exceptional and dire nature of the circumstances in Germany in the autumn of 1918. In this setting it is easy to view the Scheer Program as a pointless, desperate measure. This was not the case. The Scheer Program evolved out of a process of strategic natural selection that culminated at Jutland in May 1916. This battle destroyed once and for all the fantasy that Germany could defeat the Royal Navy on its own terms and replaced von Tirpitz and the risk theory with Reinhard Scheer and the submarine war against commerce.

Bernd Stegemann has suggested in his *Die deutsche Marinepolitik, 1916–1918*, that the SKL never intended to carry out the Scheer Program. Rather, the navy proposed to underscore its own determination for the benefit of supporters at home and adversaries abroad. If this view is accurate, the Imperial Navy must bear an extraordinary portion of the guilt for the intense suffering of the German people in the last year of the war. Neither Scheer and his supporters nor the OHL sufficiently realized the true physical and material exhaustion of Germany during 1917 and 1918. Could skilled workers return from the front and not disrupt the defense against the Allies in the west? Would these repatriated workers have the necessary skills? Did the desired raw materials exist in sufficient quantities so late in the war? Where would the crews for the new U-boats come from? If Admiral Scheer pushed these questions aside because he never intended the program to begin, is not the historian obliged to question the exaggerated value placed upon naval morale and reputation when it is purchased at such a high price?

Therefore, the thesis that the Scheer Program primarily played the role of morale booster presumes too much. Did the German naval leadership already recognize the certainty of Germany's defeat on the western front in the autumn of 1918? Are we to assume that the intricate planning of September and October formed the last act of a quickly concocted, elaborate charade? The answer to both of these questions is no.[1]

The SKL genuinely felt, as Scheer certainly did, that the process of defining a new strategy for the Imperial Navy had come to a dramatic climax at Jutland. In a new variation on Aubé, a submarine campaign against British commerce would take the place of von Tirpitz's strategy and the risk theory. At this point, the only valid question in the collective mind of the SKL concerned time and resources. Could they find the labor and materials to build a sufficient number of submarines in time? Had the answer to their strategic dilemma come too late for effective action?

These naval officers, faced with the grim possibility of defeat, believed there still was time to fulfill the program's goals. The facilities to build the boats were available, the Austro-Hungarians offered significant additional plant space and labor, and the army already had Germany living under the discipline of a relatively successful total mobilization program which strictly controlled and managed material resources. The priority of U-boat construction and the possibility of returning labor from the front seemed guaranteed by General Ludendorff and the OHL. Above all, the submarine offered a tried and tested, familiar technology for the Imperial Navy.

Furthermore, planning well into 1919 did not seem foolish, even to those officers fully aware that Germany had already approached her human and material limits after the army's failed spring offensive in 1918. By the autumn of the previous year, the Hindenburg Program had astonishingly surpassed the army's expectations in machine gun and artillery production. Ludendorff, as quartermaster general, spent 1918 energetically trying to sustain and extend this level of productivity in face of diminished resources.[2]

For its part, the army air force continued its construction well into 1919 for many of the same reasons that made the Scheer Program seem feasible to the SKL. Indeed, in an effort to minimize unemployment, the Ministry of Munitions used war-break clauses in its contracts to permit the aircraft companies to extend three months of their production over the six months following the war's end. In May 1919, the German government was still receiving nearly three hundred airplanes per week.[3]

Thus, to those naval officers laboring under the pressure of war and determined to see their cherished institution safely into the postwar world, the goals of the Scheer Program seemed attainable. The RMA and the U-Boat Office, as well as the civilian industrialists, acted with this understanding and attempted to execute the program as planned, in spite of the inevitable feeling of anxiety and uncertainty about resources and the future. The leaders of the German Imperial Navy did not perceive the true extent of their nation's physical and material exhaustion any more than did their counterparts in the OHL or the civilian administration of the Reich.[4] Indeed, in his memoirs Scheer recalls discussing with Ludendorff the latter's realization that the war was lost. Then, a few paragraphs further on, the admiral describes the activities surrounding the Scheer Program without ever placing them in the context of impending defeat.[5] Clearly, the SKL still expected to fight its final battle of the war either on the North Sea with a substantially increased U-boat force or, failing this, at the peace table, where the new submarines might bring the German navy a more palatable peace.

In addition, both the Scheer Program and the abortive "death sortie" outlined in Operations Plan 19 of 24 October 1918 take on an interesting common significance if viewed as expressions not only of eleventh-hour resolve but also of future planning and institutional preservation. In his analysis of Operations Plan 19, Holger Herwig concluded that the entire High Seas Fleet was committed to a suicide sortie "for reasons of honor and future naval building." These same motives, which nearly carried the fleet into a final pitched battle with the British and Americans, certainly contributed to the serious pursuit of the goals outlined in the Scheer Program. The navy sought to alter the course of the war if possible. But at the very least, it desired to mold its postwar reputation, increase its credibility, and preserve its industrial base well beyond 1918. In this context, and as a culmination to the arduous wartime process of redefining naval strategy, the Scheer Program should assume a greater significance for our understanding of Germany during and beyond the Great War.

From the naval-industrial perspective, the most important issue of the 1917–18 period was labor, largely because of the Scheer Program. General Groener certainly perceived that problem when he decided to support the unions so as to acquire some influence in labor circles. The RMA's "buffer projects," designed to keep valuable workers in the factories, highlighted the critical scarcity of industrial manpower and its importance as an issue late in the war. Although the RMA leadership and General Groener perceived the limits of the wartime Reich labor force, their appreciation never thoroughly penetrated official thinking and policy making. To admit the near exhaustion of Germany's most important resource brought defeat into sharp focus. This specter precipitated a busy scramble to preserve images, reputations, and institutions, rather than a frank discussion of Germany's alternatives in the ongoing crisis.

After the armistice and the demise of the monarchy, the survival of the navy became the predominant theme of demobilization. The Scheer Program fell by the wayside, and both the naval and private evaluations of the postwar situation concluded that the yards had to keep working and with them the skilled labor force. Repairs, projects still under way, and foreign contracts could occupy industry's time while a cheaper future navy took form in the minds of the surviving naval officers and the leaders of industry.

In 1897, a conflict in strategic thinking allowed Alfred von Tirpitz to emerge as the German champion of the big-gun battleship navy. His risk theory seemed to make the challenge to Britain possible, bringing with it power and influence over world affairs previously denied to a virtually landlocked power. The risk incorporated in von Tirpitz's plans was meant for Germany's adversaries. In reality, Germany herself took the risk, betting that von Tirpitz, the able politician and astute propagandist, could make reality out of the unlikely.

The element that historian Carl-Axel Gemzell left out of his Hegelian analysis of service group conflict as the crucible of successful strategic concepts is the relentless strength and optimism of ambition, whether national or personal.[6] Britain's geographical position and naval might dictated Germany's best options. The Imperial Navy had to wage a war against British commerce in the tradition of the French Young School or acquire control of the Faeroe Islands and the waters at the northern tip of Denmark, as Wegener would have it. This last option would give the High Seas Fleet the necessary position to apply greater pressure on British communications and sea lanes. The development of the U-boat at the turn of the century made the former more attractive and supported the arguments of Persius, von Maltzahn, and Galster. Wegener's alternative, first offered in 1915, offered a better strategic context for the employment of the existing fleet. In this case, however, the opposing strategic camps never truly did battle à la Gemzell because personal and national ambition presented von Tirpitz with a victory and a free hand to build his fleet before the final verbal battle ensued.

Thus the conflict remained unresolved and Germany lacked a comprehensive naval strategy well into the Third Reich. In a remarkable reprise of the 1897–1914 period, Admiral Erich Raeder, a classmate of Wegener who became head of the German navy in 1928, proposed an ambitious 365-ship construction program in 1934 without a coherent strategic context. To ensure its completion, he relied on Hitler's promise to avoid a European war. As Holger Herwig has pointed out, "no strategic design drove this massive construction program; Raeder was simply amassing ships, perhaps unable to admit that he, not Wegener, was wrong."[7] Raeder was still motivated by the decisive battle viewpoint that pervaded the Imperial Navy of his youth. In 1939 he encountered essentially the same dilemma von Tirpitz faced in 1914. War came prematurely and quickly revealed the absence of adequate and careful strategic planning beyond preparation for a surface battle with the Royal Navy or large-scale warfare against commerce.

The realities of war proved that von Tirpitz's decisive battle was a tactic without a strategy. An indecisive victory over the Royal Navy or the failure of the latter to give battle never played a part in mainstream German strategic thinking. The plausibility of the risk theory, with its decisive battle, provided the perfect political foundation for a fleet-building program, but, as a strategy, it failed utterly.[8] Germany's postwar naval leadership, determined to restore the power and numbers of the fleet after Scapa Flow, tried to copy von Tirpitz's success but could not comprehend his failure.

Appendix A

Figure and Tables

Figure 1. Organization of the German Naval Hierarchy

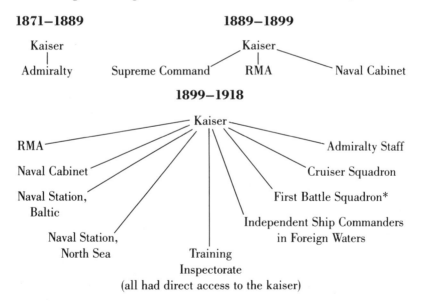

1871–1889

Kaiser
|
Admiralty

1889–1899

Supreme Command   Kaiser   RMA   Naval Cabinet

1899–1918

Kaiser

RMA

Naval Cabinet

Naval Station,
Baltic

Naval Station,
North Sea

Training
Inspectorate

Admiralty Staff

Cruiser Squadron

First Battle Squadron*

Independent Ship Commanders
in Foreign Waters

(all had direct access to the kaiser)

*Became Fleet Command when the Second Battle Squadron was added in 1903. The chief of the High Seas Fleet was the commanding officer.

Source: Gemzell, *Organization, Conflict and Innovation,* 39.

Table 1. Naval Officials in Charge of Construction Matters

RMA Construction Chiefs	State Secretaries of the RMA

Dietrich 1881–98
   Construction Office/Division
von Eickstedt 1899–1907
   Construction Division/Department
	Heusner 1889–91
	Hollmann 1891–97
	von Tirpitz 1897–1916

Rollmann 1907–14
   Construction Department
Schraeder 1914–18
   Construction Department
	von Capelle March 1916–
	   October 1918
	Behncke October 1918
	Ritter von Mann Edler von
	   Tiechler October 1918–
	   February 1919

Table 2. Vital Statistics on the Six Major Private Shipyards

Shipyard	Area (+ waterfront if available)	Work Force	Nature of Other On-Site Facilities

Germania
   (Krupp), Kiel
	220,280 sq. meters
	10 docks
		1890 = 1,409
		1899 = 2,564
		1914 = 5,000 +
			Copper, brass, iron
			   foundries
			Schultz System
			   boiler factory
			Electrical workshop
			Railroad spurs
			Beer storage
			   facilities

Howaldtswerke,
   Kiel
	155,000 sq. meters
	770 meters of
	   waterfront
	12 docks
		1890 = 1,304
		1899 = 2,370	

Schichau,
   Elbing and
   Danzig
	364,450 sq. meters
	18 docks
		1880 = 1,200[a]
		1899 = 5,820
			Factories
			Mills
			Workshops

AG Weser,
   Bremen
	38,290 sq. meters
	252 meters of
	   waterfront
		1890 = 1,178
		1900 = 1,350
			Shops
			Factories
			Storage

Table 2. (*continued*)

Shipyard	Area (+ waterfront if available)	Work Force	Nature of Other On-Site Facilities
Blohm und Voss, Hamburg	141,750 sq. meters 1,195 meters of waterfront 10 docks	1880 = 450 1890 = 2,051 1899 = 2,598	Factories Workshops Storage Workers living facilities in suburb of Wilhelmsburg
Vulcan, Stettin-Bredow and Hamburg (1906)	182,650 sq. meters 518 meters of waterfront (at Stettin) 9 docks	1899 = 6,628	Hamburg facility acquired in 1906

Source: Schwarz and von Halle, eds., *Schiffbauindustrie.*

ªElbing only.

Table 3. German Shipbuilding Firms, 1899

Baltic Sea	North Sea
Schichau, Elbing	Blohm und Voss, Hamburg
Schichau, Danzig	Reiherstieg, Hamburg
Klawitter, Danzig	Brandenburg, Hamburg
Vulcan, Stettin	Janssen and Schmilinski, Hamburg
Oderwerke, Stettin	Holtz, Harburg
Näscke, Stettin	Weser, Bremen
Neptune, Rostock	Vulcan, Vegesack (Bremen)
Koch, Lubeck	Tecklenborg, Geestemunde
Howaldtswerke, Kiel	Wencke, Bremerhaven
Germania, Kiel and Tegel	Seebeck, Gesstemunde
Flensburger Gesellschaft, Flensburg	Rickmers, Bremerhaven
	Meyer, Papenburg

Table 4. Capital Ships Built by the RMA between 1909 and 1918

Capital Ship	Company	Year
Battleships		
Kaiser	KWK	1909–12
Friedrich der Grosse	Vulcan	1910–12
Kaiserin	Howaldtswerke	1910–13
König Albert	Schichau	1910–13
Prinzregent Luitpold	Germaniawerft	1911–13
König	KWW	1911–14
Grosser Kurfürst	Vulcan	1911–14
Markgraf	Weser	1911–14
Kronprinz	Germaniawerft	1912–14
Bayern	Howaldtswerke	1914–16
Baden	Schichau	1913–16
Württemburg	Vulcan	1914–
Sachsen	Germaniawerft	1914–
Heavy cruisers		
Moltke	Blohm und Voss	1909–11
Goeben	Blohm und Voss	1909–12
Seydlitz	Blohm und Voss	1911–13
Derfflinger	Blohm und Voss	1912–14
Lützow	Schichau	1912–15
Hindenburg	KWW	1913–17
Mackensen	Blohm und Voss	1914–
Graf Spee	Schichau	1915–
Prinz Eitel Friedrich	Blohm und Voss	1915–
Fürst Bismarck	KWW	1915–
Ersatz Yorck	Vulcan	1916–
Ersatz Gneisenau	Germaniawerft	1916–
Ersatz Scharnhorst	Blohm und Voss	1916–
Light cruisers		
28 ships, 8 of which were never completed		

Source: Gröner, *Kriegsschiffe*, vol. 1. The vessels for which no end date is given were never completed.

Table 5. Metal Prices According to the Kriegsmetall AG, April 1915

Copper	350 marks per 100 kgs.
Aluminum	430
Tin	700
Nickel	1,200
Antimon	230
Lead	62
Refined Zinc	102
Raw Zinc	65

Source: RMA Dockyard Department, Berlin, to Imperial Yards et al., 4 Nov. 1915, BA/MA RM3/7771.

Table 6. Numbers of Women Workers Employed in the Imperial Shipyards

Shipyard	1 April 1916	1 October 1916	10 December 1916
Wilhelmshaven	378	500	1,084
factory	261	300	804
office	117	200	280
Kiel	172	437	1,171
factory	39	260	899
office	133	177	272
Danzig	48	272	458
factory	33	196	323
office	15	76	135
Friedrichsort	21	27	118
factory	0	0	64
office	21	27	54

Table 7. Number of U-boats Projected in Different Plans

Date	Plans, 1918–1919	Pre-Scheer	U-Boat Office 15 Aug. 1918	Scheer Proposals 12 Sept. 1918
1918				
Oct.	13	12	12	16
Nov.	12	10	13	16
Dec.	18	14	15	16

Table 7. (*continued*)

Date	Plans, 1918–1919	Pre-Scheer	U-Boat Office 15 Aug. 1918	Scheer Proposals 12 Sept. 1918
1919				
Jan.	15	11	15	20
Feb.	16.5	13	16	20
March	18	13	17	20
April	22.5	13	17	25
May	23.5	15	18	25
June	30.5	17	19	25
July	31.17	16	21	30
Aug.	33.67	15	22	30
Sept.	33.67	14	21	30
Oct.	34.67	14	22	36
Nov.	37.67	15	21	36
Dec.	35.17	16	23	36
Total	332	172	232	333

Source: Rössler, U-Bootbaus, 120.

Note: The plans for the Scheer Program in the first colum are based on six U-boat types under construction at eleven yards.

Appendix B

Structure of the RMA Protocol System

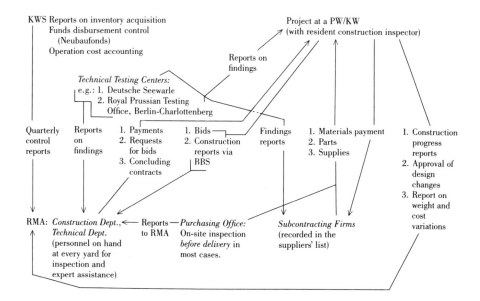

KWS Reports on inventory acquisition
  Funds disbursement control
    (Neubaufonds)
  Operation cost accounting

Project at a PW/KW
(with resident construction inspector)

Reports on
findings

Technical Testing Centers:
e.g.: 1. Deutsche Seewarle
      2. Royal Prussian Testing
         Office, Berlin-Charlottenberg

Quarterly
control
reports

Reports
on
findings

1. Payments
2. Requests
   for bids
3. Concluding
   contracts

1. Bids
2. Construction
   reports via
   BBS

Findings
reports

1. Materials payment
2. Parts
3. Supplies

1. Construction
   progress
   reports
2. Approval of
   design
   changes
3. Report on
   weight and
   cost
   variations

RMA: *Construction Dept.,* ← Reports — *Purchasing Office:*
     Technical Dept.   to RMA   On-site inspection
     (personnel on hand   *before delivery* in
     at every yard for   most cases.
     inspection and
     expert assistance)

Subcontracting Firms
(recorded in the
suppliers' list)

Notes

Introduction

1. McNeill, *Pursuit of Power*, chap. 8. In this book the term *naval-industrial complex* is understood in the sense of Samuel Huntington's definition of the military-industrial complex: "a large permanent military establishment supported by and linked to a variety of related industrial, labor, and geographical interests" ("Defense Establishment," 562–84).
2. Epkenhans, "Grossindustrie und Schlachtflottenbau."
3. Hubatsch, *Die Ära Tirpitz*; Hubatsch, *Der Admiralstab.*
4. Kehr, *Schlachtflottenbau.*
5. Herwig, *German Naval Officer Corps*; Geyer, *Deutsche Rüstungspolitik*; Lambi, *Navy and German Power Politics*; Deist, *Flottenpolitik.*
6. I corresponded with other archives in Germany before beginning research on this topic; they responded that they held no pertinent source material. These included Staatsarchiv Bremen, Staatsarchiv Hamburg, Universität Hamburg- Historisches Seminar Bibliothek, Stadtbücheri Kiel, Stadtarchiv Landeshauptstadt Kiel, Technische Bibliothek- Fachhochschule Hamburg, and Westfälisches Wirtschaftsarchiv.
7. In this sense the present study builds on the analysis of Patrick J. Kelly, who portrayed von Tirpitz as a bureaucratic empire builder. Kelly's research demonstrated that the admiral was concerned less about the operational viability of the High Seas Fleet and the risk theory than about creating an organization that would serve him and his political ambitions. See Kelly, "Naval Policy of Imperial Germany."

Chapter 1. An Ambitious Beginning, 1890–1898

1. Berghahn, *Tirpitz Plan*, 23–24. See also Hubatsch, *Der Admiralstab*. The ennobling "von" will be used throughout this study for the sake of consistency even though many members of the German naval leadership received the privilege late in their careers. Von Holtzendorff was a member of the Prussian nobility from birth, but most of the others received the title later: von Capelle in 1912, von Tirpitz and von Müller in 1900.
2. Steinberg, "Germany and the Russo-Japanese War," 1968.
3. Admiral Heusner entered the navy on 18 June 1857 and served in the Admiralty and as director of the Naval Department. In 1889 he was given the newly created position of state secretary of the RMA. He retired in 1891.

   Admiral Hollmann was von Tirpitz's immediate predecessor as state secretary of the RMA, which position he took in 1891. He had been promoted to captain 15 February 1881 and appointed commander of the First Sailor Division. He was promoted to rear admiral 14 August 1888 and served as chief of the Instruction Squadron. His final promotion to vice-admiral occurred on 18 November 1890.
4. Hurd and Castle, *German Seapower*, 195. Hollmann did not like von Tirpitz and frequently wrote about him in later letters to his close friend Fritz Krupp. See Hollmann to Krupp (on Capri), Berlin, 18, 26 April 1899, HA Krupp, FAH 111 C233. See also Owen, "Military Industrial Relations."
5. 9 Legislatur Periode, IV Session 1895–97, Kommission für den Reichshaushalts Etat 27, Sitzung, 8 March 1897, BA/MA RM3/2487 Reichstagsverhandlung. For the 1873 plan, "Denkschrift betreffend die Ausführung des Flottengrundungsplans von 1873" (Berlin, 1873), BA/MA Library.
6. Hurd and Castle, *German Seapower*, 195.
7. The kaiser was thinking about von Tirpitz for this position as early as 1896. See von Senden, on board the SMS *Hohenzollern*, to von Tirpitz, Berlin, 3 March 1896, BA/MA N160/5 Nachlass von Senden-Bibran.
8. Steinberg, *Yesterday's Deterrent*, 136–40.
9. Hurd and Castle, *German Seapower*, 307–9.
10. Hollyday, *Bismarck's Rival*, 101–2, 112–13.
11. Hurd and Castle, *German Seapower*, 311, 199. During this period Germany's arms industry experienced increased competition from France. In 1885 the Chamber of Deputies lifted its arms export prohibition against Germany. See Owen, "Military Industrial Relations."
12. Hurd and Castle, *German Seapower*, 369–71. See Germania, Berlin/Tegel to Jencke, Essen, 24 Dec. 1896, HA Krupp, WA IV 952. The Krupp firm also tried to enter into a close association with Vulcan, which the latter rejected. Then Krupp began secretly to purchase large blocks of Vulcan stock (HA Krupp, FAH III B179, passim). The yard's income from warship contracts rose from 40.5 million marks between 1871 and 1896 to 51.5 million between 1897 and 1904. In the latter period, only Schichau had greater revenue (Böhm, *Überseehandel und Flottenbau*, 147).

13. Schwarz and Halle, eds., *Schiffbauindustrie*, 58–59. The yard's dividends bounced erratically between 0 and 6.5 percent during this period. With the arrival of Krupp capital in 1896, the dividends leveled off at a steady 4.5 percent.

14. Boelcke, ed., *Krupp und die Hohenzollern*, 236.

15. Schwarz and Halle, eds., *Schiffbauindustrie*, 314, 22.

16. Ibid., 11–12, 191.

17. Schichau, Elbing, to SS/RMA Konstruktions Department, Berlin, 9 Sept. 1891, BA/MA RM3/347; Schwarz and Halle, eds., *Schiffbauindustrie*, 12, 85. In spite of its potential, Schichau's purely commercial work was modest. It was one of the three or four German companies capable of handling large transatlantic vessels, but it received no contracts between 1881 and 1890 and only six between 1891 and 1900. In this area the old Hanseatic cities monopolized the business. Between 1881 and 1890 Blohm und Voss and Reiherstiegwerft in Hamburg accounted for fourteen each out of the fifty-five ships of this type built in Germany. Vulcan, Stettin (ten), and Flensburger of Schleswig-Holstein (eight) were a close third and fourth. In the 1890s the same four firms won 121 out of 162 commercial contracts for ships over 2,000 tons displacement. Breaking into this market was difficult, even for a firm of Schichau's size (ibid., 53).

18. Schwarz and Halle, eds., *Schiffbauindustrie*, 82.

19. Ibid., 53, 57, 12, 16.

20. Gröner, *Kriegsschiffe*, 1:19–49.

21. Schwarz and Halle, eds., *Schiffbauindustrie*, 12, 17. See also Hurd and Castle, *German Seapower*, 366–67.

22. Schwarz and Halle, eds., *Schiffbauindustrie*, 50.

23. Blohm und Voss, Hamburg, to SS/RMA, Berlin, 4 June 1892, BA/MA RM3/354.

24. Gröner, *Kriegsschiffe*, 1:19–49 and passim.

25. Schwarz and Halle, eds., *Schiffbauindustrie*, 21.

26. Hurd and Castle, *German Seapower*, 362–64.

27. Ibid., 50, 19. The six were the *Preussen, Bayern, Sachsen, Danzig, Stettin,* and *Lübeck.*

28. Ibid., 15–17.

29. Ibid., 15.

30. Ibid., plan 1 (Appendix).

31. Gröner, *Kriegsschiffe*, 1:40–41. The contract for the U-42 was awarded to the Societa Fiat San Giorgio, La Spezia-Muggiano. All of these boats were very early models, either 450-ton petrol-driven vessels or 800-ton Ms-boats. See "Inbaugabe der U-boote," Berlin, 3 May 1917, BA/MA RM3/11692.

32. Schwarz and Halle, eds., *Schiffbauindustrie*, plan 3 (Appendix), plan 2 (Appendix). At the turn of the century the imperial yards had a modest work force of 15,781 (ibid., 204–5, 244–45).

33. "Protokoll über die Sitzung am 16. Juni 1900," BA/MA RM3/3699. See also BA/MA RM3/3697–98, passim, for similar examples. For the award to Schichau in the S-90 to 101 case see Gröner, *Kriegsschiffe,*, 1:34.

34. Hurd and Castle, *German Seapower*, 361.

35. KWK to SS/RMA, Berlin, 2 Oct. 1896, "Beantragung von Mitteln aus den lfd. No. 11 und 12 des Rechnungssolls von den einmaligen Ausgaben," BA/MA RM3/6071. See BA/MA RM3/7312–13 (1895-1909), passim, on budget control.

36. BA/MA RM3/6072 (1896–1900), passim.

37. Payment of 661.80 marks made to the Norddeutschen Gewerbe Ausstellung, Königsburg, 16 Oct. 1895, BA/MA RM3/6061. The American system was similar. See "Marine der Vereinigten Staaten," Construction Department, RMA, Berlin, 1896, BA/MA RM3/1073.

38. Pollard and Robinson, *British Shipbuilding Industry*, 29.

39. Leckebusch, "Beginn des deutschen Eisenschiffbaues," 191–99.

40. BA/MA RM3/3681.

41. *Nauticus* (1899), 282–83.

42. Hubatsch, *Kaiserliche Marine*; Ritter, *Staatskunst und Kriegshandwerk*.

43. Berghahn, *Tirpitz Plan*; Röhl, "Admiral von Müller," 656–67.

44. Hurd and Castle, *German Seapower*, 110. See also *Rangliste* (1890–95).

45. Böhm, *Überseehandel und Flottenbau*, 87–88. For further information on the Jeune Ecole see Bueb, *"Junge Schule."*

46. Admiral Galster was one of von Tirpitz's strongest and best-known critics. He advocated the integration of the U-boat into German naval strategy. He was promoted to rear admiral 13 September 1901 and to vice-admiral 14 March 1905. In 1904 he was appointed director of the Ship Artillery Inspectorate at the imperial shipyard in Wilhelmshaven. He retired in 1907.

   Admiral Freiherr von Maltzahn (1849–1930) began his career in 1866. He was chief of the Baltic Naval Station and participated in tactical experiments on maneuvers under Dahnhardt, Köster, and Thompson. He served as commander of the SMS *Wurttemburg*, 1893–95, and commander of the school ship *Stosch* in 1898, then transferred to the Naval Academy in 1899. He was a strategic opponent of von Tirpitz. He retired in 1903.

47. Mahan, *Influence of Seapower*. The original title of Dienstschrift IX was "Allgemeine Erfährung aus den Manövern der Herbstubungsflotte."

48. *Rangliste* (1889–97).

49. The supplements to the 1900 Naval Law came in 1906, 1908, and 1912, but under slightly different conditions. The von Bülow bloc was rocked in 1908 by a proposed increase in taxes.

50. Riezler, *Tagebücher*, 299.

51. Von Bülow, *Denkwürdigkeiten*, 1:413; Berghahn, *Tirpitz Plan*, 380–82.

52. Steinberg, *Yesterday's Deterrent*.

53. Ibid., 191; Huntington, *Soldier and the State*, 102.

54. Herwig, *German Naval Officer Corps*, 27.

55. Both of these men were frequently at von Tirpitz's side during Reichstag debates.

   Admiral von Capelle entered the German navy on 18 April 1872. He spent thirteen years working at sea. He was promoted to captain 8 October 1900, to rear admiral 7 July 1906, to vice-admiral 5 September 1909, and to admiral in 1913. He was director of the Administrative Department of the RMA from 1900 to 1914, then assistant state secretary of the RMA until 1916. On 17 March 1916 he succeeded von Tirpitz as state secretary of the RMA.

Admiral Dähnhardt was born 27 October 1863 and entered the service in April 1879. He served under Pohl in the Central Division of the RMA until 1902, when he became first adjutant to Diedrichs, chief of the Admiralty Staff. He was promoted to captain in 1905 and directed the Budget Division of von Capelle's Administrative Department until 1914, being promoted to rear admiral in 1910. On 31 March 1914 he was promoted to vice-admiral and named director of the Budget Department of the RMA. He retired 15 January 1916.

56. Kennedy, "Fisher and Tirpitz," 52.

57. Kehr, *Schlachtflottenbau;* Steinberg, *Yesterday's Deterrent.*

58. "Zusammenstellungen von Schiffsneubauten bei 1897/98 und Neubauten Schiffe Sachsen Klasse" (quoting figures from 1889 to 1898), BA/MA RM3/347.

59. Reichstag Budget Commission Hearings, 3 March 1898, BA/MA RM3/11636, Handakten Dahnhardt.

60. Steinberg, *Yesterday's Deterrent,* 186. The Reichstag was understandably concerned about obsolescence. How could appropriations for material repair and ship replacement be determined? The navy projected only a twenty-five-year service life for the new ships, and parts to repair these vessels constantly spiraled upward in price. Reichstag deputy Hammacher lamented that "we should not have to fear constantly that the prices will suddenly change. They are already high enough." The presence of State Secretary von Posadowsky-Wehner from the Reich Treasury Office as a von Tirpitz supporter during the budget debates only slightly reassured the legislators (Hearings, 2 March 1898, BA/MA RM3/11636, Handakten Dahnhardt).

61. For Bebel's speech and the Reichstag reaction see Verhandlungen des Reichstages, Stenographischer Bericht, 9. Legisl. Periode, V. Session, 68. Sitzung Wed. 23 March 1898, 1746. For Steinberg's analysis see *Yesterday's Deterrent,* 193–95.

62. For an example of a typical Sitzung see RMA Administrative Conference on Capital Ship Boilers, Berlin 13 Jan. 1904, BA/MA RM3/3691.

63. *Rangliste* (1908).

64. "Die Frage: 'Weshalb hat sich die Fertigstellung der Armierung bisher verspätet und Weshalb wird das Kommende schneller Fertig werden,' " RMA Memo An N (dept.), 27 Nov. 1899, BA/MA RM3/6650.

65. Construction Records, SMS *Wittlesbach,* 1898–1902, BA/MA RM3/443.

66. BBS, KWK, 24 Dec. 1896, to SS/RMA, Berlin, Re: Light Cruisers "K" and "N," BA/MA RM3/6071.

67. "Zusammenstellungen von Schiffsneubauten bei 1897/98 und Neubauten den Schiffe Sachsen Klasse," BA/MA RM3/347.

68. "Bericht über die Verhandlungen der internationalen Konferenz zur Vereinfachung einheitlicher Prufungsmethoden," 9–11 Sept. 1895, BA/MA RM3/2098.

69. *New York Times* article, 26 Feb. 1895, BA/MA RM3/1073.

70. Trials of the USS *Cincinnati,* BA/MA RM3/1073.

71. Report on the trials of the USS *Alabama* and *Kearsarge,* German naval attaché,

Washington, D.C., to SS/RMA, Berlin, 7 Sept. 1899, BA/MA RM3/1074.

72. Allgemeine Bedingungen, 1894, BA/MA RM3/11564.

73. See, for example, KI, KII, and KIV interoffice correspondence, BA/MA RM3/421.

74. Consideration of a firm for the Lieferantenverzeichnis (1910), BA/MA RM3/2210.

75. Von Tirpitz was familiar with French and American progress in U-boat development. RMA records for the 1890s contain many of the press reviews provided by the German Foreign Office on American submarine development. Von Tirpitz knew of the presence of the French U-boat experts d'Equevilley and Laboeuf at the Germaniawerft in Kiel. Yet RMA policy did not allow U-boat technology to emerge from the shadow of the capital ship until 1914. See von Tirpitz, *Memoirs*, 1:48.

76. "Versuche mit Materialien," BA/MA RM3/2249–52 passim.

77. Von Senden-Bibran, aboard the Imperial Yacht SMS *Hohenzollern*, to Captain Barber, U.S. naval attaché, Berlin 14 July 1898, BA/MA RM2 (Marinekabinette)/34; see technical information sent by German legation in Washington, D.C., 1895–97, RM3/1072.

78. BA/MA RM3/2106 (1897–98), passim.

79. Ibid. The Parsons Marine Steam Turbine Company was founded in Great Britain in 1897.

80. "Lieferantenliste der deutschen Kriegsmarine" (Berlin, 1907), 66 (Section No. 46), BA/MA RM3/2298; Breyer, *Battleships and Battlecruisers*, 276.

81. I take issue with P. C. Witt's assertion that the naval authorities were less than energetic in this regard. See Witt, *Finanzpolitik*, 140.

82. Bericht: KWK to SS/RMA, Berlin, 5 May 1897, BA/MA RM3/2193.

83. "Zu BII 6466 von BII 6065," 24 Nov. 1891 (RMA interoffice correspondence), BA/MA RM3/2190; "Bismarckhütte to SS/RMA, Berlin, 19 Oct. 1895, RM3/2192; "Lieferantenliste," Berlin, 1907, Sections 1, 2, 3, RM3/2298.

84. Report: KWK to SS/RMA, Berlin, 1 Sept. 1897, BA/MA RM3/2193.

85. *Krupp, 1812–1912* (Jena, 1912), 365, HA Krupp. Krupp acquired Grusson-Magdeburg on 1 May 1893.

86. *The History of Armor Plate Manufacturing by Fried. Krupp*, 17, HA Krupp WA IV 753. 420 nickel-steel armor was 150 mm. thick, in three layers, made up of 0.34 percent carbon, 0.3 percent nickel, and 2 percent chrome. The process was perfected 14 July 1894, and the first sales were in 1895. It was first used in the SMS *Freya, Hertha*, and Kaiser Class battleships. The use of nickel-steel armor reduced by almost 50 percent the amount needed to render a ship "safe." It cost over 2,300 marks per ton as opposed to about 1,500 marks for the old compound plate. Some historians see this as a true saving for the RMA and a value worth the price. The latter was definitely true, but given Krupp's excessively high prices during this period, the former was hardly the case. Armor and its foreign and domestic price will be further explored in later chapters.

87. "Gesichtspunkte, die fur die Frage der Behandlung unseres neuen Panzerplatten-Fabrikations," 1898, HA Krupp, FAH III B39.

88. Fried. Krupp, Gusstahlfabrik, Essen, to SS/RMA, Berlin, 26 Feb. 1897; Dillinger

Hüttenwerke, Dillingen, Saar, to SS/RMA, Berlin, 19 Feb. 1897; RMA Construction Division to Dillinger, 12 Jan. 1897, all in BA/MA RM3/327.

89. Armor prices sometimes forced budget amendments in the midst of construction, for example, light cruiser "K" (16 Nov. 1896). The original estimate for armor was 500,000 marks (18 Jan. 1897); for a portion 193,004.82 marks were paid, for a difference of 306,995.18 marks; price increases of 470,000 marks brought the total budget increase needed for 1898 to 163,000 marks. See KWK to SS/RMA, Berlin, 18 Jan. 1897, BA/MA RM3/6071.

90. "Denkschrift über die Entwicklung des Panzerplattenmaterials in den letzten 10 Jahren unter besonderer Berucksichtigung der Preissteigerung," Berlin, 29 Nov. 1899, Weapons Division (W), RMA, BA/MA RM3/6650.

91. Cooling, *Grey Steel and Blue Water Navy*, 120.

92. "Denkschrift über die Entwicklung des Panzerplattenmaterials in den letzten 10 Jahren unter besonderer Berucksichtigung der Preissteigerung," Berlin, 29 Nov. 1899, Weapons Division, RMA, BA/MA RM3/6650.

93. For example, in the 1890s Speck von Sternberg (the army's attaché in Washington, D.C.) sent material on U.S. armor and artillery trial results to Krupp. The naval attaché did the same on a regular basis (e.g., Krupp, Essen, to SS/RMA, 27 March 1893, BA/MA RM3/1072, acknowledging the receipt of such information). Other firms did not receive similar treatment.

94. "Versuche mit Materialien," BA/MA RM3/2552. See also BA/MA RM3/2249–51, passim, on the insulation question.

Chapter 2. Further Expansion and the Second Stage, 1899–1901

1. Bernhard Furst von Bülow served as legate in Bucharest in 1888, ambassador in Rome in 1893, foreign minister in 1897, and reichschancellor and Prussian minister president from 1900 to 1909.

2. Kennedy, *Rise of Anglo-German Antagonism*, 226.

3. Herwig, *Politics of Frustration*, 28–29.

4. Kennedy, *Samoan Tangle*.

5. Herwig, *Politics of Frustration*, 34.

6. Herwig, *German Naval Officer Corps*, 26.

7. The discussion about a man for this post involved some industrial leaders, including Hanns Jencke, director of the Krupp firm. See Jencke to Krupp, 24 March 1899, HA Krupp, FAH III B127.

8. Hurd and Castle, *German Seapower*, 328–29, contains the text of the 1898 Naval Law.

9. The term *normal* is employed to designate weight at the time of shakedown cruise, with partial complement and less than half of normal fuel load.

10. Gröner, *Kriegsschiffe*, 20.

11. Herwig, *Luxury Fleet*, Table 6.

12. Gröner, *Kriegsschiffe*, 20.

13. Preston, *Battleships of World War I*, see Wittelsbach Class.

14. Gröner, *Kriegsschiffe*, 20.

15. Berghahn, *Tirpitz Plan*, 618 (Table 34).

16. Gröner, *Kriegsschiffe*, 23.

17. Berghahn, *Tirpitz Plan*, 618 (Table 34).

18. Gröner, *Kriegsschiffe*, 27, 34. The one exception to Schichau's virtual monopoly of torpedo boats between 1886 and 1900 was the D-10, built by Thornycroft, London.

19. The Prussian War Ministry determined the military code violations in the area of supply. See "Mittellungen über Ausschiliessungen und Wiederzulassen von Lieferern und Unternehemern," Berlin, 3 July 1914, BA/MA RM3/2304.

20. See BA/MA RM3/2294 regarding controls developed during the formation of the suppliers' list.

21. For example, Torpedo Inspectorate, Kiel, to SS/RMA, Berlin, 16 Sept. 1916, BA/MA RM3/2307.

22. Kaiserliches Marine Abnahmeamt (ABA), Graf Adolfstrasse 53, Düsseldorf.

23. Max Krause (director of Borsig Bergund Hüttenverwaltung) to Herrn Langner, Geheime Admiralitätsrat, RMA, Berlin, 1 Oct. 1901, BA/MA RM3/2066.

24. Vulcan, Hamburg, to SS/RMA, Berlin, 25 April 1900, BA/MA RM3/458.

25. British Admiralty Contract Forms, Correspondence between KII and KIV, April 1901, BA/MA RM3/6007.

26. Correspondence between Schichau and BBS, Danzig, 26−29 Aug. 1901, BA/MA RM3/452.

27. Cooperation between von Tirpitz and the Construction Department was the basis for contract awards. See, e.g., Construction Department Memo to SS/RMA, May 1901, BA/MA RM3/471.

28. SS/RMA, Berlin, to Germania-Tegel, Berlin, 24 May 1901, BA/MA RM3/471.

29. Naval attaché, U.S. Embassy, Berlin, to SS/RMA, Berlin, 6 July 1903, BA/MA RM3/1077.

30. BA/MA RM3/6026−27−28 passim. Final ship prices were usually higher than original bids but neither figure varied dramatically from PW to PW on any given project.

31. Blohm und Voss, Hamburg, to SS/RMA, Berlin, 8 May 1901, BA/MA RM3/471.

32. Germania, Tegel-Berlin, to SS/RMA, Berlin, 11 May 1901; Vulcan-Stettin to SS/RMA, Berlin, 10 May 1901, both in BA/MA RM3/471.

33. For example, see "Räthenwertheilungsplan, 1901," BA/MA RM3/6029.

34. One such case developed with Krupp armor in 1901; see Krupp, Essen, to SS/RMA, Berlin, 14 March 1901, BA/MA RM3/6073.

35. Von Tirpitz to SS/RMA, Berlin, 22 Dec. 1901, BA/MA RM3/6029. Von Thielmann served as state secretary of the Imperial Treasury from 1897 to 1903.

36. Construction Department, Berlin, to KWW, 16 March 1900, BA/MA RM3/458; Allgemeine Bedingungen, 1900, RM3/277.

37. For example, Schichau, Elbing, to SS/RMA, 29 Sept. 1899, BA/MA RM3/360. Schichau complained that light cruisers could not be built at less than 3,100 tons, let alone the 3,000 tons the RMA wanted. "Bericht des Marineattaches des Kaiserlichen Botschaft zu Washington #77. Die neue Kreuzer von Denver Klasse,"

Washington, D.C., 19 July 1899, RM3/360. American light cruiser tonnage averaged between 2,500 and 3,400 tons for the Denver Class.

38. Allgemeine Bedingungen, 1900, BA/MA RM3/277.

39. Construction Department, Berlin, to Schichau, Danzig, 28 Dec. 1901, BA/MA RM3/452.

40. For example, Vulcan, Hamburg, to SS/RMA, 29 June 1900, BA/MA RM3/458. See also RM3/449 and 285 passim.

41. Die Frage: "Weshalb hat sich die Fertigstellung der Armierung bisher verspätet und weshalb wird das Kommende schneller Fertig werden?" RMA Memoranda, "An Nachrichten Bureau," 27 Nov. 1899, BA/MA RM3/6650.

42. Correspondence between Schichau, von Eickstedt, and Boekholt (BBS, Danzig), August to December 1901, re: Wittelsbach Class, BA/MA RM3/452.

43. For a few illustrations see KWW to SS/RMA, 7 Dec. 1900, BA/MA RM3/441.

44. Schwarz and Halle, eds., *Schiffbauindustrie*, 208–9.

45. "Denkschrift uber die Entwicklung des Panzerplattenmaterials in den letzten 10 Jahren unter besonderer Berucksichtigung der Preissteigerung," Berlin, 29 Nov. 1899, signed "Sack" for the Weapons Division, BA/MA RM3/6650.

46. Report, Chief of the Admiralty Staff to SS/RMA, Berlin, 24 Oct. 1901, BA/MA RM3/3701; Construction Department to every yard, Berlin, 5 April 1897, RM3/327; Vulcan, Stettin-Bredow, to SS/RMA, Berlin, 5 July 1900, RM3/458.

47. Construction Department to Germania, Schichau, Vulcan, and Blohm und Voss, Berlin, 3 April 1901, BA/MA RM3/470; Construction Department, Berlin, to Vulcan, Stettin-Bredow, 5 Oct. 1900, RM3/458.

48. Dillinger to SS/RMA, Dillingen-Saar, 28 March 1899, BA/MA RM3/439.

49. Dillinger to SS/RMA, Dillingen-Saar, 25 Jan. 1900, BA/MA RM3/440.

50. For example, Vulcan, Stettin-Bredow, to SS/RMA, Berlin, 21 Dec. 1899, BA/MA RM3/440.

51. Notes on armor contracts for Wittelsbach Class 1901, BA/MA RM3/6029.

52. Cooling, *Grey Steel and Blue Water Navy*, 154.

53. Werftdepartment an Zentralabteilung, 31 March 1900, BA/MA RM3/2.

54. Trebilcock, "British Armaments and European Industrialization," 256.

55. Witt, *Finanzpolitik*, 140.

56. SS/RMA, Berlin, to Krupp, Essen, 4 April 1900, BA/MA RM3/2.

57. Jencke, Essen, to von Tirpitz, Berlin, 30 March 1900; Krupp, Capri, to von Tirpitz, 6 April 1900, both in BA/MA RM3/2.

58. Jencke to Krupp, Berlin, April 1900 (letter draft, undated), ibid.

59. Krupp, Capri, to von Tirpitz, Berlin, 6 April 1900, ibid.

60. HA Krupp, FAH III B36, passim.

61. Jencke, Essen, to von Tirpitz, Berlin, March 1900, ibid.

62. Weckruf Nr. 77, 1 April 1900, ibid.

63. Ibid., 74–75.

64. Press clippings from Feb., March, and April 1900, ibid.

65. Krupp, Capri, to Jencke, Essen, 17 April 1900, ibid.

66. Fritz Krupp's account of the meeting with the kaiser and von Senden, ibid. The

Krupp firm did become a joint stock company, but in 1903, many months after Fritz's death.

67. Manchester, *Arms of Krupp*, 217.

68. Nachlass von Tirpitz, Berlin, to Krupp, Essen, 23 Jan. 1899, BA/MA N253/4.

69. Leckebusch, "Seeschiffswerften," 64.

70. HA Krupp, FAH III B36, 74–75; Handakten Dähnhardt: "Panzer: Ubersicht uber die Panzerpreise in verschiedenen Landern," 3 March 1915, BA/MA RM3/11634.

71. Jencke, Essen, to von Tirpitz, Berlin, 27 Feb. 1900, and telegram 27 Feb. 1900, BA/MA RM3/6648.

72. Von Tirpitz to RMA Budget Department, Berlin, 18 Nov. 1899, BA/MA RM3/3699.

73. Press clippings, 1901, HA Krupp FAH III B40.

74. Krupp Direktorium to SS/RMA, 5 March 1901, ibid.

75. Krupp Direktorium to von Tirpitz, 5 March 1901, HA Krupp FAH III B40. Rebates, for example, were often considered in RMA-Krupp business relations but were not popular with Krupp. See also H. Jencke to Krupp, Essen, 10 April 1900, FAH III B127.

76. Report by the *Norddeutsche Allgemeine Zeitung*, 8 March 1901, on the Reichstag meeting of 7 March 1901, 1 P.M. (63d session), ibid.

77. KWK to SS/RMA (Construction Department), Berlin, 11 May 1901, BA/MA RM3/6042.

78. HA Krupp, FAH III B40. A study of these papers shows just how self-justified Krupp felt. He was not merely presenting a facade.

79. KWK to SS/RMA Technical Department, 17 June 1901, BA/MA RM3/2196.

80. KWW to SS/RMA (Construction Department), Berlin, 11 May 1901, BA/MA RM3/1231.

81. *Brockhaus Enzyklopädie*, 17:404.

82. BA/MA RM3/1229–33 passim, for example, KWW to SS/RMA (Technical Department), 26 June 1901, RM3/1229.

83. KWW to SS/RMA, Berlin, 5 Oct. 1900, BA/MA RM3/1230.

84. Schwarz and Halle, eds., *Schiffbauindustrie*, 253.

85. BA/MA RM3/2248 (1900–1901), passim.

86. BA/MA RM3/1002–15 (1900–1910), passim.

87. North German Lloyd, Bremerhaven, to SS/RMA, 16 July 1900, 14 Jan., 15 April, 18 June 1901, BA/MA RM3/272.

88. Schiffbautechnischen Gesellschaft, 1899, BA/MA RM3/90.

89. Fact-finding trip report by Construction Inspectors Edgar and Schumann to SS/RMA, Berlin, 8 July 1901, BA/MA RM3/272.

90. K (Construction Department) to M (Central Section), Berlin, 27 March 1901, BA/MA RM3/2492.

91. Brown and Boveri, Mannheim, to RMA, 23 Aug. 1900, BA/MA RM3/2107.

92. Schiff- und Maschinenbau Germania, Kiel, to Imperial Torpedo Inspectorate, Kiel, 23 Nov. 1900, BA/MA RM3/2107.

93. Ibid.; see also the source cited in note 94.

94. "Verhandlung mit der Firma Brown und Boveri über Parsons Turbinen," Torpedo Inspectorate, Kiel, to SS/RMA, Berlin, 13 Oct. 1900, BA/MA RM3/2107.

95. John J. Thornycroft and Company, London, to Vulcan, Stettin, 27 Sept. 1899; Vulcan, Stettin, to SS/RMA, Berlin, 12 Feb. 1900, both in BA/MA RM3/1244.

96. *Daily Graphic* clipping, 3 Feb. 1899, BA/MA RM3/3685.

97. Naval attaché, Paris, to SS/RMA, 13 Feb. 1900, BA/MA RM3/1049.

98. Naval attaché, London, to SS/RMA, Berlin, 9 Nov. 1900; naval attaché, Paris, to SS/RMA, Berlin, 10 Jan. 1901, both in BA/MA RM3/3876.

99. BA/MA RM3/6062, passim.

100. Published account of U-boat development at the Germaniawerft, HA Krupp, WA Xa 4,160; ibid., WA IV 714. Barandon was the chairman of the two sections of Germania, Tegel-Berlin and Kiel. Each section had its own director.

101. Handakten von Gohren, "U-bootsdebatten im der Budgetkommission von 1900–1903," BA/MA RM3/11603.

102. *Daily Mail*, 2 March 1901; naval attaché, Paris, to SS/RMA, Berlin, 10 Jan. 1901, both in BA/MA RM3/3876.

103. Kennedy, "Tirpitz, England and the Second Naval Law," 34, 35; Witt, *Finanzpolitik*, 142.

104. Kennedy, "Tirpitz, England and the Second Naval Law," 34.

105. Hurd and Castle, *German Seapower*, 119; Kennedy, *Rise of Anglo-German Antagonism*, 417.

106. Deist, *Flottenpolitik*, 140–42.

107. Marienfeld, *Wissenschaft*, 83. Membership statistics from 1 Jan. 1900 to 31 Dec. 1900 rose as follows: single from 93,991 to 269,370; organizations from 152,890 to 329,771; *Die Flotte* circulation from 125,000 to 300,000.

108. Deist, *Flottenpolitik*, 81–82.

109. Berghahn, *Tirpitz Plan*; Kehr, *Battleship Building*.

110. Witt, *Finanzpolitik*, 139–41.

111. Berghahn, *Tirpitz Plan*, 285–86.

112. Gröner, *Kriegsschiffe*, 20.

113. Preston, *Battleships of World War I*, see the section on the Braunschweig Class.

114. Gröner, *Kriegsschiffe*, 23.

115. Ibid., 27.

116. Ibid., 31. *Eber* was 1,193 tons and cost 1,632,000 marks; *Tsingtau*, 280 tons at a cost of 497,000 marks; *Vaterland*, 280 tons and a cost of 492,000 marks.

117. While a torpedo boat was still under construction, its designation revealed the yard responsible for it, thus the S (Schichau) 114 through 131 or the G (Germania) 132 through 136. Upon commissioning the prefix "T" replaced the first initial of the yard (ibid., 34).

118. Von Tirpitz to Wilhelm II, Berlin, 17 Oct. 1900, BA/MA RM3/2.

Chapter 3. Business as Usual? 1902–1904

1. Kennedy, *Rise of Anglo-German Antagonism*, 265.
2. Naval attaché in London to Kaiser Wilhelm II, 18 Nov. 1904, in Lepsius, Mendelssohn-Bartholdy, and Thimms, eds., *Grosse Politik*, vol. 19, pt. 2, no. 6149, pp. 353–56; Maj. Graf von der Schulenberg, military attaché in London, to Chancellor von Bülow, Berlin, 13 Dec. 1904, ibid., no. 6154, pp. 360–65; Chancellor von Bülow to Kaiser Wilhelm II, 26 Dec. 1904, ibid., no. 6157, pp. 372–73.
3. Kennedy, *Rise of Anglo-German Antagonism*, 265.
4. "Politische und Militärische Beatractungen über einen english-deutschen Krieg," Berlin, 27 Nov. 1904, BA/MA N253/21 Nachlass von Tirpitz.
5. Kennedy, *Rise of Anglo-German Antagonism*, 268–73. The traditional Continental and later colonial antagonisms between England and France had been a basic assumption of German foreign policy since 1871.
6. Diary excerpt, 11 Jan. 1902, no. 221; Holstein to Bülow, 21 Aug. 1908, no. 496; Holstein to Bülow, Dammhaus, 13 Sept. 1908, no. 510, all in von Holstein, *Geheimen Papiere*.
7. Wilhelm II to von Tirpitz, aboard the SMS *Hohenzollern* (the kaiser's yacht), Kiel, 28 June 1902, BA/MA RM3/108.
8. Von Tirpitz to von Eickstedt, Berlin, 20 June 1902, BA/MA RM3/2493.
9. Gemzell, *Organization, Conflict and Innovation*, 103.
10. For example, "Neubau 107, Turretdampfer für die Erzfahrt an die Herrn L. Posschl and Co., Lübeck," 17 March 1904, BA/MA RM3/6008.
11. RSA (Imperial Treasury) to SS/RMA, Berlin, 7 April 1904; ibid.
12. Witt, *Finanzpolitik*, 112–13.
13. *Nauticus* (1904), 18. In 1904 the following represent proposed and (granted) funds in millions of marks: continued projects, 99.3 (99.3); shipbuilding and arming, 100.4 (94.9); special projects, 25.7 (21.2); totals, 225.4 (215.4).
14. *Nauticus* (1904), 439.
15. Jürgen Rohwer, "Kriegschiffbau und Flottengesetze um die Jahrhundertwende," in Schottelius and Deist, eds., *Marine und Marinepolitik*, 215–27.
16. Ibid.
17. *Nauticus* (1904), 439.
18. Rohwer, "Kriegschiffbau," 215–27.
19. *Nauticus* (1904), 439.
20. 1902 edition of the *Lieferantenverzeichnis* (suppliers' list or *LV*), BA/MA RM3/2296. Other prewar editions included one for 1905, in RM3/2297–98, and 1907 in RM3/2298.
21. Revisions for the 1902 suppliers' list, RMA Construction Department, Berlin, 28 April 1903; Richard Lehman, Dresden, to RMA, Berlin, 5 June 1903; both in BA/MA RM3/2294.
22. BA/MA RM3/2295, passim (1904).
23. Von Tirpitz to von Eickstedt, Berlin, 3 April 1903, BA/MA RM3/328.

24. Carl Flohr Maschinenfabrik to SS/RMA, Berlin, 4 April 1903, BA/MA RM3/2294.
25. 1904 edition of the *Vorschriften für die Lieferung und Abnahmeprüfung von Materialen und Apparaten*, BA/MA RM3/301.
26. KWK to SS/RMA, Berlin, 28 July 1904, BA/MA RM3/2295.
27. Richard Gradenwitz Company to RMA, Berlin, 2 Sept. 1903, ibid.
28. *LV* (1907), BA/MA RM3/2298.
29. *LV* (1902), BA/MA RM3/2294.
30 ABB = General construction regulations. See list of abbreviations.
31. SS/RMA, Berlin: "Auf die Schreiben vom 7 April 1904 und vom 10 September 1904," to Budget Department, and KWK to Vulcan, Stettin, 8 June 1904, BA/MA RM3/6008.
32. "Grundzüge für elektrischen Anlagen," BA/MA RM3/1170.
33. RMA, Berlin, to North German Lloyd, Bremen, 21 June 1902, BA/MA RM3/328; Berlin to Germaniawerft, Kiel-Gaarden, 8 Jan. 1903, RM3/502.
34. RMA, Construction Department, Berlin, to Schichau, Elbing, 22 Feb. 1902, BA/MA RM3/1238.
35. "Materialabnahme für die kleine Kreuzer 'G' und 'H,' " Berlin, 11 Jan. 1902, BA/MA RM3/2040.
36. KWK to RMA, Technical Department, Berlin, 4 Aug. 1902; correspondence between the Technical Department and the six major shipyards, Oct. 1901–June 1902; Handelskammer für den Kreis, Essen, to SS/RMA, Berlin, 1902, all ibid.
37. RMA Construction Department, Berlin, to KWK, 7 Nov. 1903, ibid.
38. KWK to SS/RMA, Berlin, 3 Feb. 1904, BA/MA RM3/2100.
39. *Der Grosse Brockhaus*, 16th ed., vol. 3 (Wiesbaden, 1953), see entry on crucible steel.
40. Ibid.
41. Commander of the First Squadron, North Sea, to SS/RMA, Berlin, 5 Sept. 1902, BA/MA RM3/3701.
42. RMA Construction Department, Berlin, to Vulcan, Stettin, 31 Jan. 1902, BA/MA RM3/483; Germaniawerft, Kiel-Gaarden, to SS/RMA, Berlin, 4 Nov. 1904, BA/MA RM3/480; RMA, Berlin, to KWW, 27 April 1904, RM3/446.
43. For example, see BA/MA RM3/500–511, passim.
44. F. A. Krupp, Villa Hügel, to Direktorium, Essen, 2 Nov. 1898, HA Krupp, FAH III C181.
45. Direktorium to F. A. Krupp, Essen, 7 Dec. 1898, ibid.
46. "Bericht betreffend die verspäteten Lieferungen des Artillerie-Materials für SMS *Kaiser Friedrich III*," Direktorium to Krupp, Essen, 7 Dec. 1898, ibid.
47. Vulcan, Stettin, to SS/RMA, Berlin, 24 June 1904, BA/MA RM3/488.
48. Krupp to SS/RMA, Berlin, 4 Nov. 1902; "Notizen zum Immediatverträge über der Inbaugabe von Kriegschiffen, die 1903 neu gefordert werden," Berlin, 30 Oct. 1902, both in BA/MA RM3/502.
49. KWK to RMA Construction Department, Berlin, 14 May 1904, BA/MA RM3/1100.

50. Vulcan, Stettin, to Kaiserliche Marinebaurath Flach, Berlin, 10 Sept. 1902, BA/MA RM3/462; "Rückstandige Angaben für den Bau SMS *Wettin*," Danzig, 29 March 1902, BA/MA RM3/453.

51. KWK to SS/RMA, Berlin, 19 July 1902, BA/MA RM3/453.

52. Krupp, Essen, to SS/RMA, Berlin, 8 April 1902; KWK to SS/RMA, Berlin, 3 April 1902; both in BA/MA RM3/286.

53. Schichau, Danzig, to SS/RMA, Berlin, 17 Feb. 1902, BA/MA RM3/453.

54. KWK to SS/RMA, Berlin, 15 May 1903, BA/MA RM3/455.

55. KWK to RMA Construction Department, 20 Dec. 1904 (telegram), BA/MA RM3/517; Haniel and Lueg, Düsseldorf, to SS/RMA, Berlin, 16 Dec. 1904, and RMA Construction Department, Berlin, to KWW, 23 Dec. 1904, RM3/527.

56. Schichau, Danzig, to SS/RMA, Berlin, 7 Oct. 1903, BA/MA RM3/495; KWK to RMA Construction Department, Berlin, 25 Feb. 1904, RM3/481.

57. KWW to SS/RMA, Berlin, 20 March 1902, BA/MA RM3/444; Germaniawerft, Kiel, to SS/RMA, Berlin, 4 Feb. 1904; BA/MA RM3/478.

58. Vulcan, Stettin, to RMA, Berlin, 31 Oct. 1903, BA/MA RM3/463.

59. Vulcan, Stettin, to RMA, Berlin, 20 July 1903, BA/MA RM3/462.

60. RMA, Berlin, to Krupp, Essen, 16 Feb. 1904, BA/MA RM3/360.

61. BA/MA RM3/460–61, passim; "Vierteljährliche Ausgabekontrolle über den Fonds für den Neubau des Linienschiffs 'Mecklenburg' für das 3. vierteljahr 1903" (KWW), RM3/6112; Vulcan, Stettin, to SS/RMA, Berlin, 17 Dec. 1904, RM3/489; RMA, Berlin, to Germaniawerft, Kiel, 11 Feb. 1904, RM3/504.

62. KWD to SS/RMA, Berlin, 7 April 1904; KWK-BBS to SS/RMA, Berlin, 6 April 1904; Krupp, Essen, to SS/RMA, Berlin, 16 April 1904; Vulcan-BBS, Stettin, to SS/RMA, Berlin, 22 April 1904, all in BA/MA RM3/6007.

63. Von Tirpitz to Construction Department, RMA (handscript notations), Berlin, 16 Feb. 1903, BA/MA RM3/462; von Tirpitz to Kaiserliche Kommando des 1. Geschwader, Berlin, 23 May 1903, RM3/455.

64. Abschrift zu KIV 3457, zu EI 1625/03, Berlin, 26 Sept. 1903, BA/MA RM3/6008.

65. KWK to RMA Construction Department, Berlin, 14 Nov. 1904, BA/MA RM3/6078.

66. Firma B. Koch, Stettin, to RMA, Berlin, 27 Feb. 1905, "Beschwerde gegen die Handlungsweise der Kaiserlichen Werft, Danzig"; KWD to SS/RMA Technical Department, Berlin, 27 March 1905; *Mitteilungen des Verbandes des deutschen Tiefbauunternehmer*, no. 3, March 1905, all in BA/MA RMA/10857.

67. Firma B. Koch, Stettin, to RMA, Berlin, 17 April 1905, BA/MA RM3/10857.

68. Reichswerft, Danzig, to Reichswehrministerium, Berlin, 3 March 1921, ibid.

69. "Vergebung der grossen Kreuzer 'C' und 'D' an Privatwerften," Berlin, 2 June 1904, Shipyard Department to SS/RMA, BA/MA RM3/6033.

70. "Vergleich der Neubaukosten auf Kaiserlichen und Privatwerften," Berlin, 24 Sept. 1902, BA/MA RM3/6030. This was a constant concern for the RMA. Von Tirpitz sent a Professor Bernhardt to Britain to evaluate the Royal Navy's state shipyards in 1904. Bernhardt thought their machinery was a bit out of date but

concluded that they bore a heavier burden for the British than the KWs did for the
RMA. See Prof. Bernhardt to SS/RMA, Essen, Report on his fact-finding trip of
June 1904, BA/MA N253/7, Nachlass von Tirpitz.

71. Gustav Hartmann, Dresden, to Rötger, Essen, 5 Nov. 1903; Rötger, Merau,
    Habsburger Hof, to Hartmann, Essen, 9 Nov. 1903, both in HA Krupp FAH IV
    C16; Gustav Hartmann, generalia, WA Xa 3,7 and FAH IV C276. See also FAH
    IV C13 and WA IV 1264. Hartmann was a member of the Krupp Board of Gover-
    nors from 1903 to 1909. Max Rötger was born 27 August 1860 in Wittenberg and
    died 7 April 1923 in Berlin-Grünewald. He succeeded Hanns Jencke as chair-
    man of the Krupp Direktorium, serving from 1 June 1901 to 1 October 1909. See
    HA Krupp FAH III B261.

72. Rötger to Hartmann, Baden-Baden, 30 April 1904, HA Krupp FAH IV C16.

73. Von Maltzahn, Oberpräsident of Pommern, to Chancellor von Bülow, Berlin,
    1903, BA/MA RM3/514. By comparison, Germaniawerft's contracts between
    1900 and 1905 were as follows: 1900, six torpedo boats; 1901, one battleship;
    1902, one battleship; 1903, one battleship; 1904, one U-boat; 1905, one battle-
    ship. The greater frequency of contracts and the overlapping of projects made it
    less likely that Germania would have difficulty keeping its workers on the job. See
    Gröner, *Kriegsschiffe*, passim.

74. Vulcan, Stettin, to SS/RMA, Berlin, 4 Jan. 1902, BA/MA RM3/460; Vulcan,
    Stettin, to Krupp, Essen, 26 June 1902, RM3/461.

75. Rötger to Hartmann, Baden-Baden, 30 April 1904, HA Krupp FAH IV C16. See
    also Epkenhans, "Grossindustrie und Schlachtflottenbau," 82–86. This article
    was very disappointing. I have corresponded since 1986 with Epkenhans, a stu-
    dent at the University of Münster, discussing our respective opinions on the his-
    tory of heavy industry and the RMA during this period. In this matter of Krupp
    and Vulcan, we continue to differ. Our disagreement is based on interpretation
    and certainly not on mistranslation. Epkenhans believes that Krupp simply
    wanted to exert influence over the decision-making process at Vulcan to reduce
    the competitive pressure on Germaniawerft during this very disruptive period of
    naval expansion. My interpretation is somewhat stronger because of the awkward
    and vulnerable position in which Vulcan found itself during this period, which
    the Krupp leadership could not have failed to appreciate. Given both the circum-
    stances I described in the text and the very mercurial situation in the shipbuild-
    ing industry at this time, Krupp's stock purchases, together with its monopoly of
    the armor plate and naval gun industry, placed it in a position to exert extraordi-
    nary pressure on Vulcan without having to approach majority stock interest. This
    is the threat Vulcan's directors had to face.

   Epkenhans's research is excellent, and I long ago became acquainted with the
    documentation he cites. But he consistently fails to evaluate Krupp as a multi-
    faceted industrial concern in the larger context of the shipbuilding industry. He
    prefers instead to discuss the firm's component parts independently, as if they
    had no effect on each other, on Krupp's industrial policy, or on the behavior of von
    Tirpitz and the RMA. Indeed, his article virtually ignores the navy's opinion and

NOTES TO PAGES 69–71

the formulation of the RMA's viewpoint. It is essential that historians evaluate the impact of the ambitious naval expansion on the Germaniawerft in the context of the RMA's policy, the company's place in the constellation of Krupp interests, and within the shipbuilding industry at large.

Epkenhans also argues that a takeover of Vulcan would disturb the Krupp Directorate because it would cause an outcry over monopoly. Since there was a regular outcry in the government and press regarding Krupp's other monopolies, why would the company suddenly become sensitive? Neither its reputation nor its support in high political and economic circles would have been significantly altered.

76. KWK to RMA Construction Department, Berlin, 9 May 1904, BA/MA RM3/2290.
77. Leckebusch, "Seeschiffswerften."
78. Schichau, Danzig, to SS/RMA, Berlin, 28 Feb. 1903, BA/MA RM3/494.
79. Hoerder Bergwerks- und Hütten Verein, Hoerde, to RMA, Berlin, 4 March 1903, BA/MA RM3/485.
80. Vulcan, Stettin, to SS/RMA, Berlin, 28 June, 31 July, 10 Dec., 6 May 1902, BA/MA RM3/484.
81. Construction inspector, Stettin, to RMA Construction Department, Berlin, 16 Sept. 1904, BA/MA RM3/2040.
82. "Protokol über die Sitzüng am 27. Oktober 1902," RMA, Berlin, BA/MA RM3/2527.
83. Germaniawerft, Kiel-Gaarden, to SS/RMA, Berlin, 30 April 1904, BA/MA RM3/479; KWK to SS/RMA Construction Department, Berlin, 2 Jan. 1903, RM3/6076. Information on F. A. Krupp is from von Alten, *Handbuch für Heer und Flotte*, vol. 5.
84. Weapons Department to Central Division RMA, Berlin, 2 April 1903, BA/MA RM3/2527; "Zusammenstellung des Gesamtverbrauchs an Krupp'schen Vertikalpanzermaterial" (survey of cost between 1894 and 1906), BA/MA N253/7, Nachlass von Tirpitz.
85. RMA memo regarding 24-centimeter guns for battleships, Berlin, 26 Sept. 1904; "Aufstellung der Artillerie in Kasematten, Einzeltürmen und Zwillingstürmen," Berlin, 3 Nov. 1904; RMA memo: Construction Department on 21-centimeter guns for new battleship contracts, Berlin, 13 Dec. 1904, all in BA/MA RM3/329; "Protokoll über die Sitzung am Montag den 24. November 1902," RM3/3701.
86. Hubatsch, *Der Admiralstab*, 115–16.
87. Blohm und Voss, Hamburg, to SS/RMA, Berlin, 4 May 1903, BA/MA RM3/1077.
88. Report by Oberleutnant z. S. von Löwenfeld regarding his experiences on board the battleship *Tsarevitch* at Tsingtau (Kiaochow), 20 Aug. 1904; BA/MA RM3/1002.
89. "Beobachtung auf Cesarewitsch," Tsingtau (Kiaochow), 1 Sept. 1904, ibid., written by Vice-Admiral von Prittwitz.
90. "Bericht der nach Schottland und England zum Studium der Parsonsturbinen entsandten Kommission" to SS/RMA, Berlin, 16 May 1902, BA/MA RM3/2108.

91. Promotional brochure for Turbina, Deutsche Parsons Marine AG, 1902, ibid.
92. Clipping from the *Berliner Tageblatt*, 15 Feb. 1904, BA/MA RM3/2109.
93. "Bericht der nach Schottland und England zum Studium der Parsonsturbinen entsandten Kommission," Berlin, 16 May 1902, BA/MA RM3/2108.
94. Hubatsch, *Kaiserliche Marine*, 375–84.
95. BA/MA RM3/1171–72, passim (1903–4).
96. KWK to RMA Technical Department, Berlin, 3 Oct. 1902, BA/MA RM3/1173.
97. RMA Construction Department, Berlin, to Siemens and Halske, Berlin, 30 April 1902; Construction Department to Weapons Division, RMA (eight-page memo), Berlin, 1902, both in BA/MA RM3/1232.
98. Dockyard Department, section VII to section V, RMA, Berlin, 3 Jan. 1904, BA/MA RM3/1100.
99. "Generalle Vorschriften über Einrichtung von Funkentelegraphenkammern," Berlin, 8 Nov. 1902, ibid.
100. Techel, *Unterseebooten*, 5.
101. *Nauticus* (1904), 103–10; BA/MA RM3/3877 British Submarine Boat Company, Ltd., London to SS/RMA, Berlin 6 Oct. 1902. RM5/1947, passim; comparative notes on U-boat development in: France, Britain, U.S.A., Japan, and Germany.
102. Fortschritte in Bau der Unterseeboote, 1904, BA/MA RM5/1947.
103. Techel, *Unterseebooten*, 5. To maximize profits, Krupp hoped to rely on a bare minimum of subcontractors, but it had to procure a light, reliable diesel engine for surface running from MAN, Fiat (Turin), or Körting. Krupp spent the better part of the next decade unsuccessfully trying to surpass the four-cycle designs these firms had to offer.
104. Rötger and Eccius, Essen, to Hartmann, Dresden, 20 Dec. 1904, HA Krupp FAH IV C13.
105. Abschrift: Fortschritte in Bau der Unterseeboote—1904, BA/MA RM5/1947.
106. Techel, *Unterseebooten*, 101; Gröner, *Kriegsschiffe*, 40–45.
107. All technical information on these vessels came from Gröner, *Kriegsschiffe*, 20–40; and Breyer, *Battleships and Battlecruisers*, 262–63.

Chapter 4. Criticism, Continuity, and Legislative Success, 1905–1908

1. Kennedy, *Rise of Anglo-German Antagonism*, 251–52.
2. Metternich, London, to Chancellor von Bülow, Berlin, 11 Jan. 1905, *Die Grosse Politik*, vol. 19, pt. 2, no. 6159, pp. 375–77.
3. Von Tirpitz to von Bethmann-Hollweg, Berlin, 20 April 1907, BA/MA RM3/11710.
4. Ritter, *Staatskunst und Kriegshandwerk*, 192–93.
5. Kennedy, "German Naval Operations Plans against England," 71.
6. Breyer, *Battleships and Battlecruisers*, 263.
7. Von Holstein to von Bülow, Berlin, 29 Aug. 1907, in von Holstein, *Geheimen Papiere*, 4:439–40. Cecil, *Albert Ballin*, 350–51.
8. Marienfeld, *Wissenschaft*, 83.

9. For example, see News Bureau (Boy-Ed) to SS/RMA, Berlin, 2 Dec. 1907, BA/MA RM3/10148.
10. Berghahn, *Germany and the Approach of War in 1914*, 92.
11. Von Tirpitz, *Memoirs*, 1:203; "Begrundung zur Novelle 1908," BA/MA RM3/6674.
12. Berghahn, *Tirpitz Plan*, 474.
13. Secretaries of the Imperial Treasury Office (RSA) von Stengel (1903–8) and Reinhold von Sydow (1908–9).
14. Witt, *Finanzpolitik*, 141.
15. Deist, *Flottenpolitik*, 99.
16. Hallgarten, *Imperialismus*, 2:544.
17. Witt, *Finanzpolitik*, 142.
18. RMA interoffice correspondence: Budget Department to Dockyard Department, RMA, Berlin, 20 Feb. 1905, BA/MA RM3/3609.
19. "Notiz zum Immediatbericht, betreffend Vergebung der Linienschiffe 1907," BA/MA RM3/2528; Construction Department to Central Division, RMA, Berlin, 25 June 1908, RM3/578.
20. "Denkschrift betreffend den Ausbau der Werften. Stand im Mai 1908 und nachstliegende Zukunftsbedurfnisse," Berlin, 16 May 1908, BA/MA RM3/3610.
21. BA/MA RM3/3608–10, passim.
22. Berghahn, *Tirpitz Plan*, 485ff.
23. For the debates on the passage of the 1906 and 1908 supplements, see the *Verhandlungen des Reichstags (Stenographische Berichte)* for 25 June 1906 and 6 April 1908, as well as the preliminary sessions just before these dates.
24. Hurd and Castle, *German Seapower*, 335–36.
25. BA/MA RM3/1002–15, passim.
26. "Denkschrift über die Notwendigkeit einer Marine-Versuchsanstalt," Berlin, 11 Oct. 1907, BA/MA RM3/1006; RM3/1008, passim.
27. KWK to Construction Department, RMA, Berlin, 21 July 1907, BA/MA RM3/2204.
28. BA/MA RM3/2066–67, passim. For example, KII to Dockyard Department, RMA, Berlin, 20 June 1906.
29. See, for example, the case of the firm Posnansky and Strelitz doing work on insulation materials: KWD to RMA, Berlin, 14 Jan. 1903, BA/MA RM3/2249.
30. BA/MA RM3/1003, passim.
31. RMA Construction Department to Weapons Division, Aug. 1905, BA/MA RM3/329.
32. RMA, Berlin, to Vulcan, Stettin, and Germaniawerft, Kiel, 4 Dec. 1906, BA/MA RM3/2528.
33. SS/RMA to Construction Department, Berlin, 2 Oct. 1906, BA/MA RM3/2531.
34. Marine Oberbaurat Prof. Otto Kretschner, Baden-Baden, to RMA, Berlin, Aug. 1905, BA/MA RM3/348.
35. Construction Department to SS/RMA, Berlin, 10 June 1905, BA/MA RM3/357.

36. RMA, Berlin, 18 April 1907, "Armierung der 1908 Linienschiffe an Seiner Excellenz dem Herrn Staatssekretar vorzulegen," BA/MA RM3/577.

37. Max Krause to RMA, Berlin, 1 March 1905, BA/MA RM3/302.

38. Correspondence between RMA and Vulcan, Howaldtswerke, Blohm und Voss, Schichau, Germaniawerft, and Weser, Nov.–Dec. 1907, BA/MA RM3/279.

39. "Denkschrift betreffend Erhohung der Geschwindigkeit der kleinen Kreuzer," Berlin, 16 Dec. 1905, BA/MA RM3/361. One badly needed improvement had to await further exploration. The increasing weight of capital ships required a better form of propulsion. The obvious answer—the turbine engine—was not applied uniformly in German battleships until the 1909 Kaiser Class. Meanwhile, the conventional engines required to power the new dreadnoughts took up an extraordinary amount of room.

40. Schiffsform Guljaeff, Kiel, to SS/RMA, Berlin, 2 Feb. 1906, BA/MA RM3/331.

41. Correspondence between the RMA and the major private yards, Dec. 1905–Jan. 1906, BA/MA RM3/330; Hurd and Castle, *German Seapower*, 322.

42. Rössler, *Die Deutsche U-Bootbau bis Ende des 1. Weltkrieg*, 35. Note that this volume is not the same as the general history of German U-boats published by Rössler in 1975, which is cited throughout this work as *U-Bootbaus.* "Denkschrift zum Immediatevortrag betreffend Entwicklung des U-bootwesens," Berlin, 10 Sept. 1909, BA/MA RM3/4915; "Fortschritte im Bau der Unterseeboote," 1905, BA/MA RM5/1947; Gemzell, *Organization, Conflict and Innovation*, 62.

43. Von Tirpitz, *Memoirs*, 2:572, 1:138.

44. "U-bootsdebatten im Plenum und in der Budgetkommission von 1904–1914," BA/MA RM3/11603, Handakten von Gohren.

45. Gemzell, *Organization, Conflict and Innovation*, 60–61. Captain Persius was von Tirpitz's most relentless opponent and a U-boat advocate. Because he was professionally isolated and hounded by von Tirpitz, his career ended prematurely. He entered the service on 16 April 1883 and achieved the rank of lieutenant commander by 1903.

46. BA/MA RM3/9754. See Persius's work *Die Tirpitz Legende* (1918).

47. All technical information taken from Gröner, *Kriegsschiffe*, 40. Oberingenieur Techel was in charge of U-boat construction at the Germaniawerft from 1907 to 1918. His work with the Krupp firm extended back to 1895 (HA Krupp WA Xa 4, 187). In 1909 the Germaniawerft Direktorium members were Bauer, Huber, Steinike, Toussaint, and Richter. The last replaced Lieutenant Commander Ritter von Mann, wartime head of the U-Boat Office and later SS/RMA, who was the shipyard's liaison with the navy. See F. Krupp AG, ed., *Handbuch* (Essen, 1906 and 1909).

48. Hubatsch, *Der Admiralstab*, 121.

49. RMA to Reichshauptkasse, Berlin, 28 May 1906, BA/MA RM3/1004.

50. Von Tirpitz, *Memoirs*, 1:38–39.

51. "Fleets (Great Britain and Foreign Countries)" (London, 1904), an official publication, BA/MA RM3/3686.

52. Marine attaché, Paris, to SS/RMA, Berlin, 10 April 1906, BA/MA RM3/1050.
53. Weser, Bremen, to RMA, Berlin, 23 Jan. 1905, BA/MA RM3/278; RM3/280, passim.
54. KWW to RMA, Suggestions for the revision of the ABB, 1908, BA/MA RM3/280.
55. BBS, Stettin-Bredow, to RMA Construction Department, Berlin, 29 Feb. 1908, BA/MA RM3/1182; "Return to KI," Berlin, 28 April 1906, RM3/6009.
56. 1905 edition of the suppliers' list, BA/MA RM3/2296.
57. Postler and Co., Dresden, to RMA, Berlin, 10 Nov. 1908, BA/MA RM3/2299.
58. KWW to RMA, Berlin, 16 June 1908, ibid.
59. KWK to RMA, Berlin, 19 July 1909, ibid.
60. Construction Department report on financial difficulties confronting Becker and Ulmann, Berlin, 31 Aug. 1905, BA/MA RM3/2296; Carl Stoeckicht AG, Frankfurt a.M., to RMA, Berlin, 2 Feb. 1907, RM3/2297.
61. Blohm und Voss, Hamburg, to SS/RMA, Berlin, 28 Sept. 1909, BA/MA RM3/1185.
62. KWW to Construction Department, RMA, Berlin, 17 Oct. 1905, BA/MA RM3/2296.
63. AG Mix and Genest, Berlin-Schönberg, to SS/RMA, Berlin, 28 Oct. 1916, BA/MA RM3/2076.
64. Kaiserliche Marine Deutsche Seewarts, Hamburg, to Nautical Section, RMA, Berlin, 8 Nov. 1906, BA/MA RM3/7618.
65. Germaniawerft, Kiel-Gaarden, to SS/RMA, Berlin, 11 Feb. 1908, BA/MA RM3/6009.
66. BBS, Hamburg, to Construction Department, RMA, Berlin, 11 Feb. 1908, BA/MA RM3/348.
67. Fricke, "Eine Denkschrift Krupps," 1253.
68. Ibid., 1250–53.
69. Construction Department to Legal Section, RMA, Berlin, 22 Oct. 1907, BA/MA RM3/6009.
70. Admiral Rollmann replaced von Eickstedt as head of the RMA Construction Department in 1907 and held that position until the opening of the war in 1914. He served as a lieutenant commander in 1906; second adjutant under Captain Engel, director of the Shipyard Division of the RMA; was appointed rear admiral 27 April 1907; and director of the RMA Construction Department and vice-admiral 27 Jan. 1910.
71. Von Usedom was appointed captain 18 Sept. 1899 (*Rangliste*, 1904–7); rear admiral 14 March 1905, and director of KWK. See KWK to Construction Department, RMA, Berlin, 19 Feb. 1906, BA/MA RM3/1176.
72. Kommando der Marine Station der Ostsee, Kiel, to SS/RMA, Berlin, 28 Aug. 1907 and 21 Sept. 1905, BA/MA RM3/4851.
73. RMA Construction Department report, "Lange Bauzeit der franzoschischen Neubauten," Berlin, 10 June 1908, BA/MA RM3/1051.
74. RMA Construction Department report, "Abkurzung der Schiffbauzeiten," Berlin, 24 Jan. 1906, BA/MA RM3/6672.

75. For example, see Schichau, Danzig, to SS/RMA, Berlin, 14 Dec. 1905, BA/MA RM3/499.

76. Weapons Division to Budget Department, RMA, Berlin, 23 Dec. 1905, BA/MA RM3/6672.

77. Krupp, Essen, to SS/RMA, Berlin, 8 Jan. 1906, ibid., regarding "Termine für Lieferung von Schiffsarmierung."

78. Construction Department, "Denkschrift zum Immediatvortrag über die Fertigstellung des Linienschiffes *Pommern*," 26 May 1904, BA/MA RM3/523; Vulcan, Stettin, to SS/RMA, Berlin, 3 Nov. 1906, RM3/522.

79. Construction Department, RMA, Berlin, to Legal Section, 22 Oct. 1907, BA/MA RM3/6009.

80. "Denkschrift über Verkurzung der Bauzeiten und Verbilligung der Baukosten bei den Schiffsneubauten nach den Ausfuhrungen von Schichau," Berlin, 2 Dec. 1908, BA/MA RM3/6673.

81. Geheime Kommerzienrat Ziese, Elbing, to SS/RMA, Berlin, 19 June 1908, ibid.

82. Rollmann to SS/RMA, Berlin, 4 June 1908, ibid.

83. Vulcan, Stettin, to SS/RMA, Berlin, 27 March 1908, ibid.

84. Blohm und Voss, Hamburg, to SS/RMA, Berlin, 17 Jan. 1908, ibid.; BBS, Blohm und Voss, Hamburg, to Construction Department, RMA, Berlin, 11 Feb. 1908, RM3/348.

85. RMA, Berlin, to Vulcan, Stettin, 24 Feb. 1905, BA/MA RM3/489; Construction Department, "Gutachten zum Sonderbericht des Schiffsprufungs Kommission betreffend Bekohlungseinrichtungen SMS *Deutschland*," 1907, RM3/511.

86. KWK to Construction Department, Berlin, 19 Jan. 1907, BA/MA RM3/511.

87. KWK to Construction Department, RMA, Berlin, 10 Jan. 1905, BA/MA RM3/489.

88. Germaniawerft, Kiel-Gaarden, to SS/RMA, Berlin, 1 Feb. 1905, BA/MA RM3/481.

89. KWK to Construction Department, RMA, Berlin, 6 April 1905, ibid.

90. Germaniawerft, Kiel-Gaarden, to SS/RMA, Berlin, 19 July 1906, BA/MA RM3/510.

91. Germaniawerft, Kiel-Gaarden, to SS/RMA, Berlin, 2 Jan. 1905, BA/MA RM3/480; KWK to Construction Department, RMA, Berlin, 15 June 1905, RM3/491.

92. Ship Testing Commission, Kiel, to Construction Department, RMA, Berlin, 19 Sept. 1905, BA/MA RM3/491.

93. Vulcan, Stettin, to SS/RMA, Berlin, 21 Aug. 1907, BA/MA RM3/524. For international armor price comparisons see Cooling, *Grey Steel and Blue Water Navy*, Table 7.

94. Vulcan, Stettin, to SS/RMA, Berlin, 30 Oct. 1906, BA/MA RM3/522.

95. Krupp, Essen, to SS/RMA, Berlin, 28 March 1906, BA/MA RM3/287.

96. Handakten Dahnhardt, "Panzer: Übersicht über die Panzerpreise in verschiedenen Landern," prepared 3 March 1915, BA/MA RM3/11634; see also Epkenhans, "Grossindustrie und Schlachtflottenbau," 67ff. Epkenhans's analysis of

the possible conflict between Krupp's self-interest and the national interest is shallow at best. He is perfectly willing to allow Krupp's audience with Kaiser Wilhelm I in 1900 to stand as the revelation of the industrialist's conviction that he served the national interest by serving the needs of his company. Although he perceives the fundamental contradiction between the motives and goals of private industry and the navy, Epkenhans misses its significance. The navy's military mission and the private sector's quest for profit and growth, though both legitimate, led to contradictory perceptions of why Germany was building warships. Neither side fully appreciated the demands and risks taken by the other to implement naval expansion. Both felt that they were working in the national interest. Von Tirpitz expected a commitment from Krupp and other industrialists which would provide the RMA with the best warships of which German technology was capable. Krupp was interested in responsibility and commitment clearly defined by contract. During the imperial period in Germany's history, this conflict never resolved itself into the symbiotic relationship we now call the military-industrial complex. Most of the time, Krupp's economic, political, and royal connections gave him an advantage von Tirpitz did not have.

97. Construction Department to Weapons Division, RMA, Berlin, 9 March 1907, BA/MA RM3/2204. Von Tirpitz, von Eickstedt, and others within the RMA lacked the authority to control Krupp. Thus the significant portion of von Eickstedt's statement is not that Krupp would do everything to deliver things of quality. Rather, von Eickstedt knew all too well that the company would work primarily in its own interest, regardless of the RMA's wishes and needs, and he was sure that the company's interest and that of the navy, which he naturally equated with his country's welfare, were not necessarily the same.

98. Weapons Division, "Besprechung über den Anschluss der elektrischen Einrichtungen für schwere Artillerie der Neubauten 1906 an ihre Primarstationen," 28 April 1906, BA/MA RM3/1176.

99. Construction Department to Weapons Division, RMA, Berlin, 9 March 1907 and reply, 12 March 1907, BA/MA RM3/2204.

100. F. F. King Real Estate and Investments, Denver, to SS/RMA, Berlin, 13 Feb. 1908, BA/MA RM3/2206.

101. "Protokoll über die Sitzung von 22. September 1905 betreffend Neukonstructionen von Linienschiffen und grossen Kreuzern," BA/MA RM3/3704.

102. Admiral von Müller, Berlin, to Krupp Director Max Rötger, Berlin, 21 March 1905, HA Krupp FAH IV C7. Admiral Karl Alexander von Müller (1854–1940) entered the service in May 1871 and spent some time as a lieutenant commander in von Tirpitz's torpedo arm in 1879. Early in his career he was assigned to the German embassy in Stockholm as naval attaché. He was promoted in 1891 to commander of the cannon boat *Iltis* (China); in 1897–98 served as personal adjutant to Prince Heinrich (the kaiser's brother) in China and as chief of staff to the Cruiser Squadron; and in 1898–1900 as commander of SMS *Deutschland*. In 1900 he was promoted to captain and assigned to the Naval Cabinet. In 1902–4 he commanded SMS *Wettin*, in 1907 replaced von Senden-Bibran as chief of the Naval Cabinet, and in 1910 was promoted to admiral.

103. Weapons Division to Construction Department, RMA, Berlin, 3 Jan. 1906, BA/MA RM3/1176.
104. "Kommission zur Prüfung von Vertragen über Kriegslieferung," tenth session, 15 Nov. 1917, BA/MA RM3/7763; *Brockhaus Enzyklopädie*, 5:267.
105. AG Weser, Bremen, to SS/RMA, Berlin, 20 Aug. 1908, BA/MA RM3/600.
106. KWK to Construction Department, RMA, Berlin, 27 March 1909, BA/MA RM3/2207.
107. BBS, Bremen, to SS/RMA, Berlin, 9 March 1908, BA/MA RM3/544.
108. Bergische Stahl-Industrie, Remscheid, to SS/RMA, Berlin, 1 Oct. 1907, Bismarckhütte to SS/RMA, Berlin, 22 Nov. 1906, and RMA reply, 11 Dec. 1906, BA/MA RM3/304.
109. Blohm und Voss, Hamburg, to SS/RMA, Berlin, 29 July 1909, BA/MA RM3/1184.
110. For example, "Allgemeine Bewertung und Prüfung," May 1905, BA/MA RM3/1174.
111. Krupp, Essen, to SS/RMA, Berlin, 17 Aug. 1907; RMA Construction Department to AEG, Berlin, 23 Aug. 1907, both in BA/MA RM3/1180.
112. Telegram to RMA from Krupp, Essen, 11 Aug. 1902; Krupp, Essen, to SS/RMA, Berlin, 16 Aug. 1906; SS/RMA, Berlin, to Krupp, Essen, 25 Nov. 1906; Weapons Division to Construction Department, RMA, Berlin, 13 Nov. 1906, all in BA/MA RM3/1178.
113. Construction Department, RMA, Berlin, to Krupp, Essen, 14 July 1906; Weapons Division to Construction Department, Berlin, 29 June 1906; Construction Department to Weapons Division, Berlin, 12 July 1906, BA/MA RM3/1177.
114. AEG, Berlin, to Construction Department, Berlin, 11 Sept. 1907, BA/MA RM3/1180; KWW to Construction Department, RMA, Berlin, 4 Aug. 1906, RM3/1178.
115. KWW to Construction Department, RMA, Berlin, 28 July 1909, BA/MA RM3/1184.
116. Letters to SS/RMA, Berlin, from the major shipyards, April, May, June 1905; Gesellschaft für Drahtlose Telegraphie m.b.H., Berlin, to Construction Department, Berlin, 4 April 1905 and 26 Oct. 1905, BA/MA RM3/1101.
117. KWK to Construction Department, RMA, Berlin, 5 Feb. 1907, ibid.
118. KWK to Construction Department, Berlin, 3 March 1909, BA/MA RM3/1102.
119. KWK to Construction Department, RMA, Berlin, 3 Feb. 1905, BA/MA RM3/1174; KWK to Construction Department, Berlin, 14 Jan. 1905, RM3/1173.
120. Central Division, RMA, Berlin, to S.P.K., Kiel, 7 April 1906, BA/MA RM3/2533; KWK to Construction Department, RMA, Berlin, 25 April 1906, RM3/2111.
121. BA/MA RM3/2112, 2113, folders on research and development costs for the various steam turbine systems, passim (1906–7).
122. Turbina Deutsche Parsons Marine AG to SS/RMA, 26 Sept. 1906, BA/MA RM3/2112.

123. Press clipping from the *Daily Telegraph*, 23 Nov. 1906, sent to the RMA by the Foreign Office, ibid.
124. "Notiz zum Immediatvortrag" (signed by von Eickstedt), Berlin, 22 Sept. 1906; Admiral von Müller to von Tirpitz, Berlin, 16 Oct. 1906, ibid.
125. Germaniawerft, Kiel-Gaarden, to SS/RMA, Berlin, 20 Oct. 1906, ibid.; KWK to Construction Department, RMA, Berlin, 7 May 1907; SSW, Berlin, to SS/RMA, Berlin, 4 April 1906, and reply, 10 April 1906, RM3/1176.
126. AEG Turbinenfabrik, Berlin, to SS/RMA, Berlin, 17 Sept. 1906, BA/MA RM3/2112.
127. Vulcan, Stettin-Bredow, to SS/RMA, Berlin, 29 May 1906; Construction Department, RMA, Berlin, to Vulcan, Stettin-Bredow, 14 June 1906, ibid.
128. AG Weser, Bremen, to SS/RMA, Berlin, 3 Nov. 1906, ibid.
129. Between 1905 and 1908 six different shipyards shared construction of the battleships of the Nassau and Helgoland classes. The imperial yard in Wilhelmshaven, which had the cheapest construction costs of any yard, was given the SMS *Nassau* and *Ostfriesland*. AG Weser, in Bremen, received contracts for the SMS *Westfalen* and *Thuringen*, and the SMS *Rheinland* went to Vulcan. The SMS *Posen* and *Oldenburg* went to the Germaniawerft and Schichau, respectively. All of these ships were dreadnoughts, ranging in cost between 37 and 47 million marks, and they entered naval service by 1912. The imperial yard at Kiel and Blohm und Voss began building the heavy cruisers SMS *Blucher* and *von der Tann* in 1907 and 1908. Kiel produced the *Blucher* for 28.5 million marks, but the *von der Tann* proved more expensive. The first of the larger ships to employ a Parsons turbine, the *von der Tann* cost the navy 36.5 million marks.

 The RMA also occupied the imperial yard at Kiel with the light cruisers SMS *Königsberg* and *Nürnberg*, while the *Stuttgart* and the *Emden* went to Danzig. The SMS *Nautlius*, *Albatross*, *Stettin*, *Dresden*, and *Kolberg* went to Weser, Vulcan, Blohm und Voss, and Schichau, respectively. These ships varied in weight and cost between 3 and 8 million marks. For all technical information regarding these ships see Gröner, *Kriegsschiffe*, 20−35.
130. Boy-Ed (News Bureau, RMA) to SS/RMA, Berlin, 4 Oct. 1907, BA/MA RM3/9757; Karl Galster, *Welche Seekriegsrüstung braucht Deutschland* (Berlin, 1907).
131. Berlin Police President to RMA News Bureau, Berlin, 5 Nov. 1909, BA/MA RM3/9753.
132. Clipping from the *Times* (London), 16 April 1909 (RMA News Bureau), ibid.
133. *Ibid.*
134. Nachlass Weichold, "Aufzeichnungen . . . Admiral (ret.) von Mantey (1938)," BA/MA N316/61.

Chapter 5. The Money Runs Out, 1909−1912

1. Handakten Dahnhardt, passim, esp. Memo on the Risk Theory, 1912, BA/MA RM3/11639.

2. Ritter, *Staatskunst und Kriegshandwerk*, 2:232–36.
3. Röhl, "Admiral von Müller," 670, 688–89, 654.
4. RMA News Bureau, Berlin, to the *Jahrbuch für deutsche Armee und Marine*, Berlin, 1 May 1909, BA/MA RM3/9753.
5. Hubatsch, "Kulminationspunkt," 296.
6. Kennedy, "German Naval Operations Plans against England," 75.
7. Hubatsch, "Kulminationspunkt," 17, 312; Jonathan Steinberg, "Diplomatie als Wille und Vorstellung: Die Berliner Mission Lord Haldanes im Februar 1912," in Schottelius and Deist, eds., *Marine und Marinepolitik*, 263–82.
8. Marder, *From the Dreadnought to Scapa Flow*, 1:153.
9. Ibid., 160–70.
10. Ibid., 177.
11. Ibid., 179–205 passim. See also Steinberg, "Diplomatie als Willie und Vorstellung," in *Marine und Marinepolitik*, 263–82.
12. Röhl, "Admiral von Müller," 661.
13. Hubatsch, "Kulminationspunkt," 319–22; von Kühlmann, London, to von Bethmann-Hollweg, Berlin, 22 Oct. 1913, BA/MA RM3/6674.
14. Jarausch, *Enigmatic Chancellor*, 94–96.
15. Riezler, *Tagebücher*, 187–88.
16. Hubatsch, "Kulminationspunkt," 301–3.
17. Speech by SPD Reichstag representative Vogtherr in the naval budget debates, 123d sess., 1 March 1913, BA/MA RM3/5997, pt. 1.
18. Speech by SPD representative Noske in the Reichstag naval budget debates, 124th sess., 3 March 1913, ibid.
19. *Nauticus* (1912), 297–98.
20. Gemzell, *Organization, Conflict and Innovation*, 81.
21. 1909 press clippings, BA/MA RM3/4742.
22. *Vossische Zeitung* clipping, 7 Dec. 1909, BA/MA RM3/4743.
23. *Der Tag*, 7 Dec. 1909, *Die Post*, 7 Dec. 1909, and 7 Dec. 1909, and *Vossische Zeitung*, 7 Dec. 1909.
24. Hubatsch, *Tirpitz Ära*, chap. 4.
25. Naval attaché, London, to SS/RMA, Berlin, 30 Oct. 1913, BA/MA RM3/3707.
26. BA/MA RM3/3694–95, passim.
27. "Bericht über die 12. Hauptversammlung des Deutschen Verbandes für die Materialprufung der Technik," 1911, BA/MA RM3/2101.
28. "Kosten für Ausarbeitung des Projekts No. 283. Schnelle Linienschiffsstudie," 1911, HA Krupp WA VII f 1479.
29. Blohm und Voss, Hamburg, to SS/RMA, Berlin, 2 Dec. 1911, BA/MA RM3/1482; RM3/7619, passim.
30. KWK to Construction Department, RMA, Berlin, 27 April 1910, BA/MA RM3/1013; F. H. Schmidt, Altona, to Rechnungsrat Dopking, Berlin, 23 April 1909, BA/MA RM3/1011.
31. KWK to SS/RMA, Berlin, 30 April 1910, BA/MA RM3/1013.
32. Von Tirpitz's statements in the Reichstag, 29 March 1909, BA/MA RM3/6674.

33. *Shipping World*, no. 875, 9 March 1910, BA/MA RM2/190.

34. "Rundschau in allen Marinen: Jahresübersicht 1909," *Marine Rundschau*, 1910, BA/MA RM2/189.

35. Verein Deutscher Schiffswerften to SS/RMA, Berlin, 28 July 1909, BA/MA RM3/280; Construction Department, RMA, Berlin, to KWW, 16 March 1911, RM3/582.

36. "Vorgehen in Ubootsbau," Berlin, 30 Nov. 1909, BA/MA RM3/4915.

37. RMA to Chief of the Admiralty Staff, Berlin, 5 Jan. 1910, BA/MA RM5/1948. These boats were at Wilhelmshaven pending completion of their pens on Helgoland.

38. Rössler, *U-Bootbaus*, 49.

39. Ibid., 40.

40. Von Tirpitz, *Memoirs*, 2:581–82; "Denkschrift zum Immediatvortrag, betreffend Entwicklung des Ubootswesens," Berlin, 10 Sept. 1909, BA/MA RM3/4915.

41. KWD to Construction Department, RMA, Berlin, 5 Jan. 1910, BA/MA RM3/2209.

42. KWD to Construction Department, RMA, Berlin, 17 March 1909, BA/MA RM3/1183.

43. SS/RMA, Berlin, to the Chief of the Admiralty Staff, Berlin, 30 Jan. 1912, BA/MA RM5/1948.

44. Rössler, *U-Bootbaus*, 51.

45. SS/RMA, Berlin, to Commander of the Baltic Naval Station, Kiel, 1 June 1913; BA/MA RM5/1948.

46. Von Tirpitz, *Memoirs*, 2:571–72; Rössler, *U-Bootbaus*, 33.

47. Rössler, *U-Bootbaus*, 37.

48. HA Krupp WA VII f 1113, passim.

49. HA Krupp WA VII f 1479, Bau 177/180 and Bau 167.

50. ABA, Düsseldorf, to Construction Department, RMA, Berlin, 30 June 1912, BA/MA RM3/1118; Weser, Bremen, to SS/RMA, Berlin, 9 July 1909, RM3/547; Weser, Bremen, to SS/RMA, Berlin, 3 Jan. 1910; RM3/550; Germaniawerft, Kiel-Gaarden, to SS/RMA, Berlin, 18 April 1911, RM3/308.

51. "Protokoll über die Sitzung am 30.3.11 Anwesend Vetreter von A,K,W, and B. Betreffend: Grossen Kreuzer K," Berlin, 5 May 1911, BA/MA RM3/3694.

52. Krupp, Essen, to SS/RMA, Berlin, 25 Sept. 1909; Dillinger Huttenwerke, Dillingen/Saar, to SS/RMA, Berlin, 2 Oct. 1909, BA/MA RM3/580.

53. "Zusammenstellung der im Rechnungsjahre 1911 entstanden Kosten der artelleristischen Armierung für Schiffsneubauten," Weapons Division, RMA, Berlin, BA/MA RM3/289.

54. Handakten Dahnhardt, "Panzer: Übersicht über die Panzerpreisen in verschiedenen Landern," 3 March 1915, BA/MA RM3/11634.

55. "Entwicklung der Panzerpreise," Budget Department, RMA, Berlin, 1915, ibid.

56. Boelcke, *Krupp und die Hohenzollern*, 206.

57. Handakten Dahnhardt, "Panzer: Übersicht über die Panzerpreisen in verschiedenen Landern," 3 March 1915, BA/MA RM3/11634. For Krupp's reaction

to the Thyssen-Midvale threats see Krupp, Essen, to SS/RMA, Berlin, 16 Dec. 1909, RM3/11712; and Handakten Dahnhardt, 26−39, RM3/11635.

58. Handakten Dahnhardt, 178−94, BA/MA RM3/11638.

59. Ibid., 16−26; "Verhandlung mit Thyssen über Aufnahme der Panzerplatten-Herstellung," Construction Department, RMA, Berlin, 1913, BA/MA RM3/11635.

60. Handakten Dahnhardt, 16−26, BA/MA RM3/11635.

61. Handakten Dahnhardt, "Panzer: Übersicht über die Panzerpreisen in verschiedenen Landern," 3 March 1915, BA/MA RM3/11634

62. Handakten Dahnhardt, Reichstag Verhandlungen, 24th Sitzung, Kommission für Reichshaushalts-Etat, 12th Legislatur-Periode, II session 1909−10, BA/MA RM3/11635.

63. Handakten Dahnhardt, M. Erzberger, Berlin, to Thyssen, Mülheim, June 1911, BA/MA RM3/11639.

64. RMA Construction Department, "Konkurrenz gegen Krupp," 1909, and "Panzerlieferungsfrage Krupp-Thyssen," Berlin, 1 Feb. 1910 (Rollmann); see also "Resume," all in BA/MA RM3/11712.

65. Von Capelle to SS/RMA, Berlin, 26 Jan. 1910, BA/MA RM3/11711 EI 182/10 1910.

66. Interoffice correspondence, BA/MA RM3/11635 EI 182/10 1910.

67. "Entwicklung der Panzerpreise," Budget Department, RMA, Berlin, 1915, BA/MA RM3/11634. See also Epkenhans. "Grossindustrie und Schlachtflottenbau," 69ff. I was disappointed to see that Epkenhans presented a series of theses in 1988 on the armor plate controversy which were astonishingly similar to my own without ever citing my dissertation (1982) or two articles which I published on the subject in 1984. For the original research on this subject and the first presentation of these arguments, which Epkenhans has altered very little, see Weir, "Imperial Naval Office" and "Tirpitz, Technology, and Building U-boats."

68. Baumeister Grundt, Danzig, to SS/RMA, Berlin, 2 Oct. 1909; correspondence between the ABA in Danzig and Wilhelmshaven and the Construction Department, RMA, Berlin, 11 May 1909, BA/MA RM3/2043.

69. ABA, Düsseldorf, to KWW, 10 March 1910, ibid.

70. Firma Carl Zeiss, Jena, to Kaiserliche Inspektion des Torpedowesens, Kiel, 23 Dec. 1913, BA/MA RM3/2044.

71. KWW to Construction Department, RMA, Berlin, 3 Feb. 1912; and BBS, Hamburg (Blohm und Voss), to Construction Department, RMA, Berlin, 15 June 1912, ibid.; KWD to Construction Department, RMA, Berlin, 22 Aug. 1910, BA/MA RM3/2043.

72. Telegrams, RMA to KWD, KWW, and KWK, 29−30 Aug. 1913, BA/MA RM3/2044.

73. "Beaufsichtigung der Panzerplattenfabrikation," Essen, to SS/RMA, Berlin, 29 July 1912, ibid.

74. Präsidialkanzeli des K.u.K. Kreigsministeriums, Marinesektion, Vienna, to German naval attaché, Vienna, 3 Oct. 1913, BA/MA RM3/1063.

75. Naval attaché in Vienna to SS/RMA, Berlin, "Probefahrten in der Österreichisch-Ungarischen Marine," 22 Sept. 1911, ibid.

76. Germaniawerft, Kiel-Gaarden, to SS/RMA, Berlin, 9 Oct. 1912; Schichau, Elbing, to SS/RMA, Berlin, 6 Nov. 1912; Vulcan, Hamburg, to SS/RMA, Berlin, 4 Nov. 1912, BA/MA RM3/6013.

77. BA/MA RM3/6198–6202, passim, 1909–18.

78. KWW to Construction Department, RMA, Berlin, 24 Jan. 1911, BA/MA RM3/6011.

79. Blohm und Voss, Hamburg, to Geheim Oberbaurat Burkner, Hamburg, 13 Sept. 1913, BA/MA RM3/363; Werkvertrag: Ersatz Kurfürst Friedrich Wilhelm (Grosser Kurfürst, König Class), 1911, RM3/381.

80. KWK to Construction Department, RMA, Berlin, 31 May 1913, BA/MA RM3/1119.

81. "Besichtigung über die Firma Wurttembergische Eisenwerke GmbH., Feuerbach-Stuttgart," 1909, BA/MA RM3/2208; KWW to Construction Department, RMA, Berlin, 9 Sept. 1909, RM3/2300.

82. Henry P. Newman, Hamburg, to RMA, Berlin, 20 Aug. 1910; HK, Hamburg, to SS/RMA, Berlin, 10 June 1910, BA/MA RM3/2256.

83. Handelskammer (HK), Frankfurt a.M. to SS/RMA, Berlin, 30 June 1910; HK, Dresden, to SS/RMA, Berlin, 1 June 1910, ibid.

84. HK, Hannover, to SS/RMA, Berlin, 23 March 1910, ibid.

85. HK, Düsseldorf, to RMA, Berlin, 3 Jan. 1910, BA/MA RM3/2255.

86. HK für den Kreis Siegen to SS/RMA, Berlin, 30 March 1910, BA/MA RM3/2209; HK, Plauen, to SS/RMA, Berlin, 3 May 1910, RM3/2256.

87. RMA, Berlin, to Germaniawerft, Kiel-Gaarden, 27 Jan. 1909; to Blohm und Voss, Hamburg, 6 Feb. 1909; to Schichau, Danzig, 25 Jan. 1909, BA/MA RM3/6010.

88. Vulcan, Hamburg to RMA, Berlin, 3 July 1913; Blohm und Voss, Hamburg, to RMA, Berlin, 12 July 1913; BA/MA RM3/284.

89. Blohm und Voss, Hamburg, to RMA, Berlin, 28 June 1910, BA/MA RM3/281.

90. Handakten von Capelle, "Notizen für Seine Exzellenz den Herrn Staatssekretar zu den Beschuldigungen im Prozess Heinrich Frankenthal. Betr: Schlendrian in der Marineverwaltung," pt. 2, "Werftorganization," 12 Nov. 1909, BA/MA RM3/11713.

91. KWK to Construction Department, RMA, Berlin, 22 April 1911, "Aufstellung der Ausgabekontrollen, Berucksichtigung von Geldüberweisung," BA/MA RM3/ 6089.

92. KWW to Construction Department, RMA, Berlin, 22 Aug. 1912, Ausgabenkontrolle für das 1. Vierteljahr 1912, BA/MA RM3/6121; KWW to Construction Department, RMA, Berlin, 10 Nov. 1911, RM3/6119; KWK, "Vierteljahrliche Ausgabekontrolle den Fonds für den Neubau des Linienschiffes Ostfriesland für das IV Vierteljahr 1911," RM3/6091.

93. Jahresausbildungsplan der Flotte, 1910, BA/MA RM3/2021.

94. "Denkschrift betreffend den weiteren Ausbau der Werften auf Grund der Flot-

tengesetznovelle 1912," Berlin, 7 May 1912, BA/MA RM3/3611.

95. "Denkschrift über die Notwendigkeit der Beibehaltung der Deckungsgemein-schaften bei den Schiffbau und Armierungsfond," 1911, BA/MA RM3/11599.

96. Krupp, Essen, to SS/RMA, Berlin, 18 June 1910, BA/MA RM3/539; BBS, Blohm und Voss, Hamburg, to SS/RMA, Berlin, 2 Dec. 1913, RM3/1480.

97. Reports to the RMA by Inspektion des Torpedowesens, Kiel, 24 Oct. 1911; KWW, 11 Nov. 1911; KWD, 24 Nov. 1911; and KWK, 30 Nov. 1911, BA/MA RM3/308.

98. Inspektion des Torpedowesens, Kiel, to Herr Ohlrich (representative of AG Weser), Friedrichsort, 19 April 1909, BA/MA RM3/548.

99. Vulcan, Stettin, to RMA, Berlin, 13 March 1909, BA/MA RM3/361.

100. KWW to Construction Department, RMA, Berlin, 11 Aug. 1911, BA/MA RM3/583.

101. "Denkschrift über die Notwendigkeit der Beibehaltung der Deckungsge-meindschaften bei den Schiffbau und Armierungfonds," 1910, p. 5, BA/MA RM3/11599.

102. Witt, *Finanzpolitik*, 261–62, 341–43.

103. Ibid., 341–43, 375, 206.

104. Ritter, *Staatskunst und Kriegshandwerk*, 2:233–36.

105. Handakten Dahnhardt, von Capelle memo to Budget Department, RMA, Berlin, 1911, BA/MA RM3/11639.

106. Berghahn, *Germany and the Approach of War in 1914*, 99.

107. Krupp to Ehrensberger, Berlin, 19 Jan. 1910, HA Krupp FAH IV E64; "Begrun-dung der Novelle in der Budgetkommission," Administrative Department, RMA, Berlin, 1912, BA/MA RM3/11594. One such example was Winston Churchill's speech in the Commons on 22 July 1912, in James, *Churchill*, 2:1981; see also his speech on the naval situation, which begins on page 1970.

108. Reichstags Verhandlungen, Kommission für Reichhaushalts Etat, 1912, BA/MA RM3/5996 pt. 2.

109. "Nachweisung der Teilnehmer an einer Reichstagsinformationsreise im Juni," 1913, BA/MA RM3/11691.

110. Handakten von Gohren, "Betrifft: Rustungsaussschuss," Berlin, 13 July 1913 (Dahnhardt to von Tirpitz, Berlin), ibid.

111. Hurd and Castle, *German Seapower*, 337–39; Handakten Dahnhardt, Scheme of fleet composition and development from 1898 to 1912, BA/MA RM3/11637.

112. Ritter, *Staatskunst und Kriegshandwerk*, 2:237–38.

113. Rollmann's personnel requests were often drastically reduced. The 1910 budget is one example. See BA/MA RM3/2500.

114. Annual Reports of the Shipbuilding Commission, 1906–15, BA/MA RM3/6673–74.

Chapter 6. The Tables Begin to Turn, 1913–1914

1. Witt, *Finanzpolitik*, 375.
2. Feldman, *Army, Industry, and Labor*, 6–7ff.
3. Müller, *Kriegsrohstoffbewirtschaftung*, is the best source on these matters.
4. Mendelssohn-Bartholdy, *War and German Society*, 205–6.
5. Jarausch, *Enigmatic Chancellor*, 162–63.
6. Riezler, *Tagebücher*, 77, 222.
7. Cecil, *Albert Ballin*, 198.
8. Jarausch, *Enigmatic Chancellor*, 265–66.
9. Röhl, "Admiral von Müller," 667.
10. Reichstag speech by Matthias Erzberger, 218th sess., 19 Feb. 1914, BA/MA RM3/5997 pt. 2.
11. Kommission zur Prüfung der Rustungslieferungen, Stenographische Berichte, 2d sess. on 8 and 9 January 1914, BA/MA RM3/9378.
12. Epstein, *Matthias Erzberger*, 74–75.
13. Gustav Noske's speech to the Reichstag, 218th sess., 19 Feb. 1914, BA/MA RM3/5997 pt. 2.
14. Speech by Representative Vogtherr before the Reichstag, 219th sess., 20 Feb. 1914, BA/MA RM3/5997 pt. 2.
15. Abschrift: "Betrifft: Rustungsausschuss," Berlin, 3 July 1913, BA/MA RM3/11691. This was sent to von Tirpitz by the Budget Department of the RMA and signed by Dahnhardt.
16. Speech by Matthias Erzberger before the Reichstag, 218th sess., 19 Feb. 1914, BA/MA RM3/5997 pt. 2.
17. Von Tirpitz's speech before the Reichstag, 219th sess., 19 Feb. 1914, ibid.
18. HA Krupp WA VIIf 1103, 27.
19. Documentation on the Russian light cruiser *Murawjeff Amurski*, BA/MA RM3/417, passim.
20. Berghahn, *Germany and the Approach of War in 1914*, 181; "Nachweisung der Teilnehmer an einer Reichstagsinformationsreise im Juni," 1913, BA/MA RM3/11691.
21. Herwig, *German Naval Officer Corps*, 179.
22. Riezler, *Tagebücher*, 219–20.
23. Kommando der Hochseestreitkräfte, Wilhelmshaven, to Admiralstabschef, Grosshauptquartier, 8 Nov. 1914, BA/MA RM3/49.
24. Gemzell, *Organization, Conflict and Innovation*, 185.
25. Müller, *Kriegsrohstoffbewirtschaftung*, 13–14.
26. Ibid. Müller is an excellent source for the proper titles and agencies related to mobilization in 1914.
27. Ibid., 32–33.
28. Feldman, *Army, Industry, and Labor*, 470.
29. Ibid., 301.
30. Bry, *Wages in Germany*, 192.

31. For labor problems 1914–16, see BA/MA RM3/5335–38, passim. The General Naval Department was in charge of labor shortage questions in consultation with the Dockyard and Construction departments from 1914 to 1918.

32. To "B" (Dockyard Department) from "K" (Construction Department), 11 April 1913, BA/MA RM3/2045.

33. Feldman, *Army, Industry, and Labor*, 65, n. 39.

34. Bry, *Wages in Germany*, 74, 4; Shortages and high prices for food, coal, and oil reported in BA/MA RM3/4661–69.

35. Speech by SPD representative Brandes before the Reichstag, 124th sess., 3 March 1913, BA/MA RM3/5997 pt. 1.

36. Leopold, *Alfred Hugenberg*, 175, n. 17.

37. Marine Indendatur, Wilhelmshaven, to SS/RMA, Berlin, 12 Dec. 1914, BA/MA RM3/7766.

38. A. Borsig, Berlin, to SS/RMA, Berlin, 12 Aug. 1914, BA/MA RM3/2045.

39. Feldman, *Army, Industry, and Labor*, 253–57.

40. Marine Indendatur, Wilhelmshaven, to SS/RMA, Berlin, 3 April 1915, BA/MA RM3/7766.

41. SS/RMA, Berlin, to all naval stations, the High Seas Fleet, Naval Depot Inspectorate (Wilhelmshaven), the Naval Indendatur (Kiel), Yard Inspectorate (Wilhelmshaven), and Construction Inspector at Blohm und Voss, Hamburg, 5 Aug. 1914; BA/MA RM3/4434.

42. Von Pohl (chief of the Admiralty Staff) to RMA, Berlin, 26 Sept. 1914; telegram from Admiralty Staff, Berlin, to RMA, Berlin, sent via Baltic Command, 5 Aug. 1914, BA/MA RM3/4434.

43. AG Weser, Bremen, to SS/RMA, Berlin, 14 Jan. 1914, BA/MA RM3/1125.

44. Vulcan, Hamburg, to RMA, Berlin, 3 July 1913; Blohm und Voss, Hamburg, to RMA, Berlin, 12 July 1913, BA/MA RM3/284.

45. Wilhelm II, Neues Palais, order splitting U-boat and torpedo affairs, 13 Dec. 1913; Organisatorische Bestimmungen fur die Inspektion des Unterseebootswesens (von Tirpitz), 13 Dec. 1913, BA/MA RM3/5014.

46. Rössler, *U-Bootbaus*, 51.

47. Ibid., 49.

48. Kennedy, "German Naval Operations Plans against England," 70.

49. Information on cost and weight overruns, 1914–18, BA/MA RM3/11276–80, 11293–97.

50. HA Krupp WA VIIf 1104, p. 5 (U-boats).

51. Angaben über U-boote und Ubootsvertrage während des Krieges und nach dem Waffenstillstand, 1919, BA/MA RM3/11599; Rössler, *U-Bootbaus*, 54; Denkschrift über die Vermehrung des Ubootsmaterials während des Krieges und den Stand der Ubootsbauen am 1 April 1916, Berlin, 8 April 1916, BA/MA RM3/4915; report, SS/RMA, Berlin, 30 Aug. 1914, BA/MA RM3/4434. Liste der im Bau befindlichen Torpedo und Unterseeboote—aufgestellt, 17 Nov. 1914, BA/MA RM3/4435.

52. Rössler, *U-Bootbaus*, 54.

53. HA Krupp WA VIIf 1113 contains profit and loss figures for Krupp on selected projects.

54. Rössler, *U-Bootbaus*, 54. Ms-boat means mobilization boat.

55. Ibid., 57, 60.

56. Ibid., 60–62.

57. Nordmann, Kiel, to RMA, 18 Aug. 1914; Krupp, Essen, to Imperial U-boat Inspectorate, n.d., HA Krupp FAH IV E67.

58. Ohl, "The Navy, the War Industries Board, and Industrial Mobilization," 18; Cooling, *Grey Steel and Blue Water Navy*, 197–98.

59. Speech by Representative Schultz (Reichspartei, Bromberg) before the Reichstag on the subject of Matthias Erzberger's proposed state testing institute and armor factory, 123d sess., 1 March 1913, BA/MA RM3/5997, pt. 1.

60. Construction inspector at Vulcan, Hamburg, to SS/RMA, Berlin, 28 March 1914, BA/MA RM3/1097.

61. Entries in von Tirpitz's war diary (Kriegstagebüch), 10 A.M., 18 Oct. 1914, and 7 P.M., 14 Sept. 1914, BA/MA RM3/2620.

62. Budget Department report regarding the Armaments Commission, Berlin, 7 May 1914, BA/MA RM3/9379.

63. Hessen, *Steel Titan*, 221.

64. Urofsky, *Big Steel*, 95, 105.

65. Müller, *Kriegsrohstoffbewirtschaftung*, 19. The Kriegsausschuss der deutschen Industrie was established on 8 August 1914 by unifying the CVDI and the Bund der Industrellen. Some of the founding members were Borsig, Gwinner (Deutsche Bank), Hugenberg (Krupp), Müller (Dresdener Bank), Schulze (Siemens), Urbig (Diskontogesellschaft), and Bleichroder.

66. Mendelssohn-Bartholdy, *War and German Society*, 231–32.

67. Müller, *Kriegsrohstoffbewirtschaftung*, 44–45.

68. Zu der Frage, ob vor Ausbruch des Krieges Festgesetzte Vertragspreise fur Lieferung an die Marine aus Anlass des Krieges erhoht werden durfen (1914), BA/MA RM3/7766; see BA/MA RM3/1815, 1798, passim, for price limits on all minor metals and all food, clothing, and personal needs in 1914.

69. HA Krupp WA VIIf 1104, 1.

70. BA/MA RM3/2316; see 2314–16, passim, on metal shortages in 1914–16.

71. For foreign sources of raw materials, 1911–14, see BA/MA RM3/2103; Vereinigte Kammerich' und Belter Schneevogel'sche Werke AG, Berlin, 30 Oct. 1914, ibid.

72. Gebrüder Körting AG Körtingsdorf to SS/RMA, Berlin, 10 Dec. 1914, BA/MA RM3/2218.

73. For Krupp prices see "to K IVa," BA/MA RM3/409.

74. Müller, *Kriegsrohstoffbewirtschaftung*, 117.

75. Krupp sales in total figures as presented to the RMA in quarterly reports, HA Krupp WA VIIf 1103, pp. 16–17; Die Kriegsmaterial Verkaufburos, vol. A, ibid.

76. Suppliers' list, 1914–18, BA/MA RM3/2304–7, passim.

77. Imperial Shipyard, Kiel, to RMA Construction Department, Berlin, 14 April 1913, BA/MA RM3/2068; Imperial Naval Purchasing Office, Düsseldorf, to RMA

Construction Department, Berlin, 2 Jan. 1914, BA/MA RM3/1119.

78. Imperial Naval Purchasing Office, Düsseldorf, to RMA Construction Department, Berlin, 10 Sept. 1913, BA/MA RM3/2214.

79. Memo-Kriegsministerium, Berlin, 9 Aug. 1914, BA/MA RM3/5309.

80. Zuweisungsamt bei der Metall Meldestelle des Kriegsministeriums, Berlin, to RMA, Berlin, 2 June 1916, BA/MA RM3/2318.

81. Howaldtswerke, Kiel, to SS/RMA, Berlin, 31 July 1913, BA/MA RM3/1865; Contract for the SMS *Bayern* (1914) sent to the author by Howaldtswerke AG.

82. Imperial Shipyard, Kiel, to RMA Construction Department, 31 May 1913 (patents), BA/MA RM3/1119; contract for the SMS *Bayern* in the possession of the author, see section IV: Patents; Werkvertrag: Ersatz Kaiser Friedrich III (Sachsen and Bayern classes)—given to Krupp Germaniawerft, BA/MA RM3/409.

83. Geheimhaltungsvorschrift fur Schiffsneubauten and Geheimhaltungsvorschrift für Unterlieferanten, both documents dated Berlin, 18 May 1914, BA/MA RM3/3688.

84. Imperial Shipyard, Wilhelmshaven, to RMA Construction Department, Berlin, 30 Jan. 1914, BA/MA RM3/1480; Arbeitsgebeit des Technischen Buros, 23 Aug. 1918, BA/MA RM3/11710.

85. Mitteilungen uber Ausschliessungen und Wiederzulassen von Liefern und Unternehmern, SS/RMA, 3 July 1914, BA/MA RM3/2304.

86. RMA Construction Supervisor, Kiel, to RMA, Berlin, 5 Nov. 1914, BA/MA RM3/2045.

87. Telegrams, RMA to Imperial Shipyards at Kiel, Danzig, and Wilhelmshaven, 29 and 30 Aug. 1913, BA/MA RM3/2044.

88. BA/MA RM3/2059, entire folio; see RM3/2050s series for the private sector's attempts to accelerate Purchasing Office testing procedures, 1914–17.

89. Wieland und Cie, Ulm a.d. Donau, to SS/RMA, Berlin, 30 Dec. 1914, BA/MA RM3/2048; Abschrift: Maschinenfabrik Augsburg-Nürnberg von Flexilis-Werke Spezial Tiegelstahlgiesserei GmbH, Berlin, 15 Dec. 1914, BA/MA RM3/2047.

90. RMA Construction Department, Berlin, to Vulcan, Hamburg, 19 Feb. 1914, BA/MA RM3/1377.

91. The construction of battleships and heavy cruisers came to an end during the war just as the production of U-boats skyrocketed.

92. Krupp, Essen, to RMA Dockyard Department, Berlin, 9 Dec. 1914; Fried. Krupp Gusstahlfabrik, Essen, to RMA Dockyard Department, Berlin, 9 Dec. 1914, BA/MA RM3/2046.

93. To "E" (Budget Department) from "K" (Construction Department), 5 Feb. 1914, BA/MA RM3/5997 pt. 2, report on the Siemens-Schuckert discount to the Japanese, who received manufactured electrical parts and systems 30 to 50 percent cheaper than the Imperial Navy.

94. Von Tirpitz to all relevant RMA departments, Berlin, 7 May 1913, BA/MA RM3/9376.

95. Naval indendant, Wilhelmshaven, to SS/RMA, Berlin, 29 Nov. 1913, BA/MA RM3/9378.

96. Ritter von Mann to Krupp von Bohlen und Halbach, Villa Hügel, Essen, 20 March

1907, HA Krupp FAH IV C49; "Tagesordnung für die Aufsichtsratssitzung am 14 Dezember 1907 um 10 uhr vormittags . . . ," HA Krupp FAH IV C14.

97. Blohm und Voss, Hamburg, to SS/RMA, Berlin, 12 July 1913, BA/MA RM3/284.

Chapter 7. The End of the von Tirpitz Era, 1915—1916

1. "Wie steht die Marine den neuen Aufgaben gegenüber," n.d. (probably 1916), BA/MA RM3/11729, Nachlass Behncke; Comments on a war at sea with Britain by Behncke, and Wilhelm II to Admiral Zenker, 16 July 1915, BA/MA RM3/11702.

2. Behncke to von Trotha, 7 Oct. 1916; Denkschrift von Trotha, "Überlegungen über die Organization der Marine," 30 Dec. 1915, BA/MA RM3/11729.

3. Wegener, *Naval Strategy of the World War.* See Holger Herwig's excellent discussion of these matters in the introduction to his new translation of Wegener's work. Wolfgang Wegener entered the naval service in 1894 and served in the Far East Cruiser Squadron from 1897 to 1899. He then returned to the Naval Academy as an instructor from 1905 to 1907 after which he served in the Second Battle Squadron from 1907 to 1908 and in the First Battle Squadron (under von Holtzendorff) from 1908 to 1909. He was with the Scout Forces from 1909 to 1910 and then served as a staff officer with the Scout Forces under Bachmann from 1911 to 1912 and then under Lans and Eckermann from 1913 to 1917. He was promoted to commander as of 26 April 1917, to captain as of 21 January 1920, and then to rear admiral on 1 March 1923. He retired as a vice-admiral on 30 September 1926.

4. Ritter, *The Sword and the Scepter*, 3:19. Admiral Henning von Holtzendorff entered the service on 11 April 1869. By 1902 he had almost twenty years of service at sea. He was promoted to captain 30 June 1897 and served as director of the imperial yard at Danzig; to rear admiral 27 January 1904 and attached to the director of the Baltic Sea Naval Station; to vice-admiral 27 April 1907 serving as chief of the First Squadron; and to admiral 27 January 1910 serving as chief of the High Seas Fleet. He retired in 1913.

5. Gemzell, *Organization, Conflict and Innovation*, 211, 232.

6. Ibid., 187—88.

7. Reichstag Budget Commission Hearing, 3 April 1916, BA/MA RM3/11526.

8. Riezler, *Tagebücher*, 342, 352.

9. "Wie steht die Marine den neuen Aufgaben gegenüber," n.d. (probably 1916), BA/MA RM3, Nachlass Behncke.

10. Williamson, *Helfferich*, 190—93.

11. "Niederschrift über die Auffuhrung seine exzellenz des Herrn Staatssekretars über den Immediatevortrag betreffend Typenfrage und Flottengesetz am 3 Mai 1916," BA/MA RM3/11599.

12. Von Tirpitz, *Memoirs*, 2:586.

13. Rössler, *U-Bootbaus*, is an excellent source for the design and purpose of the Ms, UB, and UC boats. The UB III and UC III models are discussed in the next chapter.

14. Von Bethmann-Hollweg to the Chief of the Admiralty Staff, Berlin, 7 July 1916, BA/MA RM3/55.

15. Feldman, *Army, Industry, and Labor,* 149–50, 152, 160–61.

16. SS/RMA and Admiral von Capelle in a Budget Commission Hearing, n.d. (probably late 1916), BA/MA RM3/11714.

17. HA Krupp WA VIIf 1103, 47, 54, 60.

18. Williamson, *Helfferich,* 155–57.

19. Ibid., 158; RMA Budget Department Statement for the Budget Commission Hearings, March 1916, "Unterseebootskrieg," BA/MA RM3/11688.

20. Reichstag Budget Commission Hearings, 3 April 1916, BA/MA RM3/11526.

21. Rössler, *U-Bootbaus,* 69, 76.

22. "Inbaugabe von U-booten im April 1916," Berlin, 13 May 1916; memo for the SS/RMA regarding a collective project by all RMA departments concerned with construction, BA/MA RM3/4915.

23. Rössler, *U-Bootbaus,* 85–95.

24. Feldman, *Army, Industry, and Labor.* The analysis of the Hindenburg Program starts on page 149.

25. SS/RMA, Berlin, to Chief of the Admiralty Staff, Naval Stations, North Sea and Baltic, Naval Corps, Brugge, U-boat Inspectorate, Torpedo Factory, Friedrichsort, and all Imperial Shipyards, 29 May and 17 June 1916, BA/MA RM3/4436.

26. Rössler, *U-Bootbaus,* 70.

27. UI (U-Boat Inspectorate), Melden, 20 April 1915; B.V. 2821; 24 June 1915, B.V. 4569, BA/MA RM3/4915.

28. Rössler, *U-Bootbaus,* 70.

29. Reply to a criticism on the punctuality of U-boat production by Chancellor von Bethmann-Hollweg, dated 1 November 1917, circulated within the RMA by Commander Keller, BA/MA RM3/4915.

30. RMA Construction Department, Berlin, to MAN, Augsburg, 26 April 1916, BA/MA RM3/2052.

31. Von Capelle's reply at the Reichstag Budget Commission Hearings, 3 April 1916, BA/MA RM3/11526.

32. Rössler, *U-Bootbaus,* 96–97, 99–100; Krupp von Bohlen und Halbach, Essen, to Major Meusel, 15 July 1928, HA Krupp FAH IV C54.

33. Helfferich, *Der Weltkrieg,* 2:130.

34. Rössler, *U-Bootbaus,* 97–99.

35. Handakten Dahnhardt U-boats, 1915; see copy of 1915 Budget Commission table on U-boat development and cost, 9 March 1915, BA/MA RM3/11634.

36. Report regarding labor matters at the U-boat shipyards, Berlin, 15 Aug. 1916, BA/MA RM3/4916.

37. Rössler, *U-Bootbaus,* 115–16.

38. MAN, Augsburg, to the U-Boat Inspectorate, Kiel, 15 Sept. 1915, BA/MA RM3/5336.

39. Körting, Körtingsdorf bei Hannover, to SS/RMA, Berlin, 3 Nov. 1915, BA/MA RM3/5338.

40. Report regarding labor matters at the U-boat shipyards, 15 Aug. 1916, BA/MA RM3/4916. According to this report, some of the manpower losses at the major private yards and subcontracting firms building U-boats were as follows from 1 June 1916 to 1 August 1916:

Firm	Losses to field army	Losses to domestic units	Totals
Blohm und Voss	314	382	696
Vulcan (Hamburg)	144	518	662
Bremer Vulcan	22	118	140
Howaldstswerke	10	0	10
AEG	14	19	33
AG Weser	186	407	593
Totals	690	1444	2134

41. See the file in BA/MA RM3/5707 for U-boat affairs in the occupied territories of northern Europe.
42. Communication from Admiral Hopman, Charleville (sent by the RMA Administrative Department to the Naval Department), 12 April 1915, BA/MA RM3/5709.
43. Torpedo Inspectorate, Kiel, 1 March 1915, "Regarding the Examination of the B and C Boats in Flanders after Their Assembly," BA/MA RM3/5709.
44. Vulcan, Hamburg, to SS/RMA, Berlin, 11 June 1915, BA/MA RM3/1098; Auszug aus BV 2635/15—Germaniawerft, Kiel, to RMA, Berlin, via the supervising constructor, 13 April 1915, and Auszug aus KI ASS 163/15—Proposal by Germaniawerft, Kiel, 3 May 1915, RM3/3688. See also Rössler, *Die Deutsche U-Boote*, 53–54.
45. U-Boat Inspectorate, Kiel, 31 Jan. 1915, "Betrifft: Flotillenfahrzeug fur die Unterseebootsflotille in Belgien," BA/MA RM3/5709.
46. SS/RMA to Germaniawerft and the Torpedo Inspectorate, Berlin, 10 July 1916, BA/MA RM3/6355.
47. Handakten von Capelle, "Darstellung der Handhabung ds Beschaffungswesens wahrend des Krieges," 1916, BA/MA RM3/11709.
48. Engelmann, *Krupp* (see the genealogy); correspondence between Bauer and Krupp von Bohlen und Halbach on the matter of cooperation between Germaniawerft and AG Danubius-Stabilimento Tecnico on U-boat designs, April–May 1915, HA Krupp FAH IV C49.
49. RMA Construction Department internal correspondence between KIV, KI, and KII, BA/MA RM3/421.
50. "Bemerkungen von KI zu den bisherigen Angeboten: Germania, Vulcan, Weser, Howaldt, March, 1915," BA/MA RM3/421.
51. "Abschrift: Brief von der RMA KII Dept.," Berlin, 26 Sept. 1916 (to "Akten"— i.e., for the record), signed by Schraeder, BA/MA RM3/2075.
52. KII section, "Überwachung der Arbeitsausfuhrung der elektrische Maschinen und Apparate bei den E-Firmen," 29 Sept. 1916; to KII from B (RMA interoffice

correspondence), Berlin, 13 Sept. 1916; K to B, Berlin, 20 Oct. 1916, BA/MA RM3/2074.

53. Vulcan, Stettin-Bredow, to SS/RMA, Berlin, 9 Dec. 1916; response, Berlin, 19 Jan. 1917, BA/MA RM3/2307; April–May Monthly Report by Purchasing Office Official Professor Krainer, RM3/2056.

54. RMA Construction Department, Berlin, to Howaldtswerke, Kiel, and C. August Schmidt Sohne, Hamburg, 2 Sept. 1915, BA/MA RM3/2050.

55. State Secretary of the Interior to SS/RMA, Berlin, 1 March 1915; Grand Duchal Ministry of State, Weimar, to the German Imperial Chancellor, 21 Feb. 1915; State Secretary of the Interior, Berlin, to the Grand Duchal Ministry of State, Weimar, 1 March 1915, BA/MA RM3/2304.

56. Howaldtswerke, Kiel, to SS/RMA, Berlin, via the Supervising Constructor, 23 Sept. 1915, BA/MA RM3/2306.

57. MAN, Nürnburg, to SS/RMA, Berlin, 6 Sept. 1915, BA/MA RM3/1098.

58. Vulcan, Hamburg, to SS/RMA, Berlin, 16 March 1915; Blohm und Voss, Hamburg, to SS/RMA, Berlin, 26 March 1915, BA/MA RM3/420.

59. Versuchsanstalt fur Wasserbau und Schiffbau to the RMA, Berlin, 8 Feb. 1915, BA/MA RM3/1005.

60. RMA KII Department, Berlin, to Siemens-Schuckertwerke, Siemensstadt bei Berlin et al., 19 Dec. 1916, BA/MA RM3/2076.

61. RMA KII Department, Berlin, to G. Seebeck AG in Geestemunde, 25 Dec. 1916, BA/MA RM3/2056.

62. RMA interoffice correspondence, Budget Department to Construction Department, 20 Oct. 1916, BA/MA RM3/2074.

63. RMA interoffice correspondence, Central Division to Construction Department, 5 Oct. 1915, BA/MA RM3/2052.

64. Maschinenbau Vorarbeiter Dahms et al., Oberschonenweide, to RMA, Berlin, 13 May 1916, BA/MA RM3/2053; Koerfer, Aachen-Rothe Erde, to RMA, Berlin, 10 June 1915, and Construction Department reply to Koerfer, 29 June 1915, RM3/2049; Wilhelm Schulz, engineer, Essen/Ruhr, to SS/RMA, Berlin, 18 Dec. 1914, and Construction Department to Schulz, 5 Jan. 1915, RM3/2046.

65. RMA Dockyard Department to the Supervising Constructor, Schichau et al., Berlin, 30 April 1915, BA/MA RM3/2048; M an KII Neiderschrift über die Sitzung der Abnahmebeamten am 15.11.15 betreffend Besprechung über Materialabnahme, RM3/2051; RM3/2070, passim; see also vols. 2068–71.

66. Report, Imperial Navy Yard, Kiel, to Construction Department, RMA, 13 June 1915, BA/MA RM3/2069.

67. May–June Reports of Purchasing Inspectors Heyn, Krainer, and Eyermann, 1915, BA/MA RM3/2050.

68. Vulcan, Stettin-Bredow, to Supervising Constructor "M" of the Torpedo Inspectorate, Stettin-Bredow, 19 Aug. 1915, BA/MA RM3/2050. Both volumes 2050 and 2051 contain hundreds of notices in 1915 from vendors that contracts were fulfilled and products were ready for testing; all are addressed to the RMA Construction Department.

69. Report from Purchasing Inspector Professor Francke to the RMA, Berlin, 22

Nov. 1916; RMA Construction Department, Berlin, to Siemens-Schuckertwerke, Siemensstadt bei Berlin, 19 Dec. 1916, BA/MA RM3/2076.

70. Carl Schwanitz Gummiwerke, Berlin, to Purchasing Inspector E. Heyn, Berlin-Dahlem, 14 Aug. 1915; reply by Heyn to Schwanitz, 15 Aug. 1915, BA/MA RM3/2049.

71. RMA KII Division 9 (RMA Construction Department), Berlin, to Imperial Shipyard, Kiel, 19 Dec. 1916, BA/MA RM3/2076.

72. Panzer AG, Wolgast, to Construction Department (KII-RMA), Berlin, 25 Oct. 1916; reply, 23 Nov. 1916, BA/MA RM3/2056.

73. Report of the Supervising Constructor, Schichau-Elbing, to Harburger Eisen und Bronzwerke, 21 Dec. 1916, ibid.

74. Stahlwerke zu Pirna, Pirna a.E., to RMA, Berlin, 10 April 1916, BA/MA RM3/2052. See the marginal comments on a letter from Chemisches Laboratorium fur Tonindustrie, Berlin, to SS/RMA, Berlin, 26 Aug. 1916, RM3/2054; "Protokoll über die Sitzung der Abnahmebeamten am 30.12.16," RM3/2057.

75. Report of the Imperial Navy Purchasing Office, Düsseldorf, to SS/RMA, Berlin, 23 Nov. 1916, BA/MA RM3/2056; Schichau, Elbing, to SS/RMA, Berlin, BA/MA RM3/2048.

76. Correspondence between Weser, Vulcan, and various companies producing brass fittings, cold water systems, bilge pumps, and other products, April–Aug. 1915; Weser Shipyard, Bremen, to the Supervising Constructor of the U-Boat Inspectorate in Bremen, 7 Sept. 1915, BA/MA RM3/2050. Weser, Bremen, to Shipyard Department, RMA, Berlin, 15 May 1915, RM3/2048.

77. AG Mix and Genest (telephone and telegraph works), Berlin-Schonberg, to SS/RMA, Berlin, 28 Oct. 1916, BA/MA RM3/2076.

78. Purchasing reports for the autumn of 1916 from Eyermann, Krainer, et al., BA/MA RM3/2055.

79. "Merkblatt Kriegswirtschaftliche Einrichtungen des Kriegsministeriums," 1915, BA/MA RM3/5311; Feldman, *Army, Industry, and Labor,* 62–63, 65, 163, 168–91, 193.

80. Müller, *Kriegsrohstoffbewirtschaftung,* 108.

81. Ibid., 19.

82. Requisition by Maffei-Schwartzkopf for copper from Hackethal, Draht, and Kabelwerke (Hannover) for manufacturing switches, April 1916, BA/MA RM3/2317.

83. Memo by the SS/RMA, Berlin, 19 Jan. 1916, BA/MA RM3/2333.

84. Schichau, Danzig, to SS/RMA, Berlin, 11 March 1916, BA/MA RM3/2314.

85. Schichau, Elbing, to SS/RMA, Berlin, 16 Oct. 1916, BA/MA RM3/2323.

86. Howaldtswerke, Kiel, to SS/RMA, Berlin, 19 Dec. 1916; supervising constructor, Kiel, to SS/RMA, Berlin, 20 Dec. 1916, BA/MA RM3/2326. Weser, Bremen, to SS/RMA, Berlin, 4 Jan. 1917, RM3/2327.

87. Fried. Krupp Gusstahlfabrik, Essen, to War Ministry, War Materials Division, 12 April 1916, BA/MA RM3/2320; see also same correspondents, 13 Sept. 1916, RM3/2322. These documents refer to the nickel shortage, and the submarines in

question, which are not mentioned in the text of the document, were the commercial U-boats *Deutschland* and *Bremen*.

88. Construction Department interoffice correspondence: KI to KII and KIVa and b, 17 May 1915, BA/MA RM3/2218.

89. Blohm und Voss, Hamburg, to SS/RMA, Berlin, 22 Aug. 1916, BA/MA RM3/2321.

90. Mannesmann Rohren-Werke, Division Grillo Funke, Gelsenkirchen-Schalke, to SS/RMA, Berlin, 26 July 1916, BA/MA RM3/2320; Blohm und Voss, Hamburg, to SS/RMA, Berlin, 31 Dec. 1915; Schichau, Danzig, to SS/RMA, Berlin, 15 Jan. 1916, BA/MA RM3/2313.

91. Metall-Beratungs- und Verteilungsstelle fur den Maschinenbau, Berlin-Charlottenburg, to SS/RMA, Berlin, 28 Nov. 1916; RMA Construction Department to all major yards, 20 Dec. 1916, BA/MA RM3/2326.

92. "Denkschrift über die Vermehrung des Ubootsmaterials wahrend des Krieges und den Stand der Ubootsbauten am 1 April 1916," Berlin, 8 April 1916, BA/MA RM3/4435.

93. "Schweiz" Monatliche Wirtschaftsberichte RMA, 1916 (Herbst-Winter); "Vereinigte Staaten von Amerika," Monatliche Wirtschaftsbericht RMA, Nov. 1916, General Naval Department, BA/MA RM3/4668.

94. Feldman, *Iron and Steel in the German Inflation*, 55.

95. "Darstellung der Handhabung des Beschaffungswesens wahrend des Krieges," 1916, BA/MA RM3/11599.

96. Marine Intendatur, Wilhelmshaven, to SS/RMA, Berlin, 11 Jan. 1915, BA/MA RM3/7766.

97. Supervising constructor, Stettin-Bredow, to RMA Construction Department, Berlin, 21 Nov. 1916, BA/MA RM3/2325.

98. HA Krupp WA IV 3096, passim, 1915–16; Imperial Shipyard, Kiel, to RMA Construction Department, Berlin, 7 April 1916, BA/MA RM3/2070.

99. Feldman, *Army, Industry, and Labor*, chap. 7.

100. Memo to the Torpedo Inspectorate, Kiel, from supervising constructor, Vulcan, Hamburg, 24 July 1917, BA/MA RM3/6588.

101. Hessen, *Steel Titan*, 231.

102. Imperial Shipyard, Wilhelmshaven, to RMA Dockyard Department, Berlin, 6 June 1915, BA/MA RM3/5334.

103. Marinebaurat Diese to Torpedo Inspectorate, Kiel, 14 Jan. 1916, BA/MA RM3/6355.

104. Supervising constructor, Howaldtswerke, Kiel, to SS/RMA, Berlin, 26 April 1916, BA/MA RM3/1866; Imperial Shipyard, Kiel, to RMA Construction Department, Berlin, 19 July 1915, RM3/1867.

105. Torpedo Work Station, Friedrichsort, 26 Jan. 1915, Germaniawerft, Kiel, 11 Feb. 1915, Westfalische Maschinbau-Industrie, Gustave Moll AG, 13 Feb. 1915, all to SS/RMA, Berlin; RMA (A IV) (telegram) to all private yards and machine contractors, 24 Feb. 1915; KWK to SS/RMA, 30 Jan. 1915; Schichau, Danzig, to SS/RMA, 26 Jan. 1915, BA/MA RM3/5333.

106. Telegram from Ludendorff to the Admiralty Staff, 13 Nov. 1916, BA/MA RM3/3688.
107. War Ministry, General War Department, to RMA, Berlin, 11 Sept. 1915, BA/MA RM3/5336.
108. Marinebaurat Diese to Torpedo Inspectorate, Kiel, 14 Jan. 1916, BA/MA RM3/6355.
109. Feldman, *Army, Industry, and Labor,* 312–13.
110. Replacement Worker Requisition Approval, Army "Ersatzkommission," 1915, BA/MA RM3/5338; Notice to the RMA from Germaniawerft, Kiel, 25 June 1915, RM3/6355.
111. "Richtlinien fur eine einheitliche Handhabung des Zuruckstellungsverfahrens," Berlin, 9 May 1915, esp. pp. 10–11, BA/MA RM3/5311.
112. Vulcan, Hamburg, to SS/RMA, Berlin, 19 June 1915; supervising constructor, Kiel, to SS/RMA, 1 July 1915; Berliner Maschinenbau AG to RMA (A IV), Berlin, 28 July 1915, BA/MA RM3/5335.
113. War Ministry, Berlin, to SS/RMA, Berlin, 4 April 1915, BA/MA RM3/5334; telegram from Brugge to RMA (A), Berlin, 22 May 1915, RM3/5709; RMA (A) to Commanders of the Naval Stations at Kiel (Ostsee) and Wilhelmshaven (Nordsee), 3 Sept. 1915, RM3/5335; "Arbeiterstand auf den Kaiserlichen Werften und Privatewerften," Berlin, 13 March 1915, RM3/5334.
114. War Ministry, Berlin, to SS/RMA, Berlin, 4 April 1915, BA/MA RM3/5334; telegram from Brugge to RMA (A), Berlin, 22 May 1915, RM3/5709; RMA (A) to Commanders of the Naval Stations at Kiel (Ostee) and Wilhelmshaven (Nordsee), 3 Sept. 1915, RM3/5335; "Arbeiterstand auf den Kaiserlichen Werften und Privatewerften," Berlin, 13 March 1915, RM3/5334.
115. Supervising constructor at AG Weser, Bremen, to SS/RMA, Berlin, 11 March 1915, BA/MA RM3/420.
116. Krupp, Essen, to RMA, Berlin, 22 July 1915, BA/MA RM3/5335; Krupp von Bohlen und Halbach, Essen, to von Tirpitz, 8 June 1915, HA Krupp FAH IV E67.
117. Siemens-Schuckertwerke, Siemensstadt bei Berlin, to U-Boat Inspectorate, Kiel, 26 Aug. 1915, BA/MA RM3/5337.
118. Ordnance Depot, Berlin, to RMA, Berlin, 28 July 1915, BA/MA RM3/5336.
119. Handakten Spindler, "Zahl der in den Werften beschaftigen Frauen," RMA Budget Department, Oct. 1916, BA/MA RM3/11698.
120. RMA interoffice correspondence, B VII to B III, 21 April 1915, BA/MA RM3/5334.
121. RMA interoffice correspondence, B to K, 14 Oct. 1915, BA/MA RM3/5338; AG Weser, Bremen, to SS/RMA, Berlin, 9 July 1915, and RMA (A IV) to AG Weser, Bremen, 17 July 1915, RM3/5335.
122. "Besprechung mit der Fabrikenkommission des Reich Marine Amts am 6. Oktober 1915 vormittags 9 1/4 Uhr," BA/MA RM3/6355.
123. "Stellungsnahme von K zur Frage: Ersatzbauten fur verloren gegangene Schiffe," 6 Jan. 1915, BA/MA RM3/3689.

124. "Kriegsausschluss fur die Metalbetriebe Gross-Berlins," Berlin, 19 Feb. 1915, BA/MA RM3/2305.
125. Gesellschaft fur Drahtlose Telegraphie, Berlin, to SS/RMA (A IV), Berlin, 28 July 1915, BA/MA RM3/5335.
126. Supervising constructor, Kiel, to SS/RMA, Berlin, 31 July 1915, ibid.; Germaniawerft, Kiel, to Direktorium, Essen, 15 June 1915, HA Krupp WA IV 1245.
127. Feldman, *Iron and Steel in the German Inflation*, 65.

Chapter 8. The Unexpected End, 1917–1918

1. Feldman, *Army, Industry, and Labor*, 270, 385–404.
2. Kosyzk, *Pressepolitik im Ersten Weltkrieg*, 37, n. 47.
3. For von Tirpitz's activities after 1916, see BA/MA RM3/11628, passim. Admiral Paul Behncke (13 Aug. 1866–4 Jan. 1937) entered the navy on 4 April 1883 and by 1911 had accumulated fourteen years and two months of sea duty. He was promoted to captain 12 September 1908, serving as head of the Admiralty Staff Department; to rear admiral 14 July 1914, serving as the official representative of the Admiralty Staff from 1914 to 1915; then to vice-admiral 25 November 1916 with the same duties until January 1916, and commanded the Third Battle Squadron until September 1918.
4. Folio of writings by Kapitan zur See Lothar Persius (Ret.), BA/MA RM3/9754.
5. Feldman, *Army, Industry, and Labor*, 363–64.
6. Correspondence between state secretary of the Imperial Office of Justice and the SS/RMA, Admiral von Capelle, BA/MA RM3/11728.
7. Feldman, *Army, Industry, and Labor*, 365.
8. Report from the RMA News Bureau on an article written by Matthias Erzberger in *Germania*, 23 Sept. 1917, BA/MA RM3/11728.
9. Herwig, *German Naval Officer Corps*, 238, n. 3.
10. Ibid., 238.
11. Deist, "Die Politik," 347; Stegemann, *Deutsche Marinepolitik*, 138.
12. Herwig, *Luxury Fleet*, 222; Deist, "Die Politik," 347.
13. Herwig, *Luxury Fleet*, 222.
14. Ibid., 181.
15. Scheer, *Germany's High Seas Fleet*, 177.
16. Rössler, *U-Bootbaus*, 69, 85–95; "Inbaugabe von U-booten im April 1916," Berlin, 13 May 1916, BA/MA RM3/4915 (memo for the state secretary of the RMA regarding a collective project by all RMA departments concerned with construction).
17. Herwig, *German Naval Officer Corps*, chap. 10, section A.
18. Lundeberg, "German Naval Critique," 107.
19. State Secretary of the RMA von Capelle, Berlin, to Chief of the Naval Cabinet von Müller, Grosses Hauptquartier, 3 Sept. 1917, BA/MA RM3/11612.
20. Rössler, *U-Bootbaus*, 117–18.
21. Nachlass Behncke, "Besprechung mit den Vertretern der Werften und Industrie

uber die Möglichkeit zur Durchfuhrung des von der Seekriegsleitunggeforderten U-bootsbauprogramms am 19.9.18," BA/MA N173/12.

22. Nachlass Behncke, "Niederschrift über die Besprechung bei der SKL am 14.9.18 über einen neuen U-bootsbauplan," BA/MA N173/2.

23. Nachlass Behncke, "Erklarung des Chefs des Admiralstabes der Marine anlasslich der Besprechung des Reichs Marine Amts mit Herrn der Industrie über das grosse Ubootsprogramm," 18 Sept. 1918, BA/MA N173/12.

24. RMA U-Boat Office, "Betr: Hauptangaben fur die Uboote UF 33/48," Berlin, 4 May 1918, BA/MA RM3/4915; "Aktennotiz uber die Besprechung am Montag, den 23. September 1918, vormittags 10 1/2 Uhr auf der Werft Blohm und Voss," 24 Sept. 1918, RM3/11227.

25. "Zusammenstellung der Firmen, die sich bis heute bereit erklart haben, Uboots-Arbeitern zu ubernehmen," Berlin, 26 Oct. 1918, BA/MA RM3/11228.

26. Rössler, *U-Bootbaus*, 119ff.

27. U-Boat Office to the State Secretary of the RMA, Berlin, 7 Sept. 1918, BA/MA RM3/11272.

28. Deutsche Werft, Hamburg, to State Secretary of the RMA, Berlin, 6 July 1918, ibid.

29. Austria Shipyard AG, Vienna, to Technical Department of the Mediterranean U-Boat Command, Pola, via the supervising constructor, Trieste, 31 Oct. 1918, BA/MA RM3/6570.

30. Supervising constructor, Kiel-Gaarden, to SS/RMA via the U-Boat Inspectorate, Berlin, 2 July 1917, 17 April 1918; AG Weser, Bremen, to SS/RMA, Berlin, via Supervising constructor, Bremen, 7 June 1915, BA/MA RM3/1099.

31. Appendix to a report on the Austrian shipyards by a representative of the German U-Boat Office, 28 July 1918; inspection tour report by an RMA Dockyard Department representative stationed in Vienna, October 1918; RMA Dockyard Department, Berlin, to the U-Boat Inspectorate, Kiel, 13 July 1918; "Protokoll über die Sitzung am 18. September 1918 mit der Firma Ganz und Co. Danubius für die Lieferung der grossen U-boote der zweiten Serie," all in BA/MA RM3/11273.

32. "Besprechung bei Seiner Exzellenz dem Herrn Staatssekretar von 10. Mai 1918 über Vergebung von U-booten an Tecklenborg und Bremer Vulcan," Berlin, 10 May 1918, BA/MA RM3/4915.

33. Rössler, *U-Bootbaus*, 123 and appendix.

34. "Unterlagen für Beantwortung von Anfragen im Reichstage betreffend Ubootsbau," RMA Dockyard Department, Berlin, 2 March 1917, BA/MA RM3/11595.

35. Handakten von Gohren, "Unser U-bootbau wahrend des Krieges" by Dr. Struve (SPD, Kiel), BA/MA RM3/11692; Reichstag Budget Commission Hearing, 10 May 1917, RM3/11691.

36. Reichstag Appropriations Debates, Sept.–Oct. 1918, BA/MA RM3/11596.

37. "Berechnung der Jahrkosten für Bau und Armierung von Schiffen und Fahrzeugen zu Lasten des Kriegsfonds," 1 Feb. 1918, BA/MA RM3/11726.

38. "Niederschrift über den Immediatvortrag von 22 Januar 1918 betreffend die Entwurfe L20e und L24 und die Torpedoarmierung für neue Grosskampfschiffe," BA/MA RM3/3707.

39. RMA interdepartmental correspondence, Jan. 1917, BA/MA RM3/3707.

40. "Bericht-betrifft: Fortgang der Arbeiten an den Schiffsneubauten (Linienschiffe, Grosse Kreuzer, Kleine Kreuzer)," Berlin, 1 Feb. 1918, BA/MA RM3/11726.

41. Von Capelle's presentation at Reichstag Budget Commission session, 26 April 1917, BA/MA RM3/11604.

42. Tecklenborg AG, Bremerhaven, to Kapitan z. S. Eberius, U-Boat Office, Berlin, 29 May 1918, BA/MA RM3/11228.

43. "Bestimmung über die Beteiligung der Marine-Bauaufsichtigung . . . ," 31 March 1917, BA/MA RM3/3688.

44. Denkschrift über die Entwicklung der Kaiserlichen Werften nach dem Kriege, Berlin, March 1917, BA/MA RM3/3611.

45. Denkschrift Schraeder, "Zum Immediatvortrag über deutsch-turkische Werftanlagen am Bosporus," Berlin, 8 Feb. 1918, BA/MA RM3/11726.

46. Supervising constructor, Howaldtswerke, Kiel, to SS/RMA, Berlin, 9 Oct. 1918, BA/MA RM3/1871.

47. BA/MA RM3/6627, passim; VU-496-98 "Mehr- und Minderkosten über die Akkumulatoren- Batterien . . . ," 11 July 1917, BA/MA RM3/6627.

48. Herwig, *German Naval Officer Corps*, 190.

49. "Einige Bemerkungen zu der vom Kabinettschef uberrichten neuen Dienstanweisung für den Chef des Admiralstabs der Marine," Berlin, 5 Sept. 1917, BA/MA RM3/11628.

50. See BA/MA RM3/11319, passim, for 1918–19. The cancellation of contracts and the reduction in the pace of construction forced some of the smaller firms to lay off workers.

51. RMA to the Imperial U-Boat Inspectorate, Berlin, 5 Nov. 1918, BA/MA RM3/11227.

52. "Niederschrift uber die Besprechung auf der UI betreffend Einbau der 3000 PSe- M.A.N.- Ölmaschinen am 3. September 1917," BA/MA RM3/6589.

53. To A from B5 (RMA interoffice correspondence), Berlin, 28 Aug. 1917; Abschrift: Betr.: Fortgang der Arbeiten an Schiffsneubauten (Linienschiffe, Grosse Kreuzer, Kleine Kreuzer), Berlin, 22 Sept. 1917, BA/MA RM3/3688.

54. Handakten Spindler, Admiral Kraft's report: "Betrifft: Hilfsdienstgesetz. Material für Reichstag," Berlin, 16 Feb. 1917, BA/MA RM3/11698.

55. Feldman, *Army, Industry, and Labor*, 310.

56. Rössler, *U-Bootbaus*, 113.

57. Feldman, *Army, Industry, and Labor*, 326, 321.

58. Bry, *Wages in Germany*, 7.

59. Ibid., 196–97.

60. Reichstag Proceedings, 104th sess., 9 May 1917, BA/MA RM3/11595.

61. Howaldtswerke, Kiel, to SS/RMA, Berlin, 16 Nov. 1918; Germaniawerft, Kiel-Gaarden, to RMA, Berlin, 13 Nov. 1918, BA/MA RM3/11320.

62. Blohm und Voss, Hamburg, to U-Boat Office, Berlin (telegram), 12 Nov. 1918, BA/MA RM3/11318.

63. Special report attached to Ruppel's February (monthly) report, Frankfurt a.M. to the RMA Construction Department, Berlin, 28 Feb. 1918, BA/MA RM3/2084.

64. "Weiterbau von U-booten und sonstigen Marinebauten nach Erlass des Demobil-machungsamtes über Beginn der Friedenswirtschaft," Berlin, 25 Nov. 1918 (U-Boat Office), BA/MA RM3/1338.

65. Handakten Behncke, "Vortrag des Inspekteurs der S.A.I." (Ship's Artillery Inspectorate), July 1918, BA/MA RM3/11701.

66. BA/MA RM3/2080. For the RMA's effort to avoid a Siemens monopoly in certain areas of electrical equipment see the 2060, 2070, and 2080 series in the RM3 collection.

67. "Kommission zur Prufung von Vertragen über Kriegslieferungen," 10th session, 15 Nov. 1917, BA/MA RM3/7763; *Brockhaus Enzyklopedie*, 5:267.

68. RMA Interoffice Memo A IV, Berlin, 31 July 1917, BA/MA RM3/5723.

69. RMA Construction Department, Berlin, to Schichau, Elbing et al., 21 April 1917, BA/MA RM3/2057.

70. "Besprechung uber offene oder geheime Herausgabe der Lieferanten-Liste der deutschen Kriegsmarine am 15.1.18," RMA, Berlin, BA/MA RM3/2307; RMA Construction Department to all Imperial Shipyards, 13 June 1918, RM3/2085.

71. Blohm und Voss, Hamburg, to SS/RMA, Berlin (telegram), 11 Jan. 1917, BA/MA RM3/2327.

72. Ohl, "The Navy, the War Industries Board, and Industrial Mobilization," 18.

73. MAN Director Lauster, Augsburg, to the Directors of the Vulcan Shipyard, Hamburg, 22 Dec. 1917, HA Krupp WA IV 3105.

74. Lauster, Augsburg, to the U-Boat Inspectorate, Kiel, 29 May 1918; Lauster, Augsburg, to Regenbogen at Germaniawerft, 17 April 1918, HA Krupp WA IV 3097.

75. Regenbogen at Germaniawerft to the U-boat Inspectorate, Kiel, 5 June 1918, regarding diesel contracts for June delivery, ibid.

76. Lauster, Augsburg, to Regenbogen at Germaniawerft, 11 May 1918, ibid.

77. U-Boat Inspectorate (Richter, chief of staff) to Germaniawerft, Kiel, 7 June 1918, ibid.

78. "Auszug aus dem Aktenvermerk über Verhandlung mit der UI Neubestellungen Bauprogramm 1920 am 4 Juli 1918, Kiel," ibid.

79. Ludendorff, General Headquarters, to RMA et al., Berlin, 10 Feb. 1918, BA/MA RM3/11227.

80. Notes from a meeting between Purchasing Office personnel and the RMA at the Construction Department (KIIe), Berlin, 3 March 1917, BA/MA RM3/2057; notes from a conversation among Purchasing Office and RMA officials at the Construction Department (KIIe), Berlin, 17 July 1918, RM3/2087.

81. Captain Paul (Naval Reserve), Monthly Report, February 1917, Berlin, 5 March 1917, BA/MA RM3/2078; report on the acceptance of the Main electric motors, GV 370, at the Siemens-Schuckertwerke in Nürnberg, 27–28 Feb., 7–8 March 1917, RM3/2081; Ruppel, Frankfurt a.M. to Oberbaurat Grauert, RMA, Berlin, 28 March 1918; Ruppel to Brown and Boveri Company, Frankfurt, a.M., 23 March 1918; RMA Construction Department (KIIe) to Brown and Boveri, Berlin, 8 May 1918, RM3/2085.

82. Remark attached to the November Monthly Report of Paul from RMA Construction Department (KIIe), Berlin, 2 Jan. 1918, BA/MA RM3/2084.
83. RMA Construction Department to F. Schichau, Berlin, 29 Dec. 1917, BA/MA RM3/2083; correspondence with various firms wanting inspections to clear their products for shipment, RM3/2059, passim.
84. BA/MA RM3/2062; see the 2050 and 2060 series, passim, for Purchasing Office trip and inspection reports, especially for duration and region; Fried. Krupp AG Grusonwerke, Magdeburg-Buckau, to RMA Construction Department, Berlin, 25 Oct. 1917 BA/MA RM3/2060, and 2060, passim; notice of an inspection day trip to the Firma Hirsch to be made by Purchasing Inspector Wägler departing from the Heegermuhle Brass Company sent by the RMA Construction Department (KII), RM3/2061.
85. RMA Construction Department to Siemens-Schuckertwerke, Berlin, 23 March 1918, BA/MA RM3/2084.
86. Paul's report for the month of December 1917, Berlin, 5 Jan. 1918, BA/MA RM3/2084.
87. Gesellschaftstelle der Kriegsmetall AG, Hamburg, to RMA, Berlin, 6 March 1917, BA/MA RM3/2057.
88. Report of the supervising constructor at Germaniawerft, Kiel, to SS/RMA, Berlin, 14 March 1917, BA/MA RM3/2057.
89. Meeting at the Naval Purchasing Office in Düsseldorf, 13 Dec. 1917, BA/MA RM3/2065.
90. Supervising constructor, Kiel, to RMA Construction Department, Berlin, 4 April 1917, BA/MA RM3/2080; letter from the U-Boat Inspectorate to over thirty companies, inspectors, and yards, Kiel, 7 Aug. 1917; U-boat Inspectorate, Kiel, to RMA Construction Department, Berlin, 28 July 1917, RM3/2081; U-Boat Inspectorate, Kiel, to RMA Construction Department, Berlin, 5 Feb. 1917, RM3/2078.
91. Note from Marinebaumeister (ret.) Carl Schulthes to RMA Construction Department (KIIe), Berlin, 7 Feb. 1917; Construction Department interoffice correspondence on the Schulthes letter between KIIA and KIIe, BA/MA RM3/2059.
92. Weise und Monski, Halle a.S., to RMA Material Purchasing Station, Attention: Construction Secretary Herrmann, 20 June 1917, BA/MA RM3/2058.
93. Meeting of the Purchasing Office representatives on 2 July 1918, BA/MA RM3/2065.
94. "Ausschuss von Kesselrohren," Berlin, 10 April 1918; Report: Reichswerft, Danzig, to SS/RMA, 14 Dec. 1918; Weser, Howaldtswerke, et al., complaints to the SS/RMA over late Mannesman deliveries (October 1918); Imperial Shipyard, Danzig, to RMA Construction Department, Berlin, 18 May 1918; AG Weser, Bremen, to SS/RMA, Berlin, 25 April 1918; Germaniawerft, Kiel-Gaarden, to SS/RMA, Berlin, 17 April 1918; exchanges between Phoenix, Mannesmann, and the RMA Construction Department, April 1918, all in BA/MA RM3/2104.
95. Ruppel to RMA Construction Department, Berlin, 2 April 1918, BA/MA RM3/2085; supervising constructor, U-Boat Inspectorate, Blohm und Voss,

Hamburg, to RMA Construction Department, Berlin, 5 Feb. 1918; RMA Construction Department (KIIe), Berlin, to Purchasing Office, Düsseldorf, 11 April 1918, RM3/2062.

96. Krupp, Essen, to RMA, Berlin, 18 Jan. 1917, BA/MA RM3/2328; Memorandum, RMA, Berlin, 6 July 1917, RM3/2338.

97. "Kommission zur Prufung von Vertragen über Kriegslieferungen," 11th sess., 16 Nov. 1917, BA/MA RM3/7763.

98. RMA, Berlin, to Deutsche Erdöl AG, Vienna, 20 April 1917; Deutsche Erdöl AG to RMA, 23 Aug. 1917; RMA to Deutsche Erdöl, 9 April 1918, BA/MA RM3/6395.

99. Reports for 1916–17 by the Hamburg-Amerika Line, Captain Gleichmann, 6 July 1917; RMA A Department Memo, Berlin, 20 July 1917; account of a verbal transmission to the German Foreign Office from the Swedish consulate in Berlin, 13 July 1917, BA/MA RM3/4399.

100. See BA/MA RM3/2339, passim, for the standard method of metals procurement; SS/RMA, Berlin, to Bremer Vulcan, Vegesack, 12 July 1918, BA/MA RM3/6442.

101. SS/RMA, Berlin, to all RMA departments and divisions, 16 Dec. 1917, BA/MA RM3/6581.

102. See BA/MA RM3/6581, passim, for details on firms that were closed down by cutting off their power and raw material supplies in 1917–18.

103. AG Weser, Bremen, to SS/RMA, Berlin, 13 Jan. 1917, BA/MA RM3/2327; supervising constructor, Bremer Vulcan, Vegesack, to RMA U-Boat Office, Berlin, 5 Oct. 1918, RM3/11227.

104. "Niederschrift der Besprechung zwischen UI und M.A.N. über Verträgliche Bestellung am 12.2.18," HA Krupp WA IV 3105; correspondence between MAN and the U-Boat Inspectorate, April–May 1918, passim, ibid., 3097; Director of the Gussstahlfabrik to Krupp von Bohlen und Halbach et al., Essen, 2 March 1918, ibid., 3105.

105. MAN Director Lauster to U-Boat Inspectorate, 31 Jan. 1918, HA Krupp WA IV 3105; Daimler Motoren Gesellschaft, Berlin-Marienfelde to Torpedo Inspectorate, Kiel, 16 Sept. 1918, BA/MA RM3/11228.

106. "Betrachtungen zum Aufbau unserer Marine" (Johannes Horn), 1919, BA/MA RM3/11706.

107. SS/RMA, Berlin, to the National Government via the Peoples' Deputy Herr Gustav Noske, Berlin, 7 Feb. 1919, BA/MA RM3/4916; "Niederschrift einer Besprechung im Konstructions Department des RMA über die Forderung der im Bau befindlichen Kriegsschiffe," 26 Feb. 1919, RM3/3688; RMA Memorandum: "Weiterbau und Annullierung der U-boote," Berlin, Nov. 1918, RM3/11319.

108. "Grundsatzliches fur die Beschäftigung der Staats- und Privatwerften in der nächsten Zeit," 14 Nov. 1918, BA/MA RM3/11320; Memorandum from A Department (General Naval Department, A IV) #8002, Berlin, 31 July 1917, RM20/47 (same as RM3/4252).

109. RMA Notice, Berlin, 20 Dec. 1918 (Committee for Demobilization in the Shipbuilding Industry), BA/MA RM3/11319; inventory and review of the shipyards by

the War Committee of German Shipyards, Hamburg, 1919, RM3/11320.

110. Rössler, *U-Bootbaus*, 126.

111. See BA/MA RM3/11347, passim, for some of the duties of the Reichsverwer-
tungsamt in 1919. It was responsible for the accounting, distribution, or disposal
of assets the navy had left over from the construction program. Volume 6326
holds material from the Reich Trust Company, which took care of the debts accumulated during the war. It was the source of all settlements between the RMA
and the private yards and contractors.

112. For the closing of wartime debts to private yards and contractors see BA/MA
RM3/6403–6411, 6439, and 6440–67. For example, "Auszug aus dem Abkom-
men zwischen der Friedrich Krupp A.G. Germaniawerft und dem Kommissar des
Reichsfinanzministeriums für Rechtsangelegenheiten aus dem Krieg," 1919,
RM3/6442.

113. The Reichsamt für die Wirtschaftliche Demobilmachung or Imperial Office for
Economic Demobilization was led in 1918–19 by Köth and worked under the au-
thority of the Imperial Chancellory. See Feldman, *Iron and Steel in the German
Inflation*, 92; RMA Memo, A IV #10076, Berlin, 10 Sept. 1917, BA/MA
RM3/4252 (same as RM20/407). Control over all labor matters remained in the
hands of those in the War Ministry.

Conclusion

1. For a similar interpretation accenting the social and economic implications of the
Scheer Program see Stjerna's article "Scheer-programmet." In a recent communication with the author, Stjerna commented that "under no circumstances did the navy
regard the program as a propaganda trick. Even as the peace talks took place, there
was not a sign or willingness of wanting to put the program aside."

2. Feldman, *Army, Industry, and Labor*, 492ff.

3. Morrow, *German Airpower in World War One*, 140, 199.

4. Feldman, *Army, Industry, and Labor*. The concluding chapters of Feldman's book
bring home the fact that very few of Germany's leaders knew, or wanted to know, the
desperation of Germany's economic and military situation. General Groener was a
possible exception, but he fell victim to a general wish to avoid coming to grips with
the reality of critical shortages and labor unrest.

5. Scheer, *Germany's High Seas Fleet*, 342–47.

6. Gemzell, *Organization, Conflict and Innovation*, introduction and statement of
method.

7. Wegener, *Naval Strategy of the World War*, xliv. The quote is from the fine introduction by Holger Herwig.

8. For the complete story behind the von Tirpitz–Raeder connection see the works of
Wegener, Salewski, and Dülffer listed in the bibliography.

Bibliography

Primary Sources

Unpublished

Bundesarchiv-Militärarchiv, Freiburg im Breisgau
   Imperial Admiralty to 1889 (RM1)
   Naval Cabinet (RM2)
   Imperial Naval Office (RM3)
   Imperial Naval High Command 1889–99 (RM4)
   Admiralty Staff, from 1899 (RM5)
   Office of the Naval Command, post-1918 (RM20)
   General Naval Office, post-1918 (RM21)
   Office of Naval Administration, post-1918 (RM23)
Private Papers
   Alfred von Tirpitz (N253)
   Eduard von Capelle (N170)
   Gustav von Senden-Bibran (N160)
   Paul Behncke (N173)
Historisches Archiv Fried. Krupp, Villa Hügel, Essen
   Works Archive (WA)
   Family Archive (FAH)

Published

von Alten, Georg. *Handbuch für Heer und Flotte*. Vol. 5. Berlin: Deutsches Verlag Bong, 1913.

Breyer, Siegfried. *Battleships and Battlecruisers, 1905–1970*. Garden City, N.Y.: Doubleday, 1973.

von Bülow, Bernhard Fürst. *Denkwürdigkeiten*. Vol. 1. Berlin: Ullstein AG, 1930.

Görlitz, Walter, ed. *Der Kaiser . . . Aufzeichnungen des Chefs des Marinekabinettes Admiral Georg Alexander von Müller über die Ara Wilhelms II.* Göttingen: Musterschmidt Verlag, 1965.

————. *Regierte der Kaiser? Kriegstagebücher, Aufzeichnungen und Briefe des Chefs des Marinekabinettes Admiral Georg von Müller, 1914–1918.* Göttingen: Musterschmidt Verlag, 1959.

Gröner, Erich. *Die deutsche Kriegsschiffe, 1815–1945*. 2 vols. Munich: J. F. Lehmann, 1966.

Hohenlohe-Schillingsfürst, Chlodwig K. V., Fürst zu. *Denkwurdigkeiten der Reichskanzlerzeit.* Edited by Karl Alexander von Müller. Stuttgart: Deutsche Verlags Anstalt, 1931.

————. *Memoirs of Prince Chlodwig of Hohenlohe-Schillingsfürst.* Edited by Friedrich Curtius. New York: Macmillan, 1906.

von Holstein, Friedrich. *Die Geheimen Papiere Friedrich von Holsteins.* Vol. 4. Edited by Norman Rich and M. H. Fisher. Göttingen: Musterschmidt Verlag, 1963.

James, Robert Rhodes. *Winston S. Churchill: His Complete Speeches, 1897–1963.* Vol. 2, 1908–13. New York: Chelsea House, 1974.

Krupp. *Handbuch*. Essen: Krupp, 1906, 1909.

Lepsius, Johannes, Albert Mendelssohn-Bartholdy, and Friedrich Thimme, eds. *Die grosse politik der europäischen Kabinette, 1871–1914.* Berlin: Deutsche verlagsgesellschaft für politik und geschichte, 1924.

Nauticus. Jahrbuch für Deutschlands Seeinteressen. Berlin: Ernst Siegfried Mittler und Sohn, 1900ff.

Preston, Anthony. *Battleships of World War I.* Harrisburg, Pa.: Stackpole Books, 1972.

Rangliste der kaiserlichen deutschen Marine. Berlin: Ernst Siegfried Mittler und Sohn, 1890–1918.

Riezler, Kurt. *Tagebücher, Aufsätze, Dokumente.* Edited by Karl D. Erdmann. Göttingen: Vandenhoeck and Ruprecht, 1972.

Scheer, Reinhard. *Germany's High Seas Fleet in the World War.* New York: Peter Smith, 1934.

von Tirpitz, Alfred. *Erinnerungen*. Leipzig: K. F. Koehler, 1919.

————. *My Memoirs*. 2 vols. London: Hurst and Blackett, 1919.

————. *Politische Dokumente*. 2 vols. Stuttgart: Cotta, 1924–26.

Verhandlung des Reichtages, Stenographische Berichte. 1898, 1900, 1906, 1908, 1912.

Wegener, Wolfgang. *The Naval Strategy of the World War*. Translated with an introduction by Holger H. Herwig. Annapolis: Naval Institute Press, 1989.

Weslicenus, Georg. *Deutschlands Seemacht sonst und jetzt*. Leipzig, 1896.

Secondary Sources

Baecker, Thomas. "Mahan über Deutschland." *Marine Rundschau* 73 (Jan.– Feb. 1976): 10–19, 86–102.

Berghahn, Volker R. "Flottenrustung und Machtgefüge." In *Das kaiserliche Deutschland: Politik und Gesellschaft, 1870–1918*. Edited by M. Stürmer. Düsseldorf: Droste Athenäum, 1970.

————. *Germany and the Approach of War in 1914*. New York: St. Martin's Press, 1973.

————. *Der Tirpitz Plan: Genisis und Verfall einer innpolitischen Kreisenstrategie unter Wilhelm II*. Düsseldorf: Droste Verlag, 1971.

————. "Zu den Zielen des deutschen Flottenbaus unter Wilhelm II." *Historisches Zeitschrift* 210 (Feb. 1970): 34–100.

Berghahn, Volker R., and Wilhelm Deist. "Kaiserliche Marine und Kriegsausbruch 1914." *Militärgeschichtliches Mitteilungen* 7 (1970): 37–58.

Boelcke, Willi A., ed. *Krupp und die Hohenzollern in Dokumenten: Krupp-Korrespondenz mit Kaisern, Kabinettschefs und Ministern 1850–1910*. Frankfurt a.M.: Akademische Verlagsgesellschaft Athenian, 1970.

Böhm, Ekkehard. *Überseehandel und Flottenbau. Hanseatische Kaufmannschaft und deutsche Seerustung, 1879–1902*. Düsseldorf: Bertelsmann Universitätsverlag, 1972.

Born, Karl E. *Moderne deutsche Wirtschaftsgeschichte*. Cologne: Kiepenheuer und Witsch, 1966.

Boyd, Carl. "The Wasted Ten Years, 1888–1898: The Kaiser Finds an Admiral." *Royal United Services Institution Journal* 3 (1966): 291–97.

Brockhaus Enzyklopädie. Wiesbaden: Brockhaus, 1968.

Bry, Gerhard. *Wages in Germany, 1871–1945*. Ann Arbor: University Microfilms, 1960.

Bueb, Volkmar. *Die "Junge Schule" der franzosischen Marine. Strategie und Politik, 1875–1900*. Boppard a.Rh.: H. Boldt, 1971.

Cecil, Lamar. *Albert Ballin*. Princeton: Princeton University Press, 1967.

Cooling, Benjamin Franklin. *Grey Steel and Blue Water Navy: The Formative Years of America's Military-Industrial Complex, 1881–1917*. Hamden, Conn.: Archon Books, 1979.

Deist, Wilhelm. *Flottenpolitik und Flottenpropaganda: Das Nachrichtenbüro des Reichsmarineamtes, 1897–1914.* Stuttgart: Deutsche Verlagsanstalt, 1976.

———. *Militär und Innenpolitik im Weltkrieg, 1914–1918.* 2 vols. Düsseldorf: Droste Verlag, 1970.

———. "Die Politik der Seekriegsleitung und die Rebellion die Flotte Ende Oktober 1918." *Vierteljahrshefte für Zeitgeschichte* 14 (Oct. 1966): 341–68.

Dülffer, Jost. *Weimar, Hitler und die Marine: Reichspolitik und Flottenbau, 1920–1939.* Düsseldorf: Droste Verlag, 1973.

Engelmann, Bernt. *Krupp.* Munich: Deutsche Taschenbuchverlag, 1978.

Epkenhans, Michael. "Grossindustrie und Schlachtflottenbau, 1897–1914." *Militärgeschichlichtes Mitteilungen* 1 (1988): 65–140.

Epstein, Klaus. *Matthias Erzberger and the Dilemma of German Democracy.* Princeton: Princeton University Press, 1959.

Feldman, Gerald. *Army, Industry, and Labor in Germany, 1914–1918.* Princeton: Princeton University Press, 1966.

———. *Industrie und der Inflation: Studien und Dokumente zur Politik der deutscher Unternehmer, 1916–1923.* Hamburg: Hoffmann und Campe, 1977.

———. *Iron and Steel in the German Inflation.* Princeton: Princeton University Press, 1977.

———. "The Large Firm in the German Industrial System." In *Industrielle Gesellschaft und Politisches System,* edited by Dirk Stegmann et al. Bonn: Verlag Neue Gesellschaft, 1978.

Fraley, J. David. "Government by Procrastination: Chancellor Hohenlohe and Kaiser Wilhelm II, 1894–1900." *Central European History* (1974): 159–83.

Fricke, Dieter. *Die deutsche Arbeiterbewegung, 1869–1914.* Berlin: Dietz Verlag, 1976.

———. "Eine Denkschrift Krupps aus dem Jahre 1912 über den Schutz der Arbeitswilligen," *Zeitschrift für Geschichtswissenschaft* 6 (1957): 1245–53.

Gemzell, Carl-Axel. *Organization, Conflict and Innovation: A Study of German Naval Strategic Planning, 1888–1940.* Lund: Esselte Studien, 1973.

Geyer, Michael. *Deutsche Rüstungspolitik.* Frankfurt a.M.: Suhrkamp Verlag, 1984.

Graham, Gerald S. *The Politics of Naval Supremacy.* Cambridge, Mass.: Harvard University Press, 1965.

Der Grosse Brockhaus. 16th ed. Wiesbaden: Brockhaus, 1953.

Hallgarten, George W. F. *Imperialismus vor 1914.* 2 vols. Munich: Beck, 1963.

Hallgarten, George W. F., and Joachim Radkau. *Deutsche Industrie und Politik von Bismarck bis heute.* Frankfurt a.M.: Europäische Verlagsanstalt, 1974.

Helfferich, Karl. *Der Weltkrieg*. Vol. 2. Berlin: Ullstein and Co., 1919.

Herwig, Holger. "Feudalization of the Bourgeoisie: The Role of the Nobility in the German Naval Officer Corps, 1890–1918." *Historian* 38 (Feb. 1976): 268–80.

———. *The German Naval Officer Corps: A Political and Social History*. Oxford: Oxford University Press, 1973.

———. *Luxury Fleet: The Imperial German Navy, 1888–1918*. London: George Allen & Unwin, 1980.

———. *Politics of Frustration*. Boston: Little, Brown, 1976.

Herwig, Holger, and David F. Trask. "Naval Operations Plans between Germany and the United States of America, 1898–1913: A Study of Strategic Planning in the Age of Imperialism." *Militärgeschichtliches Mitteilungen* 8 (1970): 5–32.

Hessen, Robert. *The Steel Titan: The Life of Charles M. Schwab*. New York: Oxford University Press, 1975.

Hollyday, Frederic B. M. *Bismarck's Rival: A Political Biography of General and Admiral von Stosch*. Durham: Duke University Press, 1960.

Hubatsch, Walther. *Der Admiralstab und die obersten Marinebehörden in Deutschland, 1848–1945*. Frankfurt a.M.: Verlag für Wehrwesen Bernard und Graefe, 1958.

———. *Kaiserliche Marine*. Munich: Lehmann in Komm, 1975.

———. "Der Kulminationspunkt der deutschen Marinepolitik im Jahre 1912." *Historische Zeitschrift* 422 (Oct. 1953): 291–332.

———. *Die Ära Tirpitz: Studien zur deutschen Marinepolitik, 1890–1918*. Berlin: Musterschmidt Verlag, 1955.

Huntington, Samuel P. "The Defense Establishment: Vested Interests and the Public Interest." In *The Military Industrial Complex and U.S. Foreign Policy*, ed. Omer L. Carey, 562–84. Pullman: Washington State University Press, 1969.

———. *The Soldier and the State: The Theory and Politics of Civil-Military Relations*. Cambridge, Mass.: Belknap Press of Harvard University Press, 1957.

Hurd, Archibald, and Henry Castle. *German Seapower: Its Rise, Progress, and Economic Basis*. New York: Scribner, 1914.

Jarausch, Konrad. *The Enigmatic Chancellor: Bethmann-Hollweg and the Hubris of Imperial Germany*. New Haven: Yale University Press, 1972.

Kaeble, Hartmut. *Industrielle Interessenpolitik in der Wilhelminischen Gesellschaft. Centralverband deutscher Industrieller, 1895–1914*. Berlin, 1967.

Kaulisch, Baldur. *Alfred von Tirpitz und die Imperialistische Flottenrüstung*. Berlin: Militärverlag der Deutschen Demokratischen Republik, 1982.

Kehr, Eckart. "The Munitions Industry." *Encyclopedia of Social Sciences.* New York: Macmillan, 1930–35. 11:132.

———. *Primat der Innenpolitik.* Berlin: Walter de Gruyter, 1970.

———. "Schlachtflottenbau und Parteipolitik, 1894–1901." *Historische Studien,* 197. Berlin: E. Ebering, 1930.

Kelly, Patrick J. "Naval Policy of Imperial Germany, 1900–1914." Ph.D. dissertation, Georgetown University, 1970.

Kennedy, Paul. "The Development of German Naval Operations Plans against England, 1896–1914." *English Historical Review* 89 (Jan. 1974): 48–76.

———. "Fisher and Tirpitz: Political Admirals in the Age of Imperialism." In *Naval Warfare in the Twentieth Century, 1900–1945. Essays in Honor of Arthur Marder,* edited by Gerald Jordan. London: Croom Helm, 1977.

———. *The Rise of Anglo-German Antagonism, 1860–1914.* London: George Allen & Unwin, 1980.

———. *The Samoan Tangle.* New York: Barnes and Noble, 1974.

———. "Tirpitz, England and the Second Naval Law." *Militärgeschichtliches Mitteilungen* 2 (1970): 33–57.

Kosyzk, Kurt. *Deutsche Pressepolitik im Ersten Weltkrieg.* Düsseldorf: Droste Verlag, 1968.

Kuczynski, Jurgen. *Studien zur Geschichte des deutschen Imperialismus.* Vol. 1. Berlin: Dietz Verlag, 1951.

Lambi, Ivo N. *The Navy and German Power Politics, 1862–1914.* Boston: George Allen & Unwin, 1984.

Langer, William L. *The Diplomacy of Imperialism, 1890–1902.* Vol. 2. New York: Knopf, 1935.

Leckebusch, Günther. "Der Beginn des deutschen Eisenschiffbaues, 1850–1890." In *Moderne deutsche Wirtschaftsgeschichte,* edited by Karl E. Born. Cologne: Kiepenheuer und Witsch, 1966.

———. "Die Beziehungen der deutschen Seeschiffswerften zur Eisenindustrie an der Ruhr in der Zeit von 1850 bis 1913." *Schriften zur rheinisch-westfälischen Wirtschaftsgeschichte.* Vol. 8. Rheinisch-Westfälischen Wirtschaftsarchiv zu Köln. Cologne: Kiepenheuer und Witsch, 1963.

Leopold, John A. *Alfred Hugenberg: The Radical Nationalist Campaign against the Weimar Republic.* New Haven: Yale University Press, 1977.

Lundeberg, Philip. "German Naval Critique of the U-boat Campaign." *Military Affairs* 27 (Fall 1963): 105–18.

Mahan, Alfred T. *The Influence of Seapower upon History.* Boston: Houghton Mifflin, 1890.

Manchester, William. *The Arms of Krupp.* Boston: Little, Brown, 1968.

Marder, Arthur J. *From the Dreadnought to Scapa Flow: The Royal Navy in the Fisher Era, 1904–1914.* London: Oxford University Press, 1961.

Marienfelde, Wolfgang. *Wissenschaft und Schlachtflottenbau in Deutschland, 1897 bis 1906.* Berlin: Ernst Siegfried Mittler und Sohn, 1957.

Marinearchiv, ed. *Der Krieg zur See, 1914–1918.* 22 vols. Edited by Rear Admiral E. von Mantey. Berlin: Ernst Siegfried Mittler und Sohn, 1920.

McNeill, William. *The Pursuit of Power.* Chicago: University of Chicago Press, 1982.

Mendelssohn-Bartholdy, Albrecht. *War and German Society.* New Haven: Yale University Press, 1971.

Mommsen, Wolfgang J. "Domestic Factors in German Foreign Policy before 1914." *Central European History* 6 (1973): 3–43.

Morrow, John H., Jr. *Building German Airpower, 1909–1914.* Knoxville: University of Tennessee Press, 1976.

―――. *German Airpower in World War One.* Lincoln: University of Nebraska Press, 1982.

Müller, Alfred. *Die Kriegsrohstoffbewirtschaftung 1914–1918 im Dienst des deutschen Monopolkapitals,* Berlin: Akademie Verlag, 1955.

Nichols, John A. *Germany after Bismarck: The Caprivi Era, 1890–1894.* Cambridge, Mass.: Harvard University Press, 1958.

O'Byron, Leonhard. *Die Beurteilung der deutschen Flottenpolitik in Amerikanischen Zeugnissen der Vorkriegszeit.* Historische Studien, 257. Berlin: E. Ebering, 1934.

Ohl, John K. "The Navy, the War Industries Board, and Industrial Mobilization for War, 1917–1918." *Military Affairs* 40 (Feb. 1976): 17–22.

"150 Jahre Fried. Krupp." *Krupp Mitteilungen,* no. 50, 1961.

Owen, Richard. "Military Industrial Relations: Krupp and the Imperial Naval Office." In *Society and Politics in Wilhelmine Germany,* edited by Richard J. Evans. London: Croom Helm, 1978.

Pistorius, F. "Die Vulcan-Werke A.G., Stettin. Aufstieg, Gluck, und Ende einer grossen deutschen Werft." *Marine Rundschau* 35 (July 1930): 312–22.

Pollard, Samuel, and Paul Robinson. *The British Shipbuilding Industry, 1870–1914.* Cambridge, Mass.: Harvard University Press, 1979.

Rahn, Werner. "Wilhelm und seine Marine." *Marine Rundschau* 73 (May 1976): 285–91.

Ritter, Gerhard. *Staatskunst und Kriegshandwerk.* Vol. 2. Munich: R. Oldenbourg Verlag, 1965.

―――. *The Sword and the Scepter.* Vol. 3. Translated by Heinz Norden. Coral Gables: University of Miami Press, 1972.

Röhl, John C. G. "Admiral von Müller and the Approach of War, 1911–1914." *Historical Journal* 12 (1969): 651–73.

―――. *Deutschland ohne Bismarck: Die Regierungkrise im zweiten Kaiserreich, 1890–1900.* Tübingen: Ranier Wunderlich Verlag H. Leins, 1969.

Rosenberg, Hans. "Political and Social Consequences of the Great Depression of 1873–1896 in Central Europe." *Economic History Review* 13 (1943): 58–73.

Rosinski, Herbert. "German Theories of Sea Warfare." In *Brassy's Naval Annual*, 88–101. London: Brassy's, 1940.

Rössler, Eberhard. *Die deutsche U-Bootbau bis Ende des 1. Weltkrieg*. Munich: J. F. Lehmann Verlag, 1979.

————. *Die deutsche U-boote und ihre Werften*. Munich: Bernard Graefe Verlag, 1979.

————. *Geschichte des deutschen U-Bootbaus*. Munich: J. F. Lehmann Verlag, 1975.

Salewski, Michael. *Die deutsche Seekriegsleitung, 1935–1945*. Frankfurt a.M.: Bernard und Graefe, 1970.

Saul, Klaus. *Staat, Industrie, und Arbeiterbewegung im Wilhelminischen Reich*. Düsseldorf: Bertelsmann Universitätsverlag, 1974.

Schorske, Carl. *German Social Democracy, 1905–1917*. Cambridge, Mass.: Harvard University Press, 1955.

Schottelius, Herbert, and Wilhelm Deist, eds. *Marine und Marinepolitik im kaiserlichen Deutschland, 1871–1914*. Düsseldorf: Droste Verlag, 1972.

Schröder, Ernst. *Albrecht von Stosch*. Historische Studien 353. Berlin: E. Ebering, 1939.

Schüssler, Wilhelm. *Weltmachtstreben und Flottenbau*. Witten a. Ruhr, 1956.

Schwarz, Tjard, and Ernst von Halle, eds. *Die Schiffbauindustrie in Deutschland und im Ausland*. 2 vols. Berlin: R. Oldenbourg, 1902.

Stearns, Peter N. "Adaption to Industrialization: The German Workers as a Test Case." *Central European History* 3 (Dec. 1970): 303–31.

Stegemann, Bernd. *Die deutsche Marinepolitik, 1916–1918*. Berlin: Duncker und Humblot, 1970.

Steinberg, Jonathan. "Germany and the Russo-Japanese War." *American Historical Review* 75 (1970): 1965–86.

————. *Yesterday's Deterrent*. New York: Macmillan, 1965.

Stjerna, Leif. "Scheer-programmet. Krigsmakten, industrin och planerna på en utbyggnad av ubåtsvapnet i Tyskland år 1918." *Bihäfte, Aktuellt och historiskt* (1978): 3–35.

von Strandmann, Hartmut P. *Unternehmenspolitik und Unternehmensführung*. Düsseldorf: Droste Verlag, 1978.

Stumpf, Richard. *War, Mutiny, and Revolution in the German Navy*. Edited by D. Horn. New Brunswick: Rutgers University Press, 1967.

Stürmer, Michael, ed. *Das Kaiserliche Deutschland*. Düsseldorf: Droste Athenäum, 1970.

Techel, Hans. *Der Bau von Unterseebooten auf der Germaniawerft*. 1923. Reprint. Munich: J. F. Lehmann Verlag, 1969.

Thalheimer, Siegfried. *Das deutsche Flottengesetz von 1898*. Düsseldorf: Otto Fritz, 1926.

Trebilcock, Clive. "British Armaments and European Industrialization, 1890–1914." *Economic History Review* 26 (May 1973): 254–72.

Urofsky, Melvin I. *Big Steel and the Wilson Administration*. Columbus: Ohio State University Press, 1969.

Vagts, Alfred. "Hopes and Fears of a German American War, 1870–1915." *Political Science Quarterly* 54 (1939): 514–35.

Wagner, Lt. Capt. "75 Jahre Marinewerft Wilhelmshaven." *Marine Rundschau* 36 (1931): 320–23.

Weir, Gary E. "The Imperial Naval Office and the Problem of Armor Prices in Germany." *Military Affairs* 48 (April 1984): 62–65.

———. "Tirpitz, Technology, and Building U-boats, 1897–1916." *International History Review* 6 (May 1984): 175–90.

Widenmann, Wilhelm. *Marine-Attaché an der kaiserlich-deutschen Botschaft in London, 1907–1912*. Göttingen: Musterschmidt Verlag, 1952.

Williamson, John G. *Karl Helfferich, 1872–1924*. Princeton: Princeton University Press, 1971.

Witt, Peter-Cristian. *Die Finanzpolitik des deutschen Reiches von 1903 bis 1913*. Historische Studien 415. Lübeck: Matthiesen Verlag, 1970.

Zmarzlik, Hans-Günther. *Bethmann-Hollweg als Reichskanzler, 1909–1914*. Düsseldorf: Droste Verlag, 1957.

Index

About the Author

Gary E. Weir graduated from Manhattan College with a B.A. in history in 1973. He studied German history and naval-industrial relations under Professor John H. Morrow, Jr., at the University of Tennessee, Knoxville, and received his doctorate in history in 1982. After year on the faculty of the U.S. Naval Academy, Dr. Weir joined the newly established Contemporary History Branch of the Naval Historical Center in 1987. In this capacity he is preparing a history of naval-industrial relations in the construction of the American submarine fleet from 1914 through 1960. The first portion of this study, titled *Building American Submarines, 1914–1940*, appeared in June 1991 as part of NHC's Contributions to Naval History series. His work has also appeared in *Military Affairs*, *Naval War College Review*, *International History Review*, *U. S. Naval Institute Proceedings*, *Naval History*, and the *Naval Engineers' Journal*. He is an associate professor of history at the University of Maryland University College and the recipient of fellowships from the McClure Foundation and the DAAD.

The Naval Institute Press is the book-publishing arm of the U.S. Naval Institute, a private, nonprofit professional society for members of the sea services and civilians who share an interest in naval and maritime affairs. Established in 1873 at the U.S. Naval Academy in Annapolis, Maryland, where its offices remain today, the Naval Institute has more than 100,000 members worldwide.

Members of the Naval Institute receive the influential monthly magazine *Proceedings* and discounts on fine nautical prints, ship and aircraft photos, and subscriptions to the quarterly *Naval History* magazine. They also have access to the transcripts of the Institute's Oral History Program and get discounted admission to any of the Institute-sponsored seminars offered around the country.

The Naval Institute's book-publishing program, begun in 1898 with basic guides to naval practices, has broadened its scope in recent years to include books of more general interest. Now the Naval Institute Press publishes more than sixty new titles each year, ranging from how-to books on boating and navigation to battle histories, biographies, ship and aircraft guides, and novels. Institute members receive discounts on the Press's nearly 400 books in print.

Full-time students are eligible for special half-price membership rates. Life memberships are also available.
For a free catalog describing the Naval Institute Press books currently available, and for further information about U.S. Naval Institute membership, please write to:

Membership & Communications Department
U.S. Naval Institute
118 Maryland Avenue
Annapolis, Maryland 21402-5035
Or call, toll-free, (800) 233-8764.

THE NAVAL INSTITUTE PRESS

BUILDING THE KAISER'S NAVY
The Imperial Navy Office and German Industry
in the von Tirpitz Era, 1890–1919

Set in Bodoni Book and Bodoni Bold
by Brushwood Graphics, Inc.
Baltimore, Maryland

Printed on 50-lb. Penntech Eggshell Cream
and bound in Holliston Roxite A
by The Maple-Vail Book Manufacturing Group
York, Pennsylvania